T0321925

Emerging Trends and Applications of the Internet of Things

Petar Kocovic
Union – Nikola Tesla University, Serbia

Reinhold Behringer
Leeds Beckett University, UK

Muthu Ramachandran
Leeds Beckett University, UK

Radomir Mihajlovic
New York Institute of Technology, USA

A volume in the Advances in
Wireless Technologies and
Telecommunication (AWTT)
Book Series

www.igi-global.com

Published in the United States of America by
    IGI Global
    Information Science Reference (an imprint of IGI Global)
    701 E. Chocolate Avenue
    Hershey PA, USA 17033
    Tel: 717-533-8845
    Fax: 717-533-8661
    E-mail: cust@igi-global.com
    Web site: http://www.igi-global.com

Library of Congress Cataloging-in-Publication Data

Library of Congress Cataloging-in-Publication Data

Names: Kocovic, Petar, 1959- editor. | Behringer, Reinhold, editor. |
    Ramachandran, Muthu, editor. | Mihajlovic, Radomir, editor.
Title: Emerging trends and applications of the Internet of things / Petar
    Kocovic, Reinhold Behringer, Muthu Ramachandran, and Radomir Mihajlovic,
    editors.
Description: Hershey, PA : Information Science Reference, [2017] | Includes
    bibliographical references.
Identifiers: LCCN 2017002925| ISBN 9781522524373 (hardcover) | ISBN
    9781522524380 (ebook)
Subjects: LCSH: Internet of things.
Classification: LCC TK5105.8857 .E44 2017 | DDC 004.67/8--dc23 LC record available at https://
lccn.loc.gov/2017002925

This book is published in the IGI Global book series Advances in Wireless Technologies and Telecommunication (AWTT) (ISSN: 2327-3305; eISSN: 2327-3313)

British Cataloguing in Publication Data
A Cataloguing in Publication record for this book is available from the British Library.

All work contributed to this book is new, previously-unpublished material.
The views expressed in this book are those of the authors, but not necessarily of the publisher.

For electronic access to this publication, please contact: eresources@igi-global.com.

Advances in Wireless Technologies and Telecommunication (AWTT) Book Series

ISSN:2327-3305
EISSN:2327-3313

Editor-in-Chief: Xiaoge Xu, The University of Nottingham Ningbo China, China

MISSION

The wireless computing industry is constantly evolving, redesigning the ways in which individuals share information. Wireless technology and telecommunication remain one of the most important technologies in business organizations. The utilization of these technologies has enhanced business efficiency by enabling dynamic resources in all aspects of society.

The **Advances in Wireless Technologies and Telecommunication Book Series** aims to provide researchers and academic communities with quality research on the concepts and developments in the wireless technology fields. Developers, engineers, students, research strategists, and IT managers will find this series useful to gain insight into next generation wireless technologies and telecommunication.

COVERAGE

- Broadcasting
- Mobile Web Services
- Mobile Technology
- Wireless Sensor Networks
- Global Telecommunications
- Telecommunications
- Radio Communication
- Wireless Broadband
- Network Management
- Virtual Network Operations

IGI Global is currently accepting manuscripts for publication within this series. To submit a proposal for a volume in this series, please contact our Acquisition Editors at Acquisitions@igi-global.com or visit: http://www.igi-global.com/publish/.

Titles in this Series

For a list of additional titles in this series, please visit:
http://www.igi-global.com/book-series/advances-wireless-technologies-telecommunication-awtt/73684

Resource Allocation in Next-Generation Broadband Wireless Access Networks
Chetna Singhal (Indian Institute of Technology Kharagpur, India) and Swades De (Indian Institute of Technology Delhi,India)
Information Science Reference ● ©2017 ● 334pp ● H/C (ISBN: 9781522520238) ● US $190.00

Multimedia Services and Applications in Mission Critical Communication Systems
Khalid Al-Begain (University of South Wales, UK) and Ashraf Ali (The Hashemite University, Jordan & University of South Wales, UK)
Information Science Reference ● ©2017 ● 331pp ● H/C (ISBN: 9781522521136) ● US $200.00

Big Data Applications in the Telecommunications Industry
Ye Ouyang (Verizon Wirless, USA) and Mantian Hu (Chinese University of Hong Kong, China)
Information Science Reference ● ©2017 ● 216pp ● H/C (ISBN: 9781522517504) ● US $145.00

Handbook of Research on Recent Developments in Intelligent Communication Application
Siddhartha Bhattacharyya (RCC Institute of Information Technology, India) Nibaran Das (Jadavpur University, India) Debotosh Bhattacharjee (Jadavpur University, India) and Anirban Mukherjee (RCC Institute of Information Technology, India)
Information Science Reference ● ©2017 ● 671pp ● H/C (ISBN: 9781522517856) ● US $360.00

Interference Mitigation and Energy Management in 5G Heterogeneous Cellular Networks
Chungang Yang (Xidian University, China) and Jiandong Li (Xidian University, China)
Information Science Reference ● ©2017 ● 362pp ● H/C (ISBN: 9781522517122) ● US $195.00

Handbook of Research on Advanced Trends in Microwave and Communication Engineering
Ahmed El Oualkadi (Abdelmalek Essaadi University, Morocco) and Jamal Zbitou (Hassan 1st University, Morocco)
Information Science Reference ● ©2017 ● 716pp ● H/C (ISBN: 9781522507734) ● US $315.00

For an enitre list of titles in this series, please visit:
http://www.igi-global.com/book-series/advances-wireless-technologies-telecommunication-awtt/73684

www.igi-global.com

701 East Chocolate Avenue, Hershey, PA 17033, USA
Tel: 717-533-8845 x100 ● Fax: 717-533-8661
E-Mail: cust@igi-global.com ● www.igi-global.com

Table of Contents

Section 2
Internet of Things Development, Tools, and Techniques

Detailed Table of Contents

Section 1
The Concept

The Internet that most of us knows as the World Wide Web is expanding beyond PCs and mobile devices. Called the "Internet of things", this movement will link consumer devices, enterprise assets, media and everyday items, such as packaged goods, to the Internet at an increasing rate. Why the push? New business models and new ways of interacting with customers, employees and suppliers are possible when physical items are linked to the Internet. In theory, the Internet of things will make it possible for a connected refrigerator to automatically order milk. However, history has shown that, even though a technology can be transformational, it takes a series of many small evolutions before the consumer and business world are ready for transformational models like this. We believe that, at first, the sweet spot for the Internet of things will be to use it in simple ways that extend or enhance an existing process. For example, a washing machine that has a 2D bar code can enable a smartphone user to view the instruction manual, or a service person to view the service history and parts list. In contrast, using the Internet of things technologies to make a washing machine that can auto-detect clothes by reading the RFID tags on the garments' labels, and consequently run at the right settings, is less likely to gain adoption.

Iva Vojinović, University of Belgrade, Serbia
Dušan Barać, University of Belgrade, Serbia
Ivan Jezdović, University of Belgrade, Serbia
Milica Labus, University of Belgrade, Serbia
Filip Jovanović, Project Management College, Serbia

This chapter will foster the understanding of the structure of business model elements in Internet of things field. Business model provides an efficient way to analyze, understand and manage strategically oriented goals for one or more stakeholders in order to create some value for end-users, but in the Internet of things there is not clear path for its development. An approach that will be used is the generally accepted principle of forming business model, Canvas template, which is a strategic template for understanding the relation between key partners, key activities, customers and clients, key resources, value proposition for customers in the form of products or services, relationships with customers, sales and distribution channels, cost structure, income flow. Presented is an integrated model with main aspects that should be covered when it comes to the Internet of things business model development, combining Canvas template, inside organizational structure and ecosystem restrictions.

Dragorad Milovanović, University of Belgrade, Serbia
Vladan Pantović, Faculty of Business Economics and Entrepreneurship,
*   Serbia*
Gordana Gardašević, University of Banja Luka, Bosnia and
*   Herzegovina*

The Internet of Things (IoT) is the concept of linking various objects to the Internet that sense/acquire and transmit data in the environment to create a new application. From a standardization perspective, the IoT can be viewed as a global infrastructure, enabling advanced services by interconnecting (physical and virtual) objects based on evolving interoperable information and communication technologies (ICT). The success of the IoT will depend strongly on the existence and effective operation of global standards. The standardization initiative, research projects, national initiatives and industrial activities are outlined in this chapter. There are already many standardization activities related to the IoT, covering broad research areas: wireless and cellular technologies, networking protocols, emerging applications, media-centric IoT. What is needed, therefore, are a harmonization of standards and effective frameworks for large-scale deployment.

Section 2
Internet of Things Development, Tools, and Techniques

Chapter 4

In this paper, two assistive projects on the spatial cognition by blind and visually impaired (B&VI) people are presented using the sound patterns and ultrasonic sensing. The first device supports the sport activities of B&VI, the golf game specifically. Every golf flagstick has the sound marking device with the active buzzer and WiFi remote control by the person with good vision. The NodeMcu Lua ESP8266 ESP-12 WiFi boards in devices are controlled by the cross-platform HTML web-sites, and hence any WiFi smartphone and / or computer can be in use to start the HTML web-page. Mini portable WiFi router links all devices in the network. End-users are securely connected using the password to wireless router. Ten assistive devices were handed in Instituto para Ciegos y Débiles Visuales "Ezequiel Hernández Romo" together with WiFi router. The second device supports the orientation of B&VI by measuring the distance to the obstacle based on the ultrasonic sensor HC-SR04 and Arduino Uno. The distance is pronounced to the B&VI using headphone and MP3 player with SD card. Nowadays, Universidad Politécnica de San Luis Potosí is negotiating with several organizations to create a production line. All devices are of the budget price up to USD 10. All devices were tested successfully. This is joint work of Instituto para Ciegos y Débiles Visuales "Ezequiel Hernández Romo", Universidad Politécnica de San Luis Potosí, and Tecnológico de Monterrey with ongoing project "Artificial Eyes" based on Raspberry Pi 3 Model B board with an ultrasonic sensor and camera for the image and/or video processing of the surrounding environment, as well as the friendly integration into the local networks using onboard WiFi and Bluetooth.

Chapter 5

IoT tools and techniques can be split into three main categories – infrastructure (i.e. hardware like Arduino Uno), software apps (e.g. Arduino C/C++ sketch), and lightweight protocols (e.g. MQTT and CoAP) for the connection of the heterogeneous components. Nowadays, they allow to develop fully functional smart systems. In this chapter, Arduino open-source computer soft- and hardware are discussed for the remote LED control, the web-server development, the design of the dual axis solar tracker with energy saving algorithm, the smart city's natural environment component based on Arduino weather station, the aid systems (in the mobility) for the visually impaired and blind people. In addition, the connection of the heterogeneous soft- and hardware is presented based on MQTT protocol.

    László Lengyel, Budapest University of Technology and Economics,
      Hungary
    Péter Ekler, Budapest University of Technology and Economics,
      Hungary
    Imre Tömösvári, Budapest University of Technology and Economics,
      Hungary
    Tamás Balogh, Budapest University of Technology and Economics,
      Hungary
    Gergely Mezei, Budapest University of Technology and Economics,
      Hungary
    Bertalan Forstner, Budapest University of Technology and Economics,
      Hungary
    Hassan Charaf, Budapest University of Technology and Economics,
      Hungary

The Internet of Things (IoT) is the network of physical objects embedded with electronics, software, sensors, and network connectivity, which enables these objects to collect and exchange data. The chapter introduces the Model-driven Multi-Domain IoT concept and provides a method and a supporting framework. Multi-Domain IoT as the actual frontier for innovation, competition, and productivity. The method supports effective service and application development and therefore covers connected devices, data collection, data access and complex analytics. The efficiency of the method and the framework is confirmed by several projects. Selected parts of these projects are introduced as innovation projects and case studies.

    Branka Rodić Trmčić, Medical College of Applied Studies in Belgrade,
      Serbia
    Aleksandra Labus, University of Belgrade, Serbia
    Svetlana Mitrović, Project Management College, Serbia
    Vesna Buha, Project Management College, Serbia
    Gordana Stanojević, Health Center Zvezdara, Serbia

The main task of Internet of Things in eHealth solutions is to collect data, connect people, things and processes. This provides a wealth of information that can be useful in decision-making, improving health and well-being. The aim of this study is to identify framework of sensors and application health services to detect sources of stress and stressors and make them visible to users. Also, we aim at extracting relationship between event and sensor data in order to improve health behavior. Evaluation of the proposed framework model will be performed. Model is based on Internet of Things in eHealth and is going to aim to improve health behavior. Following the established pattern of behavior realized through wearable system users will be proposed a preventive actions model. Further, it will examine the impact of changing health behavior on habits, condition and attitudes in relation to well-being and prevention.

Chapter 8

Oleksandr Rolik, National Technical University of Ukraine "Igor Sikorsky Kyiv Polytechnic Institute", Ukraine

Sergii Telenyk, National Technical University of Ukraine "Igor Sikorsky Kyiv Polytechnic Institute", Ukraine & Cracow University of Technology, Poland

Eduard Zharikov, National Technical University of Ukraine "Igor Sikorsky Kyiv Polytechnic Institute", Ukraine

The Internet of Things (IoT) is an emerging technology that offers great opportunities that is designed to improve the quality of consumers' lives, and also to improve economic indicators and productivity of enterprises, and more efficient use of resources. IoT system refers to the use of interconnected devices and distributed subsystems to leverage data gathered by sensors and actuators in some sort of environment and to take a proper decision on a high level. In this chapter, the authors propose an approach to Microcloud-based IoT infrastructure management to provide the desired quality of IT services with rational use of IT resources. Efficiency of IT infrastructure management can be estimated by the quality of services and the management costs. The task of operational service quality management is to maintain a given level of service quality with the use of minimum IT resources amount in IoT environment. Then, the maximum efficiency can be achieved by selecting such control when actual level of service corresponds to the coordinated with business unit and can be achieved by minimal costs. The proposed approach allows the efficient use of resources for IT services provision in IoT ecosystem through the implementation of service level coordination, resource planning and service level management processes in an integrated IT infrastructure management system based on hyperconvergence and software-defined principles. The main goals of this chapter are to investigate the state of art of the IoT applications resource demands in the context of datacenter architecture deployment and to propose Microcloud-based IoT infrastructure resource control method.

Chapter 9

Goran Vorotović, University of Belgrade, Serbia
Nebojša Petrović, University of Belgrade, Serbia
Časlav Mitrović, University of Belgrade, Serbia
Vesna Šešum-Čavić, Vienna University of Technology, Austria

This chapter identifies and describes the key concepts and techniques for BLOB and CLOB integration into the IoT core. Data system centralization has sped up the solution of problems with large amounts of data storage and processing, particularly if the data is large by its nature. In that sense, everyday stream of photos, audio and video content, large textual data files led to new concepts BLOB and CLOB. Adequate examples of stored procedures, views, C#, JAVA, HTML5 i PHP languages, follow the establishing communication methods. Finally, the chapter will illustrate two practical examples of IoT: the example for pagination on a large database with million BLOB and CLOB objects, and the example for dynamic mechatronic system of a fire truck with feedback.

Chapter 10

Gopal Singh Jamnal, Edinburgh Napier University, UK
Xiaodong Liu, Edinburgh Napier University, UK
Lu Fan, Edinburgh Napier University, UK
Muthu Ramachandran, Leeds Beckett University, UK

In today's world, we are living in busy metropolitan cities and want our homes to be ambient intelligent enough towards our cognitive requirements for assisted living in smart space environment and an excellent smart home control system should not rely on the users' instructions. The ambient intelligence is a sensational new information technology paradigm in which people are empowered for assisted living through multiple IoTs sensors environment that are aware of inhabitant presence and context and highly sensitive, adaptive and responsive to their needs. A noble ambient intelligent environment are characterized by their ubiquity, transparency and intelligence which seamlessly integrated into the background and invisible to surrounded users/inhabitant. Cognitive IoE (Internet of Everything) is a new type of pervasive computing. As the ambient smart home is into research only from a couple of years, many research outcomes are lacking potentials in ambient intelligence and need to be more dug around for better outcomes. As a result, an effective architecture of CIoE for ambient intelligent space is missing in other researcher's work. An unsupervised and supervised methods of machine learning can be applied in order to classify the varied and complex user activities. In the first step, by using fuzzy set theory, the input dataset value can be fuzzified to obtain degree of membership for context from the physical layer. In the second step, using K-pattern clustering algorithms to discover pattern clusters and make dynamic rules based on identified patterns. This chapter provides an overview, critical evaluation of approaches and research directions to CIoE.

Foreword

The Internet of Things is an emerging topic of technical, social, and economic significance.

Consumer products, durable goods, cars and trucks, industrial and utility components, sensors, and other everyday objects are being combined with Internet connectivity and powerful data analytic capabilities that promise to transform the way we work, live, and play. Projections for the impact of IoT on the Internet and economy are impressive, with some anticipating as many as 100 billion connected IoT devices and a global economic impact of more than $11 trillion by 2025.

Where is the value potential of the Internet of Things? Here is the list of some facts: (1) interoperability required to capture 40% of the total value, (2) less than 1% of data currently used, mostly for alarms or real-time control; more can be used for optimization and prediction, (3) today we have two times more value from B2B applications than from consumer, and (4) estimations are that we developed 60% of the ideas. The rest 40% has to be developed.

When we are speaking about market segments, without any doubts, the first place belongs to optimization of factories, and includes elements of Industry 4.0. An estimated value for this segment is 1.2-3.7 trillion USD. Silver and bronze medals in the IoT business are reserved for: smart cities (public health and transportation), and human area (health and fitness industry). Both of them are calculating with 1.7 and 1.6 trillion USD, respectively. The fourth place belongs to retail environments, almost 1.2 trillion USD. The remaining five areas are: (5) worksites (operations optimization plus health and safety, with 930 billion USD), (6) autonomous and near autonomous vehicles (740 billion USD), (7) logistics and navigation, (8) core automation and security of homes, and (9) energy efficiency in offices. Potential impact of all nine segments is between 3.9 and 11 trillion USD per year until 2015.

Many people, including myself, share the view that cities in particular and the world in general will be overlaid with sensing and actuation, much of that embedded in "things" creating what is referred to as Smart World. But it is important to note that one key issue is the degree of the density of sensing and actuation coverage. I believe that there will be a transition point when the degree of coverage triples or quadruples what we have today. At that time, there will be a qualitative change. For example, today many buildings already have sensors for attempting to save energy; home automation is occurring; cars, taxis, and traffic lights have devices to try and improve safety and transportation; people that have smartphone with sensors for running many useful apps; industrial plants are connecting to the Internet; and healthcare services are relying on increased home sensing to support remote medicine and wellness. However, all of these are just the tip of an iceberg. They are all still at early stages of development. The steadily increasing density of sensing and the sophistication of the associated processing will result a significant qualitative change in how we work and live. We will truly have systems-of-systems that synergistically interact, to form totally new and unpredictable services.

The book, *Emerging Trends and Applications in the Internet of Things*, is a series of studies systematically introducing general notions of Internet of Things. The book is written by renowned experts of the field, who bring out the intrinsic challenges of this concept. The book can be read cover to cover or selectively in the areas of the interest for readers.

The Book is intended for (a) novel readers who could benefit from understanding general concept of the IoT, (b) general practitioners who seek guidance into IoT field, and (c) experts in the field who could benefit from detailed analysis of the IoT field. The authors introduced blends of scientific and engineering concept together with a good coverage on the turbulent events covering this innovative area.

Veljko Milutinovic
University of Novi Pazar, Serbia

Preface

Internet of Things (IoT) and Internet of Everything (IoE) have emerged to address the need for connectivity and seamless integration with other devices. However, there are potential challenges ahead meeting the growing need for IoT based applications. This includes design and implementation challenges, various applications, connectivity, data gathering, storing and analyzing in a cloud based solution, and IoT Security and Privacy issues. When we look at some of the benefits of IoT, billions of smart and embedded IoT devices will be immersed in the environment (all devices including travel, entertainment systems, heath care systems, wearables, smart work place, smart public and society, smart communities, smart social-media, smart home, etc.), sensing, interacting, and cooperating with each other to enable efficient services that will bring tangible benefits to the environment, the economy and the society as a whole.

On the other hand, IoT Technology will be extremely diverse and heterogeneous in terms of resource capabilities, lifespan and communication technologies, further complicating the scenario. As a result, new problems and challenges arise spanning different areas: architecture, communication, addressing, discovery, data and network management, power and energy storage, security and privacy, to cite a few. Classic Internet approaches are not sufficient to solve these unprecedented issues, and need to be revised to address the complex requirements imposed by IoT. This paves the way for the development of intelligent algorithms, novel network paradigms, intelligent predictive algorithms can be created with the big data and analytics generated in the peta-byte and tera-byte rate with volume, velocity, and veracity (V3) and new services.

One of the main objectives of this is to provide researchers and educators with basic concepts of IoT technology, and its Development, Tools and Techniques Therefore, we believe this book will provide an insight for researchers and developers. The book consists of two sections.

Section 1," IoT Concepts," provides chapters on:

Chapter 1 provides a historical perspective on concepts, introduction, and landscape of research issues whereas Chapter 2 on "An Approach to Designing IoT-Based Business Models" provides the understanding of the structure of business model elements in Internet of things field. Chapter 3, "Converging Technologies for the IoT: Standardization Activities and Frameworks," focusses on the perspective of technical standardization, the IoT can be viewed as a global infrastructure for the information society, enabling advanced services by interconnecting (physical and virtual) things based on existing and evolving interoperable information and communication technologies (ICT).

Section 2 on "Internet of Things Development, Tools, and Techniques" provides Chapter 4 to Chapter 10. There are seven interesting chapters. Chapter 4 provides a case study on the spatial cognition of surrounding objects by the B&VI (Blind and Visually Impaired) people using sound patterns and ultrasonic sensing. In this paper, two assistive projects on the spatial cognition by blind and visually impaired (B&VI) people are presented using the sound patterns and ultrasonic sensing. Chapter 5 provides building IoT application with Aurdino processor and Chapter 6 on using model-driven approaches to build IoT applications. Chapters 7-10 provide wealth of applications based on IoT with Cloud computing, Cognitive IoE (Internet of Everything), etc.

Petar Kocovic
Union – Nikola Tesla University, Serbia

Muthu Ramachandran
Leeds Beckett University, UK

Reinhold Behringer
Leeds Beckett University, UK

Radomir Mihajlovic
New York Institute of Technology, USA

Section 1
The Concept

Chapter 1

From Ubiquitous Computing to the Internet of Things

Bozidar Radenkovic
University of Belgrade, Serbia

Petar Kocovic
Union – Nikola Tesla University, Serbia

ABSTRACT

The Internet that most of us knows as the World Wide Web is expanding beyond PCs and mobile devices. Called the "Internet of things", this movement will link consumer devices, enterprise assets, media and everyday items, such as packaged goods, to the Internet at an increasing rate. Why the push? New business models and new ways of interacting with customers, employees and suppliers are possible when physical items are linked to the Internet. In theory, the Internet of things will make it possible for a connected refrigerator to automatically order milk. However, history has shown that, even though a technology can be transformational, it takes a series of many small evolutions before the consumer and business world are ready for transformational models like this. We believe that, at first, the sweet spot for the Internet of things will be to use it in simple ways that extend or enhance an existing process. For example, a washing machine that has a 2D bar code can enable a smartphone user to view the instruction manual, or a service person to view the service history and parts list. In contrast, using the Internet of things technologies to make a washing machine that can auto-detect clothes by reading the RFID tags on the garments' labels, and consequently run at the right settings, is less likely to gain adoption.

DOI: 10.4018/978-1-5225-2437-3.ch001

INTRODUCTION

The Internet of Things (IoT) is a new hot buzzword and like most buzzwords, its purpose and definition are grossly misunderstood. When some people hear the term IoT they immediately associate it with famous 19-century novel "The Idiot" from Fyodor Dostoyevsky (1821-1881). Situation is very different – IoT referring to the world of smarties. Smart Energy. Smart Parking. Smart Homes. Smart Grid. Smart Lighting. Smart Cars. Smart Tags. Smart Health, Figure 1.(What the Internet of Things (IoT) needs to be a Reality, 2014)

The problem with IoT is a lack of education, marketing and PR. The majority of people have not been informed on what use cases are driving these astounding revenue predictions. Sure, we have all heard of connected cars, wearable devices, and appliances with sensors, but what has not been marketed enough is the real business value that these "things" create.

Figure 1. Word of smart services, technologies, meanings for everyone
(Reproduced from ARM/Freescale)(What the Internet of Things (IoT) Needs to Become a Reality, 2014)

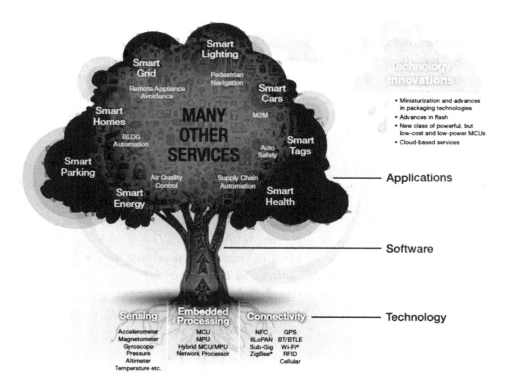

Today Internet "Sans Frontiers" consists of:

- Asset tracking of goods on the move.
- Automatic traffic management.
- Continuous monitoring of, and firmware upgrades for, vehicles.
- Environmental monitoring and control.
- Home and industrial building automation.
- Machine-to-machine communication.
- Machine-to-infrastructure communication.
- Remote security and control.
- (World of) Sensors.
- "Smart" applications, including cities, water, agriculture, buildings, grid, meters, broadband, cars, appliances, tags, animal farming and the environment, to name a few.
- Tele-health: remote or real-time pervasive monitoring of patients, diagnosis and drug delivery.

Most of the specified classes of devices and systems use PLCs (Programmable Logic Controllers) and protocols for building automation such as BACNet (ASHRAE, ANSI, ISO 16484-5 standard). Other standards for non wireless devices are: ModBUS RS 485, VDC and 12-24V VDC.

Almost all of mentioned is in wireless world. THE UBIQUITOUS sensor-rich mobile devices (e.g. smartphones, wearable devices, and smart vehicles) have been playing an increasing important role in the evolution of the Internet of Things (IoTs), which bridges the digital space and physical space at a societal scale.

The spectrum of research required to achieve IoT at the scale envisioned above requires significant research along many directions. In this section, problems and required research are highlighted in eight topic areas: massive scaling, architecture and dependencies, creating knowledge and Big Data, robustness, openness, security, privacy, and human-in-the-loop.(Stankovic, 2014) Many important topics such as the development of standards, the impact of privacy laws, and the cultural impact on use of these technologies are outside the scope of the paper.

Internet of Things also belongs to the group of twelve disruptive technologies that will play significant role in the future: (James Manyika, Michael Chui, Jacques Bughin, Richard Dobbs, Peter Bisson, Alex Marrs, 2013)

1. **Mobile Internet:** Increasingly inexpensive and capable mobile computing devices and Internet connectivity.

2. **Automation of Knowledge Work:** Intelligent software systems that can perform knowledge work tasks involving unstructured commands and subtle judgments.
3. **The Internet of Things:** Networks of low-cost sensors and actuators for data collection, monitoring, decision making, and process optimization.
4. **Cloud Technology:** Use of computer hardware and software resources delivered over a network or the Internet, often as a service.
5. **Advanced Robotics:** Increasingly capable robots with enhanced senses, dexterity, and intelligence used to automate tasks or augment humans.
6. **Autonomous and Near-Autonomous Vehicles:** Vehicles that can navigate and operate with reduced or no human intervention.
7. **Next-Generation Genomics:** Fast, low-cost gene sequencing, advanced Big Data analytics, and synthetic biology ("writing" DNA).
8. **Energy Storage -** Devices or systems that store energy for later use, including batteries.
9. **3D Printing:** Additive manufacturing techniques to create objects by printing layers of material based on digital models.
10. **Advanced Materials:** Materials designed to have superior characteristics (e.g., strength, weight, conductivity) or functionality.
11. **Advanced Oil and Gas Exploration and Recovery:** Exploration and recovery techniques that make extraction of unconventional oil and gas economical.
12. **Renewable Energy:** Generation of electricity from renewable sources with reduced harmful climate impact.

Potential economic impact of IoT until 2020 is estimate on 11.1 trillion USD.

History

If we looking for the very beginning, we must go to the year 1832. Baron Schilling in Russia created an electromagnetic telegraph, and in 1833, Carl Friedrich Gauss and Wilhelm Weber invented their own code to communicate over a distance of 1200 m within Göttingen, Germany. Baron Pavel L'vovitch Schilling (5 April 1786, Reval (now, Tallinn), Russian empire – St. Petersburg, Russia, 25 July 1837) first time in the history of telecommunications was set up cable in his apartment in St Petersburg. His device was first electromagnetic telegraph in the world – in two different apartments in his room. Baron Schilling was the first person who put into practice the idea of binary system of signal transmission. He was recognized. (IEEE Global Hostory Network, 2009)

Figure 2. Pavel L'vovitch Schilling (left), and his telegraph (right)

Two years later, two German scientists built their own functional telegraph. Carl Friedrich Gauss (1777-1855), director of Gottingen observatory and Wilhelm Weber (1804-1891) invented one of the first telegraphs and used it to communicate with each other on the distance of three kilometers. They invented their own code for communication, Figure 3.

Morse Telegraph(Morse, 1840) with Alfred Veil code (known as Morse code) came nine years later. Alfred Veil financially supported by his brother, start to build network of telegraph lines, after first success on the line between Baltimore and Washington. Morse and Veil established first telegraph company in the world – Western Union.

Three years after Morse patented his telegraph, on 1847, Alexander Graham Bell was born in Edinburgh, UK (March 3, 1847, August 2, 1922). He was awarded the US Patent for telephone in 1876.(Bell, 1876) Note that patent name was Telegraphy, but he invented telephony. Spreading of telephone network was very slow.

Next big step was made on rainy September day, 1898. On Madison Square Garden Exhibition, Nikola Tesla (1856, Smiljan, Austrian Empire – 1943, New York, USA) publicly demonstrated for the first time the use of radio waves. He controlled small unmanned boat, Figure 4.(Tesla, Method of and apparatus for controlling mechanism of moving vessels or vehicles, 1898)

On January 30, 1926, Nikola Tesla gave an interview to John B. Kennedy, from Colliers magazine(Tesla, When Woman is Boss, 1926). He stated:

Figure 3. Gauss-Webber telegraph code

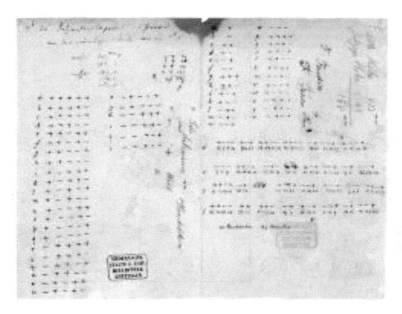

Figure 4. Nikola Tesla (left), and Madison Exhibition (right)

When wireless[1] is perfectly applied the whole earth will be converted into a huge brain, which in fact it is, all things being particles of a real and rhythmic whole......... and the instruments through which we shall be able to do this will be amazingly simple compared with our present telephone. A man will be able to carry one in his vest pocket.

However, nothing was happened until August 1942. Long time, nobody knows who are George Antheil and Hedy Markey Kisler, authors of US Patent No 2292387 A. Shortly after approval of patent, it was found right name of Hedy Markley Kisler – this was famous Austro-Hungarian actress Hedy Lamarr. She escaped from Mirabel Castle in Salzburg to Hollywood. They patented o called Secret Communication System, Figure 5. (George Antheil, 1942)

Later, their principle of wireless transferring got today name – Frequency Hopping. However – no one device that work on this (or similar principle) was produced until

Figure 5. Antheil-Kisler patent (left) and Hedy Lamarr (right)

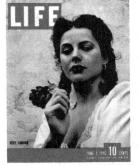

1965. Patent rights for this technology was expire, so Hedy Lamarr (1914-2000) did not have any benefit from her patent.

First light came on 1990. There really was an Internet toaster. Dan Lynch, President of the Interop Internet networking show, told John Romkey at the 1989 show that he would give him star billing the following year if he connected a toaster to the Internet. Who could have resisted a challenge like that?

Working together with his friend Simon Hackett, John Romkey rose to the occasion and connected a Sunbeam Deluxe Automatic Radiant Control Toaster to the Internet, becoming the hit of the 1990 Interop. The toaster was connected to the Internet with TCP/IP networking, and controlled with a Simple Networking Management Protocol Management Information Base (SNMP MIB), Figure 6. It had one control, to turn the power on, and the darkness of the toast was controlled by how long the power was kept on. However, a human being still had to insert the bread. At the 1991, Interop a small robotic crane was added to the system, also controlled from the Internet, which picked up a slice of bread and dropped it into the toaster, automating the system from end-to-end.

Next 1991 year, Timothy Berners-Lee created first web page during Christmas holidays in December. Few months before, Mark Weiser (1952-1999), professor at University of Maryland, coined term ubiquitous computing. In Scientific American magazine(Weiser, 1991) he stated:

The most profound technologies are those that disappear. They weave themselves into the fabric of everyday life until they are indistinguishable from it.

Ubiquitous computing! We were very close to the today technology! On the market, we had more and more innovations, but penetration was low. Maybe, problem was in the name. New name, in today meaning, The Internet-of-Things (IoT) was coined on 1999 by Kevin Eshton(Ashton, 2009), at this time in Procter & Gamble, and revolution started:

I could be wrong, but I'm fairly sure the phrase "Internet of Things" started life as the title of a presentation I made at Procter & Gamble (P&G) in 1999. Linking the new idea of RFID in P&G's supply chain to the then red-hot topic of the Internet was more than just a good way to get executive attention. It summed up an important insight which is still often misunderstood.

Internet refrigerator, ambient orb (Ambient Devices, n.d.) (16Ap1), Nabaztag rabbit (n.d.) (16Ap)... were next steps. Few classes of new devices were developed from these first trials.

Figure 6. John Romkey (left), and his toaster from 1990 (right)

The Internet-of-Thing hit another level when International Telecom Union (ITU) published its first report on the specified topic (REports, 2005). To understand how the number of connected devices could reach more than 50 billion until 2020, it is worth considering some high-level, macro-economic trends and statistics. As a few examples, by 2020 there will be:

- 3 billion subscribers with sufficient means to buy information on a 24-hour basis to enhance their lifestyles and improve personal security. In mature markets, these customers will possess between 5-10 connected devices each.
- 1.5 billion Vehicles globally, not counting trams and railways. (Gardner, 2009)(Brown, 2010)
- 3 billion utility meters (electricity, water and gas).
- A cumulative 100 billion processors shipped, each capable of processing information and communicating.

In 2011, John Timmer wrote an article that in 2007, "...the $6.4*10^{18}$ instructions per second that human kind can carry out on its general-purpose computers in 2007 are in the same ballpark area as the maximum number of nerve impulses executed by one human brain per second."(Timmer, 2011). Using the data about worldwide CPU selling, multiplying with CPU increasing power this number in 2015 was 20 times higher than in 2007.

Visionary words of Marc Weiser that quiet technology which working in the background will be dominant factor in 21st century. His words were visible in 2005 when number of mobile phones passes number of 2 billion. Number of citizens in the Earth and number of mobile devices were equal in 2005. Trends are shown on the Table 1. (Evans M., 2011)

Internet of Things Today

Today, many cities around the world are overlaid with sensors and actuators, forming fine skin of "things", referred as *smart world*. Many buildings have sensors in the attempt to save energy. Cars and trucks have sensors trying to improve safety. Apple iPayment is first of few software that will eliminate credit cards. Applications on mobile phones measuring heart rate – very soon will control heart rate 24x7. Insurance company will organize network of hospitals for the users of their cardio program who paid policy of social insurance. In the future, the scope of IoT is enormous and will affect every aspect of all our lives.

Development of the networked world is progressing through a number of waves, as shown in Figure 7.

Distribution per industries, services and government are shown in the Figure 8. Specified verticals will undergo significant transformations in coming years.

Using PEST analysis, we will derive drivers of the Embedded Internet, Table 2.

We will go back to the Figure 8. On this figure, and in other part of this chapter, we will see that many different industrial segments are affected by IoT technology. This fact-triggered professor Detlef Zühlke, from RWTH Aachen University in Germany, to state that forth industrial revolution started in 2015.(Temperton, 2015) (Previous three Industrial Revolutions started: First – between 1820 and 1840; Second – between 1870-1914, Third – around 1950)

At some point of the growth in the electronic power within things, the ability to start to consider and negotiate for resources grows. At first, it is about simple things: I need electrical power — where can I get it? (Investment banker J.P. Morgan did not understood ideas of Nikola Tesla at the end of 19th century for free (even wireless) electrical energy). It quickly advances to higher-order things, such as prices,

Table 1. Internet of Things- Figures

	2003	2010	2015	2020
World Population	6.3 bn	6.8 bn	7.2 bn	50 bn
Number of connected devices	500 mil	12.5 bn	25 bn	50 bn
Connected devices per person	0.08	1.84	3.24	6.58

Figure 7. Three waves of connected devices
(Courtesy: Ericsson)(Paper, 2011)

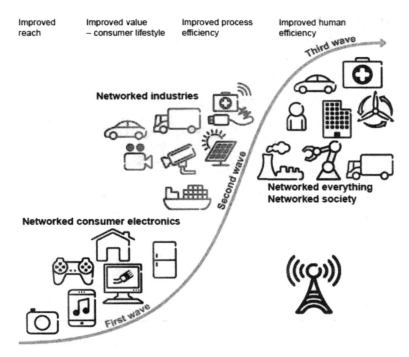

availability, forecasting, replenishment and demand. It starts with a self-awareness or self-definition of what resources it needs before it can procure them.

Things also know where they belong. For example, use a specialty part for a 1947 Ford truck will not let itself for a 1960s International tractor unless it is told to allow it. This ability to negotiate is predicated on the advancement of standards due to the long-term trend of quality programs, as well as the centralization and consolidation of back-office systems that forced broad acceptance of standard processes.

The new capabilities for negotiation provide an opportunity to analyze the forces ahead for business and government. The following is a matrix of two key forces: (1) intelligence, which recognizes the level needed for negotiation; and (2) the possible ways it is organized, from centralized to distributed. These result in the emergence of some new capabilities, depending on how the business approaches its organization. As we look at the four scenarios that emerge, a different reality emerges:

1. **Ordinary Things**: This is the world of things as they have been for centuries: some identification that a person who is physically present can read. The

Figure 8. Heating map: Distribution per industries of IoT
(Courtesy: Ericsson(Paper, 2011)

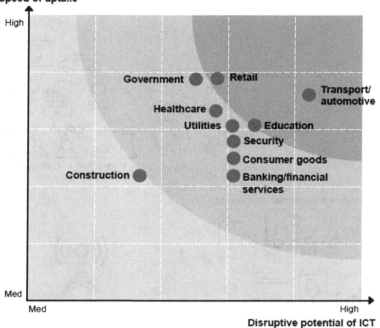

information can contain serial numbers or other tracking numbers that are then entered in another system. This requires low intelligence and is very distributed.

2. **Current State of the Art**: This is the world where all items have a bar code and their movements, when recorded, are sent to centralized systems for further processing and actions, if needed. This would also include the world of Kanban manufacturing (author Shigeo Shingo [1909-1990], Kanban was initially introduced in Toyota), where things are identified and their local movements are determined by visual inspection. All items that have a bar code, especially consumer products.

3. **Centralized Brokerages**: In this scenario, the intelligent things that are moving communicate with a central brokerage via mesh networks or other easily configured networks and seek to fulfill needs and resources through that centralized system. The system will take care of most negotiations between the individual things. In this scenario, the individual items will not be of very much value, so managers will see a centralized brokerage approach as the most rational and cost-effective one.

12

Table 2. Drivers of the Embedded Internet, PEST analysis

Political	Legislative Initiatives & Incentives: Broadband, E-Governance, E-Call, Smart Metering, E-Health
Economic	**Operational Efficiency:** Increased ARPU, lower TCO, increased Productivity
Social	**Smart Spaces:** Intelligent networked embedded devices adapt to human needs, RFID, video analytics, speech recognition and other sensing applications
Technological	**Pervasive Connectivity + Compute Growth:** LTE, GSM, WiMAX, Wi-Fi, Bluetooth*, ZigBee, Z-Wave*[2]

(Intel, 2009)

4. **Peer-to-Peer Intelligence**: In this scenario, the different devices have a built-in sense of their needs and resources within their advancing intelligence. The devices do not need the central brokerage as much as they need an information bank to know more about prices and costs. With items that are high in value, a peer-to-peer intelligence requires additional investment that can be justified with the higher risk of damage or theft to those items.

As the infrastructure of the next few years starts to build itself out, it leads to a number of new industries that have the potential to grow to a size equal to or greater than current industries:(Lopez, 2012; Mark Raskino & Hung LeHong, 2011)

- Centralized Internet Brokerage Services
- Peer-to-Peer Brokerage Services
- Self-Managed Logistics
- Design Services

Finally, the Internet consists of multiple Internets. It consists of six areas(John Mahoney, Hung LeHong, 2012):

- **Internet of Information:** The traditional Internet known to most of us — the World Wide Web.
- **Internet of Systems:** The network of business and consumer applications. With the Internet, these types of data exchanges between systems can occur over the Web. Email, video games and all kinds of other consumer applications connect and interact with each other over the Internet.
- **Internet of People:** The network of relationships created in social networks.
- **Internet of Places:** Commercial and public places are starting to become nodes on the Internet.

- **Internet of Things (Here we are):** This is an Internet of physical items, with sensors, consumer devices and enterprise assets connected both to the Internet and each other.
- **Internet of Virtual Entities:** Consists of "intelligent" digital entities.

This scenario demonstrates how the convergence of multiple Internets provides an outcome not possible by any individual implementation. Since everything has or is capable of having an IP address, the Internet of Things can apply to almost all industries:

- Heavy engineering.
- Process-based industries, such as mining and construction.
- Electronics.
- Manufacturing.
- Media and entertainment.
- Education.
- Transport.
- Healthcare and life sciences.
- Finance.
- Sport and leisure.

Internet of Things Vision and Future

As Dave Evans stated: "We evolve because we communicate!"(Evans D., 2011). Humans evolve because they communicate. Once fire was discovered and shared, for example, it did not need to be rediscovered, only communicated. A more modern-day example is the discovery of the double-helix structure of DNA, molecules that carry genetic information from one generation to another. After James Watson and Francis Crick published the article in a scientific paper in April 1953, the disciplines of medicine and genetics were able to build on this information to take giant steps forward.(The DIscovery of the Molecular Structure of DNA - The Double Helix, 2003), (Crick and Watson) This principle of sharing information and building on discoveries can best be understood by examining how humans process data, Figure 9.

From bottom to top, the pyramid layers include data, information, knowledge, and wisdom. Data is the raw material that is processed into information. Individual data by itself is not very useful, but volumes of it can identify trends and patterns. This and other sources of information come together to form knowledge. In the simplest sense, knowledge is information of which someone is aware. Wisdom is then born from knowledge plus experience. While knowledge changes over time, wisdom is timeless, and it all begins with the acquisition of data.

Figure 9. Humans turn data into wisdom
(Courtesy: Cisco)(Evans D., 2011)

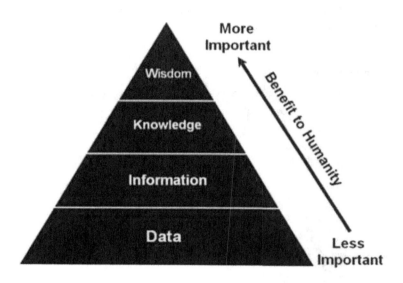

Most IoT technologies are either just emerging or at or near the peak of "hype":(Alfonso Velosa, W. Roy Shulte, Benoit J. Lhereux, 2015)

- Establish realistic expectations
- Expect some "reality checks"

Figure 10 , showing where some of the technologies were in the middle of 2015. Internet-of-Things is at the top of the Hype cycle. This means that very soon this technology can go down. Today, every attempt for automation have prefix – IoT. This is not realistic. Most of the technologies does not have place on the market. One of the reasons is – standardization. Big fight in the field of standardization is on the market. Expectations going to the surviving on only two to three main standards. This also means that huge amount of installed things will soon go to the history. Without possibility for repairing or replacement.

From other side, more intelligent tools most of them belong to the advanced analytics, artificial intelligence or Big Data, can support existing IoT projects. Era of intelligent Internet of things is in front of us. As the planet's population continues to increase, it becomes even more important for people to become stewards of the earth and its resources. In addition, people desire to live healthy, fulfilling, and comfortable lives for themselves, their families and those they care about. By combining the ability of the next evolution of the Internet (IoT) to sense, collect, transmit, analyze,

Figure 10. Hype Cycle for the IoT, 2015 The dark colored arrow represents some form of IoT platform is typically required to help enable IoT business solutions, while the light colored arrow represents other key IoT technologies are also needed to fully realize most IoT projects
(Courtesy: Gartner)

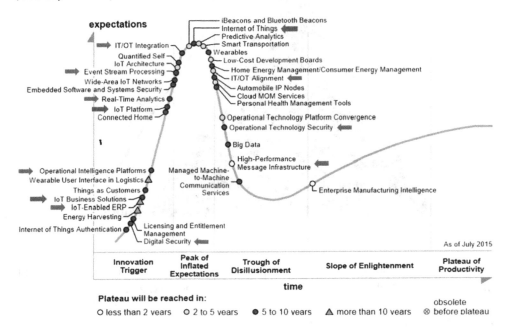

and distribute data on a massive scale with the way people process information, humanity will have the knowledge and wisdom it needs not only to survive, but to thrive in the coming months, years, decades, and centuries.

Connecting figures from Figure 11 we saw that IoT leads to the exploding world of connected people, processes, data, and things that, in general, includes:

- **Smart Grids:** Smart utility grids are increasing efficiency in energy distribution.
- **Intelligent Vehicles:** Examples include cars that self-diagnose, communicate with service centers, inform other vehicles of their existence, monitor safety, and have the latest road and weather conditions.
- **Connected Healthcare and Patient Monitoring:** Examples include smart pills that patients can ingest to help doctors diagnose and treat diseases.
- **Sensors:** Extremely small sensors can be placed on plants and animals, and then connected to the Internet, revolutionizing food production.

Figure 11. Words a) Internet of Things, b) Ubiquitous computing, c) Wireless sensors shown on Google Trends from 2005-2016

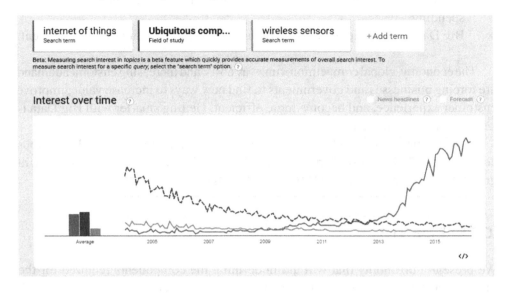

- **"Internet Routing in Space":** A program from Cisco designed to launch the Internet into space.
- **Connected Education:** Better use of technologies will help scale teachers, faculty, and educational content, increasing new ways of learning and giving students the flexibility to learn at their own pace, anywhere, anytime, using any device.

As it was mentioned earlier, Big Data is new oil for 21st century. This sophisticated analysis and insights that can be derived from the mountains of digital information created daily—is a huge trend that is influencing all parts of business and society, and it is only going to increase. Figures from the McKinsey Global Institute emphasize the power of Big Data: (James Manyika, Michael Chui, Brad Brown, Jacques Bughin, Richard Dobbs, Charles Roxburgh, Angela Hung Byers, 2011)

- Facebook has more than 2.5 billion pieces of content and ingests more than 500 terabytes of new content daily.
- Enterprises around the world stored more than 7 exabyte of new data in 2010; while consumers stored more than 6 exabyte (1 exabyte is equivalent to four times the entire content of the U.S. Library of Congress).
- For less than $600, consumers can buy a disk drive that can store all of the world's music.

- McKinsey estimates that U.S. healthcare providers can save more than $300 billion annually through Big Data—more than double Spain's annual health spending.
- Big Data could help retailers increase their operating margins by 60 percent.

The economy, global competition, runaway costs, and increasing customer demand are forcing businesses and governments to find new ways to increase value, improve customer experience, and become more efficient. Getting smarter with Big Data is key to addressing these issues.

If we looking trends and compare three words: Internet of Things, Ubiquitous computing and wireless sensors, we can get bigger picture – Internet-of-Things will grows up on Internet, Figure 11. (Google Trends)

IOT ELEMENTS

We present a taxonomy that will aid in defining the components required for the Internet of Things from a high-level perspective. Specific taxonomies of each component can be found elsewhere. There are three IoT components which enables seamless ubiquitous computing: (a) Hardware—made up of sensors, actuators and embedded communication hardware (b) Middleware—on demand storage and computing tools for data analytics and (c) Presentation—novel easy to understand visualization and interpretation tools which can be widely accessed on different platforms and which can be designed for different applications. In this section, we discuss a few enabling technologies in these categories which will make up the three components stated above.

Few words about addressing scheme: existing iPv4 does not have enough space. New 128-bit address scheme iPv6 has 655 x 10^{21} addresses. This will be more than enough for all things in next 50 years. The architecture of IPv6 addressing is described in RFC 2373, "IP Version 6 Addressing Architecture."(Hinden, 1998)

Next generation of mobile networks going to 5G mobile network. Some characteristics of 5G network are:

- More than 50 Mbps everywhere.
- Support to dense areas and crowds (up to 150,000 people/km).
- Support to fast moving vehicles (cars, high speed trains, and airplanes).
- Coverage of indoor areas with shared bandwidth of up to 1Gbps.
- Ultra low latency (latency less than 1ms) and ultrahigh reliability.
- Resilience and support to traffic surges.

- Support to massive low-cost/long-range/low-power machine type communications.
- And much more. (Minerva, September 2015).

Data storage and analytics is next point in IoT development. Creation of an unprecedented amount of data is one of the most important outcomes. Storage, ownership and expiry of the data become critical issues. The Internet consumes up to 5% of the total energy generated today. It is sure that with this amount of demand will go. Hence, data centers must ensure energy efficiency as well as reliability. Era of data stored and used on intelligent way is in front of us. It is important to develop artificial intelligence algorithms that could be centralized or distributed based on the need.

Visualization is critical for an IoT application as this allows the interaction of the user with the environment. With recent advances in touch screen technologies, use of smart tablets and phones has become very intuitive.

Finally, Cloud centric Internet of Things will play bigger role in the future. The vision of IoT can be seen from two perspectives—'Internet' centric and 'Thing' centric. The Internet centric architecture will involve internet services being the focus while the objects contribute data. In the object centric architecture, the smart objects take the center stage.

Internet of Things in Digital Business Technologies

Estimations are that Internet of Thing include between 26(Peter Middleton, Peter Kjeldsen, Jim Tully, 2013) and 50(Evans D., 2011) billion units until 2020. Where is the value potential of Internet of Things? McKinsey report stated:(James Manyika, Michael Chui, Peter Bisson, Jonathan Woetzel, Richard Dobbs, Jacques Bughin, Dan Aharon, 2015)

- Interoperability requires capturing (40% of total value). Of the total potential value that can be unlocked with IoT, 40 percent of this value, on average, requires multiple IoT systems to work together. In the worksite setting, 60 percent of the potential value requires the ability to integrate and analyze data from various IoT systems. Interoperability is required to unlock more than $4 trillion per year in potential economic impact from IoT use in 2025, out of a total potential impact of $11.1 trillion across the nine settings that we analyzed.
- Less than 1% of data currently used (mostly for alarms and control). More can be used for optimization and prediction.

- Two times more value from B2B than B2C applications.
- Estimation is that 60% is developed – 40% is in developing.

It will result in $1.9 trillion in global economic value-add through the sales in 2020,(Peter Middleton, Peter Kjeldsen, Jim Tully, 2013) and $3.9 – $11.1 trillion in 2025(James Manyika, Michael Chui, Peter Bisson, Jonathan Woetzel, Richard Dobbs, Jacques Bughin, Dan Aharon, 2015). "Settings" will affect following industries:

- **Offices:** Space where knowledge workers work - (Security and Energy) - $70-$150B
- **Worksites:** Custom production environment - (Operation optimization/ health and safety) - $160B – $930B
- **Human:** Devices attached to or inside the human body - (Health and fitness) - $170B-1.6T
- **Home Automation and Security:** Buildings where people live - $200B-$350B
- **Vehicles**: Systems inside moving vehicles - (Autonomous vehicles and condition-based maintenance) - $210B - $740B
- **Retail Environments (Automated Checkout):** Spaces where consumers engage in commerce- $410B - $1.2T
- **Outside:** Between urban environments - (Logistics and navigation) - $560B -$850B
- **Cities:** Urban environments - (Public health and transportation) - $930 - $1.7T
- **Factories:** Standardized production environment - (Operations and equipment optimization) - $1.2T – $3.7T

Growth of Internet of things is rapid, Figure 12. (Peter Middleton, Peter Kjeldsen, Jim Tully, 2013) Due to the low cost of adding IoT capability to consumer products, we expect that ghost devices with unused connectivity will be common. This will be a combination of products that have the capability built in but require software to "activate" it and products with IoT hardware/software that customers do not actively leverage. Depending on the usage model, much effort will be required to educate consumers about the utility they will derive from using IoT products. Companies may offer different product tiers, with the higher-end products offering IoT-enabled services, and mid-tier products sold with the inherent hardware capability and needing only a remote software upgrade to unlock the IoT capabilities.

Figure 13 shows a distribution of shipments of things by category in 2020, ranked by volume.(Peter Middleton, Peter Kjeldsen, Jim Tully, 2013)

Using specified Gartner forecast, in the graph are presented only few of about 60 different categories. The highest volume shipments will come from connected

Figure 12. Growth of things will be rapid

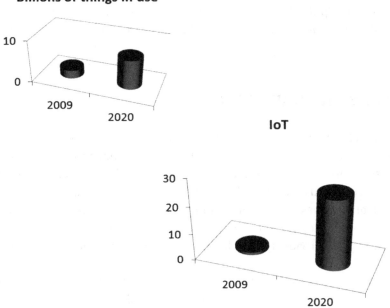

Figure 13. Shipment of things in 2020
(Courtesy: Gartner)

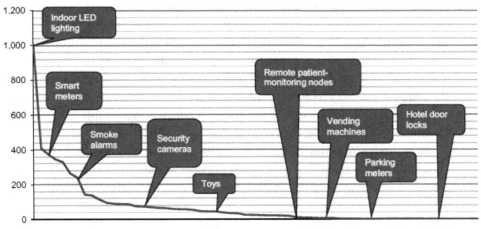

light-emitting diode (LED) interior light bulbs. Other areas with high shipment volumes include connected set-top boxes and TVs, wireless peripherals, smart meters, and smart pills. As we move to the right of the graph, the number of things in these categories falls off into a long tail composed of a great variety of different applications.

ENABLERS AND BARRIERS

For the Internet of Things to deliver its maximum economic impact certain conditions would need to be in place and several obstacles would need to be overcome. Some of these issues are technical. Some are structural and behavioral—consumers, for example, need to trust IoT-based systems, and companies need to embrace the data-driven approaches to decision making that IoT enables. In addition, regulatory issues need to be resolved, such as determining how autonomous vehicles can be introduced to public roadways and how they will be regulated and insured:

- **Technology:** The cost of basic hardware must continue to drop. Low-cost, low-power sensors are essential, and the price of MEMS (micro-electromechanical systems) sensors has dropped by 30 to 70 percent in the past five years. A similar trajectory is needed for radio-frequency identification (RFID)(Evan Welbourne, Leilani Battle, Garret Cole, Kayla Gould, Kyle Rector, Samuel Raymer, Magdalena Balazinska and Gaetano Borriello, 2009) tags and other hardware. Progress in inexpensive, low-cost battery power is also needed to keep distributed sensors and active tags operating, as well as low-cost data communication links (both short distance and long distance).
- **Interoperability:** The ability of IoT devices and systems to work together is critical for realizing the full value of IoT applications. Without interoperability, at least 40 percent of potential benefits cannot be realized. Adopting open standards is one way to accomplish interoperability. Interoperability can also be achieved by implementing systems or platforms that enable different IoT systems to communicate with one another.
- **Privacy and Confidentiality:** The types, amount, and specificity of data gathered by billions of devices create concerns among individuals about their privacy and among organizations about the confidentiality and integrity of their data.
- **Security:** Organizations need to deal with new categories of risk that the Internet of Things can introduce. Extending information technology (IT) systems to new devices creates many more opportunities for potential breaches, which must be managed. Furthermore, when IoT is used to control physical

assets, whether water treatment plants or automobiles, the consequences associated with a breach in security extend beyond the unauthorized release of information—they could potentially cause physical harm.

- **Intellectual Property:** A common understanding of ownership rights to data produced by various connected devices will be required to unlock the full potential of IoT.
- **Organization and Talent:** IoT combines the physical and digital worlds, challenging conventional notions of organizational responsibilities. Organizations also need the capacity and mindset to use the Internet of Things to guide data-driven decision-making, as well as the ability to adapt their organizations to new processes and business models.
- **Public Policy:** Certain IoT applications cannot proceed without regulatory approval. The most obvious is self-driving cars. Policy makers also often have a role to play in shaping market rules that affect IoT adoption, such as creating appropriate incentives in health care. Finally, government can play a role in setting rules for data practices regarding collection, sharing, and use of IoT data.

R&D IN INTERNET-OF-THINGS

As professor John Stankovic stated – there are eight R&D areas (Stankovic, 2014):

- Massive scaling (see IoT Elements).
- Architecture and dependencies.
- Creating knowledge and Big Data.
- Robustness.
- Openness.
- Security.
- Privacy.
- Human-in-the-loop.

Some of the topics we discussed earlier, so other we can discuss in this section.

Architecture and Dependences

Trillions of things, connected to the Internet need an adequate architecture that permits easy connectivity, control, communications, and useful applications. How will these objects interact between themselves? Some things must be disjoint and protected from other devices. Other makes sense to share devices and information.

One possible architectural approach for IoT is to borrow idea for sharing information is from the smartphone where, applications are available from an app store. Various standards and automatic checks are made to ensure that an app can execute on a given platform. A similar architectural approach for IoT would also have similar advantages. However, IoT platform is much more complicated than for smartphone. While each application must solve its own problems, the sharing of a sensing and actuation utility across multiple simultaneously running applications can result in many systems-of-systems interference problems, especially with the actuators. Interferences arise from many issues, but primarily when the cyber depends on assumptions about the environment, the hardware platform, requirements, naming, control and various device semantics.

Let us consider one example. Assume that we integrate several systems responsible for energy management (controlling thermostats(Smart Hotel Control, 2015), windows, doors, and shades)(Engineering Recommendations and Minimal Standards v4.0, 2011). If information can be shared, this would allow the energy management system to adjust room temperature depending on the physiological status of the residents as detected by the home health care system. In addition, integration will allow avoiding negative consequences. Integrating multiple systems is very challenging as each individual system has its own assumptions and strategy to control the physical world variables without much knowledge of the other systems, which leads to conflicts when these systems are integrated without careful consideration.

Creating Knowledge of Big Data

It will be necessary to develop techniques that convert this raw data into usable knowledge. For example, in the medical area, this concept is not new.(Vladimir Brusic, 1999) Main challenges for data interpretation and the formation of knowledge include addressing noisy, physical world data and developing new inference techniques that do not suffer the limitations of Bayesian or Dempster-Shafer schemes. These limitations include the need to know a priori probabilities and the cost of computations. Rule based systems may be used, but may also be too ad hoc for some applications.

The amount of collected data will be enormous. It can be expected that a very large number of real-time sensor data streams will exist, that it will be common for a given stream of data to be used in many different ways for many different inference purposes, that the data provenance and how it was processed must be known, and that privacy and security must be applied. Data mining techniques are expected to provide the creation of important knowledge from all this data. Consequently, uncertainty in interpreted data can easily cause users not to trust the system. However, in many other situations it will be necessary to combine a set of current sensor readings with a trace of the recent past readings and utilize a history of a given user's activities and personal characteristics to arrive at an accurate data assignment. More research is necessary on this problem.

Robustness

One of the most common (and simple) example of this deterioration problem is with clock synchronization. Over time, clock drift causes nodes to have different enough times to result in application failures. While it is widely recognized that clock synchronization must re-occur, this principle is much more general. One of the solution is RingBUS system for cabling systems, where responding time on the wide area location, such are airports are in milliseconds.(Fire and Smoke Protection Control System, 2010) This includes formal methods to develop reliable code, in-situ debugging techniques, on-line fault tolerance, in-field-maintenance, and general health monitoring services.

INTERNET-OF-THINGS IN INDUSTRY

Deployments of solutions in today applications are focused on:

- **Smart Cities:** Smart city construction depends on many IoT applications for different industries. Smart city development plans are divided into three stages: 1) the stage for initial infrastructure construction; 2) the stage for data-processing facility construction; and 3) the stage for end-phase service platform construction. A large number of smart city projects provide huge opportunities for telecom OEM, systems integration enterprises, data aggregation and analysis/service enterprises, and telecom operators.
- **Intelligent Transportation:** Many countries around the world need a solution to solve the problems of increased amount of traffic congestion in urban areas using new technologies such as IoT.
- **Intelligent Coal Mine:** In 2011, The State Administration of work safety and State Coal Mine Safety Supervision Bureau in China regulated that all coal mines in china must complete the construction of "Mine Six-Hedge Safety Systems" until the end of 2013. The Six-Hedge underground systems include: 1) general monitoring and controlling system; 2) personnel positioning system; 3) emergent shelter systems; 4) oxygen provision monitoring system; 5) water supply and drainage monitoring system; and 6) mine cable and wireless communication system.(Shanzhi Chen, Hui Xu, Dake Li, Bo Hu, and Hucheng Wang, 2014)

- **Intelligent Oil Field:** Intelligent oil field (IOF) consists of a distributed system, holding frequently captured data. The data are evaluated and acted upon real-time information. IOF brings lower operational costs, lower capital investment, and increased yield of oil and gas.

Internet-of-Things HUBS

IoT HUBs are general purpose and product specific devices with the main task to aggregate representation of things and their (meta) data. Typically, they do not operate with each other. This means that standardization process is necessary for avoiding "islands" of things. General concept is shown in Figure 14. Few companies still going one-step further – they produced their own hubs which working on their own standards. Possible largest community is Samsung SmartThings(One App + One Hub + All Your Things, 2016), Figure 15. Whether you have two smart devices or 200, all you need is one Hub to create a smart home.

Few companies still going one-step further – they produced their own hubs which working on their own standards. Possible largest community is Samsung SmartThings(One App + One Hub + All Your Things, 2016), Figure 15. Whether

Figure 14. IoT HUB concept

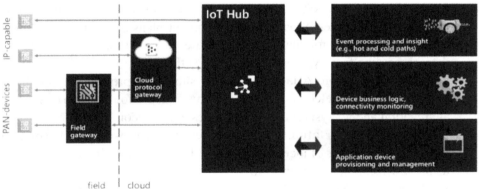

Figure 15. Samsung SmartThings

you have two smart devices or 200, all you need is one Hub to create a smart home. Like a live-in translator, the Hub communicates with all of your different connected products–regardless of their wireless protocol–so that you can easily monitor and control them from the SmartThings app. Samsung hub contains ZigBee and Z-Wave radios, and is also compatible with IP-accessible devices. There is no hard wiring or installation needed. Simply connect it to your Internet router using the included Ethernet cable, attach the power cord to the back of the Hub, and you are ready to start creating a safer, smarter home. \

Next is Nest(2016). What is most intriguing about the Nest Thermostat is how it has become the center of a connected Nest home ecosystem. The company Nest Labs (which is part of Google or Alphabet) recently added a video camera to its product lineup, which includes the thermostat and a smoke and carbon monoxide detector, Figure 16.

Of course, everything works together. Should Nest's smoke and carbon monoxide detector sense carbon monoxide in your home, for example, it will immediately tell the thermostat to shut down your heat in case the furnace is the culprit. Alternatively, should the Nest Cam sense movement in your home when the thermostat believes nobody's there, alerts can be sent to your phone.

There is a platform called Works With Nest that makes the thermostat interoperable with compatible devices. In addition, even if your smart home devices do not have the Works With Nest logo on the box, you can still integrate them into your setup using some web-based software.

Figure 16. Nest thermostat and HUB

To make all of your devices talk to each other, look to the cloud. A service called If This Then That (IFTTT)(Connect the apps you love, 2016) has pre-made recipes that can connect your devices. You can use the service to program your devices to run routines, react to triggers, or pass commands to other devices in your home. The Internet of Things is a string of connections between pieces of hardware, so set them up to control each other.

Microsoft Azure is next sample of IoT HUB.(Azure IoT HUM, 2016) Azure if fully managed service that enables reliable and secure bidirectional communications between millions of IoT devices. How does IoT Hub Work Azure IoT? Hub implements the service-assisted communication pattern to mediate the interactions between your devices and your solution back end. The pattern establishes the following principles:

- Security takes precedence over all other capabilities.
- Devices do not accept unsolicited network information.
- Devices should only connect to or establish routes to well-known services they are peered with, such as IoT Hub.
- The communication path between device and service or between device and gateway is secured at the application protocol layer.
- System-level authorization and authentication are based on per-device identities. They make access credentials and permissions nearly instantly revocable.
- Bidirectional communication for devices that connect sporadically due to power or connectivity concerns is facilitated by holding commands and device notifications until a device connects to receive them. IoT Hub maintains device specific queues for the commands it sends.

ARTIK is a family of modules (ARTIK 1, ARTIK 5, and ARTIK 10) tailored for the Internet of Things (IoT). With a tiered architecture built for performance, optimized power consumption, and memory utilization and footprint, ARTIK is designed specifically for a variety of applications, from low-end wearables to powerful hubs with local processing and analytics. The best-in-class security solution includes a hardware Secure Element (SE), with machine learning for anomaly detection, and a software Trusted Execution Environment (TEE).(Artik, 2016)

INTERNET-OF-THINGS AND SMART CITIES

Over the past few years, the definition of "Smart Cities" has evolved to mean many things to many people. Yet, one thing remains constant: part of being "smart" is

Figure 17. IoT logo (left). Microsoft Azure IoT concept (right)

utilizing information and communications technology (ICT) and the Internet to address urban challenges.

The number of urban residents is growing by nearly 60 million every year. In addition, more than 60 percent of the world's population will be living in cities by 2050. As a result, people occupying just 2 percent of the world's land will consume about three-quarters of its resources. Moreover, more than 100 cities of 1 million people will be built in the next 10 years.(State of the World Cities 2012/2013, 2013) Today's cities face a variety of challenges, including job creation, economic growth, environmental sustainability, and social resilience. Given these trends, understanding where we are in the evolution of the Internet is critical to future city-planning processes.

IAs things add capabilities like context awareness, increased processing power, and energy independence, and as more people and new types of information are connected, IoT becomes an Internet of Everything — a network of networks where billions or even trillions of connections create unprecedented opportunities as well as new risks.

In fact, we are seeing the emergence of a new imperative from public leaders and industries. "Digital urbanism" is rapidly becoming a central pillar for urban planners, architects, developers, and transportation providers, as well as in public service provision.

One challenge in smart city applications and services will be the reach and the details of service information to be utilized in the context of the regulatory framework. Over time, utilities, healthcare providers, transportation providers and government agencies will require massive storage and IT processing capabilities that will partially rely on a secure and flexible cloud-based infrastructure and service delivery mechanism. Another challenge is time needed for implementation, since the large scale for the physical infrastructure (such as that for automotive applications) will encounter careful yet slow and linear implementation approaches from government and industry.

From a public sector leadership perspective, cities can be viewed as microcosms of the interconnected networks that make up IoE. In fact, cities serve as "fertile ground" for realizing IoE value.

For this to happen, however, city leadership must understand how the components of IoE — people, process, data, and things — play specific roles, and work together, to enable our future cities and communities. The development of smart grids, data analytics and autonomous vehicles will provide an intelligent platform to deliver innovations in energy management, traffic management and security, sharing the benefits of this technology throughout society, Figure 18.

Here are some examples of Smart Cities:

- The city of Amsterdam's broader objective is to connect all of its citizens by 2018. Once connected, residents and businesses will be able to access rich information and media resources, friends and colleagues, and a wealth of innovative services that improve life across the city.(Bryant, 2015).
- In Chicago, consortium of companies promoted Smart City concept.(The City of Chicago Technology Plan, 2013).

Figure 18. Example IoT smart cities applications
(Source: KcKinsey Internal research, GSMA)

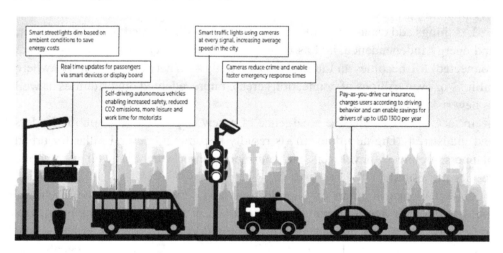

- New York – launched City 24/7, an interactive platform that integrates information from open government programs, local businesses, and citizens to provide meaningful and powerful knowledge anytime, anywhere, on any device.

Gartner position 34 most important technologies that can be used to implement smart city, Figure 19.

STATE OF THE ART AND THE ROLE OF STANDARDS

In 2016, everything going digital. Just imagine sport equipment.(Lightman, 2016). A sampling of sensor-laden sports equipment shows the range of athletic activity being, measured, analyzed and affected by the technology. Golf stick, tennis racket with movement control, balls for basketball, Figure 20 (Wilson X Connected Basketball - All Day, 2015), softball and baseball with moving sensors and distance measurement sensors together with GPS locator, are technology examples built in standard sport equipment. This so-called sensor fusion presented a real hurdle to developing sports training products that used such data.

Figure 19. Gartner hype cycle for smart city technologies and solutions
(Source: Gartner, 2011)

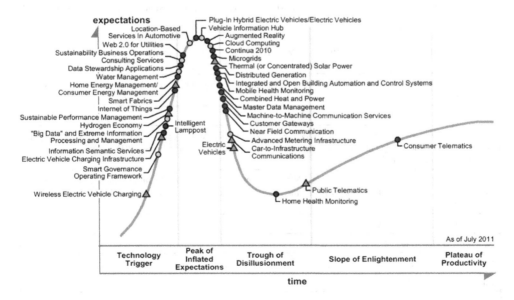

Figure 20. Wilson X connected with sensor. The battery inside the sensor is not replaceable

Main part of this ball is low power short-range Bluetooth sensor. In the Table 3, you can find latest technology regarding to Low Power Short Range Networks.

Looking through some characteristics of Low Power WAN, we can find that this technology is in the mid phase of development. We have to expect further improvement of all of the features in all standards. Table 4 showing the state of the art in this field.

Which Wireless Technologies should one Chose?

Figure 21 show a graphic representation of the short-range technologies that support the main part of the drivers and requirements listed above. This graph mainly shows technologies that are available in mobile devices such as smartphone, laptops, etc.

Table 3. Low power short range technology

IEEE 802.15.4(IEEE Standard for Local and metropolitan area networks— Part 15.4: Low-Rate Wireless Personal Area, 2011)
ANT[3]
ZWave/G9959(G 9959-SERIES G: TRANSMISSION SYSTEMS AND MEDIA, DIGITAL SYSTEMS AND NETWORKS - Short range narrow-band digital radiocommunication transceivers – PHY, MAC, SAR and LLC layer specifications, 01.2015)
IEEE 802.11ac - Wi-Fi(Part 11: Wireless LAN Medium Access Control (MAC) and Physical Layer (PHY) Specifications Amendment 4: Enhancements for Very High Throughput for Operation in Bands below 6 GHz, 2013)
Bluetooth LE(Bluetooth, 2016)
New Bluetooth variants (Long variant, Mesh)
DASH-7(DASH 7 Alliance)
Enocean (Enocean Alliance)
ISM Point-to-Point

Table 4. Low power WAN

	Proprietary LPWAN	**2G/3G**	**NB-IoT**
Availability	Now	Now	2017
Coverage	■□□	■■■	-
Low Risk	■□□	■■□	■■■
Affordable end point	■□□	■□□	■■□
Quality of Service	■■□	■■■	■■■
Business model	Operator or private	Operator	Operator
Standardized	□□□	■■■	■■■

Figure 21. Short-range technologies with power consumptions, distances and data rates

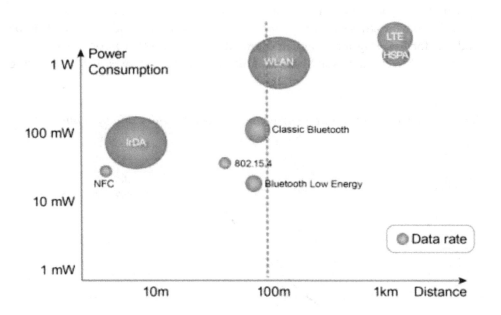

The reason for only showing wireless technologies available in mobile devices is the above mentioned requirement on an available ecosystem. One exception to the rule is 802.15.4 that both fulfills the requirement on an internationally used standard and is widely used in early IoT use cases for example building automation and smart energy.

The illustrated range is point-to-point and heavily depends on the individual devices' radio design and shall thus be considered as an indication only. The same concept applies for power consumption since the actual power consumption is use case dependent. Our illustration indicates how well the different technologies support low power applications. Most of the manufacturers today are focusing on the "last 100 meters," we will look more into the wireless technologies situated to the left of the red line.

New processor for Internet-of-Things is microcontroller. Even more – programmable logical controller (PLC) is next candidate. Reason? PLC has built in almost everything for controlling processes. Latest development reduces size of PLCs to the size of CPU. Really! Moreover, some (read all) technologies mentioned in Table 4 are embedded into microcontroller case, or even in microcontroller alone.

Very cheap Arduino microcontroller, with simple, clear programming environment, cross platform (Windows, Linux), with open source and extensible software... and hardware... That's it! Forecasts for microcontroller and embedded microcontrollers shipments are shown on Figure 22.

In previous paragraphs, terms microcontroller and PLC are mentioned. This means that few programs for programming microcontrollers and PLCs tends to be standards for IoT programming language. All devices have more or less memory. In Figure 23 check the ration between built-in memory and level of IoT operating

Figure 22. Microcontroller and embedded microcontrollers shipment until 2020

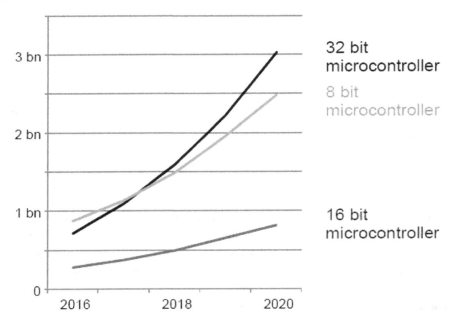

Figure 23. IoT operating systems

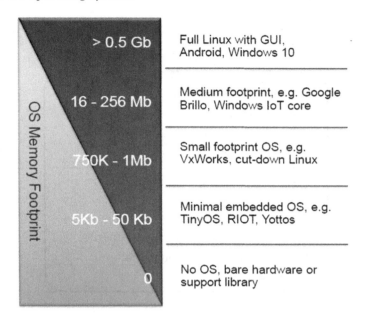

systems used for programming such devices. Full Linux with GUI, Android and Windows 10 in microcontroller or PLC is fantastic achievement. Some 20 years ago, PLCs were like small refrigerator, with no memory. Today they are of microchip size with more than 0.5 GB memory, and with operating systems.

This leads to new type of devices – HUBs that will connect tens of devices, now of one manufacturer. Samsung Smart HUB today is very big promise in the field of IoT devices. We have to expect HUBS what will connect devices from multiple companies. Alliances still exists, ant in coming period we will have significant results in this field.

IoT Platforms, Standards, and Ecosystems

First, we will discuss platforms, see Figure 24. In the middle are Data acquisition & management and Data integration systems. On one side are enterprise systems. Connection between middle area and enterprise systems are possible through: gateways/adapters, event processing, application development, analytics and visualization. On other side are, what we call "Things". Three main branches are focus of development: device provisioning and management, networking and communication and cyber security.

Figure 24. IoT platforms

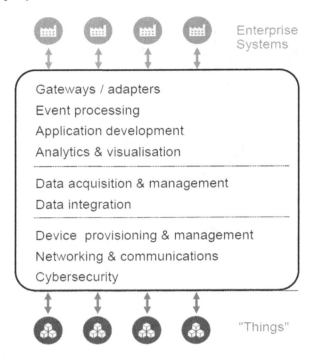

Second, we can discuss standards. Some of them we discussed earlier in this section see, Table 3. However, one standard (and alliance) we can mention her before others-LoRa(LoRa Technology, 2016).

LoRaWAN™ is a Low Power Wide Area Network (LPWAN) specification intended for wireless battery operated Things in regional, national or global network. LoRaWAN target key requirements of Internet of things such as secure bi-directional communication, mobility and localization services. This standard will provide seamless interoperability among smart Things without the need of complex local installations and gives back the freedom to the user, developer, businesses enabling the roll out of Internet of Things.

Sigfox is French company that builds wireless networks to connect low energy object, such are smart watches, smart metering devices... Ludovic le Moanand Cristopher Fourtet founded Sigfox at 2009. They charge $1 per connected device per year.(SIGFOX - The Global Communication Service Provider) Zigbee, Bluetooth, WiFi and Lte are known from earlier.

Third, important component of this mash are alliances and ecosystems. Maybe most promising is Allseen Alliance(Allseen aliance), because of Microsoft presence in Linux community. It is obvious that Microsoft saw power of Linux environment.

In October 10th, 2016, two largest alliances, OCF, sponsor of IoTivity project, and Allseen Alliance, which provides AllJoyn open source IoT framework, announced merging. Two organizations will merge ad operate under the OCF name and bylaws. (Unification Will Combine the Best of Both Organizations under Open Connectivity Foundation Name and Bylaws, 2016) Companies involved in the new standards groups expanded board include Samsung, Microsoft, AB Electrolux, LG, Canon, Cisco, GE Digital, Haier, Intel and Qualcomm.

Other alliances are: Samsung Smart Thing(Samsung Smart Thing, 2016)(one of the most powerful), Apple, Google, ZWave(ZWave Alliance, 2016), Thread Group(Thread Group, 2016), Open Interconnect Consortium, IoT Forum, OpenFog(OpenFog Consortium, 2016), and many others. IoT and Security

CONCLUSION

The Internet of Things has transformative potential for many types of participants and stakeholders. Technology suppliers are presented with the opportunity to develop new and valuable systems and create new sources of revenue and lines of business. Businesses that adopt IoT systems can improve operations and gather greater insights for data driven decision-making; some will have the opportunity to build new businesses with IoT technology and data. Consumers will have the most to gain—perhaps years of life from IoT health applications and safer transportation, greater convenience and time savings, and less costly goods and services.

To build competitive advantage in the IoT market, technology suppliers will need to create distinctive technology, distinctive data, software platforms, or end-to-end solutions. Those that fail to do so risk commoditization and loss of business. Business users of IoT technology will need to change their systems and organizations in order to make the most of the Internet of Things. They will need to invest in capabilities, culture, and processes as well as in technology. Businesses that fail to do so are likely to fall behind competitors that do. Smaller companies will need to find ways to obtain data on the scale required to compete with larger companies that will have access to sufficient data in-house.

While consumers stand to reap the greatest benefits from the Internet of Things, they will have to balance potential benefits with privacy concerns. They can gain access to an unprecedented amount of information about themselves and the world around them that can improve their quality of life. However, consumers will have to be discerning about how they engage with that information and with whom they share it.

Finally, policy makers and governments will have to ensure that these new systems are safe and that IoT data are not being stolen or abused. They can help to balance the needs for privacy and protection of private data and intellectual property with the demands of national security. With vital infrastructure connected to the Internet, security threats will multiply, which governments will need to address. Policy makers also have an important role in enabling the Internet of Things by leading and encouraging standards that will make interoperability and widespread adoption possible.

REFERENCES

Allseen aliance. (n.d.). Retrieved April 5, 2016, from https://allseenalliance.org/alliance/members

Artik. (2016). Retrieved April 24, 2016, from https://www.artik.io/hardware

Ashton, K. (2009). *That "Internet of Things" Thing*. RFID Journal.

Azure IoT HUM. (2016). Retrieved April 24, 2016, from https://azure.microsoft.com/en-us/services/iot-hub/

Bell, A. G. (1876). *Patent No. US 174 465*. USA.

Bluetooth. (2016). Retrieved April 5, 2016, from https://www.bluetooth.com/what-is-bluetooth-technology/bluetooth-technology-basics/low-energy

Brown, L. R. (2010). *World on the Edge: How to Prevent Environmental and Economic Collapse*. New York: W.W. Norton and Company.

Bryant, M. (2015, August). *The Things Network wants to make every city smart – starting with Amsterdam*. Retrieved April 24, 2016, from http://thenextweb.com/insider/2015/08/19/the-things-network-wants-to-make-every-city-smart-starting-with-amsterdam/#gref

Chen, S., Xu, H., Li, D., Hu, B., & Wang, H. (2014). A Vision of IoT: Applications, Challenges, and Opportunities With China Perspective. *The Internet of Things Journal, 1*(4), 349–359. doi:10.1109/JIOT.2014.2337336

Connect the apps you love. (2016). Retrieved April 24, 2016, from https://ifttt.com/

DASH 7 Alliance. (n.d.). Retrieved April 5, 2016, from http://www.dash7-alliance.org/

Devices, A. (n.d.). Retrieved April 12, 2016, from http://www.ambientdevices.com/

ENDNOTES

Engineering Recommendations and Minimal Standards v4.0. (2011). Hyatt International Technical Services.

Enocean Alliance. (n.d.). Retrieved April 5, 2016, from https://www.enocean-alliance.org/en/home/

Evans, D. (2011). *The Internet of Things - How the Next Evolution of the Internet is Changing Everything*. Cisco Internet Business Solution Group.

Evans, M. (2011). *Internet of Things*. Cisco.

Fire and Smoke Protection Control System. (2010). Retrieved April 24, 2016, from http://euroicc.com/solutions/ringbus/

G 9959-Series G: Transmission Systems and Media, Digital Systems and Networks - Short Range Narrow-Band Digital Radiocommunication Transceivers – PHY, MAC, SAR and LLC Layer Specifications. (2015). ITU.

Gardner, G. (2009). *Bycicle Production Reches 30 Billion Units*. Washington, DC: Worldwatch Institute.

George Antheil, H. M. (1942). *Patent No. 2292387 A*. Washington, DC: US Patent Office.

Google Trends. (n.d.). Retrieved April 17, 2016, from https://www.google.com/trends/explore#q=internet%20of%20things%2C%20%2Fm%2F07v58%2C%20wireless%20sensors&cmpt=q&tz=Etc%2FGMT-2

Hinden, R. (1998). *IP Version 6 Addressing Architecture*. Cisco Systems. doi:10.17487/rfc2373

IEEE Global History Network. (2009, May 18). Retrieved March 1, 2016

IEEE Standard for Local and metropolitan area networks— Part 15.4: Low-Rate Wireless Personal Area. (2011). New York: IEEE Computer Society.

Intel, W. P. (2009). *Rise of the Embedded Internet*. Intel Corporation.

Lightman, K. (2016, March). Silicon Gets Sporty. *IEEE Spectrum*, 44–48.

Lopez, J. (2012). *Internet of Things Scenario: When Things Negotiate*. Stamford, CT: Gartner.

LoRa Technology. (2016). Retrieved April 5, 2016, from https://www.lora-alliance.org/What-Is-LoRa/Technology

Mahoney, J., & LeHong, H. (2012). *Innovation Insight: The 'Internet of Everything*. Stamford, CT: Gartner.

Manyika, Chui, Bisson, Woetzel, Dobbs, Bughin, & Aharon. (2015). *The internet of things: Mapping the value beyond the hype*. McKinsey Institute.

Manyika, J., Chui, M., Brown, B., Bughin, J., Dobbs, R., Roxburgh, C., & Byers, A. H. (2011). *Big data: The next frontier for innovation, competition, and productivity*. McKinsay Global Institute.

Manyika, J., Chui, M., Bughin, J., Dobbs, R., Bisson, P., & Marrs, A. (2013). *Disruptive technologies: Advances that will transform life, business, and the global economy*. Mc Kinsey Global Institute.

Middleton, P., Kjeldsen, P., & Tully, J. (2013). *Forecast: The Internet of Things, Worldwide, 2013*. Stamford, CT: Gartner.

Minerva, R. (2015). Internet of Things and the 5th Generation Mobile Network. *IEEE Internet of Things* .

Morse, S. (1840). *Patent No. US1647 A*. Washington, DC: US Patent Office.

Nabaztag. (n.d.). Retrieved April 12, 2016, from http://www.nabaztag.com/

NEST. (2016). Retrieved April 24, 2016, from https://nest.com/

One App + One Hub + All Your Things. (2016). Retrieved April 24, 2016, from https://www.smartthings.com/how-it-works

OpenFog Consortium. (2016). Retrieved April 5, 2016, from http://www.openfogconsortium.org/

Paper, E. W. (2011). *More Than 50 Billion Devices Connected*. Ericson.

Part 11: Wireless LAN Medium Access Control (MAC) and Physical Layer (PHY) Specifications Amendment 4: Enhancements for Very High Throughput for Operation in Bands below 6 GHz. (2013). New York: IEEE.

Pavel Schilling. (n.d.). Retrieved 11 1, 2015, from https://en.wikipedia.org/wiki/Pavel_Schilling

Raskino, M., & LeHong, H. (2011). *Exploit the Democratization of the Internet of*. Stamford, CT: Gartner.

Reports. I. I. (2005). Internet of Things. Geneve: ITU.

Samsung Smart Thing. (2016). Retrieved April 5, 2016, from https://www.smartthings.com/

SIGFOX - The Global Communication Service Provider. (n.d.). Retrieved April 5, 2016, from www.sigfox.com

Smart Hotel Control. (2015). Retrieved April 24, 2016, from http://euroicc.com/solutions/smart-hotel-control/

Stankovic, J. A. (2014). *Research Directions for the Internet of Things. IEEE Internet of Things Journal*.

State of the World Cities 2012/20132013United Nations.

Temperton, J. (2015, May 15). *A 'fourth industrial revolution' is about to begin (in Germany)*. Retrieved April 12, 2016, from http://www.wired.co.uk/news/archive/2015-05/21/factory-of-the-future/viewgallery/474960

Tesla, N. (1898). *Patent No. US 613809 A*. Washington, DC: US Patent Office.

Tesla, N. (1926, January 30). *When Woman is Boss*. 21st Century Books.

The City of Chicago Technology Plan. (2013). Chicago: City of Chicago.

The Discovery of the Molecular Structure of DNA - The Double Helix. (2003, September 30). Retrieved April 18, 2016, from https://www.nobelprize.org/educational/medicine/dna_double_helix/readmore.html

Thread Group. (2016). Retrieved April 5, 2016, from http://www.threadgroup.org/

Timmer, J. (2011, February 11). *World's total CPU power: one human brain*. Retrieved April 12, 2016, from http://arstechnica.com/science/2011/02/adding-up-the-worlds-storage-and-computation-capacities/

Unification Will Combine the Best of Both Organizations under Open Connectivity Foundation Name and Bylaws. (2016, October 10). Retrieved November 30, 2016, from https://openconnectivity.org/press-releases/allseen-alliance-merges-open-connectivity-foundation-accelerate-internet-things

Velosa, A., Shulte, W. R., & Lhereux, B. J. (2015). *Hype Cycle for the Internet of Things, 2015*. Stamford, CT: Gartner.

Vladimir Brusic, J. Z. (1999). Knowledge discovery and data mining in biological databases. *The Knowledge Engineering Review*, *14*(3), 257–277. doi:10.1017/S0269888999003069

Weiser, M. (1991). The Computer for 21st Century. *Scientific American, 265*(September), 94–104. doi:10.1038/scientificamerican0991-94

Welbourne, E., Battle, L., Cole, G., Gould, K., Rector, K., Raymer, S., & Borriello, G. et al. (2009). *Building the Internet of Things Using RFID - The RFID Ecosystem Experience* (pp. 48–55). IEEE Computer Society.

What the Internet of Things (IoT) needs to be a Reality 2014 Retrieved from freescale.com/arm.com.

Wilson X Connected Basketball - All Day. (2015, September 10). Retrieved April 5, 2016, from https://www.youtube.com/watch?v=qRvAXsaHNkY

ZWave Alliance. (2016). Retrieved April 5, 2016, from http://z-wavealliance.org/

ENDNOTES

[1]   Not the IEEE 802.11 standard.

[2]   See section in this chapter State of the Art and the role of Standards for more details about technology.

[3]   ANT is a proprietary (but open access) multicast wireless sensor network technology designed and marketed by ANT Wireless (a division of Dynastream Innovations, in turn a wholly owned subsidiary of Garmin.

Chapter 2
An Approach to Designing IoT-Based Business Models

Iva Vojinović
University of Belgrade, Serbia

Ivan Jezdović
University of Belgrade, Serbia

Dušan Barać
University of Belgrade, Serbia

Milica Labus
University of Belgrade, Serbia

Filip Jovanović
Project Management College, Serbia

ABSTRACT

This chapter will foster the understanding of the structure of business model elements in Internet of things field. Business model provides an efficient way to analyze, understand and manage strategically oriented goals for one or more stakeholders in order to create some value for end-users, but in the Internet of things there is not clear path for its development. An approach that will be used is the generally accepted principle of forming business model, Canvas template, which is a strategic template for understanding the relation between key partners, key activities, customers and clients, key resources, value proposition for customers in the form of products or services, relationships with customers, sales and distribution channels, cost structure, income flow. Presented is an integrated model with main aspects that should be covered when it comes to the Internet of things business model development, combining Canvas template, inside organizational structure and ecosystem restrictions.

DOI: 10.4018/978-1-5225-2437-3.ch002

INTRODUCTION

In the media and literature is constantly cited forecasts that by 2020 billion devices will be connected to the Internet (Gartner, 2015). This assumption makes the market of smart devices increasingly competitive. Companies and start-ups are competing to become a leader in the smart tech sector. This led to the new go to market strategies.

The development of technology led to changes in business processes, where business models have to adapt to the new agile way of doing business. The biggest changes are based on the introduction of the Internet into all business processes, thus leading to mandatory online communication, data storage on the cloud, as well as multiple networking business systems due to the need to develop products and services based on the Internet of things. Combining different technologies leads to their overflow into one another, thus losing a clear path for go to market strategy.

In traditional industries, with products that are not connected to the Internet, the process of placing products on the market is the same whether it is a piece of clothing, food or any other product, setting it on the shelf in a store is enough to reach consumers. The whole process of sale involved the single activity and one-time interaction with customers. Product replacement happens when the product breaks down and loses its functionality. The traditional approach to modeling business systems and creating the business models does not apply to the Internet of things business models.

Internet of things, is a blend of hardware and software connected to the cloud, which significantly changes the user experience services that the product provides. Business models in Internet of things are based on keeping users on the same product with updating its functionalities. Products that are connected to the Internet, the so-called smart devices, have hardware that is constantly active, easy to update and expandable according to customer needs and market trends, providing many more possibilities for establishing long-term relationships with customers.

High fixed costs make it difficult to enter to the market and to be competitive. This provides a greater chance for more proven players to move to the IoT sector, because they are already supported by the experience and have the thrust of users that can deliver quality product.

This chapter will foster the main aspects of influencing technology on business models, and the authors aimed to analyze business models in Internet of things. Therefore, the chapter will start with an introduction of business models and business models in Internet of things, their basis through literature review. Main part of the chapter is preview of the business model Canvas applied in IoT and the overall model with the advices for business model development in IoT. At the end of this chapter authors concluded guidelines for IoT business models.

BACKGROUND

The market has become competitive for most products and services. As a result, the development of the business model is necessary to be constantly monitored and to invest resources in it based on the directions indicated by market analysis. Constant monitoring of the market and whether it is possible to promote a product or service at a given time is a prerequisite for continuous business growth. The same need for monitoring arises to the company as well, so that if there is a need for system changes it can be effectively adapted to the new situation. Monitoring the competition and find differentiation in relation to their offer is another step in the development of the business model.

Business model is a description of the value that company offers to customers including network partners and company architecture that generate sustainable revenue streams (Osterwalder, Pigneur, & Tucci, 2005). Business model can be described as the way in which the system creates, delivers and captures value. Developing a business model is a cyclic process, continuous in time. The term business model in literature interpreted differently. Various authors state that the business model is equal to the company strategy, while others see the business model as another name for sale. As today sales and marketing sectors go together, this leads to the conclusion that the development of the business model includes marketing as one of the segments that describes this term. The base of each approach is how the business system by providing value to customers creates a profit.

Business model changes over time, so the default setting of resources and activities does not apply for the whole product cycle. This occurs due to changes in technology, globalization and the need of entering the markets of developing countries.

The business model no matter how well designed it will always depend on users needs and competing business models. Safety in the success of the business model is possible only with companies that are unique in the market and have no competitors in the field. Changes in the value that the system creates for end users have become the main innovation for companies. Innovation in product or service leads to changes in the structure of the business model. All this leads to the need for system agility and sustainability of the business model.

Business development is monitored through a detailed business plan that clearly presented how and in which direction the operating system needs to be developed. It is necessary to make at least a three-year plan with geographical regions that shows the product or service plan to cover, in which industry can further expand the product or service and which communication and distribution channels should be used.

Every business model is divided into different elements (Chesbrough & Rosenbloom, 2002; Morris, Schindehutte, & Allen, 2005). Accepted elements of the business model widely spread through literature are nine building block of the Canvas model made by Osterwalder et al., (2005). The author stated that the Canvas template, with its nine building blocks, can be used as a set of assumptions and hypotheses about the value being created. The first block is a segment of users, which concerns delivering products or services to one or more users. The second block refers to the value proposition that solves user's problem and meets the need of using the product or service. It is further important to set the distribution, communication and sales channels. In contact with the user, it is important to pay attention to maintaining long-term relationships with them, which brings us to the fourth block of the business model and that is the relationship with customers and users. All transactions with the customer's business system that generates revenue, which represents the fifth block model. To the previously mentioned elements and processes successfully implemented it is necessary to plan and provide key resources. In addition to the key resources company has to have a list of key activities necessary for value creation. Partnerships can significantly improve the business model, which makes it the eighth block of the business model. Last, the ninth block of the Canvas template is cost structure.

Dijkman et al., (2015) presented the framework for a business model development for the Internet of things applications. Basis of their research is Canvas business model and analysis of its building blocks. They conducted 11 interviews and survey among 72 companies in Internet of things field. Companies are acrossed between diversified sectors such as energy, healthcare, transportation, smart home, etc. First they've presented the business model framework for Internet of things by showing the building blocks. Second, they've presented the relative importance of the building blocks and types. Their results showed that the value proposition is the most important building block, same as it is shown in the literature (Chesbrough & Rosenbloom, 2002; Morris et al., 2005). Among 9 basic building blocks customer relationships and key partnerships are also considered to be important in Internet of things business models. Survey respondents answered that the convenience, performance, comfort, possibility for updates and getting the job done are the most important in the value proposition block. Considering the cost reduction in the IoT business models is valuable (Openshaw et al., 2014), but it should be expanded with different revenue models, since Internet of things is highly flexible with amount of generated data. When it comes to customer relationships block the conducted survey indicated that focus is on co-creation by users, for example in development phase of the product, and as the other option mostly used are communities or self-service. Self-service is very popular in IoT domain, and enables every individual to be involved on its best serving way. Partnerships in IoT domain are matter of thrust on a high level, and it is in increased complexity (Hui, 2014) than in regular business models. Survey showed that partnerships have to be long term oriented since the data sharing is a matter of thrust and can cause damage to the whole cycle of partners if it is not regulated the best possible way. Partnerships are also focused on the cost reduction and basis of it are the understanding of the whole cash flow cycle. IoT business models have four different types of partnerships: hardware partners, software and app developers, launching customers and data analysis. Outsourcing is showed to be most compelling in IoT business models when it comes to innovation combining software and technology (Quinn, 2000). This finding is in line with Hui (2014): IoT business models add personalization and context through information gained over time. Insight to the customer data enables quicker and more personalized contact with customer. The author also explained that value creation has changed from resolving existing problems of the consumer in a reactive manner, to resolving emergent problems in a predictive manner.

Business models in IoT have service-dominant logic (Turber et al., 2014). The need for innovation is an essential element of IoT business models, which primarily refers to the introduction of the new updates and functionalities that can be constantly improved (Sun et al., 2012). IoT business models are not one firm model based as traditional ones, but rather the whole IoT ecosystem is involved and exchanging information is another issue to analyze in order to set up the successful model (Bucherer et al., 2012). Westerlund et al., (2014) agreed with previous authors and marked three issues as the main in the IoT: the immaturity of innovation, the diversity of objects and the unstructured ecosystems.

By Gassmann et al., (2014) business models are made of Who, What, How, and Why. Concept is presented in Figure 1.

Chen (2013) presented a detailed four-layer architecture for Internet of things devices which is presented in Figure 2:

- **Object Sensing and Information Gathering:** Data collection about the environment.
- **Information Delivering:** Wireless technologies, body area networks, Bluetooth, Zigbee, GPRS, GSM, 3G, etc.
- **Information Processing:** Services are provided through ubiquitous machines in autonomic and smart manner.
- **Application and Smart Services:** Performance is improved according to different users' requirements.

Leminen et al., (2012) set up another concept for IoT business model and connected ecosystem with customers. Figure 3 presents the ecosystem parts, open networked or closed private, and customers that can be business or consumers. They explained it through automotive industry setting the four models: model I is intelligent logistics in the future car production and logistics; model II is current

Figure 1. The archetypal business model
(*Gassman, Frankenberger, & Csik, 2014*)

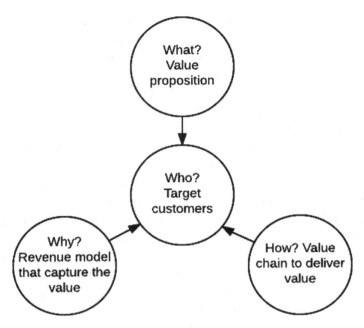

RFID usage in car production and logistics; model III is traffic safety services; and model IV is tracking and tracing in car logistics.

Rong, et al., (2015) developed 6C framework in order to improve understanding of the IoT based business system. First element is Context that is the environmental settings for the ecosystem development. The following is Cooperation that is the mechanism explaining how partners work together to reach the strategic objectives. Constructive elements are used for defining the fundamental structure and supportive infrastructure of the ecosystem. With Configuration element is seeked to identify the external relationships among partners. Capacity investigates the key success features of a supply network considering aspect of design, production, information management and inbound logistics. Change is the final element that each business ecosystem faces as challenge.

Sun et al., (2012) posited a DNA model, D-design, N-needs, and A-aspirations, addressing the How, What, and Why elements of IoT business model. Design consists of the various elements of the system such as key partners, resources, and activities which deals with the How question. Needs refer to parties in the external environment such as customer relationships and customer segments, dealing with What. Aspirations are desired results such as revenue, and deals with Why.

Figure 2. Architecture for Internet of Things
(Chen, 2013)

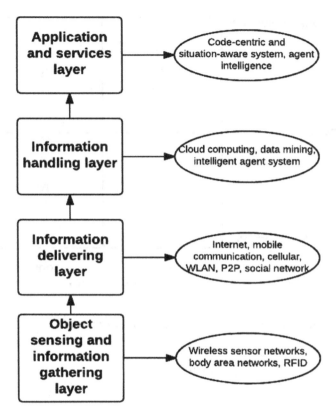

Turber et al., (2014) posited that a business model framework in IoT consists of three dimensions: Who, Where, and Why. Who describes collaborating partners, who build the Value Network, and does not only include firms who create IoT products, but also includes customers and stakeholders to reflect the network centric sentiment that customers are co-creators and co-producers of value. Where describes sources of value co-creation rooted in the layer model of digitized objects. There are four places of opportunity for value to be added by the partners. They are the device, connectivity, service and content layer (Yoo et al., 2010). The device layer comprises hardware, and an operating system; the network layer involves transmission plus network standard, and physical transport; the service layer provides direct interaction with users through application programs; while the content layer hosts the data, images and information. Why describes the benefits for partners from collaborating within the value network, both monetary benefits and non-monetary benefits. Each dimension addresses the four-layered modular architecture of digitized products.

Figure 3. Framework for analyzing diverse IoT business model
(Leminen et al., 2012)

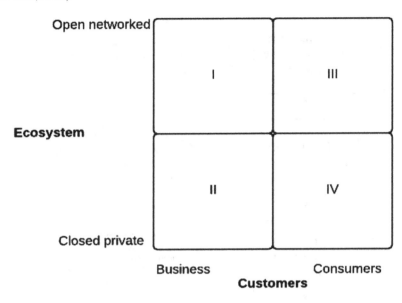

Figure 4. Framework design for a business model in the IoT
(Turber et al., 2014)

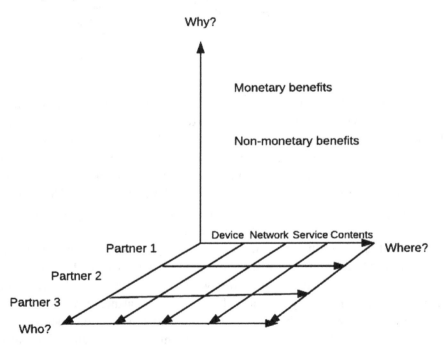

Table 1 presents perspective of business model elements based on the previous mentioned authors and their vision of what should be covered by business models and IoT business models. Osterwalder and Gassman gave the perspective of the business model concept that is universally applied. Leminen, Sun, Turber and Rong made business model concepts specifically for IoT. As we already mentioned Dijkman did not make any new business model, but presented adjusted business model Canvas in IoT and gave the most important elements for IoT business model development. Table 1 resume that the most important building block for IoT business model is partnership block. After it value proposition and customer segments are the second and third most important. Rong went further that the basic building blocks and inserted the ecosystem as one of the important blocks for business model in IoT, and named it change, considering technological and environmental changes that can influence business model.

Last perspective that needs to be covered are general business models and IoT business models accepted in literature and ready to use. Some of the basic business models by Osterwalder (2005), which authors of this chapter considered that can be used for IoT business models as well, follow:

Table 1. Summarizing business model elements based on different authors

Author	Osterwalder et al., (2005)	Leminen et al., (2012)	Sun et al., (2012)	Gassmann et al., (2014)	Turber et al., (2014)	Dijkman et al., (2015)	Rong et al., (2015)
BUSINESS MODEL ELEMENTS	Value propositions			What	Where	Value proposition	Context
	Customer relationships		Needs			Customer relationships	
	Customer segments	Customers	Who	Who	Who*		
	Channels			How			Capacity
	Key partners	Ecosystem	Design		Who*	Key Partners	Cooperation
	Key activities						
	Key resources						Construct
	Cost structure						
	Revenue streams		Aspirations	Why	Why		
							Configuration
							Change

*Same term

- **Product Cost Plus One-Off Premium Service:** Customers are paying the price of the product to which it adds a one-time premium services. An example of such a model is any wearable device that receives using, for example, one month exercise program, if it comes to a fitness device.
- **Product Cost Plus Recurring Premium Revenue:** Users buy a product for which pay full price and additionally subscribe to a service that goes along with that product as a basic service for which they purchased the product.
- **Free Product With Ongoing Revenue Stream:** In traditional products, this type of model is one of the main. However, the price of hardware for IoT device is more expensive than the cost of traditional hardware product. Therefore this model is less profitable than previously mentioned for the products connected to the Internet.
- **No Product Cost, No Service Cost:** The principle of free of charge product or services to end users is mostly applicable to health care. This model basically has B2B2C concept, where the endpoint service intended end-user is not directly payable by the manufacturer. The emphasis is on the fact that many devices which are manufactured may not be designed to end users, but can solve the problems of big companies and the system whereby they become users of smart devices.

Fleisch et al., (2015) presented six types of business models in IoT that can be charged for the digital products:

- **Physical Freemium:** There is no charge at the time of selling the device, but later service can be additionally charged for the premium users.
- **Digital Add-On:** First device is sold with inexpensively and with a thin margin, and later customer can purchase services with a higher margin.
- **Digital Lock-In:** Refers to a sensor-based, digital handshake that is deployed to define compatibility, preclude counterfeits, and assure warranties.
- **Product as Point of Sales:** Device is site of marketing services and digital sales.
- **Object Self-Service:** Refers to the ability of device to independently make requests on the Internet.
- **Remote Usage and Condition Monitoring:** Device can transmit data about their own status or their environment in real time.

To resume the previous part of the chapter, Internet of things business models introduces new segments that needs to be met in order to achieve competitiveness in the market, and the cost reduction in not the first to think of when the designing of business models starts. In the following part we will cover Canvas business model elements, explain it in detail and adjust it to IoT business model context. We selected this template as the universal for understanding and comprehensive in aspect of building block elements, but it will be expanded with ecosystem elements that are found to be missing.

AN APPROACH FOR IOT BUSINESS MODELS DEVELOPMENT

IoT devices with its spectrum of innovations during time become technically and economically feasible. This includes improvements in the performance, energy efficiency and miniaturization of sensors and batteries; low-cost computer processing power and data storage, low-cost wireless connectivity; tools that enable rapid software development; big data analytics etc.

To be able to do a business modeling it is important to have an understanding of business model aspects that needs to be explained in detail, but also to have a clear picture of the elements that every IoT device has. Those parts are the foundation of understanding how IoT business model works. Every IoT device consists of three components: physical component, smart component and the connection component. The physical components of the hardware product are its mechanical and electronic components. Smart device component represents sensors, microprocessors, data storage, an embedded operating system, controls, software and enhanced user interface or an application installed on the device. Connectivity component enables wired or wireless connections of the device to the Internet.

IoT device services can be divided into four basic capabilities that can be used for modeling service part of the device and can be used for making the revenue plan considering levels of the service that can be applied for one IoT device:

- Monitoring is a basic function of each smart device, and is characterized by monitoring the user from using the product, in what should be improved or immediately respond to user behavior. This can be easily explained by the medical devices used to monitor blood sugar levels. Monitoring improves the product so that after long-term observation of users, while using the product for a different version can improve everything turned out to be unsound products in engineering or a use case context.
- Control is the next function which represents a reaction to monitoring software, which is done from the device or the cloud system. Algorithms that detect a condition that triggers an action can not be explained by alerting device that monitors blood sugar levels, whereby when it reaches a certain level, the device responds and sends further guidance on the treatment to be applied.

- Optimization of the device is its adaptation itself to its functions on the basis of inputs received. This would mean that intelligent machines in the production itself can automatically switch blade and optimizes them according to the needs in the development of products, thus improving the efficiency of the product.
- Autonomy means the device's ability to perform all the activities itself. In this way, a vacuum cleaner and floor cleaner can clean the whole procedure by itself. In addition, these devices have the ability to learn about their environment, working self-diagnosis, repair, and adapt to the user's preference.

Whatever business model is used it is important to underline that from the beginning it is necessary to track statistics leads, referrals, all the opportunities, missed and realized with the help of various tools that can in a professional manner provide predictions and conclusions for business strategy, to be able to improve business model in every moment based on the conclusion of the previous statistics.

Canvas Building Blocks in IoT

Customer Segments

Companies need to determine for whom they are creating value and each company has to set its targeted groups or individuals. It is necessary to conduct an analysis of users on the basis that determines whether they should be divided into segments, or if the value should be placed to one group of users. Analysis needs to be done according to the behavior of individuals and the needs they have. Users can be segmented based on:

- Distribution channel that delivers value.
- Spending power.
- The various components of the same product.
- Requiring special attitude towards them.

Below is an overview of the main segments that may be considered as initial:

- **Mass Market:** The focus on the mass market is characterized by the creation of value that satisfy the needs and resolve the problems of the majority of users. Here users are directed to the same communication and distribution channels, leading to the establishment of a template for the same relationship with customers. One example of such a business model is the market of the electronic sector.

- **Niche Market:** The business model is based on a narrow segment of the market and characterized by the creation of value which is adjusted to a small percentage of users and usually can be seen in relation to supplier-buyer, for example, the manufacturer of the equipment and spare parts for cars that depend on the major car manufacturers. Niche market is flexible in communication and distribution channels to meet customer needs.
- **Segmented:** Segmented access to users relating to the adjustment of the same value to users according to their needs. Here is an example that best illustrates segmented market: bank can offers credit services to customers with different incomes and powers. In this case, special attention is paid to the way in which the revenue derived from the user.
- **Diversified:** The business model that supports diversified customers refers to two groups of users with different needs and problems which the company created by different values can meet. An example that describes this type of segmentation users is rentals for cloud computing services, where they can rent as they use, or it can take a certain space in the cloud system and use it whenever they want.
- **Multi-Sided Platform (Multi-Sided Markets):** The concept of multi-sided markets is related to the dependence of the company from several quarters of the participants. Specify in these cases, the company depends on the client and the user. An example of that can explain this principle is any service or product is offered free of charge, where on the one hand it is necessary to attract clients that a product will be interesting for advertising them. Both segments are equally important for creating value and are mutually dependent.

Users need to be in constant focus of business and communication with them has to be done continuously. It is necessary to examine how they came to a product or service the system placed on the market and thus to continue gaining new customers in the same manner. In relationship with the clients and customers it is necessary to analyze and understand their problem, build trust by having interest for their goals and how the company's' product or service can help to achieve it. When customers are targeted company have to make a plan to convert them from the initial contact to make them long-term customers.

Value Propositions

Customers and clients have needs and problems that should be solved. Solutions are implemented through single product or service that has exactly those characteristics tailored to customer requirements. Good value created for the user is the way the company that generates revenue. The value that is created for the user has quantitative and qualitative segment. In quantitative characteristic values can be adjusted to the speed of delivery and price, and it can be a qualitative user experience when using the product or service or design. The elements to be considered when creating value for users are the following:

- **Innovation:** The products can be found concerning a completely new technology which had not appeared on the market, while on the other side of innovation depends on the industry but also in the financial sector cannot make major changes in terms of added value.
- **Performance:** PC is an example of where they occurred in the past, major changes to the benefit of users, but the performance of such products in the present day become limited for the Advancement of graphics, speed and other attributes, according to attained the upper limit of its development.
- **Customization:** Customization of the product or service of different users is one of the most important elements to users to stay loyal to the brand.
- **Product Design:** In the fashion industry as well as in electronic devices design plays a decisive role and can make a product just because of his looks ranks of luxury category or as opposed to everyone's needs.
- **Brand / Status:** When a brand allocate to its exclusiveness or to the best in a field, users will feel the prestige of using a product with their logo or mark clearly highlighted on it.
- **Price:** Segment of the market that is sensitive to the price of the best can be controlled by lowering the price to provide the same service or product. Here you can talk about and totally free products that now affect telecom industry or newspapers, or variety of value-added products. It can also be used to create a product that has in itself some other product, or a set of services, of other brand, whose price is already included in the product price and not charged separately, leading to increased customer satisfaction while saving.
- **Risk Reduction - Guarantee:** Customers feel protected if the period of using the product without any additional adjustments is as much as possible.
- **Availability:** Generally refers to the provision of services such as customer service that is available any time and do not have to be adjusted to the time that is open for all other users. This may relate to the use of online banking in case of a wide segment of the market which enables transactions to realize 24 hours, or in the case of services such as private jets, where you can rent a plane at any time, which is considered a privilege for a niche that can afford it to herself.

Mejtoft (2011) classified value creation in IoT into following layers:

- Manufacturing layer where manufacturers or retailers provide items such as sensors and terminal devices.
- Supporting layer which collects data that can be utilized in the value creation processes
- Value creation layer uses IoT as a co-creative partner, because the network of things can think for itself.

Channels

Communication, sales and distribution channel that the company chooses give a different view of it, which relates to the initial presentation of the company's brand, the ways in which users can buy or use the product or service, delivering the same, as well as post-sales services such as maintenance or servicing of products.

Selecting a channel of communication, sales and distribution influence the price of a product or service. Channels can be personal or partnership, where personal channels have a larger margin, while the partner has a greater market penetration because they are used and their strength in attracting and retaining customers. The ultimate goal for the company is to maximize revenue therefore necessary to strike a balance in the channels used.

Business model in IoT changes relationship with users in its less dependence system to suppliers, by allowing companies the higher profit. On the other hand users have the advantage of understanding of product performance can take them to the producer of their choice for which manufacturers have to be careful when designing the product and its functionality. Users have the advantage because they are less dependent on the manufacturer, its advice and support in the product usage.

Business models in the IoT are changing the relationship with suppliers, due to the reduced need for delivering physical objects. IoT provides more services with a single product. Although changing the traditional suppliers for products, a new concept needs suppliers for hardware components, such as: sensors, connection, installation embedded operating system, etc.

Relationships With Customers and Clients

CRM is a term from the beginning it was used as customer relationship management, and now has a meaning, in addition to customer relationship management, managing relationships with partners, follow-up marketing and sales, support and so on. Today's Internet users are more open than ever. Companies can monitor users even before its purchase by Shopping applications that accurately detect when the user entered the store, items that looked at how long lingered in which the shelves with items etc. User behavior can be monitored with every purchase and thus improve his experience and establish a loyal relationship with them based on their needs. If the user behavior shows that he is interested in exactly one item in the store and not retained in the store out of it, then he may offer discounts application when the product is on sale or can reduce the speed queuing with such customers. On the other hand, maybe the user spends a lot of money in the store and it is useful to offer him a loyalty card. It is also possible to monitor what the user is doing after purchasing the product, do visit social networking sites that brand.

Customer relations can be established on a personal level or automatic, which can also be driven by different motivations. This may be due to the need to increase the number of users of products or services, due to the need to retain existing customers and to enhance sales channels.

There are several types that can be taken as approaches to managing relations with customers.

Personal assistance - this type of relationship with the user regards personal contact with them, where this interaction may be performed during or after completion of the sale transaction. Different communication channels can be used, such as e-mail, call center, or the point of sale. Based on the Canvas model there are five ways for building relationship with clients:

- **Dedicated Personal Assistance:** Used for long-term relationships with customers, such as customer relationships and key account managers, and communications adviser in the bank with clients who have business loans. Dedicated personal assistant is assigned an individual client and is obliged to resolve all its doubts regarding the products or services it receives.
- **Self-Service:** The company this way provides enough information and guidance, mainly online, or any recorded audio message, call center, allowing users to set the product or in any way solve the problem that they have.
- **Automated Services:** An extended version of self-service in which adjustments are possible with the support of online product platform is automated services relationship with the customer. The essence of this approach is the added value that you get online platforms. Example describing this approach is customizing the site or application used by a user and is configured independently and obtaining different suggestions for subsequent use of the product. Sites related to movies and music have such access to users.
- **Community:** Companies are using this form of customer support when they want to find out what people think should be improved with a product through the mutual exchange of user experiences, and help each other in solving problems using the product. This approach is easy to come up to the expectations that customers have when using the product.

- **Co-Creation:** User involvement in the development itself the product or service is the highest level of trust between the company and the user. In this way, users have the opportunity to provide valuable content and help manage product or service to other users. An example of such cooperation is the date the options review sites that provide users with each other as well as guidance on the content of products, such as books, music, movies.

Business development is a cyclic process that occurs continuously with analysis of feedback from customers and users, as well as market conditions. Permanent monitoring process, from initial contact with clients and customers, listening to their needs, to project implementation and successful completion, is part of the business system development. A detailed analysis has to be done for clients and customers, who are the actual users of products or services, which industry do they belong comparing vertically and horizontally. Analyzing markets and customers is determined by where you can find potential customers, and it is necessary to always be present where they are. After the analysis it is important to construct and send a clear and consistent message about the brand and quality of product or service. All these are basic steps for making some business model successful.

Revenue Streams

Company to a different segment of customers apply a special method of charging for the value it provides, through fixed price auctions, depending on the market and volumes, negotiation, management, etc. Business model can be set in two ways: one-time transaction that brings fee or permanent income in the form of extending a service or purchase a product over and over again, or customer service and maintenance after purchase. Company has to make the structure of revenues for the next year with existing and new clients, which measures the number of clients should be to maintain a positive cash flow.

The following are suggested ways of managing and generating a revenue stream:

- **Asset Sale:** The most widespread way to generate revenue is a standard sale of rights to the product, which after the transaction the product becomes the property of the customer and it has to be the way he wants. Here you can make a difference in the products that have the right to continue to use their free will, such as an electrical appliance case a hair dryer or blender, while on the other side of buying music CDs or downloading music online, the user has the right to use and no further distribution.

- **Usage Fee:** Pay-per-use services, according to the amount of utilization of services, such as hotel services, which are charged according to the number of nights spent by the postal service where the charge for sending and receiving mail in accordance with the distance.
- **Subscription Fees:** Subscription services, such as monthly or annual card for a gym, is a continuous income of revenue for the company. Some other examples can be online subscriptions and training courses, or playing video games on sites that require a subscription to use.
- **Lending / Renting / Leasing:** Renting of products for temporary use is another way of payment value to the user. This method of cash flow for the company's continuous cost-effective, because it re-rents the same product and is charged in the same fixed value according to the length of use. On the other hand it is cost effective for the user because the wages drastically lower the cost of leased product in comparison to the full price of the product. Example is car that is rented by the day or the hour.
- **Licensing:** Use of a product or service after the full right to use with the ability to cash in on the value of the licensed represents the main means of income for the owner of the product. Licensing is most often used in the media industry or technology sector, where the right to a copyright or patent is those who are content owner in pay certain fee.
- **Brokerage Fee:** Brokerage fee represents a commission to an intermediary party takes the successful execution of the transaction between the user and companies. A typical example of such a transaction is a successful match buyers and sellers in the sale of the property where the broker or sales agent takes a commission as a percentage of the total value of the property sold.
- **Advertising:** Media industry and public events that are used depend on this method of revenue collection. Placing advertising companies that are sponsors of the event or just want to have a prominent company name at an event to become recognizable to the general public, which is most popular in the media industry.

The IoT changes how companies make money, hardware and software companies, both. Hardware companies obtain profit by balancing product revenues with the costs associated with materials and manufacturing. On the other side, software companies usually leverage service business models, often with recurring revenue streams. For IoT devices, the hardware company has to start accounting the costs of tracking data and supporting a service, while the software company has to start accounting the costs of creating and distributing physical products.

Key Resources

Different industries require different resources as a key, which is why those who are engaged in product design have focus on human resources with creativity needed to come up with a solution that is ideal for some market segment, while producing companies invest huge financial part of the machinery to make the product.

The main types of resources are financial, intellectual, human and physical. All of these resources can be privately owned company, rented for a certain time period or purchased from partner companies:

- **Human Resources:** The human factor is more important for some industries than others, so the institutes depend on the scientific achievements and abilities of staff development specialist. For companies in need of creative personnel, the largest amount of administration cost of waste on their salaries. Human resources required for that 'technology stack' must have full skill set ranging from software development, data analysis, online security, etc.
- **Financial Resources:** Part of the company depends on large financial resources, roles, financial guarantors, action, etc.
- **Physical Resources:** Physical objects as buildings, vehicles, machinery, sales and distribution of the city, representing the physical resources of the company. For some industries, such as technology industry, these resources are crucial for the realization of the production of electronic devices.
- **Intellectual Resources:** The intellectual resources include patents, rights to use, brand, user base, etc. This type of resource is established hardest but once established can make a significant and sustainable value system.

IoT devices create major new human resource requirements. Engineering departments, traditionally staffed with mechanical engineers, must add talent in software development, big data, system engineering, cloud systems, agile software development etc. System should consider does it have the capacity of human resources in order to achieve its goal. Also, IoT devices require a whole set of new design principles, designs in hardware and software-based customization that enable personalization and that can easily support ongoing product upgrades.

Key Activities

Different industries rely on specific activities as a key, such as software development in the IT industry, in the production of computers in addition to production techniques the supply chain is another key activity for the business system. Main activities in IoT can be:

- **Production:** These include individual activities, such as designing, creating and delivering products with the requirement of sustainable quantity and quality of the product.
- **Problem Solving:** Typical representatives of such companies may be encountered in the consulting services of any kind, where the focus is on solving the problem for user. Here as the activities necessary for the realization are knowledge management and continuous training.
- **Platform / Network:** Networks, matchmaking platforms, software, and even brands can function as a platform. Key Activities in this category relate to platform management, service provisioning, and promotion platform.

Key Partnerships

Networking and expanding partnerships is another channel that the business has to develop in order to sustain, where their contribution to the complement system should be in the processes that the system cannot effectively implemented by itself. In order to understand a company's partnerships must be followed overall market competitiveness.

Partnerships are networking companies for the sake of mutual benefit in business. Various motives may be for the establishment of cooperation between two or more companies. Sometimes they need to reduce the risks in the business or to obtain additional human resources in the case of acquisition of smaller companies to larger. There are four basic types to which you can assign the partnerships between companies: Joint ventures in the development of new businesses, the customer-supplier coopetition in establishing partnerships competing company or strategic alliance between companies that are not competitive but they can greatly improve their business by creating value together or share resources.

Company has to expand partnerships to enable continuous business growth. Complement the partnership can be achieved in the field where one partner provides a service in the form of strategy, and the other in the form of implementation services, as well as partners where both provide the same type of service, or together proactive and efficient service delivered through a joint contract.

There are two types of partnership that can be universally applied:

- **Optimization/Economies of Scale:** Only a few companies have their own resources and all activities from beginning to end perform alone. More common are cases in which companies outsource a single activity from other companies that, for example, picked up speed when there is too much work that cannot reach, or get counseling reply from a company with which it cooperates and so solve their problems. This type of partnership is about the distribution of resources in the most common form of cooperation that is a customer-supplier relationship. It is considered unnecessary to companies all activities performed independently, which leads to this kind of cooperation. Optimization and economies of scale can significantly reduce the costs of business system because its available resources partners, such as division of infrastructure.

- **Reduction of Risk and Uncertainty:** Partnerships help reduce risk when placing new technology on the market. So many technology companies are joining in the development of a technology with which emerge on the market and remain competitive in all other products that are sold.

Internet of things business model combines the partners who together can form one or more IoT devices. In the IoT, partnerships are necessary; competitors join together and become partners in certain devices or technologies that wish to sell on the market. Because of this dependence, it is essential to know the business model of a competitor or a partner to maintain their own viability and success in the market.

Cost Structure

Each operating system in order to realize its activities have costs during the implementation thereof. Some companies, such as low cost airlines formed its values around the low cost structure while others concerning exclusive and luxury products or services are formed around the high value of the cost structure.

As previously mentioned companies formed a kind of value creation over low cost structure, to represent the Cost-driven company, while the other type of companies formed around its price value, value-driven, and their focus is not on costs.

The following are the characteristics of cost structure:

- Fixed costs are related to the costs incurred each month to the same extent as it does not depend on the volume of sales or services already affecting fixed costs incurred, and that there is no exchange value to customers. This includes salaries, infrastructure costs in case of renting space and machines. This suggests that manufacturing companies have fixed costs in the basis of their business and that they are largely the cost structure of these companies.
- Variable costs depend on the volume of sales of products or provision of services, as opposed to fixed costs. Here are typical examples service companies, such as the organization of various events.

Table 2 presents business model framework for IoT applications based on Dijkman et al., (2015) research. It is applicable for every IoT application and it listed the aspects of the IoT application that should be considered in order to place it to the market.

Table 3 more presents more detailed perspective of what indicators should be followed by setting business model for IoT startups.

Considering previous research and detail analysis, we made general model of three structures that should be covered in IoT business model development. First is organizational structure, which is divided into basic units such as IT, R&D, manufacturing, marketing, sales, service and support, finance and human resources.

Table 2. Business model framework for IoT applications

Key Partners	Key Activities	Value Propositions	Customer Relationships	Customer Segments
Hardware producers Software developers Other suppliers Data interpretation Launching customers Distributors Logistics Service partners	Customer development Product development Implementation; Service Marketing; Sales Platform development Software development Partner management Logistics	Newness Performance Customization „Getting the job done" Design Brand/status Price Cost reduction Risk reduction Accessibility Convenience/ usability Comfort Possibility for updates	Personal assistance Dedicated assistance Self-service Automated service Communities Co-creation	Mass market Niche market Segmented Diversified Multi-sided platforms
	Key Resources Physical resources Intellectual property Employee capabilities Financial resources Software Relations		**Channels** Sales force Web sales Own stores Partner stores Wholesaler	
Cost Structure Product development cost IT cost Personnel cost Hardware/production cost Logistics cost Marketing & sales cost			**Revenue Streams** Asset sale Usage fee Subscription fees Lending/renting/leasing Licensing Brokerage fees Advertising Startup fees Installation fees	

(Dijkman et al., 2015)

Table 3. Performance dashboard for lean startups

Key Partners	Key Activities	Value Propositions	Customer Relationships	Customer Segments
Suppliers Partners - No. of contracts/ agreements Investors/ Environment - Revenue (Sales) - Cash Burn Rate - Months of Cash Left - Time to Cash Flow-Breakeven -Contribution Margin -No. of Competitors	Processes -Cycle time for pivots/ prototyping/ releases -Cost per pivot cycle	-Customer Satisfaction -Customer Delight Customer Problem -Customer pain -Level of defects	-Level of Complaints -Net Promoter Score	-No. Of Prospects/ Registrations -No. Of Customers -No. Of Referrals -Cost per Acquisition(Paid/ Net) -Customer Lifetime Value -Customer Loyalty/ Retention -Average Time to First Order; Time for Follow-on Order
	Key Resources Employees/IP -Lessons learnt/ Insights -No. of interviews/pivots Machinery Product/Service -No. Of Releases/ Pivots -No. of MVPs -Total Page Views/Visits		**Channels** -Advertising Expenses -Viral Coefficient	
Cost Structure -Suppliers/Materials/Employees/Rent/Hosting -Machinery/Equipment/Design/Manufacturing -Marketing&Sales/Transportation/Miscellaneous			**Revenue Streams** -Direct Sale of Product/Service -Subscription/Leasing Fees/Licensing Fees/Royalties -Advertising/Commissions/Brokerage	

(King, 2015)

On top of that IoT organizational structure has three new units: Unified Data Organization responsible for data collection, aggregation, and analytics, and for making data and insights available across functions and business units, Dev-Ops responsible for managing and optimizing the performance of connected products after they left the factory, and last unit is Customer Success Management that is responsible for managing the customer experience (Porter & Heppelmann, 2015). Second layer is already explained Canvas model structure that can be applied with elements and indicators given in Business model framework for IoT applications in Table 2 and Performance Dashboard for Lean Startups in Table 3. Last, third layer, is ecosystem structure that includes: Technological change, Research insights, Changes in customer demand, Competition/co-opetition, Social change and Policies and legal environment (Heikkila M. & Kuivaniemi L., 2012). Third layer is the part of the model that represents restrictions every model has, but it is missed by every previous business model approach. For example policies and legal environment are different for every country.

Figure 5. 3-layered framework for IoT business model development

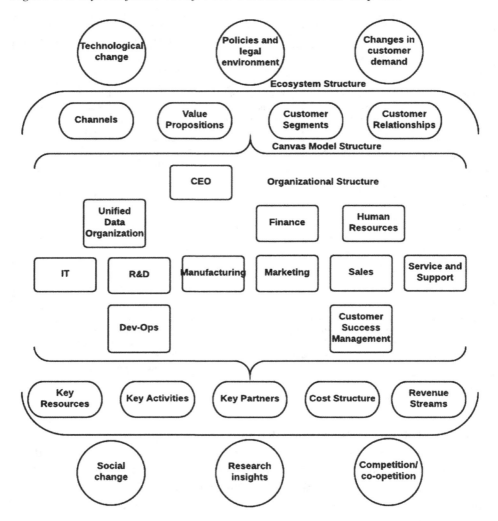

FUTURE RESEARCH DIRECTIONS

One of the main problems that arise in the designing the business models for the area of Internet of things are stakeholders and answer to a question who has the right of generated data. The stakeholders include companies that provide the service, the public sector if it holds the infrastructure, users of smart devices or services, owners of sensor networks etc. The business model may have other participants, depending on the type of the device and the industry to which it belongs. This can make the scheme of the stakeholders more complex to structure than mentioned.

Another challenge, besides the problem of ownership of the generated data and who will generate more revenue from the usage of smart device or services, is the problem of data security. Data security is important in every field, but especially has to be taken into account in healthcare when it comes to treating patients remotely, where even the smallest mistakes or interruption can sometimes have deadly consequences.

What is found to be missing by this research is that there is no clear understanding of the dynamic between the model elements. In every business model found in literature there is assumption what should be the architecture of the IoT model, but every part is given separately and real situations are that this parts should work together. Further research is going to be based on the question of the dynamic of the IoT business model components.

Also, technological changes can be motive for research how fast business model has to be innovated. This happens because of the high competitiveness on the market and users' high demand for product or service due to ability of many choices, by this factor that should be considered is time.

Limitation of this chapter is that the proposed model is based on the literature that is meta-analysis of IoT business models and in following research it should be extended with more detailed literature about IoT business models.

CONCLUSION

This chapter presents research of business models and business models in Internet of thing that leads to comprehensive approach to designing business models in IoT. To conclude, business models in IoT have few stages that have to be completed before the device is placed to the market. Compelling value propositions starts with a focus on a single customer pain point that can later be updated with more services added to the device. Then figure out how that problem can be solved in a intuitive way using hardware and software platform. Designing IoT devices requires the integration of different development skill sets and processes. First, hardware production is needed, which calls for product design and engineering in a linear, often lengthy development cycle. Secondly needed are digital and software design, which happens in short development iterations and requires support from different kinds of designers such as specialists in user interaction and programmers. While both hardware and software depends on good design to succeed, the approaches are very different, and any disruption in the development of hardware product will have three time greater impact on schedule and cost production than the estimated. The implication for most companies is that they rarely have both capabilities and partnerships are must, rather than a choice.

It should be aligned that the development of the business model for any smart device should be based on the analysis of the entire lifecycle of a product or a service that the smart device provides. Developing a business model, in the field of Internet of things, depends on the complexity of the device, whether the modeling processes for the device or service is designed for one user type, to simplify everyday life, or it is a solution designed to change the way of functioning the entire industry. For both types of smart devices is common to have the ability to be identified, to have sensors, to be networked and to have the possibility of processing information, which allows them to communicate to other objects that have compatible features, or to communicate with services via Internet. In the process of the designing and developing such a device, special attention must be paid to data security, scalability and compatibility of different device platforms that these devices are based.

Manufacturer of IoT devices has the ability to specify the product to meet customer needs much more than traditional products, even it can be adapted to the individual user, allowing easier segmentation of users in the market. The rivalry among manufacturers boils down to competitiveness to every feature and function of IoT products. Threats competitiveness can be observed and the possibility that the new IoT device replace the traditional entirely, adding more and more functionality into a product with the same basic purpose. For example, in health care, a doctor can cure more patients at the same time, establishing diagnose online and accompanying therapy in the same way.

Summarized are 7 approaches and given the preview of the basic elements that should be covered in IoT business model development. Three layers are important to be covered by every IoT business model: company structure, business model elements and ecosystem.

REFERENCES

Bucherer, E., Eisert, U., & Gassmann, O. (2012). Towards Systematic Business Model Innovation: Lessons from Product Innovation Management. *Creativity and Innovation Management*, *21*(2), 183–198. doi:10.1111/j.1467-8691.2012.00637.x

Chen, M. (2013). Towards Smart City: M2M Communications with Software Agent Intelligence. *Multimedia Tools and Applications*, *67*(1), 167–178. doi:10.1007/s11042-012-1013-4

Chesbrough, H., & Rosenbloom, R. S. (2002). *The role of the business model in capturing value from innovation: Evidence from Xerox Corporation's technology*. Academic Press.

Dijkman, R. M., Sprenkels, B., Peeters, T., & Janssen, A. (2015). Business models for the Internet of Things. *International Journal of Information Management, 35*(6), 672–678. doi:10.1016/j.ijinfomgt.2015.07.008

Fleisch, E., Weinberger, M., & Wortmann, F. (2015). Business Models and the Internet of Things. In P. Z. Ivana, P. Krešimir, & S. Martin (Eds.), *Interoperability and Open-Source Solutions for the Internet of Things, 9001* (pp. 6–10). Berlin: Springer.

Gartner. (2015). *Gartner Says 6.4 Billion Connected "Things" Will Be in Use in 2016, Up 30 Percent From 2015.* Retrieved 01.03.2016 from: http://www.gartner.com/newsroom/id/3165317

Gassmann, O., Frankenberger, K., & Csik, M. (2014). Revolutionizing the Business Model. In O. Gassmann & F. Schweitzer (Eds.), *Management of the Fuzzy Front End of Innovation* (pp. 89–98). New York: Springer; doi:10.1007/978-3-319-01056-4_7

Heikkila, M., & Kuivaniemi, L. (2012). *Ecosystem Under Construction: An Action Research Study on Entrepreneurship in a Business Ecosystem.* Technology Innovation Management Review.

Hui, G. (2014). How the Internet of Things Changes Business Models. *Harvard Business Review.*

King, R. (2015). *Performance Dashboard for Lean Startups.* Retrieved 01.03.2016 from: http://www.slideshare.net/RodKing/business-model-dashboard-for-lean-startups

Leminen, S., Westerlund, M., Rajahonka, M., & Siuruainen, R. (2012). Towards IOT Ecosystems and Business Models. In S. Andreev, S. Balandin, & Y. Koucheryavy (Eds.), *Internet of Things, Smart Spaces, and Next Generation Networking, 7469* (pp. 15–26). Heidelberg, Germany: Springer. doi:10.1007/978-3-642-32686-8_2

Mejtoft, T. (2011) Internet of Things and Co-Creation of Value. *Proceedings of the 2011 International Conference on and 4th International Conference on Cyber, Physical and Social Computing*, 672-677. doi:10.1109/iThings/CPSCom.2011.75

Morris, M., Schindehutte, M., & Allen, J. (2005). The entrepreneurs business model: Toward a unified perspective. *Journal of Business Research, 58*(6), 726–735. doi:10.1016/j.jbusres.2003.11.001

Openshaw, E., Hagel, J., Wooll, M., Wigginton, C., Brown, J. S., & Banerjee, P. (2014). The Internet of Things ecosystem: unlocking the business value of connected devices. *Technical report.* Deloitte.

Osterwalder, A., Pigneur, Y., & Tucci, C. L. (2005). Clarifying business models: Origins, present, and future of the concept. *Communications of the Association for Information Systems, 16*(1), 1.

Porter, E. M., & Heppelmann, E. J. (2015). How Smart, Connected Products Are Transforming Companies. *Harvard Business Review*.

Quinn, J. B. (2000). Outsourcing innovation: The new engine of growth. *Sloan Management Review, 41*(4), 13–28.

Rong, K., Hu, G.Y., Lin, Y., Shi, Y.J. & Guo, L. (2015). Understanding Business Ecosystem Using a 6C Framework in Internet-of-Things-Based Sectors. *International Journal of Production Economics, 159*, 41-55.

Sun, Y., Yan, H., Lu, C., Bie, R., & Thomas, P. (2012). A Holistic Approach to Visualizing Business Models for the Internet of Things. *Communications in Mobile Computing, 1*(1), 1–7. doi:10.1186/2192-1121-1-4

Turber, S., Brocke, J. V., Gassmann, O., & Flesich, E. (2014) Designing Business Models in the Era of Internet of Things. *9th International Conference, DESRIST 2014*, 17-31. doi:10.1007/978-3-319-06701-8_2

Westerlund, M., Leminen, S., & Rajahonka, M. (2014). Designing Business Models for the Internet of Things. *Technology Innovation Management Review, 4*, 5–14.

Chapter 3
Converging Technologies for the IoT:
Standardization Activities and Frameworks

Dragorad Milovanović
University of Belgrade, Serbia

Vladan Pantović
Faculty of Business Economics and Entrepreneurship, Serbia

Gordana Gardašević
University of Banja Luka, Bosnia and Herzegovina

ABSTRACT

The Internet of Things (IoT) is the concept of linking various objects to the Internet that sense/acquire and transmit data in the environment to create a new application. From a standardization perspective, the IoT can be viewed as a global infrastructure, enabling advanced services by interconnecting (physical and virtual) objects based on evolving interoperable information and communication technologies (ICT). The success of the IoT will depend strongly on the existence and effective operation of global standards. The standardization initiative, research projects, national initiatives and industrial activities are outlined in this chapter. There are already many standardization activities related to the IoT, covering broad research areas: wireless and cellular technologies, networking protocols, emerging applications, media-centric IoT. What is needed, therefore, are a harmonization of standards and effective frameworks for large-scale deployment.

DOI: 10.4018/978-1-5225-2437-3.ch003

INTRODUCTION

The Internet of Things (IoT) is a global network of connected people and devices which is enabled by converging technology, sensors, connectivity, APIs, and more. The IoT ecosystem include 6.4 billion connected things in use worldwide in 2016, a 30 percent increase since 2015, and will reach 20.8 billion by 2020 (Gartner, 2015; Cisco, 2015; Intel 2016). In 2016, 5.5 million new things will get connected every day. The IoT support total services spending of $235 billion in 2016, a 22 percent increase since 2015. Services are dominated by the professional category (in which businesses contract external providers in order to design, install and operate IoT systems), however connectivity services (through communications service providers) and consumer services grow at a faster pace. Consumer impacts include convenience, life optimization, personal data collection and efficiency. However, IoT is a large area that needs segmentation to be meaningful and effectively deployed. The major applications and deployment scenarios for IoT are smart transportation, agriculture, smart cities, buildings, rural areas, energy and smart grid, healthcare and wellbeing.

The fundamental concept behind IoT is connecting (Figure 1) the vast majority of systems to a common network and infrastructure (IEEE, 2015; Gardasevic et al., 2017):

- **Interconnectivity:** With regard to the IoT, anything can be interconnected with the global information and communication infrastructure.
- **Things-Related Services:** The IoT is capable of providing things-related services within the limitations of things, such as privacy protection and semantic consistency between physical things and their associated virtual things. In order to provide thing-related services within the limitations of things, both the technologies in the physical world and the information world have to change.
- **Heterogeneity:** The devices in the IoT are heterogeneous as based on different hardware platforms and networks. They can interact with other devices or service platforms through different networks.
- **Dynamic Changes:** The state of the devices changes dynamically, e.g., sleeping and waking up, connected and/or disconnected as well as the context of the devices including location and speed. Moreover, the number of devices can change dynamically.
- **Enormous Scale:** The number of devices that need to be managed and that communicate with each other will be at least an order of magnitude larger than the devices connected to the current Internet. The ratio of communication triggered by the devices as compared to communication triggered by humans will noticeably shift towards device-triggered communication. Even more

Figure 1. Technological and social aspects related to IoT

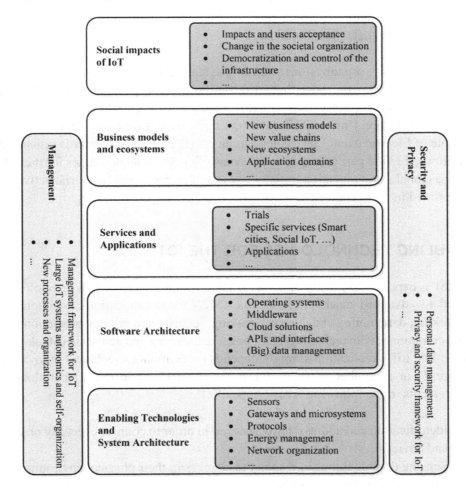

crucial will be the management of the data generated and its interpretation for application purposes. This relates to the semantics of data, as well as efficient data handling.

The characteristics of the IoT are as follows:

- Event-Driven Architecture (based on the context of processes and operations).
- Ambient Intelligence (autonomous and intelligent entities).
- IoT Complex System (due to the huge number of different links/interactions between autonomous actors).

- Semantic Interoperability (IoT objects will be able to understand each other through semantic interoperability - different stakeholders can access and interpret the data unambiguously).

Although many organizations work on the standardization process, the authors focus in this chapter on those that work on the IoT and provide a definition for it. Accordingly, we considered the IoT World Forum (IOTWF), International Telecommunication Union (ITU), Internet Engineering Task Force (IETF) and the Institute of Electrical and Electronics Engineers (IEEE). This chapter is organized as follows: the first part provides an overview of enabling technologies for the IoT, and the global standardization initiative, research projects, and industrial activities are outlined in the second part.

ENABLING TECHNOLOGIES FOR THE IOT

The IoT is expected to greatly integrate leading technologies, such as technologies related to advanced machine-to-machine (M2M) communications, autonomous networking, data mining and decision-making, security and privacy protection and cloud computing, with technologies for advanced sensing and actuation (Stankovic, 2014). The IoT's realization strongly depends on continuous technical innovation (Figure 2) in a number of fields (Gazis et al. 2015). The main technological requirements in the following areas (Appendix):

- Identification and addressability (needed in order to connect everyday objects and devices),
- Sensing (enable things to respond to changes in their physical environment),
- Embedded intelligence (empower things and devices at the edges of the network to make independent decisions),
- Miniaturization (smaller and smaller things will have the ability to interact and connect).

The Internet of Things World Forum (IoTWF) provides an essential forum for discussion and sharing of best practices on every front – flexibility, scalability, security, availability, and connectivity - as individuals, companies, and governments accelerate and optimize their IoT deployments, providing dramatic gains in efficiency, economic value, and quality of life.

The purpose of the IoTWF Reference Model is to provide clear definitions and descriptions that can be applied accurately to elements and functions of IoT systems and applications. The model aims to:

Figure 2. IoT evolution and technology roadmap

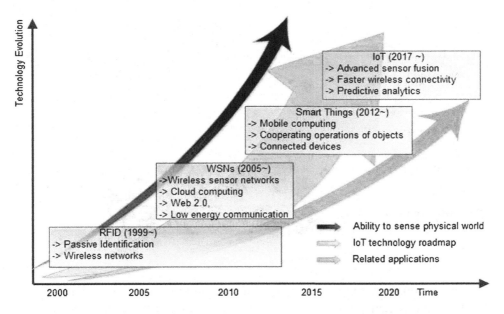

- **Simplify:** It helps break down complex systems so that each part is more understandable.
- **Clarifiy:** It provides additional information to precisely identify the levels of the IoT and to establish common terminology.
- **Identify:** It identifies where specific types of processing optimized across different parts of the system.
- **Standardize:** It provides a first step in enabling vendors to create IoT products that work with each other.
- **Organize:** It makes the IoT real and approachable, instead of simply conceptual.

The requirements of IoT middleware platforms are as follows:

- **Scale:** When performing a task over a set of millions of devices, it is practically impossible to automatically coordinate all the devices due to limitations such as time, memory, processing power and energy consumption;
- **A High Degree of Hardware and Software Heterogeneity:** Mechanisms to manage the interoperability between heterogeneous devices in several application domains must be provided.

Figure 3. Reference model (IoTWF, 2014)

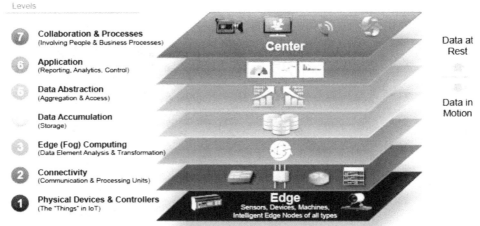

- **Uncertainties:** A major characteristic of a communication infrastructure in IoT environments is that its topology is unfamiliar and dynamic. Moreover, the devices location might not be precisely determined. Consequently, the applications often depend on services and data provided by devices that might not be reachable at the time of their use. Therefore, mechanisms to provide the dynamic discovery of devices, adaptation and context-awareness of applications are needed. Furthermore, device metadata as well as sensor readings may be inaccurate or incomplete, thus requiring, for instance, mechanisms to provide metadata reconciliation and inference.
- **Conflict Resolution:** Conflicts arise, for example, when multiple applications attempt to operate on the same device in opposite ways or try to apply mutually incompatible changes over the environment. Such a requirement demands mechanisms to specify and manage policies and relationships among different applications needs.
- **Issues Related to the Management:** Massive data, privacy, and security in the IoT context.

STANDARDIZATION INITIATIVES AND FRAMEWORKS

From the perspective of technical standardization, the IoT can be viewed as a global infrastructure for the information society, enabling advanced services by interconnecting (physical and virtual) things based on existing and evolving interoperable information and communication technologies (ICT). Through the exploitation of identification, data capture, processing and communication capabilities, the IoT makes full use of things in order to offer services to all kinds of applications, whilst ensuring that security and privacy requirements are fulfilled (Meddeb, 2016; Gazis, 2016).

The success of the IoT in business and social communities will depend strongly on the existence and effective operation of global standards. It will also depend on the application of those standards in real life for the social and economic benefit of people.

Several contributions to the full deployment and standardization of the IoT paradigm come from the scientific community. Among them, the most relevant are provided by the different sections of the Auto-ID Lab scattered all over the world, by the European Commission and European Standards Organizations (ETSI, CEN, CENELEC, etc.), by their international counterparts (ISO, ITU), and by other standards bodies and consortia (IETF, EPCglobal, etc.).

ITU-T Global Standards Initiative (IoT-GSI)

The International Telecommunication Union (ITU) published one of the first reports on *The Internet of Things* in 2005. The ITU has studied and published Recommendations in the areas of tag-based identification services, ubiquitous sensor networks (USN) and ubiquitous applications in next-generation networks (NGN) environment. IoT-GSI was established in May 2011 by TSAG (Telecommunication Standardization Advisory Group) with the aim of promoting a unified approach in ITU-T for development of technical standards (Recommendations) enabling IoT on a global scale. ITU-T Recommendations developed under the IoT-GSI by the various ITU-T Questions - in collaboration with other standards developing organizations (SDOs) – will enable worldwide service providers to offer at wide range of services expected by this technology. IoT-GSI also aimed to act as an umbrella for IoT standards development worldwide (ITU-T, 2016).

ITU produced recommendations spanning an IoT framework (basic concepts and terminology, common requirements and capabilities, ecosystem and business models etc.), various areas of applications and services (e.g. networked vehicles, e-health, home networks, machine oriented communications, sensor control networks, gateway applications) as well as testing aspects. The initial key efforts of IoT-GSI have included: IoT terminology (including the definition of IoT), IoT overview (Y.2060 *Overview of IoT*, 06/2012), ITU-T Y.2061, *Requirements for support of machine-oriented communication applications in the NGN environment*, IoT work plan (potential study items within ITU).

The IoT has been defined in Recommendation ITU-T Y.2060 (06/2012) as a global infrastructure enabling advanced services by interconnecting (physical and virtual) things based on information and communication technologies. Y.2060 provides an IoT overview, clarifies the concept and scope of the IoT, identifies the fundamental characteristics and high-level requirements of the IoT and describes the IoT reference model. The ecosystem and business models are also provided in an informative appendix. The IoT reference model is composed of four layers as well as management capabilities and security capabilities which are associated with the four layers. The four layers are as follows: application layer, service support and application support layer, network layer, and device layer.

The IoT-GSI concluded its activities in July 2015 following TSAG decision to establish the new Study Group 20 on *IoT and its applications including smart cities and communities*. All activities ongoing in the IoT-GSI were transferred to the SG20 (Table 1) (ITU-T, 2015).

Study Group 20 works to address the standardization requirements of IoT technologies, with an initial focus on IoT applications in smart cities and communities (SC&C). The group develops international standards to enable the coordinated development of IoT technologies, including machine-to-machine communications and ubiquitous sensor networks. The central part of this study is the standardization of end-to-end architectures for IoT, and mechanisms for the interoperability of IoT applications and datasets employed by various vertically oriented industry sectors.

The deployment of IoT technologies is expected to connect an estimated 50 billion devices to the network by year 2020, impacting nearly every aspect of our daily lives. The IoT contributes to the convergence of industry sectors, and SG20 provides the specialized IoT standardization platform necessary for this convergence to rest on a cohesive set of international standards.

The ITU-T layered reference model provides universally common understanding of the crucial functions and capabilities of the IoT architecture. It helps to reduce the implementation complexity and promotes interoperability among various IoT applications and communication technologies. The IoT reference model consists

Table 1. ITU-T SG20 structure: List of questions

Q1/20	Research and emerging technologies including terminology and definitions
Q2/20	Requirements and use cases for IoT
Q3/20	IoT functional architecture including signaling requirements and protocols
Q4/20	IoT applications and services including end user networks and interworking
Q5/20	SC&C (smart cities and communities) requirements, applications and services
Q6/20	SC&C (smart cities and communities) infrastructure and framework

of four horizontal layers and the common management and security capabilities associated with all layers. The top layer is the application layer that contains various IoT applications, e.g., smart home, intelligent transport systems, e-health, and smart grid. The second layer is the service and application support layer, which includes generic support capabilities as well as application-specific support capabilities. As the name indicates, the generic support capabilities are common capabilities applicable to many applications, whereas the application-specific capabilities serve a particular application's requirements. The third layer is the network layer, which includes the networking and transport capabilities. The networking capabilities come into action to connect things to networks and maintain connectivity. They include functions for access control, routing, mobility management, resource allocation, etc. Similarly, the transport capabilities include functions for transporting IoT application data as well as control and management instructions. The bottom layer is the device layer, which includes a collection of device capabilities and gateway capabilities. The device capabilities enable things to interact with a network directly or via a gateway. They are composed of ubiquitous sensor networking functions. Similarly, the gateway capabilities include protocol translation, security, and privacy protection functions to enable resource-constrained IoT devices with heterogeneous wireless technologies, such as ZigBee, Bluetooth, and WiFi, to be connected securely through a network (Kafle, 2016).

Management and security capabilities are also categorized into generic and specific capabilities. The generic management capabilities include device management functions such as remote activation, status monitoring and control, software update, network topology management, and traffic and congestion control. The generic security capabilities include access control, authorization, authentication, access control, privacy protection, confidentiality, integrity protection, etc.

ISO/IEC

The ISO/IEC Special Working Group 5 (SWG5) of the ISO/IEC Joint Technical Committee 1 (JTC1) was established in 2012 as a result of a growing interest in the IoT by other SDOs. JTC1 has a close relationship with ITU-T SG-17 on various security aspects. The relationship is at various levels, including *joint work* (Level 1), *technical collaboration by liaison mechanism* (Level 2), and *information liaison* (Level 3). ISO/IEC JTC1/SWG5 does not actually develop standards, but rather consolidates standardization activities and identifies current and future IoT trends and needs. A number of documents were issued by the SWG, including a collection of definitions and a mind map describing technologies related to the IoT, as well as application domains, requirements, and stakeholders. A list of definitions collected from various standards organizations is divided into four categories: IoT, M2M, machine type communications (MTC), and cyber-physical systems (CPS). JTC 1 Plenary 2014 approved to establish WG on IoT (WG 10). Various ISO/IEC standards related to IoT have been published or are under development (ISO/IEC 30141 *IoT Reference Architecture*, Terms and definitions for IoT Vocabularies, IoT Use-Cases, Network level technologies, Identifications, Interoperability) (ISO/IEC, 2015).

MPEG Internet of Media Things and Wearables

The Moving Picture Experts Group (MPEG) is a working group of authorities that was formed by ISO and IEC to set standards for audio and video compression and transmission. The Internet of Media Things and Wearables (IoMT&W) is the collection of interfaces, protocols and associated media-related information representations that enable advanced services and applications based on human to device and device to device interaction, in physical and virtual environments. The information refers to data sensed and processed by a device, and/or communicated to a human or another device (ISO/IEC, 2016).

The widespread adoption of the IoT will require new M2M media communication. Of the 20 billion connected *things* predicted in five years, 65% will be consumer-oriented (Gartner, 2015). All types of devices and sensors will be part of the IoT and will be able to communicate not just plain data, but also audio-visual information. Cloud computing and Big Data technologies evolve from basic data to rich audiovisual media, and enabling efficient search and discovery with everything connected will be key. This requires high levels of interoperability and efficiencies of communication to fuel market adoption and growth. The IoT encompasses a large variety of research, development and market efforts related to the communication between smart objects. An important factor contributing to the growing adoption of IoT (Internet of Things) and IoE (Internet of Everything) is the emergence of wearable devices, a category with high growth market potential. Wearable devices are commonly understood to be devices that can be worn by, or embedded in, a person, and that have the capability to connect and communicate to the network either directly through embedded wireless connectivity or through another device (primarily a smartphone) using wireless technology. In order to offer interoperability in such a dynamic market, several international consortia have emerged, like the Internet Industrial Consortium (IIC), the Alliance for Internet of Things Innovation (AIOTI), the Internet of Things Architecture (IoTA), the WSO2 reference architecture for the IoT, oneM2M and OIC. As these consortia focus on specific challenges, following their own specific requirements, MPEG identified the need for ensuring the interoperability among IoT systems, where MPEG focuses on multimedia content processing to enable an Internet of Media Things. MPEG's specific aim is to standardize the interaction commands from the user to the Media Thing or wearable device, the format of the aggregated and synchronized data sent from the Media Thing or wearable to external connected entities, as well as to identify a focused list of Media Wearables to be considered for integration in multimedia-centric systems (*MPEG Strategic Standardisation Roadmap*, June 2016).

There is an increasing interest from the industry in the IoT technologies. There are active standardization activities to define network protocols for the Internet of Things. The variety and heterogeneity of *Things* make it difficult to standardize descriptions, data formats, APIs in a global manner, however, in well-established ecosystems, this can be done. Therefore, MPEG is exploring representations of media things as part of complex distributed systems implying interaction between things and between humans and things. The Media-centric Internet of Things (MIoT) is the collection of interfaces, protocols and associated media-related information representations that enable advanced services and applications based on human to device and device to device interaction in physical and virtual environments (Figure 4). Information refers to data sensed and processed by a device, and/or communicated to a human or another device. The entity is any physical or virtual object that is sensed by and/ or acted on by Things. Thing is anything that can communicate with other Things, in addition it may sense and/or act on Entities. The Media Thing is a Thing with at least one of the audio/visual sensing and actuating capabilities (*Exploration on Media-centric Internet of Things*, Feb.2015).

Within this large field of IoTs, the MIoT applications and services that offer the provision, interpretation, representation and analysis of multi-media content

Figure 4. MPEG Media IoT reference model

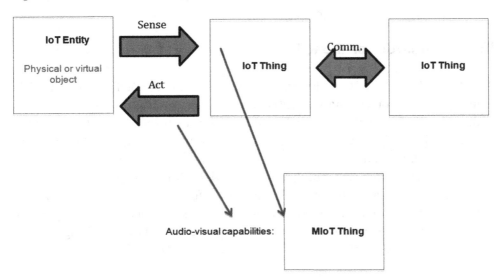

81

collected from MIoT devices (cameras, microphones) are challenging yet appealing to users. MIoT is a particular case of IoT (that by definition has the communication capability and it may sense or act on a physical or virtual object), with the specificity that an MIoT has audio-visual capabilities. MIoT applications and services can be designed and implemented if a variety of technologies are available such as information-centric networking, media analytics, cloud technologies, big data for media content, content streaming and caching. Orchestration and synchronization between these components is an absolute requirement and this can be done in a sustainable manner only by developing open standards. The objective of the MPEG standard is to contribute with major technologies in the field of data representation and APIs for MIoTs, including aggregated systems obtained by combining IoTs and MIoTs such as the Wearables (*Overview, context and objectives of Media-centric IoTs and Wearables*, Feb.2016).

The MPEG MIoT standard covers five aspects addressed in individual parts as the following:

Part 1: Global architecture, use cases and common requirements.

Part 2: System aspects (discovery, communication).

Part 3: Individual MIoTs, data formats and APIs (sensors and actuators, media processing & storage).

Part 4: Wearable MIoTs, data formats and APIs (smart glasses, camera, gesture recognizer, microphone, display, etc., smart watch, fitness tracker, smart textile (D-Shirt), sleep monitoring).

Part 5: MIoT Aggregates combining individual MIoTs, eventually with other IoTs (video surveillance systems, car sensing and communication system, smart cities - smart factory - smart offices).

IETF Standards for the IoT

The standardization activities towards the creation of a common framework for IoT communication protocols started in 2003, with joint efforts of global standardization bodies. In 2006, the IETF started working intensively on a set of IoT-related standards. The IETF already has a decade of history specifying and documenting key IoT standards and guidance. IP and particularly IPv6 are the obvious choice for the IoT networking part, but the rest of the IETF IoT stack are currently under dynamic standardization process. The core IETF IoT protocol stack, as published in RFCs, is mature and suitable for deployment. Additional needs are emerging for standardization, and the active groups at the IETF and the IRTF are working towards their identification (ISOC, 2016; IETF, 2015; IRTF, 2016).

During the past ten years there have been a variety of IETF activities initiated to enable a wide range of things to use interoperable technologies for communicating with each other. IETF has started with three IETF working groups (WGs) focusing on IoT with constrained devices and networks: 6LoWPAN, which defined the IPv6 adaptation layer and header compression suitable for constrained radio links; ROLL, which focuses on routing protocols for constrained-node networks; and CoRE, which aims to extend the Web architecture to most constrained networks and embedded devices. Today we have seven WGs (and an additional two were completed) actively working on various IoT aspects, as well as an Internet Research Task Force (IRTF) research group focusing on open and emerging IoT research issues (Burrati&Gardasevic et al., 2016).

The first IETF IoT WG, IPv6 over Low-power WPAN (6LoWPAN), was chartered in March 2005. It provides methods for adapting IPv6 to IEEE 802.15.4 (WPAN) networks by means of header compression and optimizations for neighbor discovery. The IPv6 communication requires packet sizes much larger than the IEEE 802.15.4 frame size, thus an adaptation layer is needed (RFC 4944, RFC 6282, RFC 6775). The 6LoWPAN WG concluded in 2014, and the IPv6 over Networks of Resource-constrained Nodes - 6Lo WG has replaced it by applying similar adaptation mechanisms to a wider range of radio technologies: Bluetooth Low Energy (BLE, RFC 7668), ITU-T G.9959 (as used in Z-Wave, RFC 7428), the Digital Enhanced Cordless Telecommunications (DECT) Ultra Low Energy (ULE) cordless phone standard, and the low-cost wired networking technology Master-Slave/Token-Passing (MS/TP) that is widely used over RS-485 in building automation and control networks.

The Routing Over Low-power and Lossy networks (ROLL) WG generated specifications for the RPL protocol - IPv6 Routing Protocol for Low-Power and Lossy Networks (RPL, RFC 6550) and IPv6 routing architectural framework for application scenarios for LLNs. The RPL is designed to be widely applicable; therefore many configuration options are available.

The Constrained RESTful Environments (CoRE) WG is one of the most active IoT groups, developing a framework for resource-oriented applications that run the IP protocol on resource-constrained networks. The resulting Constrained Application Protocol (CoAP, RFC 7252) overcomes some issues related to HTTP by enabling group communications (RFC 7390) and low-complexity server-push (RFC 7641). Ongoing WG activities focus on the transfer of large resources, use of resource directories for coordinating discovery, reusable interface descriptions, and the transport of CoAP over TCP and TLS. The TLS WG is defining TLS version 1.3, including DTLS 1.3, for establishing secure transport sessions better suited for IoT applications. Moreover, related activities include the selection of the appropriate data format to represent sensor measurements, such as Concise Binary Object Representation (CBOR) (RFC 7049), a JSON analog optimized for binary data and low-resource implementations.

Two IRTF research groups are also of interest: ICNRG (Information-Centric Networking) explores the applicability of their technologies for IoT scenarios, and CFRG (Crypto Forum) proposes advanced cryptographical foundations, such as new elliptic curve cryptography (ECC) curves that will be more appropriate for IoT use cases. The Internet Architecture Board (IAB has published informative documents such as Architectural Considerations in Smart Object Networking (RFC 7452).

The 6TiSCH WG (IPv6 over the TSCH mode of IEEE 802.15.4e) was chartered in 2014 to in order to accelerate the adoption of IPv6 in industrial environments. The 6TiSCH overview and problem statement document (RFC 7554) was published in 2015 followed by a specification for a minimal configuration interface.

The IETF has recently created two IoT WGs in the Security Area. The DTLS In Constrained Environments (DICE) WG (already completed) produced a TLS/DTLS profile designed particularly for constrained IoT devices. The Authentication and Authorization for Constrained Environments (ACE) WG is working on authenticated authorization mechanisms for accessing resources hosted on servers in constrained environments and a comprehensive use case document (RFC 7744) was recently completed.

The Lightweight Implementation Guidance (LWIG) WG provides documentation on CoAP and IKEv2 protocols, asymmetric cryptography, and CoAP in cellular networks. The LWIG WG published RFC 7228, which defines common terminology for constrained-node networks.

Beyond the IETF work specifically focusing on IoT scenarios, the whole Web protocol stack is evolving quickly and many of the new technologies developed in other IETF working groups will also likely end up being used for IoT (Figure 5) (Sheng et al. 2013).

Recently, the IEEE 802.15.4 physical (PHY) and medium access control (MAC) layer have been complemented by an IP-enabled IETF protocol stack. Although it is difficult to create a complete and functional IoT protocol stack based on a common networking foundation model, such as Open System Interconnection (OSI), we can still identify the main representatives within the IoT stack.

- The operations at the physical layer are defined by the IEEE 802.15.4 standard with data rate of 250 kbps, operating in the 2400-2483.5 MHz ISM (Industrial, Scientific, Medical) frequency band, for LR-WPAN. The PHY layer is responsible for the data transfer and reception, link quality indication, energy detection of current channel, and clear channel assessment. The

Figure 5. IoT stack vs. Web stack

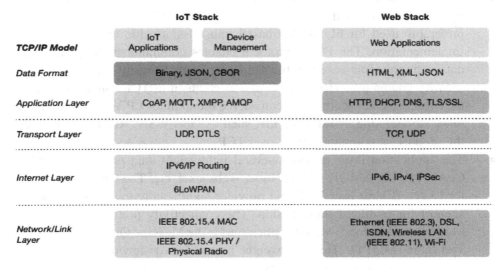

MAC layer performs the following functions: association and disassociation, channel access mechanism, acknowledged frame delivery, frame validation, guaranteed time slot management, and beacon management. The design of the MAC layer still remains an open issue, especially in non-centralized networks or large-scale networks with numerous nodes.

- The Time-Slotted Channel Hopping (TSCH) mode was recently adopted as the MAC amendment to the IEEE 802.15.4-2006, in order to provide deterministic and real-time features, and includes architecture, the information model, and configuration aspects. All communication in a TSCH networks is determined by a schedule. Time is divided in timeslots, and timeslots are grouped within a slot frame which continuously repeats over time. TSCH combines time slotted access, multi-channel communication and channel hopping, which significantly increases the robustness against external interference and multi-path fading. The adoption of TSCH accelerates the inclusion of IPv6 for industrial applications, thus creating the so-called Industrial IoT (IIoT).
- The network layer performs the IPv6-related functions, such as routing. The RPL provides a mechanism to disseminate information over the dynamically formed network topology. It is a link-independent distance vector routing protocol created specifically for LLNs, designed to discover optimal links based on an established set of criteria. The RPL supports various traffic models, such as point-to-point, point-to-multipoint, and multipoint-to-point.

- Typical representatives at the transport layer are the Transmission Control Protocol (TCP) and the User Datagram Protocol (UDP). The UDP is still preferably used for 6LoWPAN-based transmissions due to its lightweight implementation. The DTLS protocol enables communications privacy for datagram protocols based on the Transport Layer Security (TLS) protocol's security guarantees. The flow control mechanism in TCP usually generates the overhead that is commonly considered too high for LP-WPANs. Recently released operating systems for IoT, such as OpenWSN, RIOT, etc. provide the support for communications over TCP.

- The application layer provides several lightweight data protocols, such as CoAP, MQTT, AMQP, REST, Node, Websocket, etc. The CoAP, developed for LLNs, is built over UDP and provides significantly lower overhead and support for multicast transmission. The connectivity protocol for IoT and Machine-to-Machine (M2M) applications is the Message Queuing Telemetry Transport (MQTT). This lightweight protocol is designed to connect the physical devices and networks with applications and middleware used in IT and Web development. Unlike the CoAP, the MQTT runns over TCP. Additionally, this protocol provides three levels of Quality of Service (QoS) support for message delivery. The Advanced Message Queuing Protocol (AMQP) is an open standard application layer protocol for message oriented middleware. It supports queuing, routing (including point-to-point and publish-and-subscribe), reliability and security. It is also possible to use the WebSocket specification developed as part of the HTML5 initiative. The WebSocket standard simplifies the bidirectional web communication and connection management.

While the IoT-oriented IETF working groups have already produced the first wave of mature standards for IoT, new research questions are emerging. It should be emphasized that the emerging IoT standardization activities, such as ZigBee IPv6 specifications, suggest the need for coexistence of heterogeneous technologies in order to support the converged networks. The IRTF Thing-to-Thing Research Group (T2TRG) was chartered in 2015 to investigate the open research issues in IoT, focusing on issues that exhibit the standardization potential at the IETF. Topics being explored include the management and operation of constrained-node networks, security and lifecycle management, ways to use the REST paradigm in IoT scenarios, and semantic interoperability. There is also a strong interest in following and contributing to other groups that are active in the IoT area. For example, the W3C Web of Things (WoT) interest group recently began activities and the two groups have been working together to explore the future of IoT and Web technologies.

IEEE-Standard Association for the IoT

IEEE is a global, professional engineering organization whose mission is to advance technological innovation. In its special report on the IoT issued in March 2014 (IEEE, *Internet of Things*, 2014), IEEE described the phrase *Internet of Things* as: *A network of items – each embedded with sensors – which are connected to the Internet.* The primary differentiator between the traditional (legacy) Internet and the IoT is the proliferation of uniquely identifiable devices with embedded sensors and actuators.

The IEEE Standards Association (IEEE-SA), a globally recognized standards setting body within the IEEE, develops consensus standards through an open process that engages the industry and brings together a broad stakeholder community. IEEE standards set specifications and best practices based on current scientific and technological knowledge. The IEEE-SA has a portfolio of over 900 active standards and more than 500 standards under development. In its research into IoT, it has identified over 140 existing standards and projects that are relevant to the IoT (IEEE, 2016).

One project that directly relates to the IoT is IEEE P2413 *Architectural Framework*. The scope of IEEE P2413 is to define an architectural framework, addressing descriptions of various IoT domains, definitions of IoT domain abstractions, and identification of commonalities between different IoT domains. The IoT is predicted to become one of the most significant drivers of growth in various technology markets. Most current standardization activities are confined to very specific verticals and represent islands of disjointed and often redundant development. The architectural framework defined in this standard will promote cross-domain interaction, aid system interoperability and functional compatibility, and further fuel the growth of the IoT market. The adoption of a unified approach to the development of IoT systems will reduce industry fragmentation and create a critical mass of multi-stakeholder activities around the world. This standard defines an architectural framework for the IoT, including descriptions of various IoT domains, definitions of IoT domain abstractions, and an identification of commonalities between different IoT domains. The architectural framework for IoT provides a reference model that defines relationships among various IoT verticals (e.g., transportation, healthcare, etc.) and common architecture elements (Figure 6). It also provides a blueprint for data abstraction and the quality quadruple trust that includes protection, security, privacy, and safety. Furthermore, this standard provides a reference architecture that builds upon the reference model. The reference architecture covers the definition of basic architectural building blocks and their ability to be integrated into multi-tiered systems. The reference architecture also addresses how to document and, if strived for, mitigate architecture divergence. This standard leverages existing

Figure 6. Three tier architecture of IoT and vertical segmentation of sharable IoT infrastructure

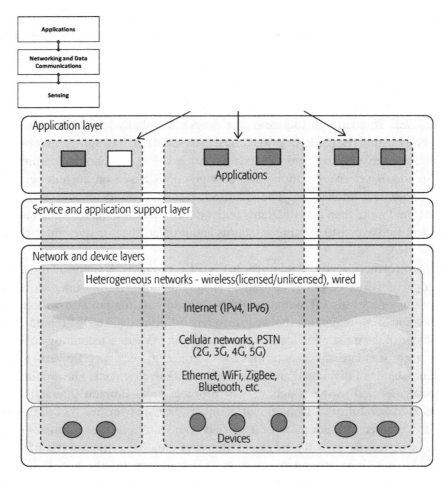

applicable standards and identifies planned or ongoing projects with a similar or overlapping scope.

The goals for the IEEE P2413 working group are to:

- Accelerate the growth of the IoT market by enabling cross-domain interaction and platform unification through increased system compatibility, interoperability and functional exchangeability.
- Define an IoT architecture framework that covers the architectural needs of the various IoT application domains.

- Increase the transparency of system architectures to support system benchmarking, safety and security assessments.
- Reduce industry fragmentation and create a critical mass of multi stakeholder activities around the world.
- Leverage the existing body of work.

Communications and IoT

A key aspect in supporting the high demand for large scale, widely available, and yet low-cost IoT-based solutions is the role played by the communication technologies to ensure that the sensed data can be reliably delivered to the applications using it.

Deterministic Ethernet refers to a networked communication technology that uses time scheduling to bring deterministic real-time communication to the standard IEEE 802 Ethernet. Deterministic Ethernet operates using a global sense of time and a schedule which is shared between network components. By using Deterministic Ethernet customers can converge real-time controls traffic with regular best effort traffic on one Ethernet network. Time-scheduled traffic is partitioned from all other network traffic and is therefore immune to disturbance. This means that in a Deterministic Ethernet network, the latency of critical scheduled communication is guaranteed. This is called Guarantee of Service. Deterministic Ethernet is used in a wide range of applications where guaranteed latency is vital, either for reasons of operational efficiency or functional safety. These include autonomous driving, machine-to-machine communication and aerospace flight control.

The two key Ethernet technologies are Time-Sensitive Networking and Time-Triggered Ethernet. IEEE Standard Ethernet for guaranteed real-time communication Time-Sensitive Networking (TSN) is a set of IEEE 802 Ethernet sub-standards that are defined by the IEEE TSN task group. This set of standards is to be completed by 2017 (IEEE, 2017).

- **Standards-Based:** Part of IEEE 802 standards suite.
- **Partitioned:** Virtual separation of traffic classes, enables convergence of other protocols on one physical network.
- **Compatible:** Integrates existing industrial Ethernet protocols including Profinet and EtherNet/IP.
- **Scalable:** Scales from small to very large systems without compromising safety, security or performance.
- **Secure:** Existing security standards and management features can be implemented, partitioning prevents denial of service.

Time-Triggered Ethernet is a scalable networking technology that uses time scheduling to deliver deterministic real-time communication over the Ethernet. It has been specifically designed for safe and highly available real-time applications, cyber-physical systems and unified networking. It is fully compatible with IEEE 802.3 Ethernet and integrates transparently with Ethernet network components. Time-Triggered Ethernet simplifies the design of fault-tolerant and high availability solutions for aerospace, automotive and industrial applications. Safety and redundancy are maintained at the network level without any need for application involvement. Functions at the network level, such as redundancy managements and fault-tolerant clock synchronization (as standardized in SAE AS6802) ease application design processes and enable faster time-to-market. Scheduled traffic in Time-Triggered Ethernet is forwarded in an extremely precise way, down to the individual packet. This enables the scheduling of very tight control loops and the certification of networks for safety systems. Time-Triggered Ethernet also includes replicated packet communication, which guarantees the transmission of messages without any additional switch-over delays, even if one channel becomes faulty. This ensures maximized availability for safety systems in the presence of faults (fail operationality) and easier failure management.

- **Standards-Based:** Based on IEEE 802.3 and standardized in SAE AS6802.
- **Partitioned:** Virtual separation of traffic classes, enables convergence of other protocols on one physical network.
- **Compatible:** Integrates installed industrial Ethernet protocols including Profinet and EtherNet/IP.
- **Scalable:** Scales from small to very large systems without compromising safety, security or performance.
- **Secure:** Existing security standards and management features implemented, partitioning prevents denial of service.
- **Safe:** Certifiable for fail-operational safety systems.

Wireless Wi-Fi HaLow variant of IEEE 802.11ah was recently released from the Wi-Fi Alliance. The IEEE standard itself is still in the IEEE-SA Sponsor Ballot stage. The first ballot is complete, and a second ballot is scheduled to come out in March, 2016. Wi-Fi HaLow follows most of the standard protocols, which helps simplify the creation of router/hub devices that handle both HaLow and conventional Wi-Fi in a single unit. The protocol commonality also means that IoT developers find it easier to create HaLow devices, leveraging their knowledge of conventional Wi-Fi. And there is little, if any, manipulation required to convert a HaLow data stream for Internet Protocol (IP) backhaul. At the same time, Wi-Fi HaLow is under no constraint to maintain absolute compatibility with conventional Wi-Fi. This frees HaLow to incorporate changes that reduce implementation complexity. The changes include more compact frame formats and reduced the protocol overhead, both of which address the standard's goal of reducing the cost and complexity of MAC-layer implementations (Wi-Fi Alliance, 2016).

The aim of the new Wi-Fi variant is also to reduce the power requirement and extend the range of Wi-Fi connectivity compared to conventional 802.11 connectivity. This is accomplished in several ways. One way is to add sub-GHz radio connectivity (900 MHz ISM band) to the mix. The lower frequencies provide a greater penetration of barriers such as walls than the 2.4 GHz and 5 GHz bands used in conventional Wi-Fi. A greater range is also obtained by lowering the data rate for HaLow. Channels defined for HaLow include 1-, 2-, 4-, 8-, and 16-MHz bandwidths compared to 20 MHz and up for Wi-Fi. The correspondingly reduced data rate allows for operation at lower signal-to-noise levels, which translates to greater range, lower transmit power, or a combination, without sacrificing data reliability.

Low-Power Wide Area Network (LP WAN) or Low-Power Network (LPN) is a type of wireless telecommunication network designed to operated in unlicensed spectrum that allows long range communications at a low bit rate among things (connected objects), such as sensors operated on a battery.

Wireless network technologies such as WiFi, ZigBee, and Bluetooth are fine for consumer applications of the IoT, but many civic, industrial, and other IoT applications need to operate over vastly greater territory than these technologies can handle. Cellular and satellite M2M technologies have traditionally filled the gap, but cost, power, and scalability concerns make these choices less appealing for the future. A number of low-power, wide-area networking (LP-WAN) alternatives have arisen that need careful consideration by developers looking to address these wide-ranging IoT applications (LoRa Alliance, 2016).

While the applications are diverse, they have many common attributes on their network wish lists. These include low cost, low energy consumption, extended range, and scalability.

Among the more established wireless networking technologies, only cellular and satellite communications offer the extended ranges that these applications require. Mesh networks such as ZigBee can potentially cover large areas but have limited scalability due to the need to forward traffic. Unfortunately cellular and satellite communications technologies fall short in the other attributes. Their radio requirements involve higher energy use and complex protocols that lower battery life and increase the cost beyond what many applications can sustain. This arises in part from their history; they were originally designed to handle voice traffic. The networks are ill adapted at to handling short data messaging.

Still, some IoT applications and M2M services did arise to leverage cellular and satellite communications networks. Many of them were based on the CDMA, or 2G cellular technology. Unfortunately, those networks are now starting to be phased out by service providers in order to free the spectrum for more advanced cellular technologies. However, the cellular community has made some strides toward improving the situation for M2M. The most recent specification for LTE (Release 12) defined communications Category 0 designed around the needs of M2M traffic. However, energy use and cost still remain concerns.

This situation has opened a door for alternative approaches to wide-area wireless networking for the IoT, approaches that focus on the low-power, low-cost requirements. At least six different approaches are currently defined with network deployment growing or getting started, and three more are in development (Weightless SIG, SigFox, LoRaWAN, LTE-Cat M, IEEE802.11ah, Dash7 Alliance Protocol, Ingenu RPMA, nWave). While all these approaches seek to provide the same key core attributes, they have different takes on numerous other system attributes that can affect their suitability for various IoT applications (Sept. 2015).

These other attributes that vary in importance among applications but still need consideration include roaming, penetration, short message handling, bidirectional communications, secure communications, and higher level services. A given wide-area IoT networking alternative may define any number of levels in the OSI model, from just the physical and data link layers to through the application layers. In some cases the network itself is operated and managed by a service provider that leases time on the network to users running their protocols and provides users with cloud services. Other alternatives define only the lower layers and have their access point connect to the Internet or to a private network, leaving the higher OSI layers to the user's choice. In such cases an ecosystem of higher-level service providers usually becomes available over time. The various low-power, wide-area networking schemes on offer address these many needs and considerations in a variety of ways. Each has made a different choice of tradeoffs among interacting attributes such as battery life, data rate, operating frequency, achievable range, and scalability. Further, they have made different choices around attributes such as security, OSI levels defined, and roaming support. This diversity makes it impossible to provide a comprehensive side-by-side comparison, but it is possible to provide a start.

3rd Generation Partnership Project (3GPP) collaboration between groups of telecommunications associations has made a major effort in Release-13 to address the IoT market (Table 2). The portfolio of technologies that 3GPP operators can now use to address their different market requirements includes:

- **eMTC:** Is the further LTE enhancements for Machine Type Communications, building on the work started in Release-12 (UE Cat 0, new power saving mode: PSM, extended DRX (Discontinuous Reception) - Connected Mode DRX). The objectives are long battery life (~10 years of operation with 5

Table 2. Summary of 3GPP protocols specification for IoT

	eMTC (LTE Cat M1)	NB-IoT	EC-GSM-IoT
Deployment:	In-band LTE	In/Guard -band LTE, standalone	In-band GSM
Coverage:	155.7 dB	164 dB for standalone, FFS others	164 dB, with 33 dBm power class 154 dB, with 23 dBm power class
Downlink:	OFDMA, 15KHz tone spacing, TurboCode, 16QAM, 1Rx	OFDMA, 15KHz tone spacing, TBCC, 1Rx	TDMA/FDMA, GMSK and 8PSK (optional), 1Rx
Uplink:	SC-FDMA, 15KHz tone spacing, TurboCode, 16QAM	Single tone, 15/3.75KHz spacing, TBCC	TDMA/FDMA, GMSK and 8PSK (optional)
Bandwidth:	1.08 MHz	180KHz	200KHz per channel (2.4MHz)
Peak rate	1 Mbps for DL and UL	DL 250kbps	DL/UL 4 time slots:
DL/UL:		UL 250kbps, 20kbps	70kbps (GMSK), 240kbps (8PSK)
Duplexing:	FH&HD (type B), FDD&TDD	HD (type B), FDD	FH, HD
Power saving:	PSM, ext. I-DRX, C- DRX	PSM, ext. I-DRX, C- DRX	PSM, ext. I-DRX
Power class:	23 dBm, 20 dBm	23 dBm, others TBD	33 dBm, 23 dBm

Watt Hour battery, depending on traffic and coverage needs), low device cost (comparable to that of GPRS/GSM devices), extended coverage (>155.7 dB maximum coupling loss MCL), variable rates (~10 kbps to 1 Mbps depending on coverage needs). It can be deployed in any LTE spectrum (it can coexist with other LTE services within the same bandwidth), support FDD, TDD and half duplex (HD) modes, and reuse existing LTE base stations with software update.

- **NB-IoT:** Is new radio added to the LTE platform optimized for the low end of the market. The objectives are an even lower cost than eMTC, extended coverage (164 dB maximum coupling loss,at least for the standalone), long battery life (10 years with 5 Watt Hour battery, depending on traffic and coverage needs), and support for massive number of devices (~50.000 per cell). The main simplification is reduced data rate/bandwidth, mobility support and further protocol optimizations. NB-IoT supports 3 modes of operation: stand-alone (utilizing stand-alone carrier, e.g. spectrum currently used by GERAN systems as a replacement of one or more GSM carriers), guard band (utilizing the unused resource blocks within a LTE carrier's guard-band), and in-band (utilizing resource blocks within a normal LTE carrier).

- **EC-GSM-IoT:** Is an EGPRS enhancements which in combination with PSM makes GSM/EDGE markets prepared for the IoT. The objectives are long battery life (~10 years of operation with 5 Watt Hour battery, depending on traffic pattern and coverage needs), low device cost compared to GPRS/GSM devices, extended coverage (164 dB MCL for 33 dBmUE, 154 dB MCL for 23 dBmUE), variable rates (GMSK: ~350bps to 70kbps depending on the coverage level, 8PSK: up to 240 kbps), support for massive number of devices (~50.000 per cell), and improved security compared to GSM/EDGE.

Protocol specifications are due to be finalized in Q2-2016. NB-IoT is the telecommunication operators attempt to exploit the forthcoming IoT opportunities without having to design and deploy separate networks. The reuse of existing LTE infrastructure and core networks enables operators to target low cost service offerings within the licensed portions of their spectrum (3GPP, 2016).

IoT ECOSYSTEM STUDY

The IoT ecosystem is hard to define. It is complex, and it is difficult to capture due to the vastness of possibility and the rapidity with which it is expanding. However, there is no doubt that IoT is changing the world. It is shaping the evolution of the Internet. The IoT is creating numerous challenges and opportunities for engineering and science (Vermesan et al., 2013; Hersent, Boswarthick, &Elloumi, 2012; Buyya, &Dastjerdi, 2016)

- Technological advances are fueling the growth of IoT. Improved communications and network technologies, new sensors of various kinds, and improved-cheaper, denser, and more reliable and power efficient storage both in the cloud and locally are converging to enable new types of products that were not possible a few years ago.
- The success of the IoT depends strongly on standardization, which provides interoperability, compatibility, reliability, and effective operations on a global scale. Most current standardization activities are confined to very specific domains and stakeholder groups. They therefore represent islands of disjointed and often redundant development. One solution is creating an IoT environment through scenarios. It objective is to collect a wide set of use cases, service descriptions, business models, and reference implementations

related to IoT. The community is looking for a set of compelling examples and possible services from which it will be possible to derive an IoT architecture and describe its components. The solid base can help the community to progress towards the realization and implementation of a vibrant IoT industry (IEEE-SA *Internet of Things (IoT) Ecosystem Study*, 2015).

- The IoT market is burgeoning but fragmented. Early players are active and currently creating products for which they see a market. In order to get products to market, these players are implementing proprietary solutions, some of which may evolve into *de facto* standards. Currently, IoT is trending toward vertical applications.

The IoT environment consists of a large number of embedded devices, like sensors and actuators that generate big data which in turn requires complex computations to extract knowledge. Therefore, the storage and computing resources of the cloud are the best choice for the IoT to store and process big data. In the following, we discuss the relation between the IoT and big data analytics, cloud and edge computing. Through cloudlets or edge/fog computing, it is possible to extend cloud computing services to the edge devices of the network (Al-Fuqaha et al., 2015).

Instead of providing application specific analytics, IoT needs a common big data *analytic platform* which can be delivered as a service to IoT applications. Such an analytic service should not impose a considerable overhead on the overall IoT ecosystem. Recent research has proposed such an IoT big data analytics service known as TSaaS using time series data analytics to perform pattern mining on a large amount of collected sensor data. One viable solution for IoT big data is to keep track of just the interesting data only. Existing approaches can help in this field like principle component analysis (PCA), pattern reduction, dimensionality reduction, feature selection, and distributed computing methods.

Cloud computing offers a new management mechanism for big data that enables the processing of data and the extraction of valuable knowledge from it. Employing cloud computing for the IoT is not an easy task due to the following challenges (Taivalsaari, &Mikkonen, 2015):

- Synchronization between different cloud vendors presents a challenge to provide real-time services since services are built on top of various cloud platforms.
- Standardizing CC also presents a significant challenge for IoT cloud-based services due having to interoperate with the various vendors.
- Making a balance between general cloud service environments and IoT requirements presents another challenge due to the differences in infrastructure.

- Security of IoT cloud-based services presents another challenge due to the differences in the security mechanisms between the IoT devices and the cloud platforms.
- Managing CC and IoT systems is also a challenging factor due to the fact that both have different resources and components.
- Validating IoT cloud-based services is necessary to ensure providing good services that meet the customers' expectations.

The IoT can utilize numerous cloud platforms with different capabilities and strengths such as ThingWorx, OpenIoT, Google Cloud, Amazon, GENI, etc. For example, Xively (formerly known as Cosm and Pachube) represents one of the first IoT application hosting service providers allowing sensor data to be available on the web. Xively aims to connect devices to applications securely in real-time. Xively provides a Platform as a Service (PaaS) solution for the IoT application developers and service providers. It is able to integrate devices with the platform by ready libraries (such as ARM mbed, Electric Imp and iOS/OSX) and facilitate communication via HTTP(S), Sockets/Websocket, or MQTT. It could also integrate with other platforms using Java, JS, Python, and Ruby libraries. The automated parking lot is a sample of using Xively to implement IoT applications.

As another example, Nimbits is an open source Platform as a Service (PaaS) that connects smart embedded devices to the cloud. It also performs data analytics on the cloud, generates alerts, and connects with social networks and spreadsheets. Moreover, it connects to websites and can store, share and retrieve sensors' data in various formats including numeric, text based, GPS, JSON or XML. To exchange data or messages, XMPP is a built-in service in Nimbits. The core of Nimbits is a server that provides REST web services for logging and retrieval of raw and processed data.

Table 3 summarizes some characteristics of several publicly available Cloud platforms for IoT. The evaluation metrics include: supporting gateway devices to bridging the short range network and wide area network, supporting discovery, delivery, configuration and activation of applications and services, providing proactive and reactive assurance of platform, support of accounting and billing of applications and services, and finally support of standard application protocols. All the platforms support sensing or actuating devices, a user interface to interact with devices, and a web component to run the business logic of the application on the cloud.

CONCLUDING REMARKS

The Internet of Things can be defined as the interconnection of uniquely identifiable devices within the Internet infrastructure. Although the standardization activities are

Table 3. IoT cloud platforms

Platform	Gateway	Provision	Assurance	Billing	REST App Protocol	CoAP App Protocol	XMPP App Protocol	MQTT App Protocol
Arkessa	-	+	+	-	+	-	-	+
Axeda	+	+	+	+	+	-	-	-
Etherios	+	+	+	-	+	-	-	-
LittleBits	-	-	-	-	+	-	-	-
NanoServices	+	+	+	-	+	+	-	-
Nimbits	-	-	-	-	+	-	+	-
Ninja Blocks	+	-	-	-	+	-	-	-
OnePlatform	+	+	+	-	+	+	+	-
Real Time.io	+	+	-	-	+	-	-	-
SensorCloud	+	+	-	-	+	-	-	-
Smart Things	+	+	-	-	+	-	-	-
TempoDB	-	-	-	-	+	-	-	-
Thingworx	-	+	+	-	+	-	-	+
Xively	+	+	+	+	+	-	-	+

very intensive, the proposed IoT frameworks still lack global adoption, mainly due to opposite requirements of consumer and industrial IoT models. Moreover, there is an urgent need for the harmonization of standards in order to provide a global interconnection of devices. The rapidly increasing data volume calls for new event processing algorithms and analytics. Special attention in ongoing standardization activities is given to security and privacy issues.

Internet traffic has started to shift away from non-multimedia data to multimedia traffic, particularly, the video data. Existing research on IoT mainly focuses on the sensing capabilities and networking techniques. Future technical challenges in communicating real-time multimedia data over wired and/or wireless links within the IoT are as follows: multimedia data acquisition techniques for devices, protocols and standards of communication in the IoT, multimedia content analysis and event detection, security and forensics, multimedia processing and storage, applications of communication, experimental measurement of multimedia communication, distributed/centralized multimedia coding, scalable and low-delay source coding, distributed multimedia compression, communication and cooperation through multimedia, scalable big data management in the IoT, and social multimedia.

REFERENCES

3rd Generation Partnership Project. (2016). *Specification Release 13*. Retrieved from http://www.3gpp.org/release-13

Al-Fuqaha, A., Guizani, M., Mohammadi, M., Aledhari, M., & Ayyash, M. (2015). Internet of Things: A survey on enabling technologies, protocols, and applications. *IEEE Communications Surveys and Tutorials*, 4(17), 2347–2376. doi:10.1109/COMST.2015.2444095

Buratti, C., & Gardasevic, G. (2016). Testing protocols for the Internet of Things on the EuWin platform. *IEEE Internet of Things Journal*, 3(1), 124–133. doi:10.1109/JIOT.2015.2462030

Buyya, R. V., & Dastjerdi, A. (2016). *Internet of Things: Principles and paradigms*. Morgan Kaufmann.

Cisco. (2015). *IoT System*. Retrieved from http://www.cisco.com/c/m/en_us/solutions/internet-of-things/iot-system.html

Gardasevic, G., Veletić, M., Maletić, N., Vasiljević, D., Radusinović, I., Tomović, S., & Radonjić, M. (2017). The IoT architectural framework, design issues and application domains. *Springer Journal Wireless Personal Communications*, 92(1), 127–148. doi:10.1007/s11277-016-3842-3

Gartner (2015). Retrieved from http://www.gartner.com/newsroom/id/3165317

Gazis, V. (2016). A survey of standards for Machine to Machine (M2M) and the Internet of Things. *IEEE Communications Surveys and Tutorials, 99*.

Gazis, V., Gortz, M., Huber, M., Leonardi, A., Mathioudakis, K., Wiesmaier, A., & Vasilomanolakis, E. et al. (2015). A survey of technologies for the Internet of Things. *Wireless Communications and Mobile Computing Conference (IWCMC)*, 1090–1095. doi:10.1109/IWCMC.2015.7289234

Hersent, O., Boswarthick, D., & Elloumi, O. (2012). *The Internet of Things: Key applications and protocols* (2nd ed.). Wiley.

Institute of Electrical and Electronics Engineers. (2015). *Towards a definition of the Internet of Things (IoT)*. Retrieved from http://iot.ieee.org/definition

Institute of Electrical and Electronics Engineers. (2016). *Internet of Things (IoT) related standards*. Retrieved from http://standards.ieee.org/innovate/iot/stds.html

Institute of Electrical and Electronics Engineers. (2017). *Time-Sensitive Networking Task Group*. Retrieved from http://www.ieee802.org/1/pages/tsn.html

Intel. (2016). *IoT Platform: Secure, scalable, interoperable.* Retrieved from http://www.intel.com/content/www/us/en/internet-of-things/overview.html

Internet of Things World Forum. (2014). *Reference Model.* Retrieved from https://www.iotwf.com/resources

Internet Research Task Force. (2016). *Thing-to-Thing Research Group.* Retrieved from https://irtf.org/t2trg

Internet Society. (2015). *The Internet of Things (IoT): An overview - Understanding the issues and challenges of a more connected world.* Retrieved from http://www.internetsociety.org/doc/iot-overview

Internet Society. (2016). *Internet of Things: Standards and guidance from the IETF.* Retrieved from https://www.internetsociety.org/publications/ietf-journal-april-2016/internet-things-standards-and-guidance-ietf

ISO/IEC JTC1/SC29/WG11 MPEG. (2016). *Internet of Media Things and Wearables.* Retrieved from http://mpeg.chiariglione.org/standards/exploration/internet-media-things-and-wearables

ISO/IEC JTC1/WG10. (2015). *Internet of Things.* Retrieved from http://isotc.iso.org/livelink/livelink/open/jtc1wg10

ITU-Telecommunication Standardization Sector. (2015). *Study Group 20 at a glance.* Retrieved from http://www.itu.int/en/ITU-T/about/groups/Pages/sg20.aspx

ITU-Telecommunication Standardization Sector. (n.d.). *Internet of Things: Global Standards Initiative.* Retrieved from http://www.itu.int/en/ITU-T/gsi/iot/

Kafle, V. P., Fukushima, Y., & Hara, H. (2016). Internet of Things Standardization in ITU and prospective networking technologies. *IEEE Communications Magazine, 54*(9), 43–49. doi:10.1109/MCOM.2016.7565271

LoRa Alliance. (2016). *Technology.* Retrieved from https://www.lora-alliance.org/what-is-lora/technology

Meddeb, A. (2016). Internet of Things standards: Who stands out from the crowd?. *IEEE Communications Magazine - Communications Standards Supplement, 7*(54), 40–47.

Sheng, Z., Yang, S., Yu, Y., Vasilakos, A., Mccann, J., & Leung, K. (2013). A survey on the IETF protocol suite for the internet of things: Standards, challenges, and opportunities. *IEEE Wireless Communications, 20*(6), 91–98. doi:10.1109/MWC.2013.6704479

Stankovic, J. A. (2014). Research directions for the Internet of Things. *IEEE Internet of Things Journal, 1*(1), 3–9. doi:10.1109/JIOT.2014.2312291

Taivalsaari, A., & Mikkonen, T. (2015). Cloud technologies for the Internet of Things: Defining a research agenda beyond the expected topics. *Proc.Euromicro Conference on Software engineering and advanced applications (SEAA)*, 484–488.

Vermesan, O. (2013). Internet of Things beyond the Hype: Research, innovation and deployment. In O. Vermesan & P. Friess (Eds.), *Internet of Things: Converging technologies for smart environments and integrated ecosystems* (pp. 15–118). Aalborg, Denmark: River Publishers.

Wi-Fi Alliance. (2016). *Introduces low power, long range Wi-Fi HaLow*. Retrieved from http://www.wi-fi.org/news-events/newsroom/wi-fi-alliance-introduces-low-power-long-range-wi-fi-halow

ADDITIONAL READING

Atzori, L., Iera, A., & Morabito, G. (2010). The Internet of Things: A survey. *Elsevier Computer Networks, 54*(15), 2787–2805. doi:10.1016/j.comnet.2010.05.010

Granjal, J., Monteiro, E., & Silva, J. S. (2015). Security for the Internet of Things: A survey of existing protocols and open research issues. *IEEE Communications Surveys and Tutorials, 3*(17), 1294–1312. doi:10.1109/COMST.2015.2388550

Haller, S. *The things in the Internet of things*, in Proc. IoT2010, Tokyo, Nov. 2010.

IoTBD 2016. 1st International conference on Internet of Things and Big Data. Retrieved from https://www.iotwf.com/resources and http://www.iotbd.org/?y=2016

Rao, K. R., Bojkovic, Z. S., & Milovanovic, D. A. (2002). *Multimedia communication systems: Techniques, standards and networks*. Upper Saddle River, NJ, US: Prentice Hall.

Rao, K. R., Bojkovic, Z. S., & Milovanovic, D. A. (2006). *Introduction to Multimedia Communications: Applications-Middleware-Networking*. Hoboken, NJ, US: Wiley.

Rao, K. R., Bojkovic, Z. S., & Milovanovic, D. A. (2008). *Wireless multimedia communications*. Boca Raton, FL, US: CRC Press.

Riazul, S. M., Kwak, D., Humaun, M. D., Hossain, M., & Kwak, K.-S. (2015). *The Internet of Things for Health care: A comprehensive survey*. IEEE Access.

Want, R., Schilit, B. N., & Jenson, S. (2015). Enabling the Internet of Things. *IEEE Computer*, *1*(48), 28–35. doi:10.1109/MC.2015.12

Zanella, A., Bui, N., Castellani, A., Vangelista, L., & Zorzi, M. (2014). Internet of Things for Smart cities. *IEEE Internet of Things Journal*, *1*(1), 22–32. doi:10.1109/JIOT.2014.2306328

APPENDIX

Table 4. IoT technological development

Areas	Before 2010	2010-2015	>2016
Standardization	RFID security Passive RFID with expanded memory and read/write capability	IoT standardization M2M Interoperability	Standards for cross interoperability with heterogeneous networks
IoT architecture technology	IoT architecture specification Context-sensitive middleware Intelligent reasoning platforms	IoT architecture developments Network of networks architecture IoT architecture in the FIF-O-T platforms interoperability	Adaptive, context based architectures Self- properties Cognitive architectures Experiential architecture
Identification technologies	Different Schemes Domain specific IDs ISO, GS1, u-code, IPv6...	Unified framework for unique identifiers Open framework for IoT URIs	Identity Management Semantics Privacy-awareness *Things DNA* identifier
Communication technology	RFID, UWB, Wi-Fi, WiMax, Bluetooth, ZigBee, ISA100, 6LoWPAN	Ultra low power chipsets, system on chip On chip antennas Millimeter wave single chips Ultra low power single chip radios Ultra low power system on chip MobilityHeterogeneity	Wide spectrum and spectrum aware protocol Unified protocol over wide spectrum
Network technology	Sensor networks	Ultra low power chipsets, system on chip On chip antennas Millimeter wave single chips Ultra low power single chip radios Ultra low power system on chip Mobility Heterogeneity	Network context awareness Network cognition Self learning, self repairing network
Software and algorithm	Relational database integration IoT oriented RDBMS Event-based platforms Sensor middleware Sensor network middleware Proximity / localization algorithms	Large scale, open semantic software modules Next generation IoT-based social software Next generation IoT-based enterprise applications	Distributed intelligence, problem solving The invisible IoT Easy to deploy IoT software Things to Human collaborations IoT for all

continued on following page

Table 1. Continued

Areas	Before 2010	2010-2015	>2016
Sensors	RFID tags and sensors Sensors build in mobile devices NFC in mobile phones Smaller and cheaper MEMs technology	Multi protocol, multi standards reader More sensors and actuators Secure, low cost tags, sensors	Smart sensors (Bio-chem) More sensors and actuators (tiny sensors) Nano-technology and new materials
Data & signal processing technology	Serial data processing Parallel data processing Quality of services	Energy, frequency spectrum aware data processing, Data processing context adaptable	Context aware data processing and data responses Cognitive processing and optimisation
Discovery and search engine technology	Simple ID based object lookup Local registries Discovery services	Distributed registries, search and discovery mechanisms Semantic discovery of sensor and sensor data	Automatic route tagging and Identification Automatic route tagging and identification management centres Cognitive search engines Autonomous search engines
Power and energy storage technologies	Thin batteries Li-Ion Flat batteries Power optimized systems (energy management) Energy harvesting (electrostatic, piezoelectric) Short and medium range wireless power	Energy harvesting Printed batteries Long range wireless power	Self-Power Energy recycling Wireless power Biodegradable batteries Nano-power processing unit
Security and privacy technologies	Security mechanism and protocol defined (RFID & WSN) Security mechanisms and protocols for RFID and WSN devices	User centric context-aware privacy and policy Privacy aware data processing	Security & Privacy profiles based on needs Privacy needs automatic evaluation Context centric security Self adaptive security mechanisms and protocols

Section 2
Internet of Things Development, Tools, and Techniques

Chapter 4

A Case Study on the Spatial Cognition of Surrounding Objects by the B&VI People Using Sound Patterns and Ultrasonic Sensing

Dmytro Zubov
Universidad Politécnica de San Luis Potosí, Mexico

ABSTRACT

In this paper, two assistive projects on the spatial cognition by blind and visually impaired (B&VI) people are presented using the sound patterns and ultrasonic sensing. The first device supports the sport activities of B&VI, the golf game specifically. Every golf flagstick has the sound marking device with the active buzzer and WiFi remote control by the person with good vision. The NodeMcu Lua ESP8266 ESP-12 WiFi boards in devices are controlled by the cross-platform HTML web-sites, and hence any WiFi smartphone and / or computer can be in use to start the HTML web-page. Mini portable WiFi router links all devices in the network. End-users are securely connected using the password to wireless router. Ten assistive devices were handed in Instituto para Ciegos y Débiles Visuales "Ezequiel Hernández Romo" together with WiFi router. The second device supports the orientation of B&VI by measuring the distance to the obstacle based on the ultrasonic sensor HC-SR04 and Arduino Uno. The distance is pronounced to the B&VI using headphone and MP3 player with SD card. Nowadays, Universidad Politécnica de San Luis Potosí is negotiating with several organizations to create a production line. All devices are of the budget price up to USD 10. All devices were tested successfully. This is

DOI: 10.4018/978-1-5225-2437-3.ch004

joint work of Instituto para Ciegos y Débiles Visuales "Ezequiel Hernández Romo", Universidad Politécnica de San Luis Potosí, and Tecnológico de Monterrey with ongoing project "Artificial Eyes" based on Raspberry Pi 3 Model B board with an ultrasonic sensor and camera for the image and/or video processing of the surrounding environment, as well as the friendly integration into the local networks using onboard WiFi and Bluetooth.

INTRODUCTION

World Health Organization pointed that 285 million people are estimated to be blind and visually impaired (B&VI) worldwide in 2014 (Visual Impairment and Blindness, 2016). In particular, 39 million are blind and 246 have low vision, which means approximately 3.9% of the population (7.261 billion in 2014) around the world have the eyes problems. About 90% of the world's visually impaired live at low income. Besides the medical treatment, these people need the assistive devices for the spatial cognition. These devices play important role in the outdoor exploration of B&VI (Sonnier & Riesen, 1985). In particular, Golledge (1993) showed that an independent travel and interaction with the wider world is a significant problem for B&VI after the reading and writing. Bruce et al. (1991) found that approximately 20% of young B&VI people in the United Kingdom had not left their home, approximately 30% had travelled locally (Clark-Carter, Heyes, & Howarth, 1986), and only 41% left their home alone and walked. In addition, most of B&VI people who explore new routes feel disorientation, fear, stress, and panic associated with being lost (Golledge, 1993). To be mobile is a factor that contributes to the success of the blind adults because it directly corresponds with their employment (Goodwyn, Bell, & Singletary, 2009). The development of the assistive devices for B&VI increases the social responsibility about B&VI (Bell, 2010).

Nowadays, different hardware was developed converting the input info (images, videos, numbers, etc.) into the tactile and sound patterns. Some devices have already been released commercially, e.g. Sonicguide of price USD 500 (Marsh, 1978), iGlasses of price USD 100 (iGlasses Ultrasonic Mobility Aid, 2016), Brainport V100 of price USD 10,000 (BrainPort V100 Device, 2015). They work quite well but they are not accessible for poor people (i.e. for 90% of the visually impaired) because of the high price. Analysis of the B&VI minimum needs shows that the basic functionality includes the sound marking of the surrounding objects and the measurement of the distance to them. In Cappagli, Cocchi, and Gori (2015), a strong deficit in the audio distance evaluation for early blind children and adults is emphasized. In Jacobson and Kitchin (1997), the geographic information system

(GIS) is used by B&VI. A small experimental study that compares the ability of GIS-based and various adaptive technologies to communicate spatial information using non-visual media is presented. The main benefit of GIS usage is an improvement of the quality of life for B&VI by increasing mobility and independence. Here, GIS for B&VI is discussed in general, as well as budget solutions are not proposed. In Goria et al. (2016), different assistive devices (e.g. NavBelt, Vibe, Prizmo 3, K-sonar), apps (e.g. KNFB Reader, SmartSight, EyeMusic), and user-interface technologies (e.g. the tongue display unit, finger-braille interface, sound patterns) are discussed in detail. Here, the soft- and hardware are presented in general too, as well as budget solutions are not proposed.

Nowadays, the budget assistance devices for the B&VI can be efficiently developed using Arduino Uno/Mega (Warren, Adams, & Molle, 2011; Norris, 2015) and/or Arduino-compatible hardware like NodeMcu Lua ESP8266 ESP-12 WiFi board (User Manual for ESP-12E DevKit based on ESP8266, 2016) of the price up to USD 10. Here, the soft- and hardware is based on the technology Internet of Things (Charalampos Doukas, 2012; Norris, 2015; Dirk Slama et al., 2015). Universidad Politécnica de San Luis Potosí and Tecnológico de Monterrey (campus San Luis Potosí) developed two assistive devices – for the golf game (the sound marking of the golf flagsticks) using mobile app connected to the NodeMcu Lua ESP8266 ESP-12 WiFi boards and for the distance measurement using Arduino Uno together with an ultrasonic sensor. These devices are in use at Instituto para Ciegos y Débiles Visuales "Ezequiel Hernández Romo" nowadays.

Based on the above-stated analysis of the previous studies, this paper main goal is to present take outs of two assistive projects made by Universidad Politécnica de San Luis Potosí and Tecnológico de Monterrey (campus San Luis Potosí) for B&VI at Instituto para Ciegos y Débiles Visuales "Ezequiel Hernández Romo":

1. An assistive project for the golf game. In this project, the golf flagsticks have the sound marking devices with the active buzzer and NodeMcu Lua ESP8266 ESP-12 WiFi board, which are remotely controlled by WiFi. Hence, B&VI people play the golf almost without help. The person with good vision controls the sound of an appropriate device based on cross-platform HTML web-site.
2. An assistive project to support the orientation of B&VI by the measurement of the distance to the obstacle using an ultrasonic sensor and Arduino Uno. Then, the distance info is pronounced to the person using headphone and embedded MP3 player.

This paper is organized as follows: In Section 2, the assistive device to support the B&VI people to play the golf game using the WiFi network of the NodeMcu Lua ESP8266 ESP-12 WiFi boards with active buzzers is presented. In Section 3, the assistive ubiquitous device to support the orientation of the B&VI people by measuring the distance to the obstacle based on the ultrasonic sensor, Arduino Uno, and MP3 player is discussed. Conclusions are summarized in Section 4.

AN ASSISTIVE PROJECT FOR THE GOLF GAME

The assistive device supports B&VI to play the golf game using an appropriate sound pattern. Every golf flagstick has the sound marking device with WiFi remote control by the person with good vision. In this case, B&VI person hears the sound (five types of beep signals of different duration) from the appropriate golf stick and then kicks the ball towards it. In other words, B&VI play the golf almost without help. The NodeMcu Lua ESP8266 ESP-12 WiFi boards in devices are controlled by the cross-platform HTML web-sites, and hence any WiFi smartphone and / or computer can be in use to start the HTML web-page. Mini portable 3G/4G WiFi 150Mbps RJ45 USB wireless router with power supply 5 V links all devices in the wireless local area network. Hence, the hardware can work outdoor supplied by 5 V power banks. The manual control is provided by an additional button to the NodeMcu Lua WiFi board if the network is not working; in this case, special beep signal is generated when WiFi board starts. End-users are securely connected to the network using the password to the wireless router. Ten devices were assembled of price USD 7 each, i.e. the total budget is USD 80 including the portable wireless router and power banks. The accumulators for power banks were taken free of charge from the Fujitsu and Samsung old laptop batteries with the capacity approximately 1500 mA each, which provides about 5 hours of the stable working. The software was developed in the Arduino Integrated Development Environment (IDE) under free software license, and hence it does not affect the price.

The electronics hardware part of the assistive device for the golf game is shown in Figure 1. The main parts are the NodeMcu Lua ESP8266 ESP-12 WiFi board, active buzzer, button, and potentiometer. They are wired on the prototyping board. The device is attached to the top of the golf flagstick using velcro (see Figure 2). Figure 3 shows how the B&VI person plays the golf using the assistive device.

The software consists of two parts – Arduino sketch for the assistive devices and cross-platform HTML web-site for the management of all devices. The static local IP addresses are from 192.168.100.180 for the first WiFi board to 192.168.100.189 for the tenth. However, the end-user sees only the buttons in the web-site as shown in Figure 4. This feature is coded based on the HTML tag *href* as follows (other tags have similar codes):

Figure 1. The electronics hardware part of the assistive device for the golf game

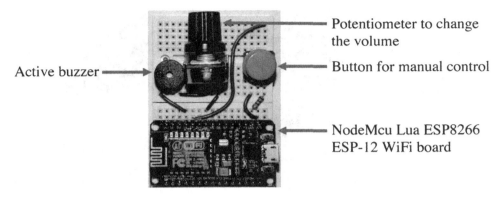

Potentiometer to change the volume

Button for manual control

Active buzzer

NodeMcu Lua ESP8266 ESP-12 WiFi board

Figure 2. The assistive device attached to the top of the golf flagstick using velcro

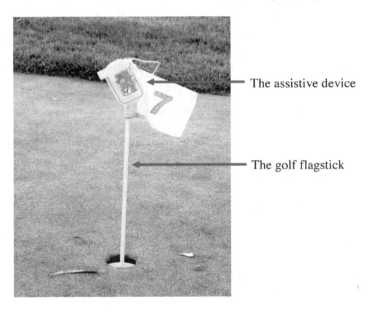

The assistive device

The golf flagstick

```
<a href="http://192.168.100.180"><button style='color:green;
font-size:30px; width:450px; height:100px; border-style:solid;
border-width:4px; border-color:green;'>Control the <b>1</
b><sup>st</sup> golf flagstick</button></a>
```

The configuration of the static local IP address in Arduino sketch for the first WiFi board is as follows (other boards are configured similarly):

Figure 3. The B&VI person plays the golf using an assistive device

The B&VI person

The golf flagstick
with assistive device

Figure 4. The screenshot of the HTML web-site for the management of all WiFi devices

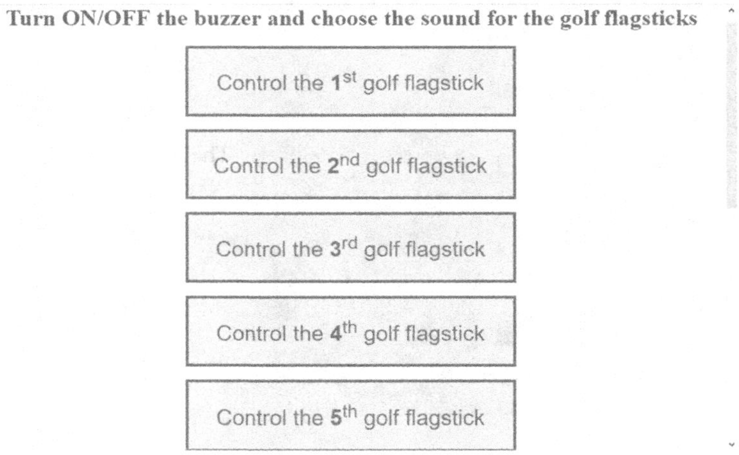

Turn ON/OFF the buzzer and choose the sound for the golf flagsticks

Control the 1ˢᵗ golf flagstick

Control the 2ⁿᵈ golf flagstick

Control the 3ʳᵈ golf flagstick

Control the 4ᵗʰ golf flagstick

Control the 5ᵗʰ golf flagstick

```
// The IP address for the WiFi board:
IPAddress ip(192, 168, 100, 180);
// Set gateway to match the network:
IPAddress gateway(192, 168, 100, 1);
// Set subnet mask to match the network:
IPAddress subnet(255, 255, 255, 0);
```

```
// Set the static local IP address:
WiFi.config(ip, gateway, subnet);
```

The screen shot of the HTML web-site hosted on the ninth WiFi board is presented in Figure 5 (other boards have similar web-sites).

The assistive device for the golf game was successfully implemented at the Instituto para Ciegos y Débiles Visuales "Ezequiel Hernández Romo", San Luis Potosí, Mexico. Three stages of the project's development are as follows: specification of the device, development of the prototype with intermediate testing, and assembling of ten assistive devices together with WiFi router and power banks.

AN ASSISTIVE PROJECT FOR THE MEASUREMENT OF THE DISTANCE TO THE OBSTACLE

The assistive ubiquitous device supports the orientation of B&VI by measuring the distance to the obstacle based on the ultrasonic sensor. Then, the distance is pronounced to the person using headphone. The electronics hardware part consists of the ultrasonic sensor HC-SR04, Arduino Uno, MP3 player with SD card, headphone, and two buttons to control the volume (see Figure 6). The red button decreases the

Figure 5. The screenshot of the HTML web-site for the management of the ninth WiFi board

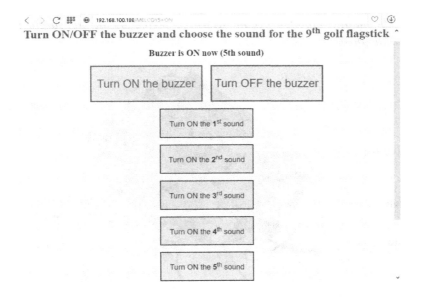

Figure 6. The electronics hardware part of the assistive device for the measurement of the distance to the obstacle

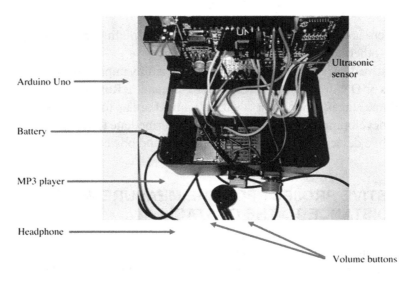

volume, the green one increases it. The device outlooks as shown in Figure 7. The hardware supplied by 5 V power bank. Three devices were assembled of price USD 8 each including the power banks. The power bank accumulators were taken free of charge from the Fujitsu and Samsung old laptop batteries as well. The testing shows that the embedded battery provides the stable power supply for at least an

Figure 7. The main components of the assistive device for the measurement of the distance to the obstacle

hour. The software was developed in the Arduino IDE under free software license, and hence it does not affect the price.

The ultrasonic sensor HC-SR04 measures the distance up to 4.5 m. Because of practical needs, this length is split into five intervals as follows: less than 1 m, greater than 1 m, 2 m, 3 m, and 4 m. MP3 files with appropriate info are written on SD card, and hence the sound patterns can be modified easily by the replacing /adding new files on SD card. In other words, this device can be adapted for the usage in many countries by simply replacing the MP3 files. Here, the main problem is about unidentified distance (usually greater than 5 m). It was found that the ultrasonic sensor HC-SR04 generates the signal about the distance less than 1 m after the unidentified one. Hence, the additional analysis of this ambiguity is implemented in Arduino sketch.

The assistive device for the measurement of the distance to the obstacle was successfully tested for the spatial cognition. Two stages of the project's development are the specification of device and the development of the prototype with intermediate testing at the Instituto para Ciegos y Débiles Visuales "Ezequiel Hernández Romo" and Lions Clubs International (Mexico, Distrito B3). Nowadays, Universidad Politécnica de San Luis Potosí is negotiating with several organizations to create a production line. Other applications were found during the testing as follows:

1. **Museums:** To tell the info about an exhibit when the visitors are near an interactive area. In this case, the loudspeaker is used instead of headphone.
2. **The Wall Installation:** The device says the distance to the person. In this case, the passive infrared sensor (Fernandez-Luque, Zapata, & Ruiz, 2013) is used to identify the biological objects.

CONCLUSION

The B&VI people at the Instituto para Ciegos y Débiles Visuales "Ezequiel Hernández Romo" say, "We are physically blind but you (i.e. people with good vision) are socially blind." In this paper, two budget solutions of the spatial cognition problem are presented for the B&VI people using sound patterns and ultrasonic sensing. These devices simplify the everyday activity of B&VI, as well as support their integration into hi-tech up-to-date environment.

Firstly, the assistive device was developed to support the B&VI to play the golf game. Here, every golf flagstick has the sound marking device with the active buzzer and WiFi remote control by the person with good vision. B&VI person hears the sound from the appropriate golf stick and then kicks the ball towards it. The NodeMcu Lua ESP8266 ESP-12 WiFi boards in devices are controlled by the cross-platform

HTML web-sites. Mini portable 3G/4G WiFi 150Mbps RJ45 USB router links all devices in the network. The hardware works outdoor using 5 V power banks. The manual control is provided by an additional button to the NodeMcu Lua WiFi board if the network is not accessible. End-users are securely connected to the network using the password to the wireless router. Ten devices were assembled of price USD 7 each, as well as they were successfully tested by the B&VI from the Instituto para Ciegos y Débiles Visuales "Ezequiel Hernández Romo", San Luis Potosí, Mexico.

Secondly, the assistive ubiquitous device was developed to support the orientation of B&VI by measuring the distance to the obstacle based on the ultrasonic sensor HC-SR04, Arduino Uno, MP3 player with SD card, headphone, and two buttons to control the volume. The distance is pronounced to the B&VI using headphone. It was successfully tested for the spatial cognition. Other applications are as follows: to tell the info about an exhibit at the museums; the wall installation – the device says the distance to the person.

The most likely prospect for the further development of this work is the project "Artificial Eyes" based on Raspberry Pi 3 Model B board with an ultrasonic sensor and camera for the image and/or video processing of the surrounding environment, as well as the friendly integration into the local networks using onboard WiFi and Bluetooth.

REFERENCES

Bell, E. C. (2010). Measuring Attitudes about Blindness: The Social Responsibility about Blindness Scale. Research Report of the Professional Development and Research Institute on Blindness. Ruston: Louisiana Tech University. Retrieved from http://www.pdrib.com/downloads/Measuring%20Attitudes%20Social%20 Responsibility%20about%20Blindness%20Scale.doc

BrainPort V100 Device Helps People who are Blind See with Tongue. (2015). Retrieved from https://brailleworks.com/brainport-v100/

Bruce, I., McKennell, A., & Walker, E. (1991). *Blind and Partially Sighted Adults in Britain: The RNIB Survey* (Vol. 1). London: Her Majesty's Stationery Office.

Cappagli, G., Cocchi, E., & Gori, M. (2015). Auditory and Proprioceptive Spatial Impairments in Blind Children and Adults. *Developmental Science*, (Nov): 1–12. doi:10.1111/desc.12374 PMID:26613827

Clark-Carter, D. D., Heyes, A. D., & Howarth, C. I. (1986). The Efficiency and Walking Speed of Visually Impaired Pedestrians. *Ergonomics*, 29(6), 779–789. doi:10.1080/00140138608968314 PMID:3743536

Doukas, C. (2012). Building Internet of Things with the Arduino. Seattle, WA: CreateSpace Independent Publishing Platform.

Fernandez-Luque, F., Zapata, J., & Ruiz, R. (2013). PIR-Based Motion Patterns Classification for AmI Systems.*Proc. of Conference on the Interplay Between Natural and Artificial Computation, IWINAC 2013*, 355-364. doi:10.1007/978-3-642-38622-0_37

Golledge, R. G. (1993). Geography and the Disabled: A Survey with Special Reference to Vision Impaired and Blind Populations. *Transactions of the Institute of British Geographers*, *18*(1), 63–85. doi:10.2307/623069

Goodwyn, M., Bell, E. C., & Singletary, C. (2009). Factors that Contribute to the Success of Blind Adults. Research Report of the Professional Development and Research Institute on Blindness. Ruston: Louisiana Tech University. Retrieved from http://www.pdrib.com/downloads/Factors%20that%20Contribute%20to%20the%20Success%20of%20Blind%20Adults.doc

Goria, M., Cappaglia, G., Tonellia, A., Baud-Bovyb, G., & Finocchietti, S. (2016). Devices for Visually Impaired People: High Technological Devices with Low User Acceptance and no Adaptability for Children. *Neuroscience and Biobehavioral Reviews*, *69*, 79–88. doi:10.1016/j.neubiorev.2016.06.043 PMID:27484870

iGlasses Ultrasonic Mobility Aid. (2016). Retrieved from https://www.maxiaids.com/iglasses-ultrasonic-mobility-aid-clear-lens

Jacobson, R. D., & Kitchin, R. M. (1997, December). GIS and People with Visual Impairments or Blindness: Exploring the Potential for Education, Orientation, and Navigation. *Transactions in GIS*, *2*(4), 315–332. doi:10.1111/j.1467-9671.1997.tb00060.x

Marsh, P. (1978). Sonic Aids for the Blinds – Do They Work? *J. New Scientist*, *13*, 114–117. Retrieved from https://books.google.com.mx/books?id=PhxDVgkDfuwC&pg=PA116&lpg=PA116&dq=Sonicguide+price+blinds&source=bl&ots=AbU1ehCMQq&sig=rSbdoz1KpJq88uHYauhoDVndf4E&hl=en&sa=X&ved=0ahUKEwjhpeerpf7PAhWJSyYKHa6PCYAQ6AEIGzAA#v=onepage&q=Sonicguide%20price%20blinds&f=false

Norris, D. (2015). *The Internet of Things: Do-It-Yourself at Home Projects for Arduino, Raspberry Pi, and BeagleBone Black*. New York: McGraw-Hill Education.

Slama, D., Puhlmann, F., Morrish, J., & Bhatnagar, R. M. (2015). Enterprise IoT: Strategies and Best Practices for Connected Products and Services. Sebastopol, CA: O'Reilly Media.

Sonnier, J., & Riesen, A. H. (1985). Developmental Brain Research, Deprivation, and Sensory Aids. In Electronic Spatial Sensing for the Blind. *Proc. of the NATO Advanced Reseasrch Workshop on Visual Spatial Prosthesis for the Blind.*

User Manual for ESP-12E DevKit based on ESP8266. (2016). Retrieved from https://smartarduino.gitbooks.io/user-manual-for-esp-12e-devkit/content/index.html

Visual Impairment and Blindness. (2016). World Health Organization. Retrieved from http://www.who.int/mediacentre/factsheets/fs282/en/

Warren, J.-D., Adams, J., & Molle, H. (2011). *Arduino Robotics.* New York: Apress Media LLC. doi:10.1007/978-1-4302-3184-4

Chapter 5
Building IoT With Arduino

Dmytro Zubov
Polytechnic University of San Luis Potosí, Mexico

ABSTRACT

IoT tools and techniques can be split into three main categories – infrastructure (i.e. hardware like Arduino Uno), software apps (e.g. Arduino C/C++ sketch), and lightweight protocols (e.g. MQTT and CoAP) for the connection of the heterogeneous components. Nowadays, they allow to develop fully functional smart systems. In this chapter, Arduino open-source computer soft- and hardware are discussed for the remote LED control, the web-server development, the design of the dual axis solar tracker with energy saving algorithm, the smart city's natural environment component based on Arduino weather station, the aid systems (in the mobility) for the visually impaired and blind people. In addition, the connection of the heterogeneous soft- and hardware is presented based on MQTT protocol.

INTRODUCTION

Wikipedia defines the Internet of Things (IoT) as "the network of physical objects – devices, vehicles, buildings and other items which are embedded with electronics, software, sensors, and network connectivity, which enables these objects to collect and exchange data" (https://en.wikipedia.org/wiki/Internet_of_Things). The IoT slogan can be formulated as "Connect uncontactable". Nowadays, IoT has reached the level of the ubiquitous devices like Arduino open-source computer soft- and hardware. Such small devices are used on almost every layer of IoT – smart power grids, smart cities, smart factories, connected vehicles, smart enterprises, etc. Experts estimate that the IoT devices will be about 50 billion by 2025 including sensors, vehicles, microwaves, fridges, and other objects run on electric power.

DOI: 10.4018/978-1-5225-2437-3.ch005

Currently, heterogeneous IoT hardware is in use. However, Arduino (https://en.wikipedia.org/wiki/Arduino) and Raspberry Pi (Norris, 2015; https://en.wikipedia.org/wiki/Raspberry_Pi) open-source computer soft- and hardware are the main options nowadays. The Raspberry Pi is a series of credit card-sized single-board computers developed by the Raspberry Pi Foundation, Wales, United Kingdom. Both have similar functionality, but the price of Raspberry Pi is several times greater than Arduino analogues usually. Other options like NodeMcu Lua ESP8266 ESP-12E WiFi development board (https://smartarduino.gitbooks.io/user-manual-for-esp-12e-devkit/content/index.html) are discussed for the wireless connection to the sensors using web-server. More details can be found in section "WiFi weather station prototype". In fact, this board is not Arduino hardware, but Arduino IDE is used for the software development.

Nowadays, different IoT devices are connected by the special type of IoT protocols because of the eal-time communication requirement. In addition, IoT hardware is of different types, as well as it has low performance and the Internet connection is slow sometimes. For instance, Arduino boards with their limited EEPROM, flash, and SRAM memory (https://www.arduino.cc/en/Products/Compare) can benefit from the IoT protocols.

In general, devices communicate with each other – it is called as D2D type of communication (http://electronicdesign.com/iot/understanding-protocols-behind-internet-things). Then, the device data are collected and sent to the server infrastructure (D2S). The server infrastructure shares the device data (S2S), possibly providing it back to devices, to analysis programs, or to people. For instance, MQTT (Message Queuing Telemetry Transport) protocol is for collecting the device data and communicating it to servers (D2S concept), AMQP (Advanced Message Queuing) is a queuing system designed to connect servers to each other (S2S concept), DDS (Data Distribution Service) is a fast bus for integrating intelligent machines (D2D concept). Nowadays, two IoT protocols, MQTT and CoAP, are in use mainly (https://eclipse.org/community/eclipse_newsletter/2014/february/article2.php, https://www.linkedin.com/pulse/iot-communication-protocols-james-stansberry). They allow the communication from Internet-based resource-rich devices to IoT-based resource-constrained devices. First one is based on the Internet TCP (Transmission Control Protocol), second one – on UDP (User Datagram Protocol).

The viable alternative of the IoT protocol depends on the app. If the message is going to be published from one node to many nodes, the MQTT protocol is recommended to use. In a system where data is very expensive, CoAP is recommended because it uses UDP, which eliminates the overhead of TCP/IP. It makes a big difference in traffic if the system has 1000s of nodes. Sometimes MQTT IoT protocol has an advantage over CoAP because of its simplicity in the usage.

Hence, the main objective is the discussion of Arduino open-source computer soft- and hardware for different IoT apps, as well as experimenting with MQTT protocol (Mosquitto broker, publisher, and subscriber more specifically) and Arduino sketch / C# console app.

BACKGROUND

The above-stated features of IoT soft- and hardware are not well documented in literature nowadays because of the diversity of IoT apps and the constant updating of technologies. In fact, the IoT info is provided by many web-sites (e.g. www.arduino. cc, mqtt.org, mosquitto.org). However, the following books present state of the art in IoT soft- and hardware adequately.

Dirk Slama, Frank Puhlmann, Jim Morrish, and Rishi M. Bhatnagar (2015) discuss different aspects of IoT in general. In particular, the smart energy, the manufacturing and industry, connected vehicles, and smart city technologies are presented. However, the concrete implementations (e.g. Arduino specific hardware, development of C# / C++ console apps, WiFi / Ethernet networks, MQTT / CoAP protocols) are shown briefly.

Norris (2015) presents several IoT apps using Raspberry Pi, Arduino, and BeagleBone Black platforms. In addition, the basics of object-oriented programming, relational databases, and machine-to-machine communications are discussed. However, the number of projects (the weather station, the web camera, the garage door opener, the irrigation control system, the lighting controller, the LCD message controller, the meteorological cloud app, and machine-to-machine communication using MQTT protocol) is limited.

Charalampos Doukas (2012) emphasizes the cloud computing and wireless technologies. Here, the main projects are as follows: Android phone collects air quality data with the help of an Arduino and Bluetooth connection; Tweet sensor readings through the Android phone using USB connection between Android phone and Arduino board; Cloud web app that visualizes sensor data from Arduino board based on Google App Engine; Process local humidity and air pressure data on the Nimbits Cloud. In this book, the number of projects is limited as well.

In this chapter, every section includes the brief analysis of previous studies for the appropriate topic with corresponding links to the Internet resources if any.

MAIN FOCUS OF THE CHAPTER

This chapter focus is the discussion of the practical experience in IoT. The main topics are as follows:

1. Intro to Arduino hard- and software.
2. Arduino IoT apps. Here, the WiFi weather station, the dual axis light tracker, the RFID control of the step motor (the simulation of the locking), and two assistive projects for the visually impaired and blind people (the sound marking of the golf flagsticks; the detection and sound signalization of the movement of humans and animals using PIR sensor) are presented.
3. Experimenting with MQTT protocol, Arduino app, and Visual Studio 2015 C# console app.

INTRODUCTION TO IOT ARDUINO HARD- AND SOFTWARE

Wikipedia defines the Arduino as "an open-source computer hardware and software company, project and user community that designs and manufactures microcontroller-based kits for building digital devices and interactive objects that can sense and control objects in the physical world" (https://en.wikipedia.org/wiki/Arduino). Since May 2015, Arduino trademark is used inside USA, Genuino – outside USA. Arduino hardware is based on microcontroller board designs, manufactured by several vendors, using various microcontrollers. These systems provide sets of digital and analog I/O pins that can be interfaced to various expansion boards ("shields") and other circuits. For programming the microcontrollers, the Arduino project provides an integrated development environment (IDE) based on the C and C++ programming languages.

Arduino open-source project points its main IoT hardware as follows (https://www.arduino.cc/en/Main/Products):

1. Arduino Yún is a microcontroller board based on the ATmega32U4 and the Atheros AR9331. The Atheros processor supports a Linux distribution based on OpenWrt named OpenWrt-Yun. The board has built-in Ethernet and WiFi support, a USB-A port, micro-SD card slot, 20 digital input/output pins, a 16 MHz crystal oscillator, a micro USB connection, an ICSP header, and three reset buttons.
2. Arduino Ethernet Shield is a board for the connection to Internet using Wiznet W5100 Ethernet chip.

3.   Arduino GSM Shield is a board for the connection to Internet using the GPRS wireless network.
4.   Arduino WiFi Shield 101 is a board for the connection to Internet based on IEEE 802.11 b/g/n for up to 72 Mbps networks.
5.   Arduino MKR1000 is a board that combines the functionality of the Arduino Zero (https://en.wikipedia.org/wiki/List_of_Arduino_boards_and_compatible_systems) and the Wi-Fi Shield.

The functionality of the above-stated boards can be realized using less expensive Arduino hardware. In spite of low frequency of the processor and absence of the wireless connection, Arduino Mega and Arduino Uno (16 MHz; Arduino Zero has the 48 MHz processor for comparison) are the core boards nowadays. They can be combined with Arduino shields (e.g. Ethernet and WiFi) and/or radio-frequency transmitter/receiver for the wireless connection. In this case, the final cost is several times less comparing with advanced boards like Arduino Yún.

The main differences between Arduino Mega and Uno (https://www.arduino.cc/en/Products/Compare) are presented in Table 1. Analysis of this table shows that all parameters of Arduino Mega board are better than Arduino Uno. The last one is in use mostly because of low cost (ratio is 2:1 approx.) and practical needs (performance and number of digital/analog pins are enough for most cases). Arduino Uno is based on ATMega328 microcontroller (see Figure 1).

Objects interact with each other using different sensors and actuators (Charalampos Doukas, 2012), which are available to buy on the Internet nowadays. In this chapter, the sensors from "Arduino Electronic Brick Advanced Kit" (http://makerstudio.cc/index.php?main_page=product_info&cPath=2&products_id=10) are used mainly. However, other kits (e.g. "Sunfounder 37 Modules Sensor Kit for Arduino", http://www.sunfounder.com/index.php?c=show&model=Sensor%20Kit&id=52) can be applied as well.

Table 1. Main differences between Arduino Uno and Arduino Mega boards

Characteristic	Arduino Mega	Arduino Uno
Processor	ATmega2560	ATmega328P
Number of analog inputs	16	6
Number of digital pins with Pulse Width Modulation (PWM)	15	6
Erasable programmable read-only memory (EEPROM), kB	4	1
Static random access memory (SRAM), kB	8	2
Flash memory, kB	256	32
Universal asynchronous receiver / transmitter (UART)	4	1

Figure 1. The specifications of Arduino Uno board

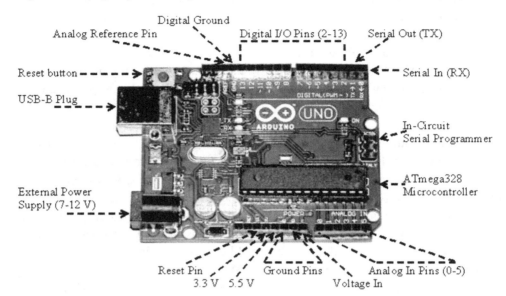

Figure 2 shows hardware from "Arduino Electronic Brick Advanced Kit". The main components are as follows:

1. Makerduino UNO (this board is compatible with Arduino UNO).
2. Makerduino Electronic Brick Shield.
3. Red Light Emitting Diode (LED).
4. RGB LED.
5. Pushbutton.
6. Momentary Pushbutton.
7. LED Button.
8. Ultrasonic Sensor.
9. PIR (Passive Infrared) Motion Sensor.
10. Light Sensor.
11. Humidity Temperature Sensor.
12. Infrared Receiver.
13. Water Sensor.
14. Toggle Touch Sensor.
15. Momentary Touch Sensor.
16. Tilt Sensor.
17. 5 V Relay.

Figure 2. Arduino electronic brick advanced kit

18. Buzzer.
19. Real-Time Clock.
20. I2C 1602 LCD (Liquid-Crystal Display).
21. 315MHz RF (Radio Frequency) Transmitter.
22. 315MHz RF Receiver.
23. 9g Servo Motor.
24. 9V Battery to DC Converter.
25. Infrared Remote Controller.

Arduino IDE version 1.6.5-r5 (release date is Aug 28, 2015) supports three types of the devices – Arduino, Arduino certified, and Partners (see Figure 3). The first position in the Board Manager is taken by installed Arduino AVR. Boards built in Arduino version 1.6.8 are Arduino Yún, Diecimila, Nano, MegaADK, Leonardo, Esplora, Mini, Ethernet, Fio, BT, LilyPadUSB, Lilypad, Pro, ATMegaNG, Robot Control, Robot Motor, Gemma, and Arduino/Geniuno Uno/Mega/Micro (see Figure 4). WiFi module from other manufacturers (e.g. NodeMcu Lua ESP8266 ESP-12E WiFi development board) can be installed as well.

Figure 3. Three types of devices (Arduino, Arduino certified, Partners) supported by Arduino IDE v. 1.6.5-r5

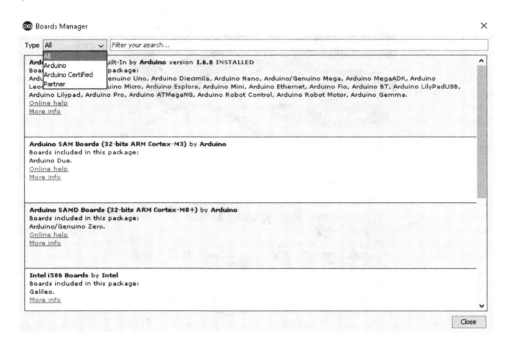

SOLUTIONS AND RECOMMENDATIONS

The preceding section presents briefly the Arduino open-source computer hard- and software for the development of the IoT solutions. In addition, the WiFi technologies are discussed in general in the context of IoT. The advanced implementations (e.g. cloud computing and mobile apps) of presented solutions can be realized as a combination of existing facilities usually. For instance, NodeMcu Lua ESP8266 ESP-12E WiFi development board can be remotely controlled using HTML5 offline web-site (smartphone part) and a simple web-server (WiFi module part).

ARDUINO IoT APPS

WiFi Weather Station

The prototype of WiFi weather station consists of two main parts:

Figure 4. Arduino AVR Boards built in Arduino version 1.6.5-r5

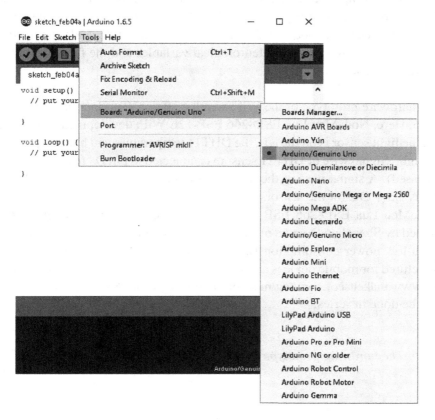

1. The outdoor unit uses sensors to measure the meteorological parameters (e.g. air temperature, humidity, rainfall, barometric pressure, light intensity). Then, WiFi module (NodeMcu Lua ESP8266 ESP-12E WiFi development board in this case) with web-server sends the data to the WiFi router located indoor usually. Web-server hosts web-site about meteorological parameters. Hence, it is possible to view the info on-line using IP address of WiFi board. If Internet provider assigns the static global IP address to the WiFi weather station, the data is accessible out of local network. The sustainable power supply can be realized using the solar panel and rechargeable batteries.

2. The indoor unit's main part is the WiFi router. Here, the web-site can be developed not only to display current meteorological parameters, but also to show other info like short- (Zubov, Volponi, & Khosravy, 2015) and long-range (Zubov, Barbosa, & Duane, 2015) weather forecast. First one uses the adiabatic

quantum computing formalism based on the Ising model with three qubits which represent three-day historical data. The second one uses a nonanticipative analog forecast method based on the identification of dependencies between the current values of two meteorological variables and the future state of the target variable.

The hardware prototype of the WiFi weather station's outdoor unit is shown in Figure 5. Here, NodeMcu Lua ESP8266 ESP-12E WiFi development board is in a center, the light sensor is on the left, the DHT11 temperature and humidity sensor is on the right. Signal wire of DHT11 sensor is connected to pin D4 (external marking is discussed). A signal wire of the light sensor is connected to pin AD0. A power supply is 3.3 V DC for the sensors.

NodeMcu Lua ESP8266 ESP-12E WiFi development board is designed and developed by Shenzhen Doctors of Intelligence & Technology (SZDOIT) based on the ultra-low power consumption UART-WiFi ESP8266 chip, which is specially manufactured for mobile devices and IoT apps. To use this board with Arduino IDE (http://www.makeuseof.com/tag/meet-arduino-killer-esp8266/), the following stages have to be done in series:

Figure 5. The hardware prototype of the WiFi weather station's outdoor unit

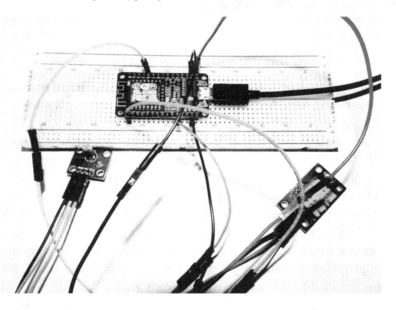

1. Installation of the serial drivers (https://www.silabs.com/products/mcu/Pages/ USBtoUARTBridgeVCPDrivers.aspx).
2. Installation of the ESP8266 in the Arduino Boards Manager. Here, it is necessary to open the Preferences dialog box (File-->Preferences option of menu) and enter the URL "http://arduino.esp8266.com/package_esp8266com_index. json" in the field "Additional Boards Manager URLs" (see Figure 6). Then, open the Boards Manager from Tools-->Board option, search for ESP8266 and install the platform (see Figure 7). Now, the option "NodeMCU 1.0" has to be accessible (see Figure 8). It is recommended to leave the CPU and upload speed as is, and select the newly installed serial port (see Figure 9).

The outdoor unit uses sketch based on C++ programming language with two libraries – *ESP8266WiFi.h* and *DHT.h* (first one is for NodeMcu Lua ESP8266 ESP-12E WiFi development board; second one is for DHT11 temperature and humidity sensor, it can be downloaded against the link http://cdn.makeuseof.com/wp-content/ uploads/2015/11/MQTT-and-DHT-for-ESP8266.zip?26523c).

Three constants are declared before *setup*() and *loop*() functions as follows:

Figure 6. Preferences dialog box in Arduino IDE

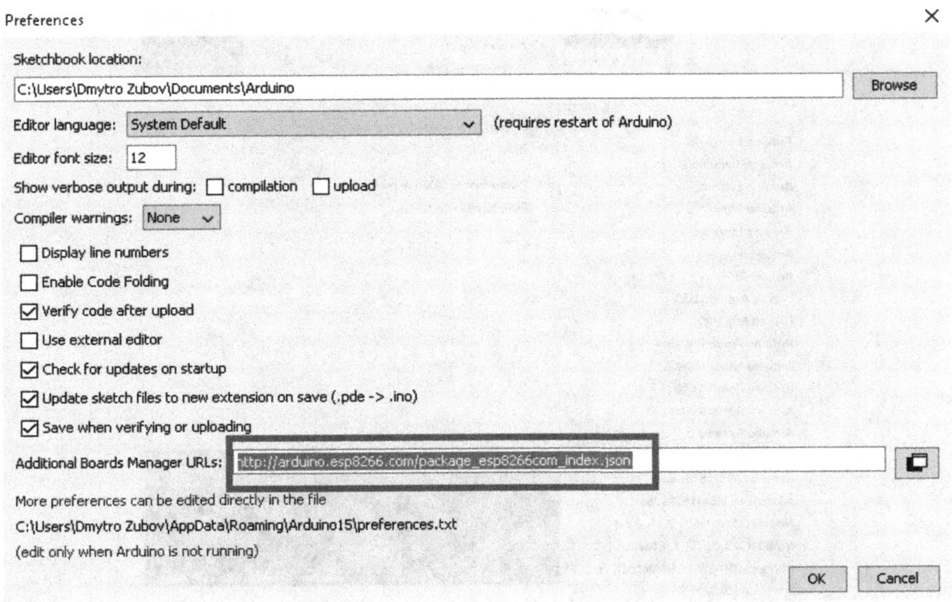

Figure 7. Installation of the ESP8266 in the Arduino boards manager

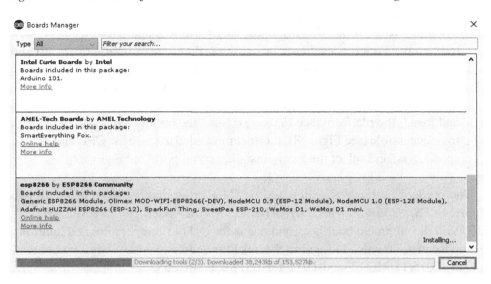

Figure 8. Selection of the NodeMCU 1.0 board for the programming

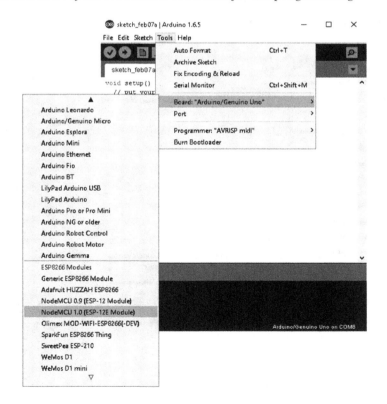

Figure 9. Example of CPU settings of the NodeMCU 1.0 board in Arduino IDE

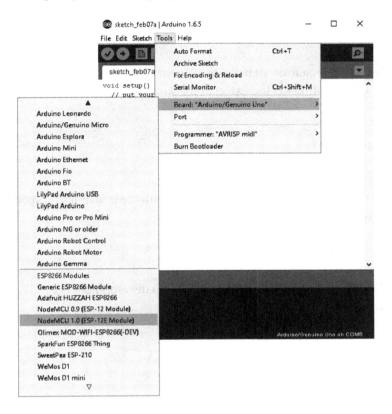

```
const char* ssid = "SSID";                    // Name of the WiFi
network
const char* password = "PASSWORD";            // Password of the
network
// Number of analog pin for the light sensor connection:
const int analogInPin = A0;
Three variables are declared as follows:
int sensorValue = 0;                          // A value read
from the light sensor
// The values of humidity and temperature read from DHT11
sensor:
float h, t;
```

The work with DHT11 sensor is based on the following declarations:

```
#define DHTTYPE DHT11
#define DHTPIN 2
DHT dht(DHTPIN, DHTTYPE,11);
```

Here, the DHT11 sensor signal wire is connected to GPIO2 (second General Purpose Input/Output; D4 is the external marking).

```
WiFi web-server is created as an instance of the server with
standard port 80:
WiFiServer server(80);
```

In *setup*() function, the serial monitor starts with the transmission speed 115200 baud as follows:

```
Serial.begin(115200);
```

Then, NodeMcu Lua ESP8266 ESP-12E WiFi development board is connected to WiFi network:

```
WiFi.begin(ssid, password);
while (WiFi.status() != WL_CONNECTED) {
  delay(500);
  Serial.print(".");
}
```

Here, the web-server and DHT11 sensor start, as well as local IP address is printed in the serial monitor:

```
server.begin();                              //
Start the server
Serial.println("Server started");
Serial.println(WiFi.localIP());         // Print the IP
address
dht.begin();                                 // DHT11
sensor starts
```

In *loop*() function, the data from the DHT11 and light sensors are read and printed in the serial monitor as follows:

```
h = dht.readHumidity();
t = dht.readTemperature();
h = h*1.23;                              // Humidity, %
t = t*1.1;                               // Temperature, oC
// Check if any DHT11 reads failed:
if (isnan(h) || isnan(t)) {
  Serial.println("Failed to read from DHT sensor!");
}
else{
  Serial.print("Temperature (oC) = "); Serial.println(t);
  Serial.print("Humidity (%) = "); Serial.println(h);
}
sensorValue = analogRead(analogInPin);     // Read the light
sensor
Serial.print("Light sensor = ");
Serial.println(sensorValue);
```

Then, program checks if a client is connected (otherwise, the *loop*() function starts from the beginning):

```
WiFiClient client = server.available();
if (!client) { return; }
```

The web-server response (i.e. HTML code for web-browser) is as follows:

```
String s = "HTTP/1.1 200 OK\r\nContent-Type: text/html\r\n\r\
n<!DOCTYPE HTML>\r\n<html>\r\n";
s += "<HEAD>\r\n<TITLE>Arduino WiFi Weather Station -
Prototype</TITLE>\r\n</HEAD>\r\n<BODY>\r\n";
s += "<H1><b>Arduino WiFi Weather Station - Prototype</b></
H1>\r\n<br>\r\n";
s += "<H2>Temperature (<sup>0</sup>C) = " + (String)t + "</
H2>\r\n<br>\r\n";
s += "<H2>Humidity (%) = " + (String)h + "</H2>\r\n<br>\r\n";
s += "<H2>Light sensor (0-1023) = " + (String)sensorValue + "</
H2>\r\n<br>\r\n";
s += "</BODY>\r\n</html>\n";
// Send the response to the client:
client.print(s);
```

```
// Wait until all outgoing characters in buffer have been sent:
client.flush();
```

If NodeMcu Lua ESP8266 ESP-12E WiFi development board is connected to the computer with Arduino IDE, the serial monitor shows the info about humidity (%), temperature (^{0}C), and intensity of the light (0 is minimum, 1023 is maximum). An example of the data is presented in Figure 10. The same info can be remotely acquired using IP address of NodeMcu Lua ESP8266 ESP-12E WiFi development board (see Figure 11).

Dual Axis Light Tracker

The alternative energetics (water, biogas, geothermal, solar, and wind mainly) is ecological, sustainable, and profitable source of renewable power nowadays.

Figure 10. Example of the data presented in serial monitor (temperature, humidity, and intensity of the light)

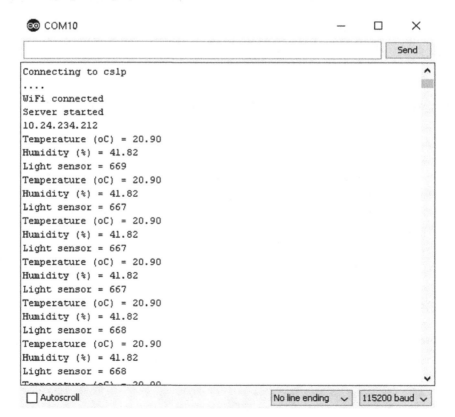

Figure 11. Example of the data presented in web-browser (temperature, humidity, and intensity of the light)

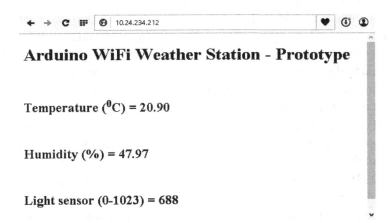

The highest average annual growth rates of renewable energy capacity is the solar photovoltaic (PV) power – 50% from end-2009 to 2014, 30% in 2014 (REN21, 2015). The similar tendency is forecasted for 2016 and 2017 yrs by U.S. Energy Information Administration (https://www.eia.gov/forecasts/steo/report/renew_co2.cfm). The solar PV panels have the maximum efficiency if they follow the sun (Gerro Prinsloo & Robert Thomas Dobson, 2014). Two main approaches are as follows:

1. Determining the sun angle using the date, time, and physical location of the solar tracker (scheduled tracking).
2. Tracking the sun using the light sensors (active tracking).

Because of the weight of solar panel (e.g. 13 kg for ECO-WORTHY 160W 12V Monocrystalline Solar Panel, http://www.eco-worthy.com/catalog/worthy-160w-monocrystalline-solar-panel-p-352.html), the energy saving algorithms are applied (Kamala & Alex Joseph, 2014). Two main methods are in use as follows:

1. Specified tolerance for the light sensors: if the light intensity is changed within the certain range, the solar panel is not moved according to the position of sun (light).
2. Specified tolerance for the motors: if the solar panel is immovable during the certain time-frame, the motors are switched off; then, if light intensity is changed greater than some value, the motors are switched on and the solar panel is moved according to position of sun (light).

Because of the sun trajectory, a two degree of freedom mechanism meets the requirements of solar panel's maximum efficiency nowadays.

Here, the dual axis light (solar) tracker using Arduino Uno and energy saving algorithm is discussed. The prototype was built using the Dual Axis "Smart" Solar Tracker (http://www.browndoggadgets.com/products/dual-axis-smart-solar-tracker) manufactured by the company "Brown Dog Gadgets" (www.browndoggadgets.com). This company provides detailed instructions to assemble the hardware, which was received in Jan 2016. However, several bugs (e.g. some designations of the connections were mixed up) were fixed during the assembling of the solar tracker. It was found that specified tolerance for the light sensors is taken into consideration by initial Arduino sketch using integer variable *tol* with the value 50 (analog input value is from 0 to 1023). In this case, if the light intensity is changed less than 50 in absolute units, the solar panel is immovable. Here, the change of the light intensity is equal to the appropriate difference of the averaged signals from four photoresistors – top left, top right, bottom left, and bottom right.

The specified tolerance for two servo motors was not realized initially. The measurement of the direct current (DC) shows the half-ampere load (approx.) on the power supply when the solar panel is moved (see Figure 12; the measured current and voltage are in the top and bottom parts of USB detector, respectively). Three integer variables *EnergySaving*, *servovprev*, and *servohprev* are used to implement the energy saving algorithm. First one reflects the time when the solar panel is immovable; if value equals 500 (the number of cycles of *loop*() function with 10 ms delay), the servo motors are switched off by *detach*() method. Second and third variables show the previous vertical and horizontal positions of the solar panel (variables *servov* and *servoh*, respectively); if current and previous values are not equal, as well as servo motors were stopped before (i.e. *EnergySaving* = 500), then servo motors are switched on by *attach*() method. The measurement of DC shows almost zero load on the power supply when servo motors are switched off (see Figure 13). The screen shot of the serial monitor is shown in Figure 14. First four numbers in the long lines represent the values read from the light sensors, the last number is the value of variable *tol*, last but one is the delay, ms. Short line represents the value of variable *EnergySaving* as follows:

```
EnergySaving = EnergySaving + 1; Serial.println(EnergySaving);
if (EnergySaving == 500) {horizontal.detach();vertical.
detach();}
if (EnergySaving > 500) {EnergySaving = 500;}
```

Figure 12. The measurement of DC when the solar panel is moved

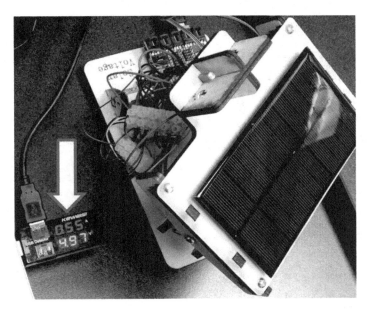

Figure 13. The measurement of DC when servo motors are switched off

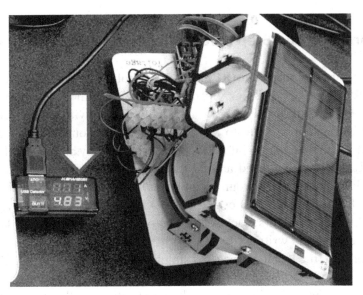

Figure 14. The screen shot of the serial monitor for the modified software

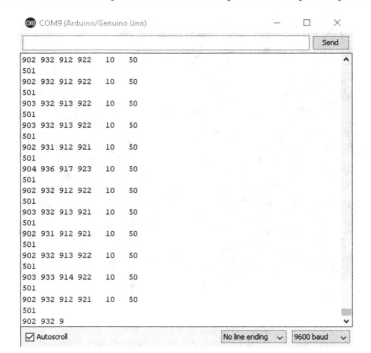

RFID Control of the Step Motor (The Simulation of the Locking)

Radio-frequency identification (RFID) is a technology that uses radio waves to automatically identify people or objects (http://www.rfidjournal.com). The info is stored in RFID card (or RFID key fob). The RFID tag with antenna enables the microchip to transmit the info to a reader. The reader converts the radio waves from the RFID tag into digital info that can be processed by computers. Nowadays, MIFARE RFID cards are used around the world based on Arduino control and MFRC522 library (http://playground.arduino.cc/Learning/MFRC522). For instance, the MIFARE Classic 1K RFID card (or RFID key fob) offers 1024 bytes of data storage, split into 16 sectors; each sector is protected by two different keys A and B (e.g. for reading and writing).

In this project, the locking process is simulated by Arduino Uno, RFID-RC522, and step motor (5 V DC). In addition, 2003 step motor driver and electronic brick boards are used. Figure 15 shows the hardware prototype for the step motor's RFID control. Digital pins 4-7 are for the step motor, 9-13 – for the RFID-RC522 module. The Arduino sketch is based on the project "How to use a stepper motor (28BYJ-48 and ULN2003APG driver)" (http://rubus.net.nz/?page_id=391) and Arduino

Figure 15. The hardware prototype for the step motor's RFID control

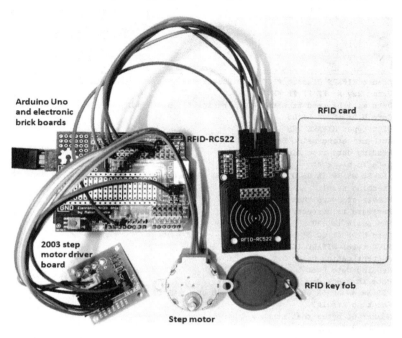

sketch "ReadAndWrite" from MFRC522 standard examples (https://github.com/ miguelbalboa/rfid). The value of step angle (90^0 in this example) is the fifth number read from the sector 1, block 4. First four numbers is a password for the operation. In this case, the password is word "STEP" represented by hexadecimal numbers 0x53, 0x54, 0x45, and 0x50 of the appropriate ASCII characters. The direction of the step angle (clockwise or counterclockwise) depends on the previous operation: if it was clockwise, the direction is counterclockwise and vice versa. Figure 16 shows the Arduino Serial monitor: rotation of the shaft 90 degrees clockwise (+90) and counterclockwise (-90). RFID key fob tests the system for security – it has the wrong password in the sector 1, block 4, and hence operation is not done.

Two Assistive Projects for the Spatial Cognition of Visually Impaired and Blind People

The Sound Marking of the Golf Flagsticks: The First Prototype (Without WiFi Control)

Nowadays, engineering science provides the technical support for the visually impaired and blind people (Hersh & Johnson, 2008; Sándor Tihamér Brassai, László Bakó,

Figure 16. The Arduino Serial monitor for the step motor's RFID control project: rotation of the shaft 90 degrees clockwise (+90) and counterclockwise (-90)

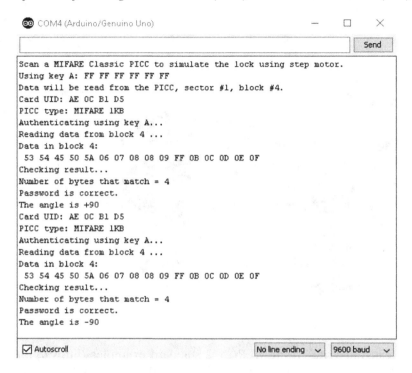

```
COM4 (Arduino/Genuino Uno)                                          —    □    ×

                                                                         Send

Scan a MIFARE Classic PICC to simulate the lock using step motor.
Using key A: FF FF FF FF FF FF
Data will be read from the PICC, sector #1, block #4.
Card UID: AE 0C B1 D5
PICC type: MIFARE 1KB
Authenticating using key A...
Reading data from block 4 ...
Data in block 4:
 53 54 45 50 5A 06 07 08 08 09 FF 0B 0C 0D 0E 0F
Checking result...
Number of bytes that match = 4
Password is correct.
The angle is +90
Card UID: AE 0C B1 D5
PICC type: MIFARE 1KB
Authenticating using key A...
Reading data from block 4 ...
Data in block 4:
 53 54 45 50 5A 06 07 08 08 09 FF 0B 0C 0D 0E 0F
Checking result...
Number of bytes that match = 4
Password is correct.
The angle is -90

☑ Autoscroll                              No line ending  ⌄   9600 baud  ⌄
```

& Lajos Losonczi, 2011). In particular, smart compact devices like Arduino can do the sound marking of the golf sticks that allows identifying their location by visually impaired and blind people. This project was done in cooperation with the Institute for Visually Impaired and Blind People (El Instituto para Ciegos y Débiles Visuales) "Ezequiel Hernández Romo", San Luis Potosi, Mexico (www.institutoparaciegos. org). Sounds with different tones are used (Jean-François Augoyard & Henri Torgue 2006). The hardware prototype is shown in Figure 17. Here, Arduino Uno controls the passive buzzer (it is on the breadboard on the right) using the pushbutton (it is on the breadboard on the left). The first pin of the buzzer is connected to a 7th digital pin, second one – to ground pin of Arduino Uno. The first wire of the pushbutton goes from one leg through a pull-up resistor 10 KOhm to the ground pin of Arduino Uno. The second wire goes from the same leg to the 2nd digital pin of Arduino Uno. The third wire of the pushbutton's diagonal leg goes to 3.3 V supply. When the end-user pushes the button, the tone is changed from lowest 261 Hz to highest 440 Hz. The final product will be based on Arduino Nano (if the wireless network is not needed).

Figure 17. The hardware prototype of the sound marking project (without WiFi control)

Five variables and an array are declared before *setup()* and *loop()* functions as follows:

```
// Number of digital pin for the pushbutton connection:
int PushButtonPin = 2;
int PushButtonVal;         // The value from the pushbutton
// Number of digital pin for the buzzer connection:
int speakerPin = 7;
int numTones = 10;         // Number of the tones
// Array with tones (i.e. frequencies, Hz):
int tones[] = {261,277,294,311,330,349,370,392,415,440};
int i=10;                           // The number of current tone
in loop() function
```

In *setup()* function, the second digital pin is assigned for the input, as well as the serial monitor starts with the transmission speed 9600 baud as follows:

```
pinMode(PushButtonPin, INPUT);
Serial.begin(9600);
```

In *loop*() function, the data from the pushbutton are read and printed in the serial monitor, as well as tone is changed if pushbutton is low (i.e. it is pressed):

```
PushButtonVal = digitalRead(PushButtonPin);
if (PushButtonVal == 1) {
  Serial.println("Button is LOW");
  i=i-1; // The tone is changed; i=10 - buzzer is off
  if (i == -1) {i = 10; noTone(speakerPin);}
  else {tone(speakerPin, tones[i]);}
}
else {Serial.println("Button is HIGH");}
delay(100);
```

Here, the *tone*() function generates a square wave of the specified frequency (and 50% duty cycle) on a pin (https://www.arduino.cc/en/Reference/Tone).

In spite of simplicity and low-cost of the hardware, the test showed an issue – it is not possible to control the sound remotely because the wireless access is not available. Hence, it was made the decision to develop other prototype based on WiFi technology with the possibility to control a device manually.

The Sound Marking of the Golf Flagsticks: The Second Prototype (With WiFi Control)

Analysis of the first prototype for sound marking of the golf flagsticks showed three obligatory features:

1. Electronic devices on the golf flagsticks must be controlled remotely. For this purpose, NodeMcu Lua ESP8266 ESP-12E WiFi development board is used. However, the manual mode must be realized as well using the pushbutton.
2. WiFi board must have beep codes. For this purpose, three types of the beep codes are used as follows: half-second beep means a normal start of the board when it is switched on; then, continuous (1.5 seconds if WiFi connection is established normally) or discontinuous (three half-second beeps and pauses if WiFi connection is not established) beep sounds.
3. Sound marks must be various for different golf flagsticks. For this purpose, six types of the sound are proposed – continuous beep plus five types of discontinuous sounds distinguished by the duration of a beep and pause. It is assumed that this number is enough for ten golf flagsticks, one or two of which will be switched on at the same time. In addition, the volume is controlled by a potentiometer.

The hardware prototype for the WiFi sound marking of the golf flagsticks is shown in Figure 18. Here, NodeMcu Lua ESP8266 ESP-12E WiFi development board is on the right, the potentiometer – top left, the pushbutton – bottom left, and the active buzzer (the passive buzzer is also discussed for the volume control) – bottom center. Buzzer is connected to pin D3 of WiFi board, pushbutton – to D4 (external marking is discussed).

The WiFi boards are controlled remotely using HTML web-site (screen shot is presented in Figure 19; 10.24.236.116 is a local IP address of WiFi board used for the testing) with following code:

```
<!doctype html>
<html lang='en'>
<head>
  <title>Turn ON/OFF the buzzers of the golf flagsticks</title>
</head>
<body style='text-align:center;background-color:lightyellow;'>
  <H1 style='color:blue;'><b>Turn ON/OFF the buzzer and choose
the sound for the golf flagsticks</b></H1></body>
  <a href="http://10.24.236.116"><button style='color:green;
font-size:30px; width:450px; height:100px; border-style:solid;
border-width:4px; border-color:green;'>Control the <b>1</
b><sup>st</sup> golf flagstick</button></a>
```

Figure 18. The hardware prototype for the WiFi remote control of the sound marking of the golf flagsticks

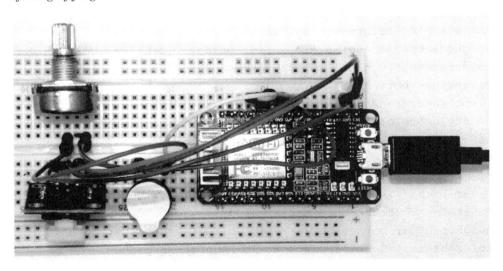

Figure 19. Screen shot of the web-site for the WiFi remote control of sound marking of the golf flagsticks (main page)

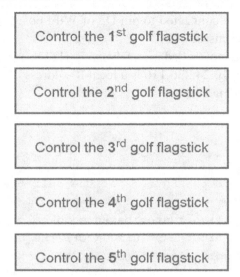

<a href="http://10.24.236.116"><butt
on style='color:green; font-size:30px; width:450px;
height:100px; border-style:solid; border-width:4px; border-
color:green;'>Control the 2nd golf
flagstick</button></a>

<a href="http://10.24.236.116"><butt
on style='color:green; font-size:30px; width:450px;
height:100px; border-style:solid; border-width:4px; border-
color:green;'>Control the 3rd golf
flagstick</button></a>

<a href="http://10.24.236.116"><butt
on style='color:green; font-size:30px; width:450px;
height:100px; border-style:solid; border-width:4px; border-
color:green;'>Control the 4th golf
flagstick</button></a>

<a href="http://10.24.236.116"><butt
on style='color:green; font-size:30px; width:450px;
height:100px; border-style:solid; border-width:4px; border-
color:green;'>Control the 5th golf

```
flagstick</button></a>
  <br /><br /><a href="http://10.24.236.116"><butt
on style='color:green; font-size:30px; width:450px;
height:100px; border-style:solid; border-width:4px; border-
color:green;'>Control the <b>6</b><sup>th</sup> golf
flagstick</button></a>
  <br /><br /><a href="http://10.24.236.116"><butt
on style='color:green; font-size:30px; width:450px;
height:100px; border-style:solid; border-width:4px; border-
color:green;'>Control the <b>7</b><sup>th</sup> golf
flagstick</button></a>
  <br /><br /><a href="http://10.24.236.116"><butt
on style='color:green; font-size:30px; width:450px;
height:100px; border-style:solid; border-width:4px; border-
color:green;'>Control the <b>8</b><sup>th</sup> golf
flagstick</button></a>
  <br /><br /><a href="http://10.24.236.116"><butt
on style='color:green; font-size:30px; width:450px;
height:100px; border-style:solid; border-width:4px; border-
color:green;'>Control the <b>9</b><sup>th</sup> golf
flagstick</button></a>
  <br /><br /><a href="http://10.24.236.116"><butt
on style='color:green; font-size:30px; width:450px;
height:100px; border-style:solid; border-width:4px; border-
color:green;'>Control the <b>10</b><sup>th</sup> golf
flagstick</button></a>
</body>
</html>
```

The WiFi remote control of the specific flagstick is realized through other HTML web-site (screen shot is presented in Figure 20 for first flagstick). Its HTML code is sent from the web-server hosted in NodeMcu Lua ESP8266 ESP-12E WiFi development board. The corresponding part of Arduino sketch is as follows (variable *value* represents six types of the sound from 0 to 5):

```
String s = "HTTP/1.1 200 OK\r\nContent-Type: text/html\r\n\r\
n<!DOCTYPE HTML>\r\n<html>\r\n";
s += "<HEAD>\r\n<TITLE>Turn ON/OFF the buzzer and choose the
sound for the 1st golf flagstick</TITLE>\r\n</HEAD>\r\n<BODY
style='text-align:center;background-color:lightyellow;'>\r\n";
```

Figure 20. Screen shot of the web-site for the WiFi remote control of the first flagstick

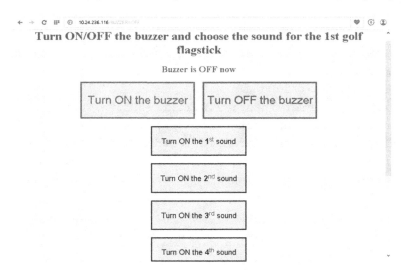

```
s += "<H1 style='color:blue;'><b>Turn ON/OFF the buzzer and
choose the sound for the 1<sup>st</sup> golf flagstick</b></
H1>\r\n";
if(value == -1) { s += "<H2 style='color:red;'>Buzzer is OFF
now</H2>";}
if(value == 0) { s += "<H2 style='color:green;'>Buzzer is ON
now</H2>";}
if(value == 1) { s += "<H2 style='color:brown;'>Buzzer is ON
now (1st sound)</H2>";}
if(value == 2) { s += "<H2 style='color:brown;'>Buzzer is ON
now (2nd sound)</H2>";}
if(value == 3) { s += "<H2 style='color:brown;'>Buzzer is ON
now (3rd sound)</H2>";}
if(value == 4) { s += "<H2 style='color:brown;'>Buzzer is ON
now (4th sound)</H2>";}
if(value == 5) { s += "<H2 style='color:brown;'>Buzzer is ON
now (5th sound)</H2>";}
s += "<a href=\"/BUZZER=ON\"\"><button style='color:green;
font-size:30px; width:300px; height:100px; border-style:solid;
border-width:4px; border-color:green;'>Turn ON the buzzer</
button></a>     ";
s += "<a href=\"/BUZZER=OFF\"\"><button style='color:red;
```

```
font-size:30px; width:300px; height:100px; border-style:solid;
border-width:4px; border-color:red;'>Turn OFF the buzzer</
button></a><br /><br />";
s += "<a href=\"/MELODY1=ON\"\"><button style='color:brown;
font-size:20px; width:250px; height:80px; border-style:solid;
border-width:3px; border-color:brown;'>Turn ON the <b>1</
b><sup>st</sup> sound</button></a><br /><br />";
s += "<a href=\"/MELODY2=ON\"\"><button style='color:brown;
font-size:20px; width:250px; height:80px; border-style:solid;
border-width:3px; border-color:brown;'>Turn ON the <b>2</
b><sup>nd</sup> sound</button></a><br /><br />";
s += "<a href=\"/MELODY3=ON\"\"><button style='color:brown;
font-size:20px; width:250px; height:80px; border-style:solid;
border-width:3px; border-color:brown;'>Turn ON the <b>3</
b><sup>rd</sup> sound</button></a><br /><br />";
s += "<a href=\"/MELODY4=ON\"\"><button style='color:brown;
font-size:20px; width:250px; height:80px; border-style:solid;
border-width:3px; border-color:brown;'>Turn ON the <b>4</
b><sup>th</sup> sound</button></a><br /><br />";
s += "<a href=\"/MELODY5=ON\"\"><button style='color:brown;
font-size:20px; width:250px; height:80px; border-style:solid;
border-width:3px; border-color:brown;'>Turn ON the <b>5</
b><sup>th</sup> sound</button></a>";
s += "</BODY>\r\n</html>\n";
```

The Detection and Sound Signalization of the Movement of Humans and Animals Using PIR Sensor

The aid systems (in the mobility) for the visually impaired and blind people are developed using heterogeneous algorithms, soft- and hardware nowadays. For instance, RFID was used in (Edoardo D'Atri, Carlo Maria Medaglia, Alexandru Serbanati, Ugo Biader Ceipidor, Emanuele Panizzi, & Alessandro D'Atri, 2007). Arduino equipment meets the following requirements – low cost, lightweight, and extensibility (e.g. ATmega328P Arduino Compatible Version LilyPad 328 Main Board: USD3, 41 grams, possible to add several sensors, sewable). The hardware prototype is shown in Figure 21. Here, Arduino Mega controls the active buzzer (it is on the breadboard on the right) based on PIR sensor signal. The pushbutton (it is on the breadboard on the left) switches off the beep if necessary. The first pin of the buzzer is connected to a 7th digital pin, second one – to ground pin of Arduino Mega. The first wire of the pushbutton goes from one leg through a pull-up resistor 10

Figure 21. The hardware prototype of the project for detection and sound signalization of the movement of humans and animals using PIR sensor

KOhm to the ground pin of Arduino Mega. The second wire goes from the same leg to the 3rd digital pin of Arduino Mega. The third wire of the pushbutton's diagonal leg goes to 3.3 V supply. The signal wire of PIR sensor (it is in the top right part of Figure 21) goes to 2nd digital pin, 5 V DC wire – to 5 V supply, ground wire – to ground pin of Arduino Mega. The signal wire of LED goes to 5th digital pin, ground wire – to ground pin of Arduino Mega. If PIR sensor detects the moving objects like humans and animals, the buzzer generates the sound and LED is switched on. If Arduino Mega is connected to a computer with Arduino IDE, the serial monitor shows the info about moving objects and the state of the pushbutton (see Figure 22). The final product will be based on Arduino Nano (if a wireless network is not necessary), or NodeMCU Lua WiFi Internet of Things Development Board with ESP8266 chip (if a wireless network is necessary), or LilyPad (the sewable solution).

The sketch includes C programming code and a library SPI.h.

Four constants and four variables are declared before *setup*() and *loop*() functions as follows:

```
const int PushButtonPin = 3;       // The number of the
PushButton pin
int PushButtonVal;                 // The value from the
pushbutton
```

Figure 22. Example of the data presented in serial monitor – the info about moving objects and the state of the pushbutton (low or high)

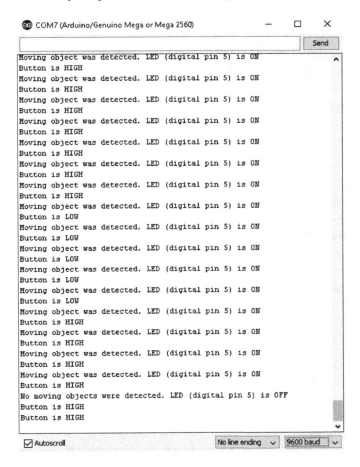

```
const int ActiveBuzzerPin = 7;        // The number of the Active
Buzzer pin
const int PIRSensorPin = 2;           // The number of the PIR
sensor pin
const int LEDSensorPin = 5;           // The number of the LED
pin
// Variable for reading the Sensor status; it will be changed:
int sensorState = 0;
// The flag is used to prevent continuous outputting
// when no moving people:
```

```
int flag = 0;
int BuzzerFlag = 1;                    // Flag for buzzer: 1 - ON,
0 - OFF
```

In *setup*() function, the serial monitor starts with the transmission speed 9600 baud, and pins are initialized as follows:

```
Serial.begin(9600);
// Pin selected to control the active buzzer:
pinMode(ActiveBuzzerPin, OUTPUT);
digitalWrite(ActiveBuzzerPin, LOW); // Buzzer is OFF initially
// Pin selected to acquire info from PushButton:
pinMode(PushButtonPin, INPUT);
// Pin selected to acquire info from PIR sensor:
pinMode(PIRSensorPin, INPUT);
pinMode(LEDSensorPin, OUTPUT);        // Pin selected to control
the LED
digitalWrite(LEDSensorPin, LOW);      // LED is OFF initially
In loop() function, the data from the PIR sensor and pushbutton
are read as follows:
PushButtonVal = digitalRead(PushButtonPin);
if (PushButtonVal == 1) {Serial.println("Button is LOW");}
else {Serial.println("Button is HIGH");}
// Read the state of the Sensor value:
sensorState = digitalRead(PIRSensorPin);
```

Then, program checks if moving objects are detected. If yes, the buzzer and LED are switched on. Otherwise, the buzzer and LED are switched off as follows:

```
if (sensorState == HIGH)                   // To turn the
buzzer ON
{
  if (BuzzerFlag == 1) {digitalWrite(ActiveBuzzerPin, HIGH);}
    Serial.println("Moving object was detected. LED (digital
pin 5) is ON");
    digitalWrite(LEDSensorPin, HIGH);      // Set LEDSensorPin
high
    flag = 0;
```

```
   if (PushButtonVal == 1 && BuzzerFlag == 1)
{digitalWrite(ActiveBuzzerPin, LOW); BuzzerFlag = 0;}
  }
  else
  {
    if(flag == 0)
    {
      digitalWrite(ActiveBuzzerPin, LOW);   // Buzzer is OFF
      Serial.println("No moving objects were detected. LED
(digital pin 5) is OFF");
      digitalWrite(LEDSensorPin, LOW);       // Set LEDSensorPin
low
      flag = 1; BuzzerFlag = 1;
    }
  }
  delay(200);
```

SOLUTIONS AND RECOMMENDATIONS

The preceding section presents the IoT projects, which are not well documented in the literature. In particular, the WiFi weather station based on NodeMcu Lua ESP8266 ESP-12E WiFi development board, the dual axis light (solar) tracker with energy saving algorithm, the RFID control of the step motor (the simulation of the locking), and two assistive projects to support the mobility of the visually impaired and blind people are discussed briefly. The examples of Arduino sketches and HTML codes are shown with comments. Users can modify the computer codes to meet their specific requirements. Hence, proposed codes can become more useful to a wider range of apps.

Experimenting With MQTT Protocol, Arduino App, and Visual Studio 2015 C# Console App

MQTT IoT Protocol

MQTT uses a "publisher/subscribers" model and requires a central broker (i.e. server) to manage and route messages among the MQTT clients. TCP stream sockets are slow but they guarantee in-order delivery of all data (Norris, 2015; http://embedded-computing.com/articles/internet-things-requirements-protocols/#) comparing with UDP datagrams. TCP needs 10 KB RAM/Flash additionally, which is suitable even for Arduino Uno. CoAP is based on the request/response without the publisher/ subscribers. In this case, the 6LoWPAN (IPv6 over Low power Wireless Personal Area Networks) with the IPv6automatic addressing is used to identify the network nodes uniquely.

MQTT has been widely implemented across a variety of devices since 1999, was published under royalty free terms in 2010. It has a client/server architecture, where the broker is a server, clients are subscribers and publisher. The publisher publishes the info with a specific topic. Subscribers receive the data according to the topic. Figure 23 shows an example of the system with three clients connected by the open-source message broker Mosquitto (http://mosquitto.org/download/). Here, publisher (Arduino Mega with Ethernet Shield, water sensor, and LEDs) sends info about the water level with topic "WaterLevel" to two subscribers (C# console app and standard Mosquitto subscriber mosquitto_sub.exe).

MQTT publisher and subscribers communicate with each other using the hierarchical topics (option "-t"). MQTT provides three levels (http://www.ibm.com/ support/knowledgecenter/SSCGGQ_1.2.0/com.ibm.ism.doc/Planning/ov00102_. html) of qualities of service (QoS; option "-q"): 0 (default) – fire and forget, where the message is delivered at most once, or it is not delivered at all, its delivery across the network is not acknowledged; 1 – the message is delivered at least once, duplicate messages can be delivered; 2 – the message is delivered exactly once, duplicate messages are not delivered. MQTT brokers may require username and password authentication from clients to connect (mosquitto_passwd.exe). In addition, TCP connection may be encrypted with SSL/TLS. More info can be found against the link http://mosquitto.org/documentation/.

Figure 23. Example of the system with three clients connected by the message broker Mosquitto

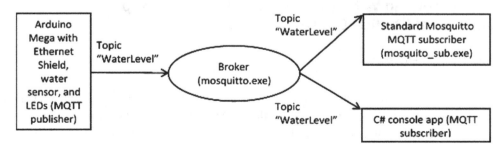

Experimenting with MQTT Protocol, Arduino Sketch, and Visual Studio 2015 C# Console App

Nowadays, computing systems with heterogeneous soft- and hardware are in use widely on the application, presentation, and session communication layers (terminology is from Open Systems Interconnection model). Here, the experiment with MQTT protocol is discussed using Arduino sketch and Visual Studio 2015 C# console app. Remote control of LEDs for the signaling (alarm, fault, water level, etc.) is based on Arduino Mega and Arduino Ethernet Shield. The info about states (ON or OFF) of LEDs is sent from Arduino Ethernet Shield (MQTT publisher) to MQTT subscribers (C# console app and standard Mosquitto subscriber mosquitto_sub.exe). The development has the following steps:

1. Download and install Arduino software (https://www.arduino.cc/en/Main/Software).
2. Download and install Mosquitto software for MQTT protocol http://mosquitto.org/download/.
3. Develop C# console app in Visual Studio 2015 (Enterprise edition was in use).
4. Download and install MQTT Arduino client.
5. Connect eight LEDs with appropriate pins on the Arduino Ethernet Shield.
6. Connect Arduino Mega and Ethernet Shield boards.
7. Connect Arduino Mega and computer by USB cable with USB-B and USB-A jacks, respectively.
8. Connect the computer and Arduino Ethernet Shield to the Internet/Intranet router by Ethernet cable.
9. Find a number of the COM port of the Arduino Mega connection in Device Manager (Microsoft Windows 7/8/10 OSs are discussed). Select port in Arduino IDE (Tools >> Port).
10. Assign MAC address and find IP address for the Arduino Ethernet Shield using the Ethernet.begin() function. Here, Ethernet is configured using DHCP (Dynamic Host Configuration Protocol) and DhcpAddressPrinter standard sketch from the Ethernet examples in Arduino IDE.
11. Identify the subnet mask and default gateway for the network. Here, the *ipconfig* command can be used for Windows 7/8/10 OSs.
12. Develop the Arduino sketch with MQTT publisher and remote control of the LEDs.
13. Start the programs.

The structure of the system is presented in Figure 24. The hardware part of the prototype is shown in Figure 25.

Figure 24. The structure of the system with web-site, MQTT protocol, Arduino sketch, and C# console app

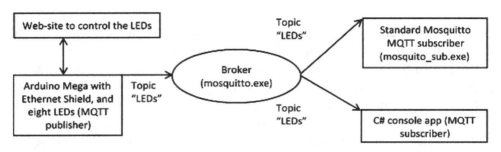

Figure 25. Hardware part of the prototype for the signaling using remote control of LEDs based on Arduino Mega and Arduino Ethernet Shield boards

The following is assumed: Arduino IDE was installed successfully (1st step); the first LED is connected to 5th digital pin of Arduino Mega, second LED – to 6th digital pin, third LED – 7th, fourth LED – 8th, fifth LED – 9th, sixth LED – 4th, seventh LED – 11th, eighth LED – 12th (5th step); Arduino Mega and Ethernet Shield boards are connected (6th step); Arduino Mega and computer are connected by USB cable with USB-B and USB-A jacks (7th step); Arduino Ethernet Shield was connected to Internet/Intranet router by Ethernet cable (8th step); number of the COM port of the Arduino Mega connection was found as well as appropriate port was selected in Arduino IDE (9th step); MAC and find IP addresses were assigned for the Arduino Ethernet Shield using the Ethernet.begin() function in DhcpAddressPrinter standard sketch (10th step); the network subnet mask and default gateway were identified using the *ipconfig* command (11th step).

In the 2nd step (Mosquitto software), OpenSSL (http://slproweb.com/products/Win32OpenSSL.html) is installed additionally (all .DLL files from OpenSSL directory must be copied into Mosquitto directory). In addition, pthreadVC2.dll file (it can be downloaded against http://www.dll-files.com) must be copied into the Mosquitto directory.

In the 3rd step, the Visual Studio 2015 C# console app is developed as follows:

```
using System;
using System.Text;
using uPLibrary.Networking.M2Mqtt;
using uPLibrary.Networking.M2Mqtt.Messages;
namespace ConsoleApplication1
{
  class Program
  {
      static void Main(string[] args)
      {
          var client = new MqttClient(System.Net.IPAddress.
Parse("192.168.0.13")); // Use IP address of your computer here
          client.MqttMsgPublishReceived += client_
MqttMsgPublishReceived;
          string clientId = Guid.NewGuid().ToString();
          client.Connect(clientId);
          client.Subscribe(new string[] { "/LEDs" }, new byte[]
{ MqttMsgBase.QOS_LEVEL_EXACTLY_ONCE });
      }
      static void client_MqttMsgPublishReceived(object sender,
MqttMsgPublishEventArgs e)
      {
          Console.WriteLine(Encoding.UTF8.GetString(e.
Message));
      }
  }
}
```

Here, IP address of the computer with MQTT broker is identified using the *ipconfig* command. uPLibrary is taken from the MQTT Client Library for .Net and

WinRT (it can be downloaded against GitHub link https://github.com/gloveboxes/ Windows-Remote-Arduino/tree/master/M2Mqtt_4.1.0.0_src).

In the 4th step, the MQTT Arduino client is installed against http://pubsubclient. knolleary.net. Zip file must be extracted into Documents->Arduino->libraries. Then, the PubSubClient library is included in the Arduino sketch.

In the 12th step, the Arduino sketch with MQTT publisher and remote control of the LEDs is developed. The C++ code is presented in Appendix 1. In this code, MQTT publisher sends and subscribers receive the byte with states (ON or OFF) of the LEDs (most significant bit corresponds to the first LED, least significant bit – eighth LED). The topic is "/LEDs". Figure 26 presents the screen shot of the web-site for the remote control of the LEDs as well as standard MQTT subscriber (mosquitto_sub.exe). Here, all LEDs are ON except the second one. Figure 27 shows four screen shots of the software apps – MQTT broker (mosquitto.exe), publisher (Arduino sketch; serial monitor of Arduino IDE presents the states of LEDs), and two subscribers (C# console app and mosquitto_sub.exe)

SOLUTIONS AND RECOMMENDATIONS

The preceding section presents the MQTT IoT protocol and its application for the remote control of the LEDs. For this purpose, the Arduino sketch, HTML web-site,

Figure 26. Screen shot of the web-site for the remote control of eight LEDs and standard MQTT subscriber (mosquitto_sub.exe)

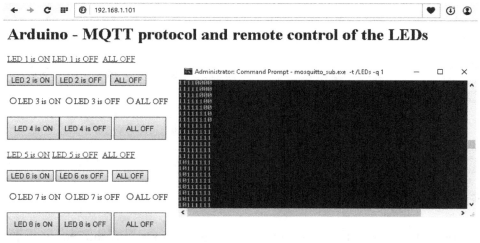

LED 1 is ON; LED 2 is OFF; LED 3 is ON; LED 4 is ON; LED 5 is ON; LED 6 is ON; LED 7 is ON; LED 8 is ON;

Figure 27. Screen shots of MQTT broker (mosquitto.exe), publisher (Arduino sketch), and two subscribers (C# console app and mosquitto_sub.exe)

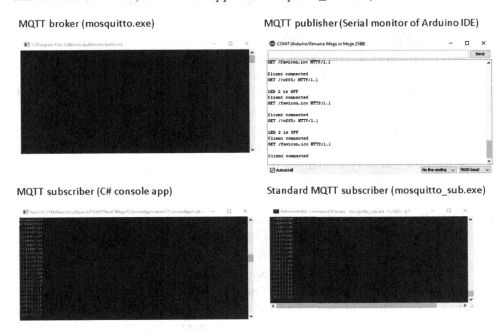

and Visual Studio 2015 C# console app were developed. MQTT server is Mosquitto broker. Arduino Mega is connected to the local network based on Ethernet shield. Users can modify these codes to develop other software.

FUTURE RESEARCH DIRECTIONS

The most likely prospect of this chapter work is to develop other apps to support the people with disabilities. For this purpose, the artificial intelligence algorithms (e.g. speech recognition and image processing) and cloud computing can be applied.

CONCLUSION

The number of IoT devices is forecasted to be about 50 billion by 2025 yr. Heterogeneous soft- and hardware are in use for the development of IoT systems nowadays, e.g. Arduino/Genuino and Raspberry Pi boards, MQTT and CoAP protocols. Nonetheless, the IoT platform and apps are not well documented in the literature for the time being. This chapter presents results of several IoT projects based on Arduino/Genuino and NodeMcu Lua ESP8266 ESP-12E WiFi boards as follows:

1. WiFi weather station consists of indoor (WiFi router) and outdoor (NodeMcu Lua ESP8266 ESP-12E WiFi development board, light sensor, DHT11 temperature and humidity sensor, and power bank) units.

2. The energy saving algorithm for the dual axis light (solar) tracker is discussed using hardware with four photoresistors and Arduino Uno board. In addition to the specified tolerance for the light sensors, the specified tolerance for two servo motors is proposed. Servo motors are switched off to save the energy if the light intensity is changed within the certain range during the particular time-frame. It was shown that the load on the power supply is almost zero in this case.

3. MIFARE Classic 1K RFID card is used to control the step motor based on the info stored in the sector 1, block 4 (four numbers represent the password for the operation, next number is the step angle for the appropriate rotation of the shaft). This project represents the simulation of the locking process.

4. The simple and budget solution for the sound marking of the golf flagsticks was developed to support the mobility of visually impaired and blind people using Arduino Uno board, pushbutton, and passive buzzer. The main disadvantage of this prototype is that there is no possibility to control devices remotely using wireless technologies.

5. The above-stated project for the sound marking of the golf flagsticks was modified for remote control using NodeMcu Lua ESP8266 ESP-12E WiFi development board.

6. The detection and sound signalization of the movement of humans and animals using PIR sensor were developed as a part of the aid systems (in the mobility) for the visually impaired and blind people. Here, Arduino Mega board controls the active buzzer based on PIR sensor signal. The pushbutton switches off the beep if necessary.

7. MQTT IoT protocol is used to connect the heterogeneous soft- and hardware based on open-source message broker Mosquitto. In this project, publisher (Arduino Mega with Ethernet Shield, water sensor, and LEDs) sends the info about the water level (topic "WaterLevel") to two subscribers (C# console app and standard Mosquitto subscriber mosquitto_sub.exe). In addition, it is shown how to control LEDs remotely using HTML web-site.

REFERENCES

Augoyard, J.-F., & Torgue, H. (2006). *Sonic Experience: A Guide to Everyday Sounds*. Quebec, Canada: McGill-Queen's University Press.

Brassai, S. T., Bakó, L., & Losonczi, L. (2011). Assistive Technologies for Visually Impaired People. *Journal of Electrical and Mechanical Engineering, 3*, 39–50.

D'Atri, E., Medaglia, C. M., Serbanati, A., Ceipidor, U. B., Panizzi, E., & D'Atri, A. (2007). A System to Aid Blind People in the Mobility: A Usability Test and its Results. In *Proceedings of 2nd International Conference on Systems (ICONS'07)*. Sainte-Luce, Martinique, France: IEEE. doi:10.1109/ICONS.2007.7

Doukas, C. (2012). Building Internet of Things with the Arduino. Seattle, WA: CreateSpace Independent Publishing Platform.

Hersh, M., & Johnson, M. A. (2008). *Assistive Technology for Visually Impaired and Blind People*. London, UK: Springer-Verlag. doi:10.1007/978-1-84628-867-8

Kamala, J., & Joseph, A. (2014). Solar Tracking for Maximum and Economic Energy Harvesting. *International Journal of Engineering and Technology, 5*(6), 5030-5037. Available from http://www.enggjournals.com/ijet/docs/IJET13-05-06-338.pdf

Norris, D. (2015). *The Internet of Things: Do-It-Yourself at Home Projects for Arduino, Raspberry Pi, and BeagleBone Black*. McGraw-Hill Education.

Prinsloo, G., & Dobson, R. T. (2014). *Solar Tracking: High precision solar position algorithms, programs, software and source-code for computing the solar vector, solar coordinates & sun angles in Microprocessor, PLC, Arduino, PIC and PC-based sun tracking devices or dynamic sun following hardware*. Available from https://www.researchgate.net/publication/263085113_Solar_Tracking_High_precision_solar_position_algorithms_programs_software_and_source-code_for_computing_the_solar_vector_solar_coordinates_sun_angles_in_Microprocessor_PLC_Arduino_PIC_and_PC-based_sun

REN21. (2015). *Renewables 2015 Global Status Report*. Available online: http://www.ren21.net/status-of-renewables/global-status-report/

Slama, D., Puhlmann, F., Morrish, J., & Bhatnagar, R. M. (2015). *Enterprise IoT: Strategies and Best Practices for Connected Products and Services*. O'Reilly Media. Available from http://enterprise-iot.org/book/enterprise-iot/

Zubov, D., Barbosa, H. A., & Duane, G. S. (2015). *A Nonanticipative Analog Method for Long-Term Forecasting of Air Temperature Extremes*. Available from http://arxiv.org/abs/1507.03283

Zubov, D., Volponi, F., & Khosravy, M. (2015). D-Wave Quantum Computing Ising Model: A Case Study for the Forecasting of Heat Waves. In *Proceedings of Fourth International Conference on Control, Automation and Information Sciences (ICCAIS 2015)*. Changshu, China: IEEE. doi:10.1109/ICCAIS.2015.7338651

KEY TERMS AND DEFINITIONS

Arduino: A term for a company and general name for the open-source computer soft- and hardware that interact, measure, and control devices.

Console App: A computer program that uses text-based user interface.

HTML: HyperText Markup Language is the standard markup language used to develop web-sites.

IoT Protocol: A software protocol intended to be used by the resource-constrained electronic devices (e.g. small memory and low power consumption) for the communication over the Internet.

Light (Solar) Tracker: A device that orients the solar panel toward the source of light (Sun for outdoor usage).

MQTT: A lightweight IoT protocol where the publisher sends the data with a specific topic and subscribers receive the data through the broker according to the topic. Currently, MQTT (Message Queuing Telemetry Transport) is ISO standard ISO/IEC PRF 20922.

NodeMcu Lua ESP8266 ESP-12E WiFi Development Board: An open source IoT platform based on the eLua project and built on the ESP8266 SDK. It includes firmware, which runs on the ESP8266 Wi-Fi SoC, and hardware that is based on the ESP-12 module.

OOP: Object-Oriented Programming (OOP) is a programming paradigm based on the concept of objects, which may contain the data and the code. Three main features (inheritance, polymorphism, and encapsulation) are discussed together with OOP usually.

RFID: Radio-Frequency Identification (RFID) is a technology to write/read the info using radio signals. ISO/IEC 18000 is a standard that describes a series of diverse RFID technologies with the unique frequency ranges.

APPENDIX

The following C++ code represents the Arduino sketch with MQTT publisher for the remote control of LEDs:

```cpp
#include <PubSubClient.h>
#include <SPI.h>
#include <Ethernet.h>
int LED1 = 5; int LED2 = 6; int LED3 = 7;  int LED4 = 8;
int LED5 = 9; int LED6 = 4; int LED7 = 11; int LED8 = 12;
byte mac[] = { 0x00, 0xAA, 0xBB, 0xCC, 0xDE, 0x02 };// Physical
mac address
byte ip[] = { 192, 168, 1, 101 };                    // IP in
lan
byte gateway[] = { 192, 168, 1, 1 };          // Internet access
via router
byte subnet[] = { 255, 255, 255, 0 };         // Subnet mask
byte serverComp[] = { 192, 168, 1, 100 };     // IP address of
the computer
EthernetServer server(80);                     // Server port
String readString, s1;
void callback(char* topic, byte* payload, unsigned int length)
{
    Serial.println((char*)payload);
}
EthernetClient ethClient;
PubSubClient MQTTclient(serverComp, 1883, callback, ethClient);
void setup(){
  pinMode(LED1, OUTPUT); //pin selected to control 1st LED
  pinMode(LED2, OUTPUT); //pin selected to control 2nd LED
  pinMode(LED3, OUTPUT); //pin selected to control 3rd LED
  pinMode(LED4, OUTPUT); //pin selected to control 4th LED
  pinMode(LED5, OUTPUT); //pin selected to control 5th LED
  pinMode(LED6, OUTPUT); //pin selected to control 6th LED
  pinMode(LED7, OUTPUT); //pin selected to control 7th LED
  pinMode(LED8, OUTPUT); //pin selected to control 8th LED
  digitalWrite(LED1, LOW); digitalWrite(LED2, LOW);
  digitalWrite(LED3, LOW); digitalWrite(LED4, LOW);
  digitalWrite(LED5, LOW); digitalWrite(LED6, LOW);
  digitalWrite(LED7, LOW); digitalWrite(LED8, LOW);
```

```
  //start Ethernet
  Ethernet.begin(mac, ip, gateway, gateway, subnet);
  server.begin();
  //enable serial data print
  Serial.begin(9600);
  Serial.println("MQTT protocol, Server, and LEDs.");
}
void loop(){
  // Create a client connection
  EthernetClient client = server.available();
  if (client) {
    while (client.connected()) {
      if (client.available()) {
        char c = client.read();
        if (readString.length() < 100) { // Read char by char
HTTP request
          readString += c; // Store characters to string
          //Serial.print(c);
        }
        if (c == '\n') {    // If HTTP request has ended
          Serial.println(readString);
          // Control Arduino pins
          if(readString.indexOf("12") >0) // Checks for 121
          {
            digitalWrite(LED5, HIGH);    // Set LED5 high
            Serial.println("LED 5 is ON");
          } else {
            if(readString.indexOf('2') >0)// Checks for 2
            {
              digitalWrite(LED1, HIGH);   // Set LED1 high
              Serial.println("LED 1 is ON");
            }
          }
          if(readString.indexOf("13") >0) // Checks for 13
          {
            digitalWrite(LED5, LOW);     // Set LED5 low
            Serial.println("LED 5 is OFF");
          } else {
            if(readString.indexOf('3') >0)// Checks for 3
```

```
    {
      digitalWrite(LED1, LOW);    // Set LED1 low
      Serial.println("LED 1 is OFF");
    }
  }

  if(readString.indexOf("14") >0) // Checks for 14
  {
    digitalWrite(LED6, HIGH);    // Set LED 6 high
    Serial.println("LED 6 is ON");
  } else {
    if(readString.indexOf('4') >0)// Checks for 4
    {
      digitalWrite(LED2, HIGH);   // Set LED 2 high
      Serial.println("LED 2 is ON");
    }
  }
  if(readString.indexOf("15") >0) // Checks for 15
  {
    digitalWrite(LED6, LOW);      // Set LED 6 low
    Serial.println("LED 6 is OFF");
  } else {
    if(readString.indexOf('5') >0)// Checks for 5
    {
      digitalWrite(LED2, LOW);    // Set LED 2 low
      Serial.println("LED 2 is OFF");
    }
  }

  if(readString.indexOf("16") >0) // Checks for 16
  {
    digitalWrite(LED7, HIGH);    // Set LED 7 high
    Serial.println("LED 7 is ON");
  } else {
    if(readString.indexOf('6') >0)// Checks for 6
    {
      digitalWrite(LED3, HIGH);   // Set LED 3 high
      Serial.println("LED 3 is ON");
    }
  }
```

```
if(readString.indexOf("17") >0) // Checks for 17
{
  digitalWrite(LED7, LOW);      // Set LED 7 low
  Serial.println("LED 7 is OFF");
} else {
  if(readString.indexOf('7') >0)// Checks for 7
  {
    digitalWrite(LED3, LOW);    // Set LED 3 low
    Serial.println("LED 3 is OFF");
  }
}


if(readString.indexOf("18") >0) // Checks for 18
{
  digitalWrite(LED8, HIGH);      // Set LED 8 high
  Serial.println("LED 8 is ON");
} else {
  if(readString.indexOf('8') >0)// Checks for 8
  {
    digitalWrite(LED4, HIGH);    // Set LED 4 high
    Serial.println("LED 4 is ON");
  }
}
if(readString.indexOf("19") >0) // Checks for 19
{
  digitalWrite(LED8, LOW);       // Set LED 8 low
  Serial.println("LED 8 is OFF");
} else {
  if(readString.indexOf('9') >0)// Checks for 9
  {
    digitalWrite(LED4, LOW);     // Set LED 4 low
    Serial.println("LED 4 is OFF");
  }
}
if(readString.indexOf("off+")>0) // Checks if LEDs to
OFF
{ digitalWrite(LED1, LOW); digitalWrite(LED2, LOW);
  digitalWrite(LED3, LOW); digitalWrite(LED4, LOW);
  digitalWrite(LED5, LOW); digitalWrite(LED6, LOW);
  digitalWrite(LED7, LOW); digitalWrite(LED8, LOW);
```

```
        Serial.println("All LEDs are OFF now");
    }
    client.println("HTTP/1.1 200 OK"); // Send new page
    client.println("Content-Type: text/html");
    client.println();
    client.println("<HTML>");
    client.println("<HEAD>");
    client.println("<TITLE>Arduino - MQTT protocol and
remote control of the LEDs</TITLE>");
    // To refresh the web-page every 10 seconds
    client.println("<meta http-equiv='refresh'
content='10'>");
    client.println("</HEAD>");
    client.println("<BODY>");
    client.println("<H1>Arduino - MQTT protocol and
remote control of the LEDs</H1>");

    // For simple testing, LEDs 1 - 8 are used in buttons
    // DIY buttons
    client.println("<a href=/?on2 >LED 1 is ON</a>");
    client.println("<a href=/?off3 >LED 1 is OFF</a>");
    client.println(" <a href=/?off+ >ALL OFF</
a><br><br>");
    // Mousedown buttons
    client.println("<input type=button value='LED 2 is
ON' onmousedown=location.href='/?on4;'>");
    client.println("<input type=button value='LED 2 is
OFF' onmousedown=location.href='/?off5;'>");
    client.println(" <input type=button value='ALL
OFF' onmousedown=location.href='/?off+;'><br><br>");
    // Mousedown radio buttons
    client.println("<input type=radio
onmousedown=location.href='/?on6;'>LED 3 is ON</>");
    client.println("<input type=radio
onmousedown=location.href='/?off7;'>LED 3 is OFF</>");
    client.println(" <input type=radio
onmousedown=location.href='/?off+;'>ALL OFF</><br><br>");
    // Custom buttons
    client.print("<input type=submit value='LED 4 is ON'
style=width:100px;height:45px onClick=location.
```

```
href='/?on8;'>");
        client.print("<input type=submit value='LED 4 is OFF'
style=width:100px;height:45px onClick=location.
href='/?off9;'>");
        client.print(" <input type=submit value='ALL
OFF' style=width:100px;height:45px onClick=location.
href='/?off+;'>");
        // DIY buttons
        client.println("<br><br><a href=/?on12 >LED 5 is ON</
a>");
        client.println("<a href=/?off13 >LED 5 is OFF</a>");
        client.println(" <a href=/?off+ >ALL OFF</
a><br><br>");
        // Mousedown buttons
        client.println("<input type=button value='LED 6 is
ON' onmousedown=location.href='/?on14;'>");
        client.println("<input type=button value='LED 6 os
OFF' onmousedown=location.href='/?off15;'>");
        client.println(" <input type=button value='ALL
OFF' onmousedown=location.href='/?off+;'><br><br>");
        // Mousedown radio buttons
        client.println("<input type=radio
onmousedown=location.href='/?on16;'>LED 7 is ON</>");
        client.println("<input type=radio
onmousedown=location.href='/?off17;'>LED 7 is OFF</>");
        client.println(" <input type=radio
onmousedown=location.href='/?off+;'>ALL OFF</><br><br>");
        // Custom buttons
        client.print("<input type=submit value='LED 8 is ON'
style=width:100px;height:45px onClick=location.
href='/?on18;'>");
        client.print("<input type=submit value='LED 8 is OFF'
style=width:100px;height:45px onClick=location.
href='/?off19;'>");
        client.print(" <input type=submit value='ALL
OFF' style=width:100px;height:45px onClick=location.
href='/?off+;'><br>");
        readString="<p>";
        if (digitalRead(LED1) == HIGH) {readString += "LED 1
is ON; "; s1 += '1';}
```

```
          else {readString += "LED 1 is OFF; "; s1 += '0';}
          if (digitalRead(LED2) == HIGH) {readString += "LED 2
is ON; "; s1 += '1';}
          else {readString += "LED 2 is OFF; "; s1 += '0';}
          if (digitalRead(LED3) == HIGH) {readString += "LED 3
is ON; "; s1 += '1';}
          else {readString += "LED 3 is OFF; "; s1 += '0';}
          if (digitalRead(LED4) == HIGH) {readString += "LED 4
is ON; "; s1 += '1';}
          else {readString += "LED 4 is OFF; "; s1 += '0';}
          if (digitalRead(LED5) == HIGH) {readString += "LED 5
is ON; "; s1 += '1';}
          else {readString += "LED 5 is OFF; "; s1 += '0';}
          if (digitalRead(LED6) == HIGH) {readString += "LED 6
is ON; "; s1 += '1';}
          else {readString += "LED 6 is OFF; "; s1 += '0';}
          if (digitalRead(LED7) == HIGH) {readString += "LED 7
is ON; "; s1 += '1';}
          else {readString += "LED 7 is OFF; "; s1 += '0';}
          if (digitalRead(LED8) == HIGH) {readString += "LED 8
is ON;</p>"; s1 += '1';}
          else {readString += "LED 8 is OFF;</p>"; s1 += '0';}
          client.print(readString);
          client.println("</BODY>");
          client.println("</HTML>");
          delay(1);
          client.stop();    // Stopping client
          if (MQTTclient.connect("arduinoClient")) {
            // Length (with one extra character for the null
terminator)
            int str_len = s1.length()+1;
            // Prepare the character array (the buffer)
            char char_array[str_len];
            s1.toCharArray(char_array, str_len);    // Copy it
over
            MQTTclient.publish("/LEDs",char_array);
            Serial.println("Client connected");
          }
          else {
            Serial.println("Client not connected");
```

```
        }
        readString = "";   // Clearing string for the next
read
        s1 = "";           // Clearing string for the next
usage
      }
    }
  }
}
```

Chapter 6
Model–Driven Multi–Domain IoT

László Lengyel
Budapest University of Technology and Economics, Hungary

Tamás Balogh
Budapest University of Technology and Economics, Hungary

Péter Ekler
Budapest University of Technology and Economics, Hungary

Gergely Mezei
Budapest University of Technology and Economics, Hungary

Imre Tömösvári
Budapest University of Technology and Economics, Hungary

Bertalan Forstner
Budapest University of Technology and Economics, Hungary

Hassan Charaf
Budapest University of Technology and Economics, Hungary

ABSTRACT

The Internet of Things (IoT) is the network of physical objects embedded with electronics, software, sensors, and network connectivity, which enables these objects to collect and exchange data. The chapter introduces the Model-driven Multi-Domain IoT concept and provides a method and a supporting framework. Multi-Domain IoT as the actual frontier for innovation, competition, and productivity. The method supports effective service and application development and therefore covers connected devices, data collection, data access and complex analytics. The efficiency of the method and the framework is confirmed by several projects. Selected parts of these projects are introduced as innovation projects and case studies.

DOI: 10.4018/978-1-5225-2437-3.ch006

INTRODUCTION

The IoT allows objects to be sensed and controlled remotely across existing network infrastructure, creating opportunities for more direct integration between the physical world and computer-based systems, resulting in improved efficiency, accuracy and economic benefit.

Technology trends continue by the unstoppable path towards cloud computing, big data, applications, mobile devices, wearable gadgets, 3D printing, integrated ecosystems, and of course the IoT as the next computing platform. (Swan 2013; Thibodeau, 2014)

This chapter introduces the *Model-driven Multi-Domain IoT* concept and provides a method and a unified framework supporting Multi-Domain IoT services, application design and development. In a multi-domain IoT environment, data comes from several sources: sensors that collect traffic, health, climate and further information, posts on social networking sites, digital images and videos, records of purchase transactions or mobile phone GPS signals to name some of the most significant.

We see Multi-Domain IoT as the actual frontier for innovation, competition, and productivity. The introduced method supports effective service and application development and therefore covers the following areas: connected devices (connectivity, intelligence), data collection (sensors, storage), data access (cloud, standards, open APIs, security), complex analytics (big data tools), and unique value (realization of the true potential driven by the connected society).

The key points of the suggested method are:

Step 1.- IoT (Sensors, Devices, Connectivity and Services): IoT is about to increase the connectedness of people and things. IoT ecosystems can help consumers achieve goals by greatly improving their decision-making capabilities via the augmented intelligence based on the collected and analyzed data.

Step 2.- Multi-Domain IoT (SensorHUB): SensorHUB (SensorHUB) is both a method and a framework to support IoT-related application and service development. Furthermore, it effectively supports the discovery of data correlations that drives the product improvement, service development and the efficiency of the business activities.

Step 3.- Model-driven Multi-Domain IoT (VMTS + SensorHUB): The utilization of software modeling and model processing techniques is provided to enrich the service and application development for the IoT area and improve its efficiency. As a result, we can increase both the development productivity and the quality of software artifacts, furthermore we can significantly reduce the time-to-market.

Our team has developed both the SensorHUB and the Visual Modeling and Transformation System (VMTS) frameworks. SensorHUB focuses on the IoT-enabled service and application development, including the multi-domain support, while VMTS is our software modeling and model-processing environment. The *Model-driven Multi-Domain IoT* concept utilizes the capabilities of both, furthermore, it realizes model-driven, quality assured service and application development for the Multi-Domain IoT area.

The chapter discusses the SensorHUB framework (Section 2), its multi-domain capabilities (Section 3), introduces the VMTS framework and the synergy of VMTS and SensorHUB, i.e. our *Model-driven Multi-Domain IoT* concept (Section 4). The efficiency of the method is confirmed by several projects. Selected parts of these projects are also discussed in order to support understanding and serve utilization of the method. Finally, concluding remarks are elaborated.

THE SENSORHUB FRAMEWORK

Software systems covering data collection, transmission, data processing, analysis, reporting, and advanced querying are usually developed by strong method and framework background. Consolidated development methods and frameworks provide the efficiency and ensure the quality of the software artifacts. SensorHUB framework is a platform as a service (PaaS) solution for IoT and data-driven application development. The strength of the framework is that it covers the whole data collection, analyzing and reporting process. SensorHUB utilizes the state-of-the-art open source technologies and provides a unified toolchain for IoT-related application and service development. SensorHUB framework, next to the IoT-related application and service development, supports the data monetization by providing a method to define data views on top of different data sources and analyzed data. (Lengyel et al, 2015b) (SensorHUB)

SensorHUB makes it possible to develop and reutilize domain-specific software blocks, for example, components of the healthcare domain or the vehicle domain that are implemented once and can be built into multiple applications. The framework makes them available by default and provides various features to support developers working in the field.

SensorHUB also provides tools to support application domain-specific service development. The architecture of the concept is depicted in Figure 1. The whole system contains the following areas:

1. Sensors, data collection, local processing, client side visualization, and data transmission (bottom left).

2.   Cloud-based backend with big data analysis and management (bottom right).
3.   Domain-specific software components (middle).
4.   Applications, services, visualization, business intelligence reports, dashboards (top).

Sensors cover different domains: health, smart city, vehicle, production line, weather and further areas. Local processing and data transmission makes up a local platform, which performs core services, i.e. data collection, data aggregation, visualization of raw measurements, secure communication, and data transmission. This component also provides information as a local service interface for different applications.

The cloud component provides historical data storage, big data management, domain-specific data analysis, and extract-transform-load (ETL) mechanisms. Its architecture was designed specifically for cloud deployments, although it can also be deployed on premises. In the core, we have designed a service layer based on the microservice architecture. The loosely coupled services make up an important part of the framework. The most notable domain-agnostic services are the data

Figure 1. Architecture of the SensorHUB

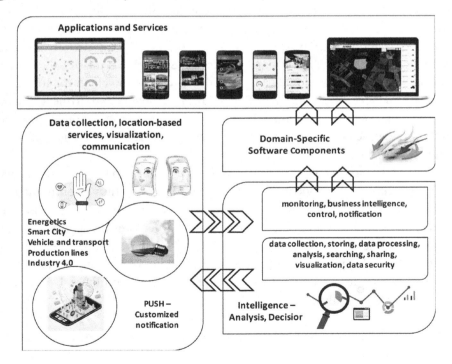

ingestion service and the general querying service. Among the more domain-specific services are the push notification service, which is applicable in all domains that have smartphones on the client side, and the proximity alert service, which can be used to determine if the sensor is located inside a predefined area and is useful in the transportation or agricultural domains.

The last layer comprises applications that implement specific user-facing functionalities. These data-driven applications, independently of their purpose, eventually face the same problems repeatedly. Without framework support, applications should find a way to collect data, to store large amounts of data reliably and in a scalable way, to transform data into a format convenient for data analysis, or present data on a dashboard. Solving these problems is not trivial, and can account for the majority of the development effort if done one-by-one for every different application. The main purpose of the SensorHUB framework is to function as a platform for these applications, providing the implementation of the previously described areas, so the application developers can focus on the domain-specific problems they intend to solve. The implementation includes client-side software components, which support easy collecting sensor data; a data processing pipeline that aids tasks from the data ingestion to the visualization of the data in an efficient, scalable way; and also several domain-specific components, which are not as commonly needed as the data processing pipeline itself, but are also reusable in different applications.

SensorHUB framework is developed in an incremental and iterative way, the loose coupling between its modules makes us able to develop and update components independently.

We utilize the following technologies and components during the implementation of SensorHUB:

- *Node.js* is applied as a cross-platform runtime environment for server-side applications. It provides an event-driven architecture and a non-blocking I/O API that optimizes an application's throughput and scalability. (Node.js)
- *Docker* is an open-source software container framework. It provides virtual machine-like separated environments with very little overhead. We used it for packaging and deploying the microservices. (Docker)
- *MQTT* is a lightweight messaging protocol based on the publish-subscribe model working on the top of the TCP/IP layer. We use an implementation of this protocol for direct two-way communication with different sensors and devices. (MQTT)
- *Apache Kafka* is applied as a central hub performing load balancing, queuing and buffering incoming data from various sources including MQTT brokers

and the microservice layer. Kafka is able to process thousands of incoming data packets per second, making it a perfect choice for this task. (Apache Kafka)

- *Apache Hadoop* is used as a software framework for distributed storage and processing of large data sets on computer clusters built from commodity hardware. It consists of a distributed file system (HDFS) and a resource management platform (YARN), furthermore, it provides a basis for a great deal of purpose-built frameworks, such as Ap*ache Spark, Apache Hive* and *Cloudera Impala*. (Apache Hadoop)
- *Apache Spark* is a high-performance cluster computing framework. We utilize the high-level functional API of Spark for data processing and Spark Streaming for effective real-time event-processing. (Apache Spark)
- *Apache Hive* is applied as a data warehouse infrastructure built on top of Hadoop. It provides an SQL interface for data stored on HDFS. We use it for ETL (extract, transform, load) batches, which require high throughput instead of low latency. We also utilize *Cloudera Impala* for this purpose, as it provides faster queries. (Apache Hive)
- *Apache Cassandra* is a distributed, massively scalable NoSQL database. SensorHUB applications can use this form of data storage for quick queries against processed data. Cassandra is capable of ingesting tremendous amounts of data very quickly; this makes it a great choice for large-scale IoT applications. (Apache Cassandra)

Detailed Framework Architecture

Given the scale the framework needs to operate on, we designed it to be deployed in cluster environments (clouds). We have organized the different functionalities into microservices. Microservices are light-weight server components that focus on a single task. This approach not only makes the services more maintainable, easier to develop independently of each other and replaceable, but also leads to components that boot fast, which is an essential requirement when deploying to the cloud, as new instances must be fired up on the run as the load increases. Most of the framework's microservices are built using the Node.js framework, because it is light-weight and excels at I/O-heavy tasks.

We made the different microservices accessible for applications through an API Gateway, which unites the microservices into a cohesive interface and hides all the service instantiation, discovery and load balancing details from the applications. Further service of the API Gateway is to authenticate applications before using the framework. Load balancing and authentication is based on the microservice repository and the application repository. These two services, running and tracing service instances, and registered client applications serve as the backbone of the framework.

The microservices are deployed in separate Docker containers. Docker is supported by all major cloud providers and using this technology makes distributing and managing the framework seamless. The clusterized running and scaling of the components can be orchestrated with tools such as Kubernetes or Docker Swarm. Based on the measurements, booting up a Node.js instance is relatively quick, compared to a Java-based solution, furthermore, by keeping the services stateless, the load balancing task is straightforward in any environment. Figure 2 provides a detailed overview of the framework architecture.

Data ingestion and data querying microservices are the two pillars. Data is uploaded into a cluster of machines running Hadoop by the Data Upload Service. Raw data can be queried using the Data Query Service.

The framework also provides an MQTT-based way for data upload. In certain cases, sensors, actuators or any client device can directly communicate with the platform, without the overhead of an application backend and layers of microservices. For these use cases, we provide the MQTT-based endpoint. Using this endpoint, the platform can receive data on large scales and is also capable of sending back control or configuration instructions.

Figure 2. The detailed architecture of the SensorHUB framework

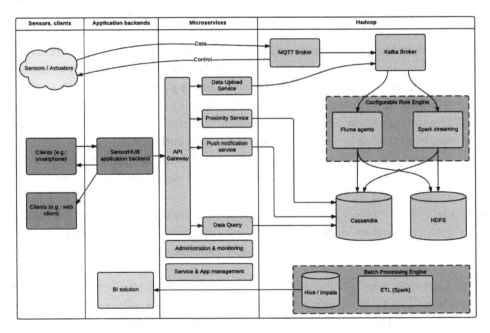

The MQTT and microservice-based ingestion methods load data into an Apache Kafka cluster, which is the entry point for the Hadoop platform.

Providing a schema for the ingested data is not required. The schema is forced on the raw data by the application itself. This method gives great flexibility, however, in certain cases, having a fixed schema provides benefits, i.e. automatic code or job generation can be performed based on schema information. Therefore, the framework allows to store schema for a given dataset or data source. A further advantage of this hybrid approach is a standard query interface for the data that has a provided schema. Applications, which do not support metadata, handle the query interface themselves. This is a reasonable tradeoff between customizability and the ability to use general services provided by the framework.

Data Processing

Although flexibility is an asset, in most cases the schema is known at the time of data ingestion. This is the reason, why we apply a hybrid approach by providing an ETL engine. In this way, application developers can configure loading their data into one of the supported query-optimized data stores. Depending on the needs of the application, the data store can be one of the followings (Figure 3):

- HDFS file system as a Data Lake (a large-scale storage repository and processing engine): this storage should never be modified and should serve as a secure and reliable historical data storage for further processing or archive purposes.
- A compressed, partitioned, columnar data store, implemented on a massively parallel processing engine (such as Apache Hive or Cloudera Impala with Parquet files) that is efficient for analytic query patterns.
- A NoSQL data store (Apache Cassandra) that is utilized for fast data retrieval, data modification and simple analytic queries, e.g. queries from client applications displaying live or historic data to end users.
- A traditional relational database (MySQL) with the advantage that it is well-known to developers, has several associated tools and scales well for medium-sized services.
- Data can be piped into a stream processing module, which can be used to detect anomalies in the incoming events and send immediate alert messages directly to client applications or do any logic required by the application.

In scenarios, where raw data is not necessarily stored, but is just processed in a streaming-like fashion, using the Data Lake is optional, but recommended. As data in the Data Lake is never modified once uploaded, application developers can

Figure 3. SensorHUB data store variations

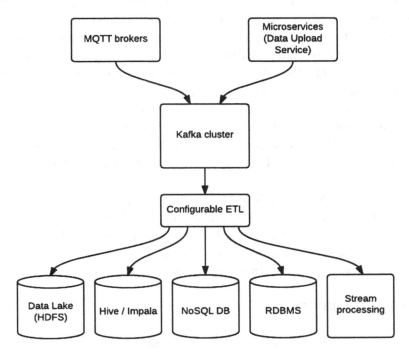

always access data with arbitrarily complex processing algorithms or by providing their own custom ETLs. These standard formats, supplemented by the capability of defining further custom processing algorithms, enable developers to focus data at the abstraction level that best fits their needs, contributing to the ease of development.

Deployment

On top of the platform, there are the domain-specific web and mobile applications and services. Special types of services are customized reports, data monitoring solutions, dashboards, and further business intelligence solutions. As the platform itself is designed to be deployed on a backend infrastructure of an internal network, it is recommended that these applications use their own separate servers to utilize the capabilities of the platform. It is also possible to simply open the internal ports to client applications, but this is not advised, because it would introduce security risks. Internal microservices are prepared to authorize requests that are coming from a relatively safe, firewall protected environment, not from the outside world. In the current architecture, application of these strong security measures is the responsibility of the application-specific web servers.

Figure 4 shows a possible setup, where the Hadoop Cluster and the SensorHUB platform are deployed on internal network servers, and the different user-facing services deploy their own web servers. An example would be an application that uses smartphones to collect data and provides services to the users. Such smartphone applications would directly connect to their own backend servers, knowing nothing about the SensorHUB framework. The application backend would wrap the services of the underlying framework, and glue them together in a way best fitting for the application. One of the main strengths of the SensorHUB framework is that it enables the application backend to remain a thin layer. In the absence of the framework, every single application would need to implement its own version of the data handling functionalities.

In many of our SensorHUB utilizations, a smartphone running Android OS serves as a bridge between a sensor and the infrastructure in the cloud. As many of these sensors have no direct internet access, but are capable of communicating using Bluetooth or Wi-Fi, an Android smartphone with the capability of Bluetooth/Wi-Fi connection and mobile internet access is ideal for this purpose.

Client-Side Support

In order to support the client application development, we provide client-side services. They are implemented on the Android smartphone platform and distributed as an application library. This library encapsulates the client-related services, and provides them as independent building blocks.

Figure 4. A possible deployment of the SensorHUB framework with client applications

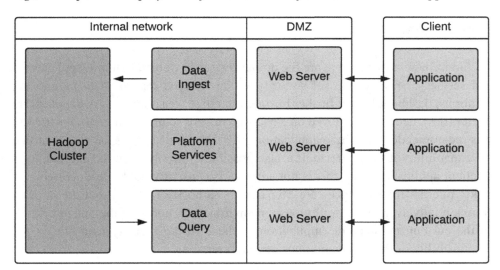

The first part of these modules are client-side counterparts of the platform services available on the infrastructure side. These are client-side utilities that support client services, such as transparent push notification handling and device registration, or data querying.

The second part of the client modules are the utilities. These modules provide services for common client-side domain-independent features, including reliable networking, secure communication, and integration with social services (Figure 5).

SensorHUB Summary

SensorHUB is a general concept with a core platform implementation. We provide different realizations (domain-specific software components), i.e. utilizations of the SensorHUB platform. The results are different specialized platforms targeting a selected area.

The framework has been successfully applied as a development accelerator framework for the smart city, vehicle, health, and production line domains. Several SensorHUB-driven systems, targeting smart city, agriculture and health areas are also under design and development. Some of them are introduced in the next two sections of this chapter.

SEVERAL DOMAINS, BIG DATA, BIG CHALLENGES, GREAT OPPORTUNITIES

Challenges of the IoT and big data areas include analysis, capture, curation, search, sharing, storage, transfer, and visualization of data, and information privacy. Management of the collected data and the attendant security concerns are among the biggest challenges. *What does data mean?* – This is a key point we often face.

Figure 5. The environment of an application that utilizes the SensorHUB framework

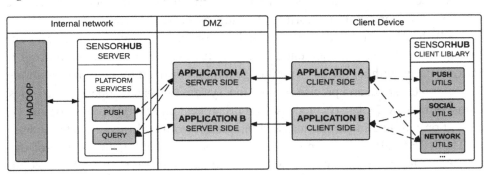

However, we believe that *big data* and the *IoT world* allow customers to get beyond reactive and even beyond proactive, to become predictive. We can take a more holistic view of the tools and their behavior.

Combining the experience and results from previous projects targeting various IoT domains, a configurable set of general modules has emerged, which we call SensorHUB. The concept continuously evolves, based on feedback from R&D and industrial projects.

VehicleICT platform is an implementation on top of the SensorHUB framework targeting the vehicle domain. The implementation of the VehicleICT platform helped to distill the architecture of the SensorHUB. VehicleICT utilizes the capabilities of the SensorHUB and provides a vehicle domain related layer with several reusable components and features. This means that VehicleICT platform itself can be considered as a test environment that verifies the different aspects of the SensorHUB framework.

Smart City Domain

The idea behind the VehicleICT platform was to identify a reasonably rich set of functionalities that typical connected car applications need and then to implement and test these functionalities and finally offer them as building blocks in a centralized manner. VehicleICT was one of the first projects, where both the client and server parts of the SensorHUB framework have been utilized (Lengyel et al, 2015a) (VehicleICT).

Within the frame of two EIT (European Institute of Innovation & Technology) Climate-KIC (EIT Climate-KIC) projects, we utilize the framework. These Climate-KIC projects are referred to as URBMOBI (Urban Mobile Instruments for Environmental Monitoring, i.e., a Mobile Measurement Device for Urban Environmental Monitoring) (URBMOBI) and SOLSUN (Sustainable Outdoor Lighting & Sensory Urban Networks) (SOLSUN).

The URBMOBI project integrates a mobile measurement unit for operation on vehicles in urban areas (i.e., local buses and trams), with data postprocessing, inclusion in enhanced environmental models and visualization techniques for climate-related services, environmental monitoring, planning, and research needs.

URBMOBI is a mobile environmental sensor that (i) provides temporally and spatially distributed environmental data, (ii) fulfills the need for monitoring at various places without the costs for a large number of fixed measurement stations, (iii) integrates small and precise sensors in a system that can be operated on buses, trams, or other vehicles, (iv) focusses on urban heat and thermal comfort, and (v) aims at providing climate services and integration with real-time climate models.

The URBMOBI solution provides a novel product that integrates state-of-the-art sensors for environmental variables embedded in a system that allows mobile usage and data handling based on geolocation technology and data transmission by telecommunication networks. Sensors can be operated on buses, trams, taxis, or similar vehicles in urban areas.

The SOLSUN project is about to demonstrate how intelligent city infrastructure can be created in a cost-effective and sustainable way by reusing existing street lighting as the communications backbone. We apply different technologies and methods to reduce energy consumption at the same time as turning streetlights into nodes on a scalable network that is also expandable for other applications. Sensors capture data on air pollution, noise pollution, and traffic density; information gathered is used to address traffic congestion, another key contributor of greenhouse gas emissions in cities. SOLSUN project develops an integrated technology platform.

Healthcare Domain

We have seen the emerging popularity of a phenomenon called „quantified self". Followers of this movement regard every aspect of their life as input data, which they record and store in order to improve daily functioning. The history of self-tracking using wearable sensors in combination with wearable computing and wireless communication already exists for many years, and also appeared, in the form of sousveillance back in the 1970s (Swan 2013). Today, healthcare sensors and different kinds of sport trackers become cheaper and affordable, and even smart devices have sensors capable of performing health related measurements.

The average user collecting self-tracking data is not medical expert, it is difficult for her to interpret her medical results or similar self-monitoring data in depth. She is not aware of the importance of the individual values or the meaning of deviance from normal intervals, nor can she combine different measured values to infer her health status. What such users can do is paying for the doctor's time or look up some uncontrolled source on the Internet to learn the meaning of these data.

Motivated by increasing healthcare costs, using medical grade sensors is also regarded as a way of cost-effectively observing the required biological signals of a patient (Pantelopoulos et al, 2010). This phenomenon transforms the healthcare industry in a form where remote experts decide, for example, on the necessity of a surgical intervention for a given patient, based on sensor data collected for days. Similar to knowledge engineering, it is possible to run learning algorithms on voluntary provided sensor data of thousands of users to infer hidden correlations. Automated processes can even warn the user if some suspicious results make it legitimate to visit a general practitioner or a specialist (Clifton et al, 2014). The experts can harness the availability of historical data during analysis.

A shortcoming of the current state-of-the-art systems for the described challenge is that they are closed proprietary solutions. Sensor data from one system cannot be used with the system of another player on the market, as the data or the provided service are holding market value. There is a couple of manufacturers providing application programming interface for their sensors or trackers, however, most of them cannot be integrated into third-party software. The reason is the sensibility of personal or medical data, as their privacy cannot be guaranteed if they are offered for third parties via uncontrolled interfaces.

Combining the SensorHUB framework with medical sensors, we are concentrating on a method, which enables the collection of various kinds of health data from different sensor sources, and then utilizing the framework to infer the health status or find correlations and predictions.

A smartphone application is used as a gateway and controller for the measurements. Information about an ongoing measurement can be shown on the mobile device of the user, together with the final result and analysis at the end of the process. Users can utilize their own sensors or trackers for this process, but it is also possible to share sensors among many users. The data analysis and storage is done on a dedicated server. In order to insure scalability of the solution SensorHUB is used as the server-side backend system.

Special care has to be taken with regard to the security of personal data. The approach also requires a complex authentication system, which would encrypt medical data and authenticate the measurement device and measurement process at the same time.

We have designed and implemented the application on the top of SensorHUB, and have named it Sensible. We have selected a set of sensor types to be integrated into the system, both wired and wireless. Wireless sensors can harness the connectivity of the smartphone device of the users. In case of the wired sensors, there is an intermediary agent that receive the signals from those sensors, and load the data into the SensorHUB. We use Raspberry Pi devices for this task, running our software and the drivers of those sensors.

A challenge was first to authenticate the patient who is initiating the measurement, and then to authorize the intermediary agent starting the process and uploading data into SensorHUB on behalf of the given patient.

We are identifying correlations between different uploaded measurement parameters and illnesses identified by doctors. Our algorithm is designed based on the model of Pearson Correlation Coefficient. It describes a linear connection between two value pairs with a number between -1 and 1. Values close to zero mean statistically not significant results, while those far from zero imply strong linear correlation.

We believe that in the near future the sensors built on advanced technology will play an important role in efficient healthcare services and also in early recognition of illnesses. Our results contribute to achieve this goal.

Besides the described domains, we are currently addressing two more domains, namely, the agriculture and the production line (industrial Internet). The architecture is similar: data is collected with domain-related sensors, locally processed and utilized, furthermore uploaded and analyzed. Services from their part are driven by the distilled data. These projects develop domain-specific solutions on top of the SensorHUB. Our experience shows that the aforementioned IoT projects, based on the utilized components and both the way and results of the development, validate the SensorHUB approach and its multi-domain capabilities. The reusability ratio of the framework components is rather high. The similarity in the architecture of the realized systems motivated us to apply a higher abstraction level development method, generate the configurable parts of the systems and increase product quality based on high-level validation methods. This led us to creation of a model-based development method.

MODEL-DRIVEN MULTI-DOMAIN IOT

The two key points in the application development are always actual: optimization of the development process, i.e. reduction of time and effort, and providing high quality artifacts. Model-driven approach addresses both issues.

The growing dimension and complexity of software systems have turned software modeling technologies into a really efficient tool in application development. Within the modeling approaches, there exists a clear trend to move from universal modeling languages towards domain-specific solutions. Domain-specific languages (DSLs) (Fowler, 2010) (Kelly et al, 2008) are strictly limited to a domain, but this limitation also makes them much more efficient than universal languages. Using domain-specific artifacts and enforcing the domain rules automatically makes DSLs useful not only for software developers, but for domain experts as well.

Domain-Specific Modeling

The key concept behind model-based software methods is to express vital information in the model and let model processors accomplish the manual work of generating the code. This approach requires the model to use a representation comfortable to express vital information, furthermore, the model and the code generator together should provide all information required by the code generation. Domain-specific modeling and model processing can successfully address these requirements.

Using DSLs has the benefit that domain experts do not have to learn new (programming) languages. They can work with the already well-known domain language. By domain-specific modeling, domain experts define the business processes and domain requirements using the concepts of the domain.

Domain-specific models are rarely the final product of a modeling scenario. We can generate reports, document templates, or statistics from models. Moreover, the specialization makes it possible to create a framework containing the base knowledge of the domain and generate code from models using this framework. The final products can then automatically be generated from the high-level specifications by domain-specific code generators. There is no need to create error-prone manual mappings from domain concepts to design or to programming language concepts.

A Modeling and Model Processing Framework

More than twelve years ago, our research team has analyzed existing modeling frameworks. We have found that it is possible to create a solution, which is highly customizable, but fast and efficient as well. We have created our own modeling and model processing framework, Visual Modeling and Transformation System (VMTS). Since then, we have fine-tuned the framework several times based on the industrial requests and the experiences gained. Current version of VMTS is heavily based on generative techniques (Czarnecki et al, 2000) and uses a modular structure. Generative techniques are used to create efficient and highly flexible APIs from domain definitions, while the modular design helps in creating a wide range of applications based on these APIs. The result is a framework, where the user can decide at *run-time* whether to use customizability features or performance optimized version, furthermore, he can also choose the appropriate storage type (e.g. file, database, cloud storage). VMTS also offers customizable graphical and textual editors for editing the domain models.

The Visual Modeling and Transformation System is a graph-based, domain-specific (meta)modeling and model processing framework, or more likely a complete domain modeling platform. VMTS addresses the diversity, various storage types, model processors and performance issues of the modeling area. During its design, we have taken into consideration the requests from our industrial partners, cutting-edge technology solutions, knowledge of other modeling frameworks, and the conclusions of workshops, where VMTS has been presented.

In VMTS, we create domain definitions in a modeling IDE referred to as VMTS Studio. Domain definitions are described by a graphical language very similar to UML Class diagram. Domain entities, relations between entities, their attributes and operations can be specified in a user-friendly way. From the domain definition, we can generate an assembly (a .dll file), which represents a domain-specific API. The domain assembly allows us to load, or save domain models (in several formats

Figure 6. VMTS domain modeling platform

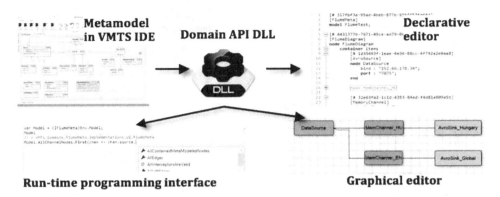

and media types) and acts as a base for all VMTS-related applications. For example, we can build or generate a graphical editor for domain models, we can edit models as a declarative document or we can also use the built-in run-time script evaluator and execute changes on models – using the domain API – on-the-fly. Although the IDE of VMTS is highly customizable for domains, we can also build a lightweight, standalone application not using the IDE, but still working on the domain models, enforcing the domain rules and supporting model storage functionality.

VMTS is used not only for modeling, but for model processing (code generation) as well. The first step here is always to ensure that the model is valid. Theoretically, the domain definition does not allow invalid models at all, however, code generators may also have certain additional requirements. By using the domain API, these validations are easy to apply. Model processing is also relatively simple, at least in case of SensorHUB, since, we have to traverse the model objects and add the appropriate code fragments to the result on each model element.

Model-Driven Multi-Domain IoT

To achieve the goals of the *Model-driven Multi-Domain IoT* concept, we apply model-based methods. The architecture of the application generation process is depicted in Figure 7. Using different domain-specific models, we describe various aspects of the IoT-based services and applications. We describe the data collection interface as the configuration of the backend system, define the data processing rules, push notification rules, data query capabilities, query parameters, service interfaces, application features, and further aspects of the envisioned IoT system. With a help of the VMTS framework, we can manage these languages and the domain models.

Figure 7. Overview of the Model-driven Multi-Domain IoT

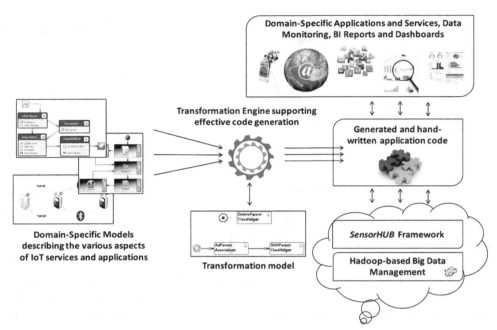

We also apply domain-specific model transformations to process system models and generate source code snippets and software components from the domain models. Custom business logic is manually added to the generated code and thus a complete source code package is created. This package relies on the SensorHUB framework, i.e. the code utilizes the framework APIs, class libraries and various services. This way, the generated code acts as a layer on top of the framework, so that we can reuse the previously prepared, well-tested and effective components of the SensorHUB framework. Usually, applications require custom design that is manually prepared and applied for the web and mobile user interface components.

Domains of SensorHUB

Regarding the SensorHUB framework, the role of domain modeling is to reduce the amount of repetitive coding tasks, decrease the time to market when introducing a new component, or changing the configuration of the framework and to increase clarity of the solutions used. At first, we have identified steps, which can be aided by domain modeling and model-based solutions. We have chosen three domains: (i) configuration files for Apache Flume, (ii) interface and data structure specification for clients and for the server side based on Swagger, (iii) filter configuration for Big Data processing. While creating environments for these domains, we consulted continuously with domain experts and fine-tuned our solutions according to their suggestions.

Configuration for Apache Flume

Flume is a distributed and reliable service for efficient collecting, aggregating, and moving large amounts of log data. Flume has a simple and flexible architecture based on streaming data flows (Apache Flume). In our solution, we have introduced a simplified graphical interface to specify Flume configuration files earlier created manually. As a result, we obtain models, which are more compact, easier to understand and faster to edit than the configuration files.

Based on the Flume specification (Apache Flume), we have created a simple, graphical DSL consisting of *Sources*, *Channels* and *Sinks*. We have also defined subtypes of these elements, where each type has attributes as defined in the specification. For example, we have an *AvroSource* (subtype of *Source*) with attributes *bind* and *port*. Note that for the sake of clarity and simplicity, only those types and those attributes were added to our language, which are used by the programmers. The language definition can easily be extended later without losing previously created models.

When the basic language was completed and tested, we have also added useful advanced features, such as multiplexing flows with selectors and Interceptors. Realizing Interceptors was challenging, since users can create an Interceptor definition (list of fields) and then use and fill out this definition (using the fields as variable slots) in Sources. E.g. a definition has two fields: *MimeType* and *Encoding*. Then, in a *HTTPSource*, we can add an Interceptor using this definition and set the concrete values as *MimeType= text/html, Encoding= UTF8*. This feature requires dynamic instance-level management of Interceptor fields, for example, in case the definition is modified. We have realized it as the part of the domain-specific modeling addon in VMTS IDE.

We have created several example models, then extended the validation logic and finally added a code generator as a part of the modeling add-on. The code generation is rather simple in this case: we have to traverse the models and for each model element generate an appropriate set of code lines. The code generator mostly consists of nested iterations listing the attributes of model elements.

The language has been tested and the solution has been verified by the developers. As a result, it become more clear and faster to apply changes in this domain environment than it was before by manual coding.

Figure 8. Model processing

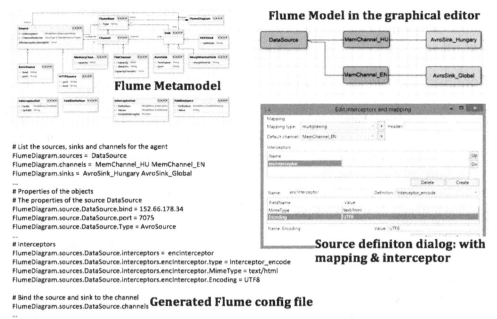

Flume Metamodel

Flume Model in the graphical editor

```
# List the sources, sinks and channels for the agent
FlumeDiagram.sources = DataSource
FlumeDiagram.channels = MemChannel_HU MemChannel_EN
FlumeDiagram.sinks = AvroSink_Hungary AvroSink_Global
...

# Properties of the objects
# The properties of the source DataSource
FlumeDiagram.source.DataSource.bind = 152.66.178.34
FlumeDiagram.source.DataSource.port = 7075
FlumeDiagram.source.DataSource.Type = AvroSource
...

# Interceptors
FlumeDiagram.sources.DataSource.interceptors = encInterceptor
FlumeDiagram.sources.DataSource.interceptors.encInterceptor.type = Interceptor_encode
FlumeDiagram.sources.DataSource.interceptors.encInterceptor.MimeType = text/html
FlumeDiagram.sources.DataSource.interceptors.encInterceptor.Encoding = UTF8
...

# Bind the source and sink to the channel
FlumeDiagram.sources.DataSource.channels
...
```

Source definiton dialog: with mapping & interceptor

Generated Flume config file

Interface Definition by Swagger

Swagger is a RESTful API representation (Swagger). Swagger definitions are used to generate interfaces for client applications and for the server-side services.

Swagger definitions can describe method calls with parameters, return types and error codes. All three parts have a type, which can be either one of the built-in primitive types, or a custom type consisting one, or more fields, e.g. a custom type *Person* with *FirstName* and *LastName* fields. Types may have additional attributes, such as *Format*, which acts as a constraint on the type (e.g. integers under 1000). Earlier, Swagger definitions were written manually, which was error-prone, since the precise usage of whitespace characters was required (e.g. the length of a tab was specified). Furthermore, there has been no autocomplete feature in the editor; thus, the spelling of type names was also a common source of errors.

We created a DSL to describe the types and the hierarchical relations between them. We have also created a built-in read-only model describing the built-in types, thus users can use (refer to) them automatically in their work. Based on this language, we built a domain environment. The environment consists of dialogs, where the selected type components can be edited in a table editor. Since type names are chosen from a dropdown list, spelling errors are automatically eliminated. Furthermore, the dialogs can validate *Format* descriptions when the users close the dialogs. The language and the environment were exhaustively tested. We can state that they are able of describing arbitrary type systems used in practical case studies.

The second step in creating the model-based solution was to extend the language with method call definitions. It was fairly simple, since method call definitions are rather similar to composite types (even if they have parameters instead of fields), but we had to add several descriptors to the definitions as well (e.g. post/get method, URL). We reused and extended our previous language in less than one day of work.

By completing the language, we moved the focus to the code generator. As in the case of the Flume domain, this step was simple: we had to traverse the model trees and generate the Swagger text by applying the *Visitor* design pattern.

Filter Configuration for Big Data

In the third domain, the basic idea is the following: we would like to process the data of the sensors. The data has a large amount of information fragments; we would like to understand these fragments, combine them and obtain answers to several questions asked by the users. While processing the fragments, we often transform them and filter out important parts while omitting everything else. For each question, we can specify the series of data manipulation tasks referred to as filters, which produce the answer. This process can be modeled quite well. Each filter has an interface definition, i.e. input and output parameters. We created a graphical language, where filters are represented by boxes. Filter definitions are managed similarly to type management in case of Swagger and boxes have input and output ports representing the parameters of filters. Boxes are connected to each other through these ports. Input and output data of the whole configuration is represented as the interface of the model itself. As the result, we have a workflow language for filters and the filter configuration can be easily described in a user friendly way.

Code generation is also possible based on the graphical models, however, it is more complex comparing to the previous two domains. For example, we have to obtain the correct sequence of execution from the model. Fortunately, this can be applied by searching for a random filter in the model with no unprocessed input and processing it. If we cannot find such a filter and there are still unprocessed filters, then the model is invalid.

CONCLUSION

There are two aspects of the IoT world: the first one is collecting data, processing and analyzing it; the second is providing services and applications to serve end users and support third-party services. The collected data represents unique fingerprints of the monitored systems and ecosystems. Data monetization is the second aspect of the IoT world: well-defined slices (views) of the data represent valuable base information for different industrial sectors.

"Data is the new oil." (Humbly, 2006) We often meet similar statements. IoT-based data collection, data transmission, big data management, trusted cloud, and privacy issues are the main challenges of this area. Frameworks help companies and research groups to contribute to the IoT ecosystem as well as to the future design and to the development platforms. Based on the development results and ongoing project activities, we can state that SensorHUB is such kind of framework.

The *Model-driven Multi-Domain IoT* concept utilizes the advantages of the model-driven system development. Based on the advantages of the VMTS and SensorHUB frameworks, the *Model-driven Multi-Domain IoT* provides a unified toolchain for IoT-related application and service development.

We have discussed the motivation, the objectives, the application areas and the domains of SensorHUB framework and its extension to the *Model-driven Multi-Domain IoT* concept. Based on present industrial trends, requirements, and needs, a SensorHUB-based method and framework is a data monetization enabler. The framework supports the collection of various sensor data, enables the processing and analysis of data, and makes it possible to define different views on top of the data combined and compiled from different data sources. These data views and collections of datasets are referred to as monetized data for various purposes, for example, supporting decision making and running smart city services.

ACKNOWLEDGMENT

This work was supported by the János Bolyai Research Scholarship of the Hungarian Academy of Sciences.

REFERENCES

Apache Cassandra Database. (2016). Retrieved from http://cassandra.apache.org

Apache Flume. (2016). *Service for collecting, aggregating, and moving large amounts of log data*. Retrieved from https://flume.apache.org

Apache Hive Data Warehouse Platform. (2016). Retrieved from https://hive.apache.org

Apache Kafka. (2016). *Publish-subscribe messaging rethought*. Retrieved from http://kafka.apache.org

Apache Software Foundation. (2016). *Apache Hadoop*. Retrieved from http://hadoop.apache.org/

Apache Spark. (2016). *General engine for large-scale data processing*. Retrieved from https://spark.apache.org

Clifton, L., Clifton, D. A., Pimentel, M. A. F., Watkinson, P. J., & Tarassenko, L. (2014). Predictive Monitoring of Mobile Patients by Combining Clinical Observations With Data From Wearable Sensors. *Biomedical and Health Informatics. IEEE Journal*, *18*(3), 722–730.

Czarnecki, K., & Eisenecker, U. W. (2000). *Generative Programming: Methods, Tools, and Applications*. Addison-Wesley.

Docker. (2016). *Platform for distributed applications*. Retrieved from https://www.docker.com

EIT Climate-KIC. (2015). *Knowledge & Innovation Community*. Retrieved from http://www.climate-kic.org/

Fowler, M. (2010). *Domain-specific languages*. Addison-Wesley Professional.

Humbly, C. (2006). *Data is the New Oil, ANA Senior marketer's summit*. Kellogg School.

Kelly, S., & Tolvanen, J. P. (2008). *Domain Specific Modeling*. Wiley. doi:10.1002/9780470249260

Lengyel, Ekler, Ujj, Balogh, & Charaf. (2015). SensorHUB – An IoT Driver Framework for Supporting Sensor Networks and Data Analysis. *International Journal of Distributed Sensor Networks*.

Lengyel, L., Ekler, P., Ujj, T., Balogh, T., Charaf, H., Szalay, Zs., & Jereb, L. (2015). ICT in Road Vehicles – The VehicleICT Platform. *4th International Conference on Models and Technologies for Intelligent Transportation Systems*, 457-462. doi:10.1109/MTITS.2015.7223294

MQTT. (2016). *A machine-to-machine (M2M)/"Internet of Things" connectivity protocol*. Retrieved from http://mqtt.org

Pantelopoulos, A., & Bourbakis, N. G. (2010). A survey on wearable sensor-based systems for health monitoring and prognosis, IEEE Trans. *Systems, Man, and Cybernetics, Part C: Applications and Reviews*, *40*(1), 1–12. doi:10.1109/TSMCC.2009.2032660

Swagger. (2016). *RESTful API representation*. Retrieved from http://swagger.io

Swan, M. (2013). The Quantified Self: Fundamental Disruption in Big Data Science and Biological Discovery. *Big Data*, *1*(2), 85–99. doi:10.1089/big.2012.0002 PMID:27442063

The SensorHUB Project Website. (2015). Retrieved from https://www.aut.bme.hu/SensorHUB/

The SOLSUN Project Website. (2015). Retrieved from http://solsun.co.uk/index.php/SOLSUN/

The URBMOBI Project Website. (2015). Retrieved from http://www.climate-kic.org/case-studies/urban-resistance-to-the-effects-of-climate-change/

The VehicleICT Project Website. (2015). Retrieved from https://www.aut.bme.hu/VehicleICT/

The VMTS Project Website. (2015). Retrieved from https://www.aut.bme.hu/VMTS/

Thibodeau, P. (2014). *The ABCs of the Internet of Things*. Computerworld US. Retrieved from http://www.techworld.com/networking/abcs-of-internet-of-things-3516134/3/

Chapter 7
Internet of Things in E-Health:
An Application of Wearables in Prevention and Well-Being

Branka Rodić Trmčić
Medical College of Applied Studies in Belgrade, Serbia

Aleksandra Labus
University of Belgrade, Serbia

Svetlana Mitrović
Project Management College, Serbia

Vesna Buha
Project Management College, Serbia

Gordana Stanojević
Health Center Zvezdara, Serbia

ABSTRACT

The main task of Internet of Things in eHealth solutions is to collect data, connect people, things and processes. This provides a wealth of information that can be useful in decision-making, improving health and well-being. The aim of this study is to identify framework of sensors and application health services to detect sources of stress and stressors and make them visible to users. Also, we aim at extracting relationship between event and sensor data in order to improve health behavior. Evaluation of the proposed framework model will be performed. Model is based on Internet of Things in eHealth and is going to aim to improve health behavior. Following the established pattern of behavior realized through wearable system users will be proposed a preventive actions model. Further, it will examine the impact of changing health behavior on habits, condition and attitudes in relation to well-being and prevention.

DOI: 10.4018/978-1-5225-2437-3.ch007

INTRODUCTION

Despite numerous definitions of Health (Eysenbach, 2001; Dzenowagis, 2005; WHO, 2006; European Commission, 2015) all of them have in common that eHealth means not only technical development but also the change of the way of thinking, positive habits, networking in order to improve healthcare on local, regional and global level.

IoT is rapid innovation that leads to radical change of information delivery to users who often have limited time and energy to collect data and make them useful.

The market of mobile devices, smart phones and wearable devices has experienced astonishing growth. That is the main reason why they should be represented in the new technological solutions for the provision of health services. Distribution and availability of mobile and wearable computers to gather and monitor relevant vital health parameters during the everyday activities.

Some predictions says that the health care system of the future will be directed to the individual, personalization, participatory and precise (Raga Lavima & Subhramanya Sarma, 2015). The idea to perform constant monitoring of well-being is becoming increasingly popular. Measurements of human behavior and external factors that influence that behavior and condition of the body can be of valuable assistance in identifying stressors.

The subjects of this paper are concepts of Internet of Things in eHealth, wearable computing in different areas of well-being and technical and technological settings that are needed for IoT solution implementation. In this paper we present a model which consists of multidimensional framework of sensors and application of health services for stress detection and monitor sources that affect changes in health behavior and occurrence of stress.

BACKGROUND

Subjective well-being is the emotional and cognitive assessment of a person about his/her life, including happiness, contentment, peace, and life satisfaction.

The occurrence of stress in any population is a common predictor of other diseases and health disorders, including mental illnesses that are often difficult to detect and treat. The most common sources of the stress are changes in habits, short deadlines, separation from home, the social environment, long queues, etc. All of that can significantly affects the reduction of academic or work performance (Sohail, 2013).

Quality of life is not just the standard of living, material wealth, and income, employment. It is constant improving of mental and physical health, build a healthy environment, learning with recreation and rest. Promoting wellness, healthy lifestyles and their impact on health, encouraged people to participate in managing their health.

Vital signs, like heart rate, blood pressure, respiration, blood oxygen, GSR can be used to detect the presence of stress. These vital parameters can be measured and monitored with different type of wearable devices, sensors or accessories that are already included in mobile devices (such as compass, accelerometer, microphone, GPS, gyroscope, front and rear cameras, etc.). All the potentials of these devices gives them important feature, inherent to people - to feel. It is the feature that permits following the patterns of behavior of an individual in order to recognize the early signs of stress.

INTERNET OF THINGS AND eHEALTH

According to European commission definition (European Commission, 2015) electronic health (eHealth) refers to tools and services using information and communication technologies (ICTs) that can improve prevention, diagnosis, treatment, monitoring and management.

Mobile health, as subset of eHealth has huge potential to establish better health communication, promotion of healthy lifestyles, facilitate decision-making processes for health workers and also for patients.

Internet of things is a network of physical objects connected via wireless or wired Internet network. It incorporates sensor technology that allows interaction with the internal state of the smart object, or with the external environment. For years, experts have predicted that the Internet of Things - a system with objects communicating with each other or with other devices – will transform a way of life (Lopez Research, 2013). The IoT has a variety of application domains, including health care and its redesigning modern health care with promising technological, economic, and social prospects (Islam, Kwak, Kabir, Hossain, & Kwak, 2015).

Recently there has been increased interest in wearable medical devices, as well as in research and in health activities (fitness, wellness, equipment for people with special needs, stress management and others) (Ranck, 2012). According to Cisco, by 2020, the connected devices will be 6.5 times more than people on earth (Evans, 2011).

THE EMERGENCE OF EHEALTH APPLICATIONS OF WEARABLES

Lately, it has been evident that a huge number of people takes care of their health and wellness. Promotion of healthy lifestyles, as well as their impact on health has encouraged people to participate in their own health management, regardless of their current health condition.

The human body signs (e.g. heart rate, blood pressure, respiration, blood oxygen, ECG, EEG, etc.) can be collected by sensors and devices and then transmitted to the devices (e.g. mobile, computer), classified and transferred to health management systems, doctors ambulances, research institutions, health analysts and so on. Mobile and wearable devices have enabled people to continually record daily life activities. Professionals or amateurs engaged in running, swimming, walking, etc., regardless of age, sex and health condition can measure and monitor vital health parameters (like speed, calorie consumption, heart rate, blood pressure, etc.). Walkers and runners can wear wearables devices on their wrist, upper arm, on the head or in the pocket. At the same places they can be used by people who are sitting, resting or doing their everyday activities on the work.

Besides monitoring through self-report applications and social networks, a large number of applications use sensors to enable passive monitoring physiological responses, movement or change of residence. An example is Jawbone UP, necklace that monitors and feel activities and bracelet that monitors physical condition. They send the result of measurement as the sum of exercise, nutrition and sleep. Systems such as Sonamba for Wellbeing monitoring (pomdevices, LLC, 2015), BreathResearch, Numera Libris i Libris+ use sensors for activity detection, respiration, behavior and monitoring of vital health parameters. The sensors that monitor posture program aimed to reduce back pain in people who spend a long time in a seated position, are also important and can be a part of intervention for the pain reduction (Morris & Aguilera, 2012). Psychological well-being through IoT and eHealth apps can provide great support via a sensor that measures and analyses the breathing such as Spire (Spire, 2015) and Muse (Interaxon Inc, 2015), headband that use brain-sensing technology to monitor brain activity during resting or various activities. According to brain activity it's able to transform signals into music.

The entire set of data that are collected provides insight into the state of one's health. Monitoring of the vital parameters and providing motivation to achieve bigger and better results (implementation of diet therapy, better results in fitness, maintaining a pulse in the range of recommended values, etc.) has big impact in successful implementation of prevention and will-being activities. Comparing and analyzing different type of collected data is very important because it can influence changes in health behavior, stress management and perform other health activities in all spheres of human life.

SOLUTIONS AND RECOMMENDATIONS

This paper will propose the framework of sensor through dimensions of wellness. Wellness is presented through seven dimensions and each individual will be the single base for Internet of Things detection and reduction stress solution. Dimensions through which it will be designed are: the social dimension, the professional dimension, the physical dimension, the emotional dimension, the intellectual dimension, the environment and a spiritual dimension. To support the proposed model we will implement an eHealth application with main health services and development a prototype of a wearable system for detection and measurement of stress level and promote healthy lifestyles among the users. The study will be designed in several phases:

Phase One: Definition of sensor framework for each dimension of wellness.
Phase Two: Developing mHealth application with main health services and development a prototype of a wearable system.
Phase Three: Integration of mHealth application with wearable system.
Phase Four: Testing and evaluation of developed model among university students.

FUTURE RESEARCH DIRECTIONS

In this paper authors propose a framework of sensors according to the dimensions of wellness. Although many predictors and stressors have been covered the list of sensors can be expanded. Future research should focus on implementing solutions not only for detecting the stressors but for providing the solutions for stress reduction. Since every individual has different manifestations in stressful situations and reacts differently, it is necessary in future steps to consider customization and personalization of such solutions.

CONCLUSION

The solution proposed in this paper can be successfully applied to many population groups and implemented through various environmental activities. In addition to the sensors implemented in this paper it is possible to implement the wearable system according to the proposed model framework by the dimensions of wellness with many different sensor nodes. The contribution of this work is in proposed model that is shaping future users well-being as they adopt healthy behavioral changes. Also the implementation of sensor framework with analyzing stressors and their interaction with contextual data will contribute to prevent the emergence of stress.

REFERENCES

Dzenowagis, J. (2005). *Connecting for Health. Global Vision, Local Insight.* Geneva: World Health Organization.

European Commission. (2015). *Policy*. Retrieved December 27, 2014, from http://ec.europa.eu/health/ehealth/policy/

Evans, D. (2011). *The Internet of Things. How the Next Evolution of the Internet Is Changing Everything*. San Jose, CA: Cisco.

Eysenbach, G. (2001). What is e-health? *Journal of Medical Internet Research*, *3*(2), 20. doi:10.2196/jmir.3.2.e20 PMID:11720962

Interaxon Inc. (2015). *Muse, the brain sensing headband*. Retrieved November 16, 2015, from http://www.choosemuse.com/

Islam, R., Kwak, D., Kabir, H., Hossain, M., & Kwak, K.-S. (2015). The Internet of Things for Health Care: A Comprehensive Survey. *IEEE Access*, *3*, 678–708. doi:10.1109/ACCESS.2015.2437951

Lopez Research. (2013). *An Introduction to the Internet of Things (IoT). Part 1. of "The IoT Series"*. San Francisco: Lopez Research.

Morris, M., & Aguilera, A. (2012). Mobile, Social, and Wearable Computing and the Evolution of Psychological Practice. *Professional Psychology, Research and Practice*, *43*(6), 622–626. doi:10.1037/a0029041 PMID:25587207

Pomdevices, LLC. (2015). *Sonamba, Medical Alert System*. Retrieved November 15, 2015, from http://sonamba.com/

Raga Lavima, P., & Subhramanya Sarma, G. (2015). Aa IoT based intelligent medicine box. *International Journal of Computer Science and Mobile Computing*, *4*(10), 186–191.

Ranck, J. (2012). *The wearable computing market: a global analysis*. San Francisco: GigaomPRO.

Sohail, N. (2013). Stress and Academic Performance Among Medical Students. *Journal of the College of Physicians and Surgeons--Pakistan*, *23*(1), 67–71. PMID:23286627

Spire. (2015). Retrieved November 15, 2015, from https://www.spire.io/

WHO. (2006). *Building foundations for eHealth: progress of Member States: report of the WHO Global Observatory for eHealth*. Geneva: World Health Organization. Retrieved December 27, 2014, from http://whqlibdoc.who.int/publications/2006/9241563354_eng.pdf

Chapter 8

IoT and Cloud Computing:
The Architecture of Microcloud–Based IoT Infrastructure Management System

Oleksandr Rolik
National Technical University of Ukraine "Igor Sikorsky Kyiv Polytechnic Institute", Ukraine

Sergii Telenyk
National Technical University of Ukraine "Igor Sikorsky Kyiv Polytechnic Institute", Ukraine & Cracow University of Technology, Poland

Eduard Zharikov
National Technical University of Ukraine "Igor Sikorsky Kyiv Polytechnic Institute", Ukraine

ABSTRACT

The Internet of Things (IoT) is an emerging technology that offers great opportunities that is designed to improve the quality of consumers' lives, and also to improve economic indicators and productivity of enterprises, and more efficient use of resources. IoT system refers to the use of interconnected devices and distributed subsystems to leverage data gathered by sensors and actuators in some sort of environment and to take a proper decision on a high level. In this chapter, the authors propose an approach to Microcloud-based IoT infrastructure management to provide the desired quality of IT services with rational use of IT resources. Efficiency of IT infrastructure management can be estimated by the quality of services and the management costs. The task of operational service quality management is to maintain a given level of service quality with the use of minimum IT resources amount in IoT environment. Then, the maximum efficiency can be achieved by selecting such control when actual level of service corresponds to the coordinated with business

DOI: 10.4018/978-1-5225-2437-3.ch008

unit and can be achieved by minimal costs. The proposed approach allows the efficient use of resources for IT services provision in IoT ecosystem through the implementation of service level coordination, resource planning and service level management processes in an integrated IT infrastructure management system based on hyperconvergence and software-defined principles. The main goals of this chapter are to investigate the state of art of the IoT applications resource demands in the context of datacenter architecture deployment and to propose Microcloud-based IoT infrastructure resource control method.

INTRODUCTION

The IoT is considered as a widely distributed and locally intelligent network of smart objects. The IoT enables many new enhancements to fundamental services such as city administration, education, healthcare, public safety, real estate, transportation and other sectors. Business success greatly depends on the IT-services quality. It makes the scientific and applied problem of development IoT infrastructure management concept important.

According to IEEE P2413 project, architecture of IoT has three main layers: Applications, Networking and Data communication, Sensing. In each layer there are many devices and protocols that interconnect through layers to deliver definite services according to specific domain. In this paper we consider the technologies that make the functioning of the Application and the Data communication layer possible.

At the same time, IT infrastructure ensures the functioning of the Application layer, and complex of low-level design and management systems ensures the functioning of Sensing layer.

The increase in business demand for IT services in the IoT area and the emergence of new services lead to the need of developing and implementing new approaches to the IT infrastructure management.

Modern IT infrastructure management systems are complex and are integrating solutions from different manufacturers. The increasing complexity of IT management is accompanied by the growth in the cost of operations. The main task of IoT infrastructure management is to maintain a coordinated level of IT services with the rational use of IT infrastructure resources in terms of virtualization, clustering, distribution and increasing the amount of user requests.

In this paper, the authors provide an overview of the vision, architecture, and benefits of the proposed IoT infrastructure management system based on the Microcloud concept.

Thus, the authors' objectives in this chapter are: 1) to analyze existing IoT solutions, 2) to analyze the use of Cloud in the IoT applications, 3) to develop an approach to service quality management in the IoT systems, and 4) to analyse the technologies that will enable developed solution.

BACKGROUND

The IoT facilitates new possibilities in many industries and creates additional load on the datacenter due to the additional number of devices being placed into the network and enormous increasing demand of data exchange and processing. IoT turns out to be much more complex than just deploying new applications, connecting more computers, mobile devices and sensors to the network.

Given the current challenges, which are created by the IoT spreading, enterprises will need to take into account relevant technology deployments and implement internal change management to be ready to the IoT load.

The Internet of Things is defined by IoT European Research Cluster (IERC) as a dynamic global network infrastructure with self-configuring capabilities based on standard and interoperable communication protocols where physical and virtual "things" have identities, physical attributes and virtual personalities, use intelligent interfaces, and are seamlessly integrated into the information network (Sundmaeker, Guillemin, Friess, & Woelfflé, 2010).

Many emergent IoT applications will be delivered on-demand through a cloud environment. Thereby, the need to employ new adequate datacenter technologies arises. They would offer high productivity, reliability and elasticity in a scalable fashion.

A significant scientific effort in the field of IoT is devoted to the Smart Environments class systems, such as the Smart Home, Smart City, Smart Office, Smart Energy & Fuel, Smart Health, environment monitoring and others. IoT evolution in this direction is very intense (Al-Fuqaha, Guizani, Mohammadi, Aledhari, & Ayyash, 2015).

The most intensively developing ecosystem is Machine-to-Machine (M2M) which services process huge amounts of data obtained from sensors (Beecham Research, 2011). Data from sensors needs to be transferred to the respective applications in compliance with security policies and priorities. In this case, cloud IoT services use stored data to perform analysis for decision-making to improve business performance. By 2020, the number of IoT objects worldwide could reach 212 billion. And by 2022 the traffic M2M services could reach 45% of all traffic on the Internet (Gantz & Reinsel, 2012).

External impacts from IoT are creating new demands to the data center. By 2020, Gartner predicts that 25 billion devices will be connected to the Internet, creating greater external demand for storage and communication with the data center.

In its documents, the European Telecommunications Standards Institute (ETSI) focuses on the M2M concept instead of using the word "Internet of Things". ETSI defines M2M as communication between two or more entities that do not necessarily need any direct human intervention. M2M services intend to automate decision and communication processes (ETSI Technical Specification, 2010).

According to Forrester (Belissent, 2010), a smart environment uses information and communications technologies to make the critical infrastructure components and services of a city administration, education, healthcare, public safety, real estate, transportation and utilities more aware, interactive and efficient.

Significant business decisions have been taken by industry leaders like IBM, Intel, Microsoft, Cisco, Google, Apple and Samsung to develop technologies and services for the IoT landscape. The EU has also invested in supporting researches and innovations in the field of IoT in different service sectors and application groups.

Telecom operators also consider that IoT and M2M are becoming a core business focus. A significant growth of connected devices and sensors is reported in their networks. Manufacturers of wearable devices anticipate a full new business segment towards a wider adoption of the IoT.

Consider the examples of the commercialization of the IoT cloud services models by leading IT companies over the globe.

IBM

IBM Watson Internet of Things Platform is a fully managed, cloud-hosted service that makes it simple to derive value from IoT devices. IBM start with client's device, be it a sensor, a gateway or something else. Using recommendations client can get it connected and start sending data securely up to the cloud using the open, lightweight MQTT messaging protocol. From there, client can setup and manage devices using online dashboard or secure APIs from IBM, so that client's applications can access live and historical data fast. Next, client start creating applications using data obtained from devices within IBM Bluemix platform, another cloud or client's servers (IBM, 2017).

Microsoft

Microsoft within Azure IoT Suite propose to create value while leveraging client's existing technology assets. Azure IoT Suite can enable client to capture and analyze untapped device data to improve results across client's business. With the Azure IoT

Suite, client can quickly get started and scale client's IoT project business needs. The Azure IoT Suite is designed to integrate with client's existing processes, devices, and systems to automate common workflows and unlock new value by making the best use of both existing and new data sources. Client of Azure IoT Suite can connect people, processes, assets, and systems to create opportunities to innovate and transform business (Microsoft, 2017).

Cisco

The IoT links smart objects to the Internet. Cisco estimates the IoT will consist of 50 billion devices connected to the Internet by 2020. Cisco's IoT System enhances productivity, creates new business models, and generates new revenue streams. It can enable an exchange of data never available before, and bring client's information in a more secure way. With the Cisco IoT System client can connect, manage, and control previously unconnected devices. Cisco's IoT infrastructure technologies and products give to client deeper insights with analytics on IoT data, better secure physical and digital assets, innovate by creating and deploying IoT applications from fog to cloud. The Cisco IoT offers industry-specific solutions that improve productivity, efficiency, mobility, and revenue in multiple industries, such as manufacturing, utilities, oil and gas, smart cities, transportation, and mining (Cisco, 2017).

Intel

Intel helps connect things to the cloud, integrate with existing infrastructure, and securely manage data. The Intel IoT Platform is an end-to-end reference model and family of products from Intel, that works with third party solutions to provide a foundation for seamlessly and securely connecting devices, delivering trusted data to the cloud, and delivering value with security, interoperability, scalability, manageability, and analytics (Intel, 2017).

Google

Google Cloud Platform gives to client the tools to scale connections, gather and make sense of data, and provide the reliable customer experiences that hardware devices require. Google's network infrastructure can sustain potentially millions of concurrent connections across a global user base. Google's backbone network has thousands of miles of fiber optic cables, uses advanced software-defined networking and has edge caching services to deliver fast, consistent and scalable performance. Google has also announced Brillo, an Android-based embedded operating system platform aimed to be used with low-power and memory constrained IoT devices. Many client's small devices are still capable of producing very large volumes of data. Google Cloud Platform is building a best in class suite of big data tools. Google also propose very flexible scheme "Pay for what you use" to adopt to client's needs (Google, 2017).

IoTivity

The IoTivity project was created to bring together the open source community to accelerate the development of the IoT ecosystem, framework and services required to connect billions of devices that they can connect securely and reliably to the Internet and to each other. The IoTivity project is sponsored by the Open Interconnect Consortium (OIC) and hosted by the Linux Foundation. IoTivity project propose many features such as: Discovery & Connectivity, Resource Management, Virtual (Soft) Sensor Manager, Protocol Plugin Manager, Things Manager, Resource Hosting service, Resource Directory, Smart Home Protocol Control Manager (IoTivity, 2017).

Apple HomeKit

HomeKit is an Apple's framework for communicating with and controlling connected accessories in a user's home. High-level device connectivity framework enables apps to interact with physical accessories in the home area providing Smart Home functionality. HomeKit Catalog demonstrates how to use the HomeKit framework for interacting with objects and performing common tasks such as: creating homes, pairing with and controlling accessories, and setting up triggers to automate actions (Apple, 2017).

Samsung SmartThings and ARTIK

SmartThings is an open platform for smart homes and the consumer Internet of Things. SmartThings is proposed by Samsung and includes an array of products such as home monitoring kit, hubs, outlets, motion sensors, multipurpose sensors, security and much more. At the center of SmartThings technology is a hub (IoT gateway) which ties together more than 200 IoT devices and products that can be controlled from a phone or tablet apps. The SmartThings Open Cloud is a cloud service based on Samsung Architecture for Multimodal Interactions (SAMI) data exchange platform and provides developers and device-makers with ready-made infrastructure for authentication, connectivity, data sharing, and security (Samsung, 2017a).

ARTIK is an open platform used in some of Samsung's consumer products. The platform will be available in three different sizes (ARTIK 1, ARTIK 5, and ARTIK 10) to fit a variety of different devices and use cases. It ships as a complete package with a processor and on-board memory, as well as integrated software and embedded hardware security technology. Samsung ARTIK 1 is the smallest IoT module form-factor available on the market, measuring just 12mm x 12mm. It interconnects using Bluetooth low energy technology, and is designed to be used in things like smart bands and activity trackers. It packs a 250MHz dual-core processor, 9-axis motion sensor, and 4MB of flash memory. Samsung's ARTIK modules can be programmed using the Arduino IDE and also come with Samsung's Secure Element, a cryptographic hardware security mechanism designed to prevent unauthorized access (Samsung, 2017b).

The considered IoT services and platforms are providing an API and open protocols to create and deploy various types of applications using common technologies (Java, Node.js, PHP, ASP.NET, Python, Ruby Sinatra and others.). Many IoT market players also provide PaaS cloud platform with dynamically additional resources allocation for critical applications, with fault tolerance and scheduler optimization based on QoS and SLA parameters in real time.

Many IoT platforms are being deployed in the cloud now, and this allows to improve the IoT properties such as availability, reliability and elasticity. Enabling technologies and application services for cloud computing and IoT integration are presented in (Gubbi, Buyya, Marusic, & Palaniswami, 2013). The authors of Botta, De Donato, Persico, and Pescapé (2014) analyze the integration of cloud computing and IoT and propose the Cloud IoT paradigm. The potential of IoT and cloud computing technologies for addressing the issues of advanced manufacturing systems is investigated, and the architecture of a cloud computing and IoT-based cloud manufacturing service system is proposed in (Tao, Cheng, Da Xu, Zhang, & Li, 2014). The key issues of IoT and cloud computing integration, such as increasing number of heterogeneous devices connected to IoT, power and bandwidth constrains along with their respective potential solutions, have been discussed in (Aazam, Khan, Alsaffar, & Huh, 2014).

Many IoT applications require location awareness, low latency, mobility support while the data need to be processed in real-time. In this case a Micro clouds or Fog computing enables new data management applications and analytics services and extends the Cloud Computing paradigm and Content Delivery Network approach to the edge of the network providing data, compute, storage, and application services to end-users (Vermesan & Friess, 2014).

Number of IoT services provided to users are growing very quickly, as well as their size. Many services are working non-stop. It also leads to an increase in volumes of stored and processed data.

One of the necessary conditions to be met by the data center architecture for IoT applications and systems is incremental deployment and inter cluster networking. We propose to use hyperconverged systems in design and implementation of Microcloud-based data centers for IoT applications.

IoT SYSTEM MODEL

Many city scale or region IoT systems may encompass part of the country, the whole country or several countries. It is recommended that such scale IoT systems are built on the basis of Cloud in conjunction with Microcloud concepts. This kind of city-scale systems include, for example, parking automation systems, road traffic monitoring systems, traffic management, security surveillance cameras, public transport management, smart public transport, etc. In this case Micro cloud may cover an administrative district of the city or part of the territory of an administrative district when one administrative area will be covered by several Micro clouds. To solve such tasks for large-scale IoT systems the authors propose Microcloud-based IoT architecture.

In addition to the vertical interaction between Cloud and Micro cloud, horizontal interaction Micro cloud - Micro cloud is proposed in the following cases:

- When it is necessary to provide low latency.
- When local Micro cloud data are used by another Micro cloud and in case of local control.
- Micro cloud mobility.
- A very large number of end nodes (sensors) to reduce global traffic.
- When one uses distributed real-time applications that require data sharing and management of multiple Micro clouds.

Generalized system model of the proposed Microcloud-based IoT architecture is shown in Figure 1.

Possible ways of communication and information exchange between Cloud and N Micro clouds are shown in Figure 2.

The interaction of the sensors and actuators within the n-th Micro cloud service Mn, $n = \overline{1, N}$, where N is the amount of Micro clouds in an IoT system, with the possibility of Cloud and other Micro clouds to be carried out through the IP-backbone or using direct data exchange between Micro clouds and within Micro clouds. A direct interaction between Micro clouds and within Micro clouds can be carried out using protocols Wi-Fi, 3G, 4G, LTE, IEEE 802.15.4, Sensor-Net, WiMAX, Ultra-Wide Band (UWB), ZigBee, Bluetooth, 6LoWPAN.

Figure 1. Generalized system model of the proposed Microcloud-based IoT architecture

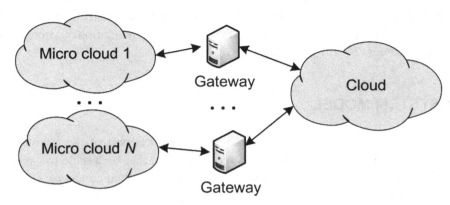

Figure 2. Possible ways of communication and information exchange between Cloud and Micro clouds in the proposed architecture

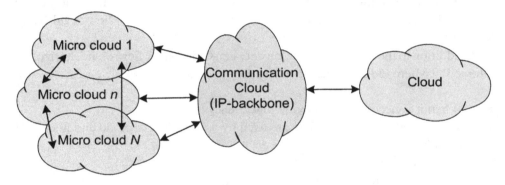

The structure of the n-th separate Micro cloud M_n, $n = \overline{1, N}$ is shown in Figure 3.

As it is evident from Figure 3 Micro cloud M_n, $n = \overline{1, N}$ contains its own local Server or Virtual Machine (VM) V_n, and Local Storage X_n, $k = \overline{1, N}$.

The interaction between the elements of the Micro cloud is implemented on the self-organization ad-hoc network principles designed and functioning according to green networking technology. Moreover, all the devices from the Micro cloud must meet the requirement to be online and ready to collaborate without further delay. Each Micro cloud can contain (or cannot contain) one or more local Servers or VMs and a local Storage. In case of local Server, VM or Storage absence in some Micro cloud computing and storage tasks are performed by servers and storages,

Figure 3. The structure and interconnection of n-th Micro cloud M_n and Cloud

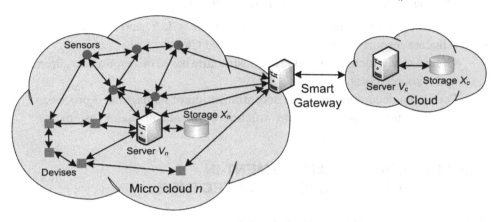

which are located in neighboring Micro clouds or by servers and storages of Cloud as shown in Figure 4.

Local servers in cooperation with one or more servers in the Cloud, as well as local storages, provide functioning of distributed applications. Distributed applications implement service S_m, $m = \overline{1, M}$, where M – the number of services in the IoT system based on Microcloud architecture.

This raises the need to solve the following problems:

Figure 4. The interaction of local servers and storage systems between Micro cloud and Cloud

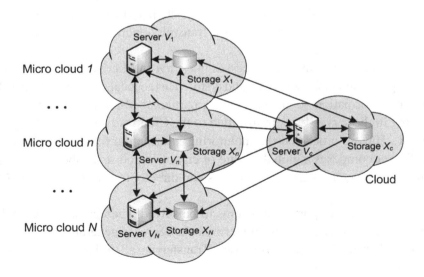

- Optimal tasks assigning between Micro cloud M_n, $n = \overline{1, N}$ and Cloud.
- Allocate functions among Micro cloud M_n, $n = \overline{1, N}$ and Cloud.
- Allocate resources among Micro cloud and Cloud.
- Optimize Microcloud-based IoT infrastructure based on resource requirements and resource costs.
- Perform a decomposition and decentralization of management processes.
- Development of principles and structure of the management system.

SERVICE QUALITY MANAGEMENT IN MICROCLOUD-BASED IOT ARCHITECTURE

Development of IoT System Based on Microcloud-Based IoT Architecture

Metropolitan scale IoT systems can be divided into two broad classes:

- Monitoring systems.
- Monitoring and management systems.

Monitoring systems include the urban systems such as road traffic monitoring systems, security surveillance cameras, firefighting and emergency, environmental and microclimate monitoring systems, workplace and home support. Monitoring and management systems are urban systems such as parking automation systems, public transport management, healthcare service, food supply chain.

The structure of the Microcloud-based IoT system performing global monitoring on the city scale, and the information flow transmission in such a system are shown in Figure 5.

Figure 5 shows information processes in each n-th Micro cloud. Data from the sensors is processed in the server V_n, and is stored in the local storage X_n. Generalized monitoring information about sensors of a particular Micro cloud, obtained after processing in the server V_n, is transmitted to the Cloud server V_c and to the Cloud storage X_c. Having processed the monitoring information from all Micro clouds, Cloud Server composes a global picture of city or region scale about the status of monitored parameters. Part of the sensors can directly transmit data to the Cloud server V_c.

One of the most important problems to be solved when creating Microcloud-based IoT monitoring systems, is to determine the degree of generality of information transmitted from the Micro cloud to Cloud. Transferring all the information extracted

Figure 5. The structure of the global monitoring system in proposed Microcloud-based IoT architecture

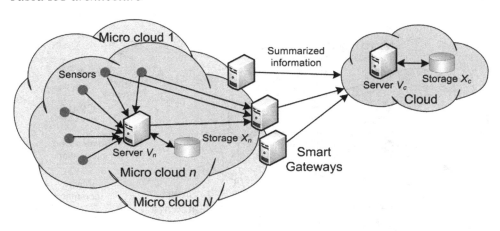

from the sensor without Micro cloud server preprocessing can cause excessive congestion of communication channels. A greater degree of generalization after processing in a local Micro cloud server leads to reduction of transmitted to the Cloud data volumes. However, the reduction of data redundancy may curtail the accuracy of the global monitoring. Data pretreatment in a Micro cloud server increases the delay in obtaining data in Cloud server.

The structure of the Microcloud-based IoT system that performs global monitoring and local control in Micro cloud coverage area is shown in Figure 6.

In global monitoring and local control processes of Microcloud-based IoT system, shown in Figure 6, each Micro cloud collects and pre-processes monitoring data coming from the sensors located in the Micro cloud area. Generalized information of the Micro cloud is transmitted to the Cloud server. Cloud server processes the data from all the Micro clouds and generates macro commands or management policy. Macro command or management policy are transmitted to Micro clouds; and corresponding Micro cloud servers generate control commands for local Micro cloud devices. In some cases, Cloud server V_c can generate control commands to Micro cloud devices directly.

Applying of the Decomposing-Compensating Approach in the Service Quality Management in Microcloud-Based IoT System

Problem solving in IoT systems based on the Microcloud architecture requires computing and storage resources. Micro cloud and Cloud both have these resources. Micro cloud resources usually are limited, so there is a problem of the development

Figure 6. Interaction of local servers and storage systems in the Microcloud-based IoT system

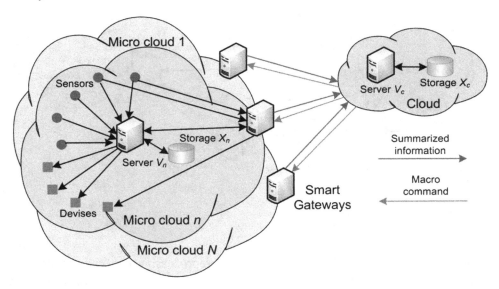

of task allocation methods between the Micro cloud and Cloud for the efficient resources use.

To solve such problems in the management of corporate IT infrastructures in the Rolik (2013a) decomposing-compensation approach is proposed. Decomposing-compensation approach can be adapted for solving resource allocation problems in Microcloud-based IoT system as follows.

To ensure the profitability of companies operating in the field of IoT, it is essential for them to receive the set $\mathfrak{S} = \{s_i\}$, $i = \overline{1, K}$ IoT necessary services of the highest quality $\mathfrak{Q}$ and at the minimum cost, $\mathfrak{C}$.

Service Level Management in the Microcloud-based IoT system is proposed to be carried out by integrated interaction of three processes: the service level coordination, resource planning level and service level management level as shown in Figure 7.

The service level coordination process is started at the initiative of IoT business managers or IoT service customers and ends up with the creation or updating of the elements of $\mathfrak{S}$ set, and the $Q = \|q_{ki}\|$ matrix. Element q_{ki}, $k = \overline{1, L_i}$, $i = \overline{1, K}$, corresponds to the k-th quality indicator of i-th service. Total number of resources r in Micro cloud and Cloud is allocated for the operation of the set of services $\mathfrak{S}$. The obtained resource set to support IoT as a system $< Q, r >$ is the basis for solving the problems on the lower layer.

Figure 7. Processes interaction in the service level management of the Microcloud-based IoT architecture

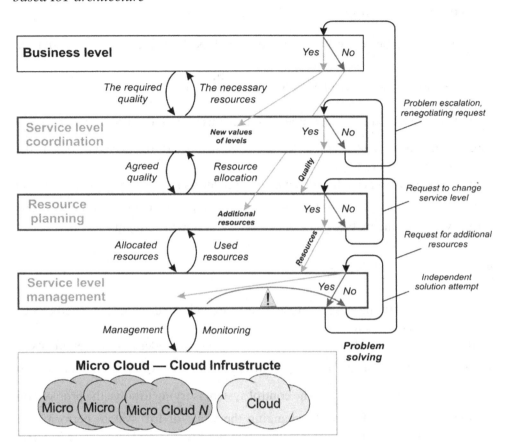

The resource planning process consists of the allocation and consolidation on each service s_i, $i = \overline{1, K}$, part of the Micro cloud and Cloud resources from the resource pool $R_1,...,R_m$, allocated for service maintenance. The volume or number $r_1,...,r_m$, of resources $R_1,...,R_m$ are defined as follows respectively:

$$r_j = \sum_1^N r_j^{(M_n)} + r_j^{M_c},$$

where $r_1^{(M_n)},...,r_m^{(M_n)}$ - resource amount allocated to the R_j, $j = \overline{1, m}$ in Micro cloud M_n, $r_j^{M_c}$ - resource amount R_j, $j = \overline{1, m}$, allocated in the Cloud. Unit of j-th resource

211

has cost c_j. In this case $c_j^{M_n}$ - the cost of j-th resource unit in Micro cloud M_n, and $c_j^{M_c}$ - the cost of j-th resource unit in Cloud.

Then the number of resources is computed as the value $r = \sum\limits_{j=1}^{m} r_j$, and the resource cost c is determined as follows $A = \sum\limits_{j=1}^{m} r_j \cdot c_j$.

The matrix $\mathrm{P} = \left\| \rho_{ij} \right\|$ determines resources used by the services, where ρ_{ij} is equal to the quantity of resource R_j, $j = \overline{1, m}$ dedicated for service s_i, or 0 if the resource is not required.

The process of service level management controls IoT system so that the actual values q_{ki}^*, $k = \overline{1, L_i}$, $i = \overline{1, K}$, of service quality indicators correspond to the agreed values of the matrix Q, i.e. to satisfy the following equality

$$q_{ki} - q_{ki}^* = 0, \forall k = \overline{1, M_i}, i = \overline{1, K}.$$

The essence of the proposed method of service quality management in Microcloud-based IoT system is as follows.

In case of non-compliance of condition (1) the system identifies the elements of the matrix of actual values of quality indicators $Q^* = \left\| q_{ki}^* \right\|$, for which $q_{ki}^* < q_{ki}$, $\forall k = \overline{1, L_i}, i = \overline{1, K}$. The control system is trying to solve the problem on the lower level (see. Figure 7), changing the value of IoT system performance parameters or reallocating resources between the Micro cloud and Cloud in order to increase the value q_{ki}^*.

If IoT system is able to ensure the condition (1) after the remedial actions, the functioning of the IoT system continues with the new settings. If authority of the lower level is not enough to achieve condition (1), problem solving is carried out at the level of resource planning.

The resource planning process is trying to solve the problem by using the following mechanisms:

- Allocation to the Micro cloud or Cloud of additional resources $R_1, ..., R_m$ for service s_i, for which the condition $q_{ki}^* < q_{ki}$ is true. A particular Micro cloud or Cloud with overloaded resources involved for providing the service s_i is localized. Resource shortage was the reason for reducing the quality of service s_i. If an additional amount of resources may be allocated in a specific

Micro cloud or Cloud, the matrix $P' = \left\| \rho'_{ij} \right\|$ is formed with the new values $\rho'_{ij} > \rho_{ij}$, $j = \overline{1,m}$, or 0, if the j-th resource is not required. An additional resource will be allocated in Micro cloud and Cloud to maintain s_i services.

- If additional resources in the Micro cloud, that has a problem, are not available, the resource planning level attempts to allocate additional resources in other Micro clouds and redirect part of the IoT management tasks to them. Resource planning level transmits monitoring data to other Micro clouds for processing, as there are no enough resources for processing in the Micro cloud with a problem.

- If it is impossible to use available resources in other Micro clouds, the resource planning level attempts to allocate additional resources in the Cloud.

- Sometimes it is impossible to allocate additional resources in the Cloud. This is either because of high cost of additional resources, that is unlikely, or due to the fact that the corporate computing center of IoT system holder is used as a Cloud and thus Cloud resources are usually limited. If Cloud does not have enough resources to allocate to Micro cloud tasks, which happens very often, the resource planning level is trying to produce a resource reallocation between services, giving more resources for essential services instead of less important ones. If the problem is solved, then the matrix $P' = \left\| \rho'_{ij} \right\|$ with new resource consolidation plan comes to the level of service management.

- If the problem can not be solved at the resource planning level, then the problem is escalated to a higher level of service level coordination.

It should be noted that in case of lack of resources in some Micro clouds, resources of the Cloud or other Micro clouds are utilized, thus it is necessary to reallocate roles and tasks in the Microcloud-based infrastructure. However, this can lead to worsening the service quality of the Micro cloud subsystem and IoT system as a whole. It is possible to reallocate tasks in Micro cloud, when a part of high-priority tasks are performed with high quality, and other tasks are performed with low quality or maintain its functionality with minimum acceptable quality.

The process of service level coordination at the initiative of resource planning level reviews values q_{ki}, for which $q^*_{ki} < q_{ki}$, and then, perhaps, values of all elements q_{ki} $k = \overline{1, L_i}$, $i = \overline{1, K}$, in quality services matrix Q in decreasing direction. If it is possible to form a matrix $Q' = \left\| q'_{ki} \right\|$ with the new values of service quality indicators, then matrix Q is transferred to the lower level, where release of resources is produced and additional resources are allocated for services, which satisfy the condition $q^*_{ki} < q_{ki}$, $k = \overline{1, L_i}$, $i = \overline{1, K}$. If the process of service level coordination does not have authority to form a new matrix $Q' = \left\| q'_{ki} \right\|$, then problem is escalated to the level of business decision that must either generate a matrix $Q' = \left\| q'_{ki} \right\|$ with the new values, or increase the total amount of resources, which leads to an increase of the values of $r_1, ..., r_m$.

The processes running at the service level coordination, resource planning level and service management level are described in Rolik (2013a).

ALLOCATION OF CONTROL FUNCTIONS IN MICROCLOUD-BASED IOT ARCHITECTURE

A Two-Tier Management System Model for Microcloud-Based IoT Architecture

Due to the fact that the current research on control theory is focused on the multi-site fact, distribution, large dimension problems, there is a need to highlight a special class of multi-site distributed management systems, which include control systems for Microcloud-based IoT architecture. One of the major issues addressed in the design and operation of such hierarchical control systems, in addition to the development of architecture, is the decision-making problem.

The complexity of decision-making process in hierarchical control systems is caused by the fact that decisions are made on most levels of management hierarchy, besides the time for decision-making being limited. In Rolik (2013b) it is proposed to consider such systems as two-tier management systems with a coordinator (Mesarovic, Macko, &Takahara, 1970).

The basis for singling out two levels in the control system is that the service level management system in the Microcloud-based IoT architecture functions in different modes in case of uncertainty, incomplete and unreliable information, the presence of risk factors, different conflicting criteria and objectives of management subsystems.

It is very difficult to achieve the optimum operation of the system, built on the Microcloud-based IoT architecture, with such control systems. Control systems in Microcloud-based IoT architecture are necessary for improving the quality metrics of IoT system. In such cases, the development of two-level systems with the coordinator are proposed in Mesarovic et al. (1970). Rolik (2013b), when the coordinator coordinate its own decisions and management actions of subsystems to improve Microcloud-based IoT system as a whole in terms of quality of services provided.

At the same time coordinator decisions should be directed at improving the global quality function of services and decision-making is carried out under uncertainty.

Figure 8 shows the structure of the control system, which manages service level in the Micro cloud-based IoT architecture in the form of a two-tier system with a coordinator (Mesarovic et al., 1970; Rolik, 2013b).

The location of control subsystems (CS) shows the hierarchical structure of the control system model. The model consists of the Coordinator as an upstream control subsystem (CS_0) and $N+1$ downstream control subsystems ($CS_1,...,CS_N,CS_C$), which directly control the process P that occurs in Micro cloud-based IoT infrastructure. Vertical interaction between CSs is as follows.

Commands, signals, feedback or interventions (inputs) $\gamma_1,...,\gamma_N,\gamma_C$, transmitted from the CS_0 to $CS_1,...,CS_N,CS_C$ are coordinating ones. The commands or impacts (inputs) $(u_1,...,u_N,u_C)$ from the $CS_1,...,CS_N,CS_C$ to process P are controlling ones. Feedback signals or data signals $v_1,...,v_N,v_C$ and $\beta_1,...,\beta_N,\beta_C$ come from bottom to top. Two-level control system can be described by the terminal variables (inputs and outputs). In this case, the CSs are described as functional subsystems, the outputs of which are uniquely determined by the inputs (Mesarovic et al., 1970).

Process P can be described as a controlled subsystem, which is affected by the control signals u from the $CS_1,...,CS_N,CS_C$, $u \in U$, U - the set of control actions;

Figure 8. Two-tier control system model with the coordinator to provide service delivery management in the Micro cloud-based IoT architecture

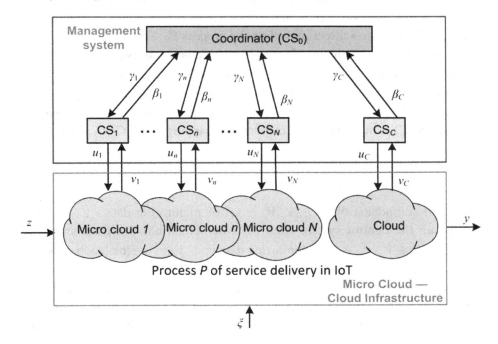

the incoming input signals z, $z \in Z$, that represent user's requests; the signals ξ, $\xi \in \Xi$, which are the disturbing influences.

Disturbing influences Ξ are the faults in the Microcloud-based IoT infrastructure, functional resource failures, requests to other Microcloud-based IoT systems sharing joint resources, or an increase of monitoring data volume, that require processing and other reasons. Requests to other IoT systems are considered to be disturbing influence towards the considered IoT system that makes it difficult to achieve management goals.

The output of the process P is y, $y \in Y$, where Y – the set of the outputs of process P, which are considered as IoT system responses to users' queries or results of IoT system operations.

Process P can be represented as a mapping based on the Cartesian product:

$$P : U \times Z \times \Xi \rightarrow Y .$$

The set of control signals U influencing the process P by $CS_1,...,CS_N,CS_C$, are represented as a Cartesian product of $N+1$ sets (Mesarovic et al., 1970).

$$U = U_1 \times U_2 \times ... \times U_N \times U_C .$$

In this case each control subsystem of $CS_1,...,CS_N,CS_C$, has the authority to select individual component $u_1,...,u_N,u_C$ of control action u from the corresponding set $U_1,...U_N$ or U_C to have a direct impact on the process P.

Two signals come at the inputs of each g-th management subsystem $CS_1,...,CS_N,CS_C$: a coordinating signal $\{\gamma_1,...,\gamma_N,\gamma_C\} \in \Gamma$ from CS_0 and feedback $\nu_1,...,\nu_N,\nu_C$ as a monitoring data. The control output of each $CS_1,...,CS_N,CS_C$ is the impact chosen by $CS_1,...,CS_N,CS_C$ from the corresponding set of $U_1,...,U_N$ or U_C. Assume that each of $CS_1,...,CS_N,CS_C$, implements corresponding mapping $C_1,...,C_N,C_C$, such that

$$C_1 : \Gamma \times V_1 \rightarrow U_1,...,C_N : \Gamma \times V_N \rightarrow U_N, C_C : \Gamma \times V_C \rightarrow U_C,$$

where each component of $V_1,...,V_N,V_C$ is set of monitoring data $v_1,...,v_N$, or v_C, coming into the control system from the Microcloud-based infrastructure, and $v_1 \in V_1,...,v_N \in V_N, v_C \in V_C$. Monitoring data $v_1,...,v_N,v_C$ are the feedback signals for the local control loop, which is based on $CS_1,...,CS_N,CS_C$.

The feedback signals $v_1,...,v_N,v_C$, as an input to the $CS_1,...,CS_N,CS_C$ are obtained by monitoring the Microcloud-based infrastructure. They contain information regarding the flow of process P. Naturally, these signals are functionally dependent on the control signals u, input signals z, disturbing influences ξ and outputs y. This relationship can be represented by a set of mappings (Mesarovic et al., 1970)

$$f_1 : U \times Z \times \Xi \times Y \to V_1,..., f_N : U \times Z \times \Xi \times Y \to V_N, f_C : U \times Z \times \Xi \times Y \to V_C.$$

Management subsystem CS_0 is a coordinator. It generates coordinate signals $\gamma_1,..., \gamma_N, \gamma_C \in \Gamma$, and each signal $\gamma_1,..., \gamma_N, \gamma_C \in \Gamma$ from a corresponding output of the CS_0 is only coming to the input of a separate downstream control subsystem $CS_1,...,CS_N,CS_C$. The coordinator CS_0 produces a signal based on an analysis of information coming to its input from the $CS_1,...,CS_N,CS_C$. The coordinator signal is representing the feedback signals and generalized information about the status and functioning of the Microcloud-based infrastructure. In this case, we can assume that C_0 mapping is implemented in coordinator such that

$$C_0 : B \to \Gamma,$$

where B is a set of information signals β, implementing feedback. Moreover, $\beta = (\beta_1,..., \beta_N, \beta_C)$ is a set of feedback signals $\beta_1,..., \beta_N, \beta_C$ coming into the coordinator CS_0 from $CS_1,...,CS_N,CS_C$ subsystems. Similarly to (5), the feedback signal β incoming to CS_0, carries information about the status of all subsystems downstream, so it is determined by mapping

$$f_0 : \Gamma \times V \times U \to B,$$

where $V = V_1 \times ... \times V_n$. Thus, B is a function of coordinating signals $\gamma_1,..., \gamma_N, \gamma_C$, feedback signals $v = (v_1,..., v_N, v_C)$ incoming to $CS_1,...,CS_N,CS_C$, and control actions $u = (u_1,..., u_N, u_C)$.

In the model in Figure 8, the interaction between subsystems $CS_1,...,CS_N,CS_C$, is not shown explicitly, as well as direct impact CS_0 on the Microcloud-based infrastructure functioning. Also, the process of receiving direct feedback signals by coordinator CS_0 from the Microcloud-based infrastructure elements is not shown, but such processes take place in real control systems.

According to Mesarovic et al. (1970) coordination is the process of impact on the $CS_1,...,CS_N,CS_C$, management subsystems, which forces them to operate consistently, subordinating the action of each of the $CS_1,...,CS_N,CS_C$, to one general policy aimed at the achievement of the global system objectives, despite the fact that this objective may conflict with the objectives of local subsystems. Coordination is carried by

CS_0, and the coordinator has to overcome the contradiction between the objectives of local subsystems $CS_1,...,CS_N,CS_C$.

The success of the coordinator activity on coordinating $CS_1,...,CS_N,CS_C$ can be measured by how successfully the global goal of Microcloud-based infrastructure management is achieved. Achieving the goal by the coordinator can be regarded as a solution to the problem, which can be formalized as the decision-making problem and lies in the assessment of coordination effectiveness. As this task is determined with respect to all subsystems, including process P, then it is called a global problem to be solved (Mesarovic et al., 1970).

For the two-level control systems two conditions must be met: to be coordinated according to the problem to be solved by CS_0, and to be coordinated in relation to the global problem (Mesarovic et al., 1970). The first means that CS_0 signals have a coordinating effect on the tasks to be undertaken by $CS_1,...,CS_N,CS_C$, and the second shows that the coordinator is able to influence the $CS_1,...,CS_N,CS_C$ so that their combined impact on the process P, executed by IoT system, is aimed at solving a global problem.

The successful operation of a management system, based on a two-level model, can be achieved only when the subsystems' objectives are coordinated with each other and aligned with the global objective of the system (Mesarovic et al., 1970; Rolik, 2013b).

In a two-level system, there are three types of objectives:

- A global objective.
- Coordinator CS_0 objective.
- Objectives of $CS_1,...,CS_N,CS_C$.

The need of objectives compatibility arises from the following specifics.

Generally, the process of P is directly affected only by $CS_1,...,CS_N,CS_C$, so the global objective can only be achieved indirectly through the actions of $CS_1,...,CS_N,CS_C$, which must be coordinated with respect to the global objective, as well as with respect to coordinator objective.

The global objective is to improve the efficiency of business processes and this objective goes beyond the immediate activity of the two-level system shown in Figure 8. And none of the subsystems $CS_1,...,CS_N,CS_C$ are focused on the achievement of the global objective or on solution of the global problem. A global problem can be solved only by joint action of all control subsystems $CS_1,...,CS_N,CS_C$.

The global objective. Given the fact that the Microcloud-based infrastructures are created to improve the functioning of IoT systems, the global objective of a management system is to provide the highest quality $\mathfrak{Q}$ of services of IoT system with minimal cost $\mathfrak{C}$. Thus, the aim of process management in accordance with

ITSM and ISO is the constant improvement of IT services level, that can be formally written as $\max \mathfrak{Q}$.

The maximum quality of service in the Microcloud-based infrastructures will be achieved in the case when

$$\max \mathfrak{Q} \Leftrightarrow \max Q_i, \forall i = \overline{1, K} \Leftrightarrow \max q_{ki}, \forall i = \overline{1, K}, \forall k = \overline{1, L_i},$$

where Q_i, $i = \overline{1, K}$ is the quality of the i-th service; q_{ki}, $k = \overline{1, L_i}$ is the value of k-th quality indicator of i-th service provided by IoT system.

To achieve the goal of process management it is necessary to continuously increase the Microcloud-based infrastructure resources, which is unacceptable, especially from the economic point of view. On the other hand, increase of the economic efficiency of doing business requires a cost reduction to the Microcloud-based infrastructure, aimed at achieving $\min \mathfrak{C}$. Maintenance of the service quality at this level is the main task of coordinator.

The objective of the coordinator. The objective of the coordinator is to maintain the quality of services $\mathfrak{Q}$ to an agreed level with a minimum $\mathfrak{C}$ of the involved resources. The purpose of the coordinator can be formalized as follows:

$$\mathfrak{Q} = \text{const}\big|_{\min \mathfrak{C}} .$$

The expression (9) means that the coordinator of all the possible procedures will select those which require minimal implementation cost. The requirement of maintaining the agreed level of services is applied to all services and individual service quality indicators:

$$\mathfrak{Q} = \text{const} \Leftrightarrow Q_i = \text{const}, \forall i = \overline{1, K} \Leftrightarrow q_{ki} = \text{const}, \forall k = \overline{1, L_i}, \forall i = \overline{1, K} .$$

It is necessary to stipulate the following fact. The main way to improve the quality of the i-th service $i = \overline{1, K}$, is the allocation of additional resources to the applications that support the i-th service. When the level of i-th service exceeds the target value, the reduction in resources allocated to the appropriate applications as required by the criterion $\min \mathfrak{C}$ is produced. At the same time the last server providing the i-th service cannot be turned off, despite the fact that the quality of the service is still higher than the desired since it will lead to a complete cessation of service. Thus, there will always be some fixed minimum cost $\mathfrak{C}$, and then a further cost reduction will be impossible.

The local objectives. The objective of the local management is to maintain preset values of functioning parameters of the Microcloud-based infrastructure at minimum cost. The model of control system shown in Figure 8, control subsystems $CS_1,...,CS_N,CS_C$ may have their own distinct operation objectives.

Coordination Principle Definition and Coordinator Synthesis

Implementation of coordinatibility and compatibility requirements are the limitations in determining the strategies that can guide the coordinator. Proposed in Mesarovic et al. (1970) the principles of coordination, based on the postulate of compatibility cannot be used in the management system of Microcloud-based infrastructure, because they assume obtaining and using accurate prediction of parameters of the process P, or require knowledge of functions or the analytical expressions for the solution of the coordination problem. For a coordination problem to be solved it is necessary to synthesis the coordinator and determine the methods, procedures or coordination algorithms after decomposition of the global objective.

Rewrite the objective (10) of coordinator in the following way

$$\min \Delta Q_i = \min(Q_i - Q_i^*), \forall i = \overline{1, K} \Leftrightarrow \min \Delta q_{ki} = \min(q_{ki} - q_{ki}^*), \forall k = \overline{1, L_i}, \forall i = \overline{1, K},$$

where Q_i and Q_i^* are the desired and the actual values of the i-th service quality indicator; q_{ki} and q_{ki}^* are the desired and actual values of the i-th service quality indicator and the actual quality is considered worse than required for $Q_i > Q_i^*$, and respectively, for $q_{ki} > q_{ki}^*$.

The inputs of the process P receive control and disturbing influences, and management system task is to choose such control that is counteracting to disturbing influences. Based on (11), the coordinator should compare current values of services quality indicators $q_{ki}^*, k = \overline{1, L_i}, i = \overline{1, K}$ provided to users by the process P, with the target (desired) values $q_{ki}, k = \overline{1, L_i}, i = \overline{1, K}$ and work out the coordination signals that minimize the deviation.

When control is aimed at maintaining the agreed service level, it is natural to use the principle of control by the deviation (Rolik, 2013b). Outputs of the process P go through appropriate transformation to bring the metrics together to determine the values $q_{ki}, k = \overline{1, L_i}, i = \overline{1, K}$. In this case, the outputs of the process P by feedback circuit come to the coordinator, and are compared with target values. On the basis of the deviation $\Delta q_{ki}, k = \overline{1, L_i}, i = \overline{1, K}$, coordinating signals are produced for $CS_1,...,CS_N,CS_C$.

Main disturbing influences can be measured by the management system. These disturbing influences are the fluctuating number of services users $\hat{a} = \{a_l, l = \overline{1, I}\}$, fault impact on the quality of service, congestion of communication channels, and others. This allows to use the control principle based on a disturbing influence together with control based on deviation and to implement in a management system a combined control. At that point, control based on deviation has more weight. Figure 9 shows the result of coordinator decomposition when coordinator implements a combined service level management principle.

The coordinator in Figure 9 contains negative feedback loop and circuits to compensate disturbing influences $\xi \in \Xi$. The compensation circuit evaluates the main disturbing influences which are taken into account when choosing a correction signal.

Global objective of Microcloud-based infrastructure management can change that arises for the coordinator by changes of application $\{A_i\}$ priorities Pr, ensuring the provision of the set $\mathfrak{S} = \{s_i\}$, $i = \overline{1, K}$, of the IoT services and targeted values Q_i, $i = \overline{1, K}$ of services level. In this case, the expression (6) takes the form

$$C_0 : Pr \times Q_i \times B \times V \times \Xi \to \Gamma, i = \overline{1, K}.$$

Once the principle of management is determined it is necessary to determine the strategy and the rules of coordinator and conditions of policies or rules application.

Figure 9. Coordinator structure, coordinator is using a feedback and taking into account the disturbing influences

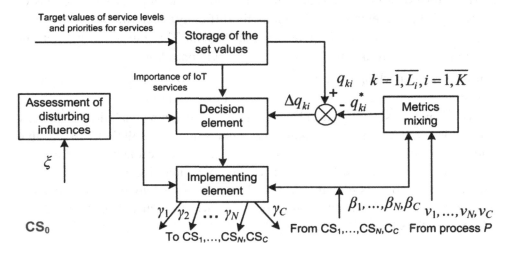

Selection of coordinating impact is determined by the system

$$< Pr, \Delta \hat{q}, \mathrm{B}, V, \Xi, \mathfrak{N} >,$$

where $\Delta \hat{q}$ is the vector of deviations; $\mathfrak{N}$ – situational uncertainty.

Let us analyze the system (13). Application priorities Pr are set by the customer of the IoT system, and take values from the set $\{1, 2, ..., Pr_m\}$, where Pr_m is the maximum value of the priority. In Microcloud-based infrastructure and IoT systems operation, the priorities of applications Pr vary, tracking importance changes in business processes or in processes utilizing the IoT system.

In order to characterize the degree of deviation values of vector $\Delta \hat{q} = (\Delta q_{1,1}, ..., \Delta q_{k,i}, ..., \Delta q_{M_K, K})$ from the target values, we introduce a function $w(\Delta q_{ki})$, $\forall k = \overline{1, M_i}$, $\forall i = \overline{1, K}$, that takes values on the interval

[-1,1] and determines the degree of proximity of the actual quality level to the target values

$$w(\Delta q_{k,i}) = (q_{ki} - q_{ki}^*) / q_{\kappa \mathrm{p}_{ki}},$$

where $q_{\kappa \mathrm{p}_{k,i}}$ is the critical value of quality index of the i-th service, in which quality is considered to be unsatisfactory. And when $w(\Delta q_{k,i}) \in (0, 1]$ the actual value of the quality index of the i-th service is better than required and when $w(\Delta q_{k,i}) \in [-1, 0)$ service quality is worse than previously agreed.

Of all the types of uncertainties typical for Microcloud-based infrastructure the most is situational uncertainty $\mathfrak{N}$, characterized by the unpredictable actions of users, unpredictable emergency situations, the difficulty of determining the resource responses on a combination of influencing factors. This raises the problem of generating the coordinating $\gamma = (\gamma_1, ..., \gamma_n)$ and control $u = (u_1, ..., u_n)$ actions considering feedback signals $v = (v_1, ..., v_n)$ and $\beta = (\beta_1, ..., \beta_n)$ under the influence of disturbances $\xi \in \Xi$ and under conditions of uncertainty $\mathfrak{N}$.

As it is not possible to determine an appropriate mapping analytically, the only way out is to use iterative coordination procedures, involving all the processes that implement the management of service level given in the diagram in Figure 7 (Mesarovic et al., 1970; Rolik, 2013b). The use of an iterative procedure allows to generate acceptable coordinating impact due to the monotony of the functions of quality indicators' dependency on resource values, as well as the monotony of influence of the situational uncertainty $\mathfrak{N}$ on the service level. Therefore, to control the quality of services provided by IoT system in Microcloud-based infrastructure for uncertainty disclosure it is advisable to use iterative procedures for the management.

The main function of the coordinator is to agree the activities of $CS_1,...,CS_N,CS_C$ while generating their own solutions so as to increase the overall impact of their joint actions. Therefore, the decisions taken by the coordinator, influence the choice of coordination actions, but not control actions (Rolik, 2013b). To select coordinating actions, it is necessary to determine the principle of coordination.

In the management system the coordinating impact indicates which of the $CS_1,...,CS_N,CS_C$ is preferred when restoring the quality of services and what methods should be used. An example of possible actions $CS_1,...,CS_N,CS_C$ is shown in Figure 10.

For example, when communication channels are overloaded allocation of additional computing resources for applications from set $\{A_l\}$ will not restore the level of service quality. Therefore, coordinator CS_0 informs appropriate subsystem $CS_1,...,CS_N,CS_C$, responsible for network flows management, the need to limit outgoing traffic from applications from $\{A_l\}$ that have the lowest priority. Such coordination may be implemented, for example, by using a coordinating principle based on productional system. The rules in notation of Backus-Naur are as follows:

$< a\_system\_of\_rules >::= [< production >]$
$< production >::=< clause >\rightarrow< consequence >$
$< clause >::= [< plain\_clause >]$
$< plain\_clause >::=< object >< attribute >< predicate >< value >$
$< object >::= CS_1,..., CS_N, CS_C$
$< consequence >::= [< directive >|< formula >|< program >]$
$< predicate >::=|\neq|<|>|\leq|\geq$
$< attribute >::=< application >|< application\_priority >|< service >|$
$|< buisness\_process >|< the\_importance\_of\_a\_process >|< parameter >|< status >$

Figure 10. An example of action selection $CS_1,...,CS_N,CS_C$ depending on the value of the function $w(\Delta q_{ki})$

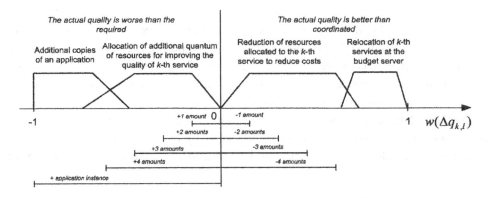

The use of a coordinating principle based on a productional system is justified in cases where the goal is to improve the quality of services, rather than to achieve optimal performance operation of the Microcloud-based infrastructure under condition with lack of information about the factors that affect the results of coordination and control actions.

Mappings (6) can have a very complex form, and for the system (13), it is impossible to obtain analytically the resulting relationship between the coordinating actions $\gamma = (\gamma_1, ..., \gamma_n)$, control actions $u = (u_1, ..., u_n)$ and process P output. In this case, the software control can be used.

The main coordination procedures are the use of iterative procedures to improve the coordinating signals based on the analysis results of the coordination or the use of feedback for the correction of coordinating signal (Rolik, 2013b). It is advisable to use both types of procedures. In both cases, to determine the error signal in assessing the impact it is necessary to make reduction of metrics measured at process P to metrics coordinator operates.

It should be noted that the coordinator is used for automatic control of service level, and for the automated management the coordinator performs the role of decision support system.

ENABLING TECHNOLOGIES FOR MICROCLOUD-BASED IOT SYSTEM REALIZATION

Data Center Architecture

Data centers remain the primary, urgent and necessary allocation unit for IT resources that provide various kinds of services. Using all sorts of server rooms and allocations will sooner or later lead to the need to review the architecture, implementation of new services, and IT infrastructure scaling. Data center that does not meet modern requirements (Turner, Seader, & Renaud, 2010) and built with not efficient topology, cannot be adapted to the new requirements.

In modern applications dataset sizes are continuing to explode with more photo/video content, produced by IoT applications, users and Internet-connected sensors. As a result, network-intensive data processing pipelines must operate over ever-larger datasets in ready-to-processing datacenters. Moreover, bandwidth demands in the datacenter are doubling every 12-15 months (Singh et al., 2015).

Modern data center has become a very complex place requiring teams of staff members to operate and control all systems at many levels. As the aforementioned performance challenges have appeared, IT administrators are working hard to find decision and as a result even more complex system is proposed that require more appliances, scripts and maintenance.

To solve or decrease influence of the performance, cost, and complexity challenges in IoT oriented ecosystem we propose to implement hyperconverged infrastructure as a Micro cloud core.

Hyperconverged systems operate by direct-attached storage running on commodity hardware, but many solutions Nutanix (2017), Scale Computing (2017), and VMware (2017) go beyond this baseline and implement additional approaches of web-scale computing and distributed systems. Baseline system consist of a set of DAS hard drives and solid state disks installed in each of the x86-based server nodes that functioning above network topology defined for set of specific apps deployment. Each of these nodes employ hypervisor, for example Hyper-V, ESXi, Xen or KVM and special software for orchestration from hyperconverged infrastructure vendor. Using modern multi-tier technologies this software aggregates all of the storage resources from across all nodes of the cluster and makes them available for consumption by virtual machines through hypervisor.

Hyperconverged infrastructure leverages not only software-defined networking, but also software-defined storage systems concepts in order to modernize and simplify the data center environment. Thereby, hyperconverged infrastructure makes it possible to ensure that IT is meeting the needs of the IoT services and business. Due to the introduction of hyper converged approach to the design of IT infrastructure in the nearest future, traditional off-the-shelf enterprise applications need to be re-architected to scale predictably on demand.

Big vendors like Microsoft start make this transition to a scale-out compatible architecture. For example, Windows Containers, Hyper-V Containers and Dockers are the next evolution in virtualization and, because of it's granularity, are isolated, resource controlled, and portable operating environment (Microsoft, 2016b; Docker, 2017).

Another step towards the scale-out compatible architecture is Nano Server, which offers a dramatically reduced footprint, resulting in lower servicing requirements and improved security. Along with Windows Server Containers, Nano Server is a key element of the modern application platform features of the Windows Server operating system ready to use in software-defined environment (Microsoft, 2016a). They all are coming to replace fat no scaled VM's from the past.

Hyperconverged Systems

Hyperconverged infrastructure is defined as a virtual computing infrastructure solution that seamlessly combines several data center services in an appliance form factor, which accelerates the speed and agility of deploying virtualized workloads, reduces complexity, improves operational efficiency, and lowers costs (ActualTech Media, 2016).

Hyperconverged systems (HCS) are now a fast-growing part of the overall converged infrastructure market, which was estimated by Gartner (which refers to it as Hyperconverged integrated system) to exceed $6 billion in revenue last year. Gartner strategic planning assumption is hyperconverged integrated systems will represent over 35% of total integrated system market revenue by 2019 and 20% of mission-critical applications currently deployed on three-tier IT infrastructure will transition to HCS by 2020 (Gartner, 2016). By 2019, approximately 30% of the global storage array capacity installed in enterprise data centers will be deployed on software-defined storage (SDS) or hyperconverged integrated system (HCIS) architectures based on x86 hardware systems, up from less than 5% today (Gartner, 2016).

Hyperconverged systems are becoming very popular and widely used in today's datacenter deployments (Kovar, 2015; Network Computing, 2015). They have a fundamentally different architecture and differ from traditional three-tier infrastructure solutions. Hyper-convergence is an architectural model for IT infrastructure that employees x86-based CPUs, SSD and HDD storages in a single building block. Next, hyperconverged systems are typically connected over IP-based networks (most commonly Ethernet) and are distributed by nature.

The usage of standard, state of the art x86-based servers instead of proprietary hardware allow decrease CapEx and OpEx. Integrated compute and storage, combined with data locality implemented in software, eliminates the complexity of modern storage networks (SAN and NAS) and decreases performance bottlenecks. Thereby, data is become closer to CPU and data movement is minimized. As a result, we get better performance at scale, lower power and space requirements of infrastructure relative to traditional three-tier systems.

Distributed nature of HCS also allows zero recovery point objectives technologies, which synchronously replicates data to another site ensuring that a real-time copy of data exists at a different location.

Thereby, virtual machines can failover from a primary site to a secondary site in the event of a disaster, guaranteeing high availability for applications.

In the event of component failure, node failure, rack/access/aggregate/core switch failure HCS allows high-level availability and resiliency by making it possible to back up VMs to local systems, to remote site, or to public cloud service providers.

HCS that use ordinary x86-based server building blocks and have a massively parallel software architecture can be scaled predictably on demand makes it possible to buy infrastructure only when needed, thereby increasing resource utilization and achieving just-in-time scaling and pay-as-you-grow economics. Therefore, the authors see the perspective of the use of HCS in the Microcloud-based IoT infrastructure design and implementation.

Integrated workflows covering administrative tasks ranging from deployment, provisioning, and scaling, to data protection and diagnostics, simplify every aspect of HCSs management. HC architectures and uniform building blocks bringing radical simplicity back to the datacenter.

Software Defined Environments

Movement of mission-critical, performance-sensitive, and other IoT applications to the cloud and, from the other hand, development and deployment new mobile, social, and analytics applications directly on cloud computing platforms leads to encouraging the shift of the value proposition of cloud computing from cost reduction to simultaneous agility and optimization. These circumstances require a changes in the architecture such as the entire computing infrastructure (compute, storage and network) is becoming software defined and dynamically programmable (Li et al., 2014). Software defined environments provide the tooling and capabilities to compose workloads from existing components that are then continuously and autonomously mapped onto the underlying programmable infrastructure (Li et al., 2014).

Software-defined approach has become pervasive methodology based on virtualization, high speed networks and massive parallelism in distributed environments. Software-defined approach has embodied in the Software defined environment (SDE) approach (Li et al., 2014) that integrates software defined compute, network, and storage and unify the control and management planes from each individual software defined component.

These unified control planes are assembled from programmable resource abstractions of the compute, network, and storage resources of a system that meet the specific requirements of individual workloads and enable dynamic optimization in response to changing business requirements (Li et al., 2014).

A workload can be specified by various applications and services as a demand of compute (CPU), RAM, network and storage resources in the form of operational requirements, such as IOPS, RAM size, CPU priorities, network bandwidth and so on that will have to be realized using the programmable abstraction level(s). As an example, a modeling language for SDE is described in (Breiter, et al, 2014), a language and runtime for continuous delivery of software and related infrastructure and the validation of workload blueprints is described in (Kalantar, et al., 2014; Arnold et al., 2014).

Software-defined approach worked out well in software-defined networks (SDN) which aims to provide a unified control framework for different networks that have complex middlebox functions (Feamster, Rexford, & Zegura, 2014). The principles of software-defined approach are beginning to be applied in the IoT as well. Jiaqiang Liu et al. proposes a software-defined IoT (SD-IoT) architecture for smart urban sensing implementation that decouples the control logic from functions of the physical devices through a logically centralized controller that manages the devices via standard interface (Liu, Li, Chen, Dong, & Jin, 2015).

IT infrastructure to be considered as hyperconvergent and web-scale if data fabric and control fabric is software-defined, fully distributed and resilient to failures. Many hyperconverged systems are positioned as completely software-defined. All of the intelligence has implemented in the software layer, and whole system does not rely on special-purpose hardware for core functions, resilience and performance acceleration. This allows new capabilities, which may be performed quickly and efficiently, such as deduplication of the capacity tier, without requiring hardware, firmware or drivers upgrades, thus eliminating the need of planned downtime. IoT infrastructure can be configured and scaled-out on-the-fly without requiring rewiring or additional hardware purchases.

With filesystems used in hyperconverged modern systems, infrastructure can be scaled out at the granularity of a single x86-based server, enabling fractional consumption and incremental growth. This simplifies infrastructure buying and lowers space and power requirements by as much as 90% versus legacy three-tier deployments. Under present conditions datacenter space and power consumption parameters are very important. According to Gartner, smarter design, energy efficiency pressures, the realities of high-density environments, and the potential of cloud computing could result in data center space requirements that will shrink dramatically before the decade is out.

Thus, in one hyperconverged system can be combined different generations of servers, servers with different combinations of compute, flash, and storage, to meet the application needs in Microcloud-based IoT infrastructure.

FUTURE RESEARCH DIRECTIONS

In recent years, IoT systems has emerged as one of the most important applied applications for modern cities and industries. Future research in the Microcloud-based IoT systems, authors propose the investigation of the following directions. First of all, due to the wide adoption of mobile devices, it is important to develop efficient resource management approaches that will take into account the mobility of sensors and devices.

As information technology services and tools continue to develop for the description of services, objects of monitoring and management, and other components of Microcloud-based IoT infrastructure can also greatly advance the efficient resource management in IoT systems, and should be addressed by future research.

Another future research direction is the development a generalized metric system for the data transmission between Micro clouds and Cloud, also the distribution of transaction processing services and batch execution jobs. Taking into account the need to ensure acceptable client latency results in the need for the distribution of the appropriate storage of hot data in Micro cloud and Cloud, based on caching.

Processing data from the massive sets of devices and sensors to operate the large amounts of augmented reality applications online, requires extensive use of large data processing and analysis methods. Appropriate Big Data processing and analysis methods in Microcloud-based IoT infrastructure should be addressed by future research.

Another important direction for future research is scaling the problem in Microcloud-based IoT systems. It is necessary to provide the increase and decrease of resources depending on quantitative indicators of the IoT service without interrupting its work. Due to the introduction of the hyper converged approach to the design of data center IT infrastructure in the nearest future, traditional off-the-shelf enterprise applications need to be re-architected to scale the predictably on demand.

How to address the information security and access issues is also an open research challenge, since Microcloud-based IoT system can serve a variety of different clients. It is necessary to eliminate their mutual influence and information leak.

Research on how to provide software-defined controllers, work and communication between controllers on control plane are needed. In this sense, focus could be on the rules and policies generated for the data plane equipment management.

IoT infrastructure management concepts include IT infrastructure management technology and synthesis of control systems technology for individual devices. The groups of devices and objects with many devices on Sensing layer.

Finally, the synthesis of IoT control systems technology for individual devices, groups of devices, integral objects with many devices can only be fully implemented with research and development towards hyperconverged systems, software-defined technologies and cloud computing. It includes: models and structures synthesis, algorithms' synthesis, parameters' synthesis, functions' separation, synthesis of control systems on the device and on the application level side.

CONCLUSION

To accommodate the increasing demand for IoT-related services, there is an increasing need of scalable and cost-efficient cloud-based architectures and data centers supporting client-centric IoT systems.

The proposed Microcloud-based IoT architecture allows the efficient use of resources for IT services provisions in the IoT ecosystem. Through the implementation of service level coordination, resource planning and service level management processes in an integrated IT infrastructure management system. It is proposed to implement a comprehensive, integrated platform on the IT infrastructure side in the IoT ecosystem. This makes it possible to develop new IoT services used in a particular domain.

In the core of the operational IT infrastructure management there is an integrated interaction of three processes. These processes include: the service level coordination, resource planning and service level management. The process of service level coordination is implemented by business managers' initiative and ends up with the creation or updating the sets of services and the sets of quality indicators for each service. A predetermined amount of IT resources is allocated to implement each service. The resource planning process is based on the allocation and assignment of IT resources from the resource pool to each of the services. Service level management process manages IT infrastructure so that the actual values of the service quality indicators correspond to the coordinated values obtained in the process of service level coordination.

It is important to implement the core of Micro cloud with the use of new technologies such as hyperconvergence and software-defined environments. Hyperconverged systems makes it possible to buy infrastructure only when needed, thereby increasing resource utilization and achieving just-in-time scaling and pay-as-you-grow economics.

Hyperconverged infrastructure leverages not only software-defined networking, but also software-defined storage systems concepts in order to modernize and simplify the data centre environment for IoT services. Hyperconverged infrastructure makes it possible to ensure that IT is meeting the needs of the IoT services and business. Therefore, the authors see the perspective of the use of hyperconverged systems in the Microcloud-based IoT infrastructure design and implementation.

The software-defined approach has become the pervasive methodology based on virtualization, high speed networks and massive parallelism in distributed environments. Many hyperconverged systems are positioned as completely software-defined and may be adopted as a core of the Micro cloud in IoT ecosystem. All of the intelligence has been implemented in the software layer, and the entire system does not rely on special-purpose hardware for core functions, resilience and performance acceleration. This allows new capabilities, which may be performed quickly and efficiently, and without requiring hardware, firmware or drivers' upgrades, thus eliminating the IoT services downtime. IoT infrastructure of Micro cloud can be configured and scaled-out on-the-fly without requiring rewiring or additional hardware purchases.

REFERENCES

Aazam, M., Khan, I., Alsaffar, A., & Huh, E. (2014). Cloud of Things: Integrating Internet of Things and cloud computing and the issues involved. *Proceedings of 11th International Bhurban Conference on Applied Sciences & Technology (IBCAST)*, 414-419.

ActualTech Media. (2016). *2016 State of Hyperconverged Infrastructure Market.* ActualTech Media.

Al-Fuqaha, A., Guizani, M., Mohammadi, M., Aledhari, M., & Ayyash, M. (2015). Internet of things: A survey on enabling technologies, protocols, and applications. *IEEE Communications Surveys and Tutorials*, *17*(4), 2347–2376. doi:10.1109/COMST.2015.2444095

Apple. (2017). *Working with HomeKit.* Retrieved Jan 12, 2017, from https://developer.apple.com/homekit/

Arnold, W. C., Arroyo, D. J., Segmuller, W., Spreitzer, M., Steinder, M., & Tantawi, A. N. (2014). Workload orchestration and optimization for software defined environments. *IBM Journal of Research and Development*, *58*(2/3), 11–1. doi:10.1147/JRD.2014.2304864

Beecham Research. (2011). *M2M Sector Map.* Beecham Research. Retrieved Jan 12, 2017, from http://www.beechamresearch.com/download.aspx?id=18

Belissent, J. (2010). *Getting Clever About Smart Cities: New Opportunities Require New Business Models.* Forrester Research.

Botta, A., De Donato, W., Persico, V., & Pescapé, A. (2014). On the integration of cloud computing and internet of things. *The 2nd International Conference on Future Internet of Things and Cloud (FiCloud)*, 23-30.

Breiter, G., Behrendt, M., Gupta, M., Moser, S. D., Schulze, R., Sippli, I., & Spatzier, T. (2014). Software defined environments based on TOSCA in IBM cloud implementations. *IBM Journal of Research and Development*, *58*(2/3), 1–10. doi:10.1147/JRD.2014.2304772

Cisco. (2017). *Internet of Things (IoT), Connecting everything drives positive business results.* Retrieved Jan 12, 2017, from http://www.cisco.com/c/en/us/solutions/internet-of-things/overview.html

Docker. (2017). *Docker Use Cases.* Retrieved Jan 12, 2017, from https://www.docker.com/use-cases

ETSI Technical Specification. (2010). *Machine-to-Machine Communications (M2M); M2M Service Requirements.* ETSI TS 102 689 V1.1.1(2010-08).

Feamster, N., Rexford, J., & Zegura, E. (2014). The road to SDN: An intellectual history of programmable networks. *Computer Communication Review, 44*(2), 87–98. doi:10.1145/2602204.2602219

Gantz, J., & Reinsel, D. (2012). The digital universe in 2020: Big data, bigger digital shadows, and biggest growth in the far east. *IDC iView: IDC Analyze the Future, 2007*, 1-16.

Gartner. (2016). Magic Quadrant for Integrated Systems. ID: G00291000

Google. (2017). *Internet of Things (IoT) Solutions.* Retrieved Jan 12, 2017, from https://cloud.google.com/solutions/iot/#learn

Gubbi, J., Buyya, R., Marusic, S., & Palaniswami, M. (2013). Internet of Things (IoT): A vision, architectural elements, and future directions. *Future Generation Computer Systems, 29*(7), 1645–1660. doi:10.1016/j.future.2013.01.010

IBM. (2017). *Simplify development for networked devices.* Retrieved Jan 12, 2017, from http://www-03.ibm.com/software/products/en/internet-of-things-foundation

Intel. (2017). *IoT Security and Scalability on Intel® IoT Platform.* Retrieved Jan 12, 2017, from http://www.intel.com/content/www/us/en/internet-of-things/iot-platform.html

IoTivity. (2017). *IoTivity, a Linux Foundation Collaborative Project.* Retrieved Jan 12, 2017, from https://www.iotivity.org/

Kalantar, M. H., Rosenberg, F., Doran, J., Eilam, T., Elder, M. D., Oliveira, F., & Roth, T. et al. (2014). Weaver: Language and runtime for software defined environments. *IBM Journal of Research and Development, 58*(2/3), 1–12. doi:10.1147/JRD.2014.2304865

Kovar, J. F. (2015). *13 Powerful Hyper-Converged Infrastructure Solutions.* Retrieved Jan 12, 2017, from http://www.crn.com/slide-shows/virtualization/300076666/13-powerful-hyper-converged-infrastructure-solutions.htm/pgno/0/13

Li, C., Brech, B. L., Crowder, S., Dias, D. M., Franke, H., Hogstrom, M., & Rao, J. et al. (2014). Software defined environments: An introduction. *IBM Journal of Research and Development, 58*(2/3), 1–11. doi:10.1147/JRD.2014.2298134

Liu, J., Li, Y., Chen, M., Dong, W., & Jin, D. (2015). Software-defined internet of things for smart urban sensing. *IEEE Communications Magazine, 53*(9), 55–63. doi:10.1109/MCOM.2015.7263373

Mesarovic, M. D., Macko, D., & Takahara, Y. (1970). *Theory of Hierarchical, Multilevel Systems.* New York, NY: Academic Press.

Microsoft. (2016a). *Install Nano Server.* Retrieved Jan 12, 2017, from https://technet. microsoft.com/windows-server-docs/get-started/getting-started-with-nano-server

Microsoft. (2016b). *Windows Containers.* Retrieved Jan 12, 2017, from https://docs. microsoft.com/en-us/virtualization/windowscontainers/about/index

Microsoft. (2017). *4 steps to start your IoT solution.* Retrieved Jan 12, 2017, from https://www.microsoft.com/en-us/server-cloud/internet-of-things/overview.aspx

Network Computing. (2015). *10 Hyperconvergence Trendsetters.* Retrieved Jan 12, 2017, from http://www.networkcomputing.com/storage/10-hyperconvergence-trendsetters/1523423309

Nutanix. (2017). *Nutanix Products Series.* Retrieved Jan 12, 2017, from https:// www.nutanix.com/products/hardware-platforms/

Rolik, A. I. (2013a). Decomposition-Compensation Method of Service Level Management of Corporate IT Infrastructures. *Visnyk NTUU "KPI" Informatics, Operation and Computer Science, 58*, 78-88.

Rolik, A. I. (2013b). Service Level Management of Corporate IT Infrastructure Based on the Coordinator. *Visnyk NTUU "KPI" Informatics, Operation and Computer Science, 59*, 98–105.

Samsung. (2017a). *SmartThings.* Retrieved Jan 12, 2017, from https://www. smartthings.com/

Samsung. (2017b). *The ARTIK End-to-end IoT Platform.* Retrieved Jan 12, 2017, from https://www.artik.io/

Scale Computing. (2017). *Hardware Platforms.* Retrieved Jan 12, 2017, from https:// www.scalecomputing.com/products/hardware-platforms/

Singh, A., Ong, J., Agarwal, A., Anderson, G., Armistead, A., Bannon, R., & Kanagala, A. et al. (2015). Jupiter rising: A decade of clos topologies and centralized control in googles datacenter network. *Computer Communication Review, 45*(4), 183–197. doi:10.1145/2829988.2787508

Sundmaeker, H., Guillemin, P., Friess, P., & Woelfflé, S. (2010). *Vision and challenges for realising the Internet of Things. Cluster of European Research Projects on the Internet of Things*. Brussels: European Commision.

Tao, F., Cheng, Y., Da Xu, L., Zhang, L., & Li, B. H. (2014). CCIoT-CMfg: Cloud computing and internet of things-based cloud manufacturing service system. *IEEE Transactions on Industrial Informatics, 10*(2), 1435–1442. doi:10.1109/TII.2014.2306383

Turner, W. P., Seader, J. H., & Renaud, V. E. (2010). *Data center site infrastructure tier standard: Topology*. New York, NY: Uptime Institute.

Vermesan, O., & Friess, P. (2014). *Internet of Things - From Research and Innovation to Market Deployment*. Aalborg: River Publishers.

VMware. (2017). *VMware Hyper-Converged Infrastructure (HCI) - VMware Products*. Retrieved Jan 12, 2017, from https://www.vmware.com/products/hyper-converged-infrastructure.html

Chapter 9

Possibilities of BLOB (Binary Large OBject) and CLOB (Character Large Object) Integration Into the Core of IoT and Using the SQL Platform for Distributing a Large Amount of Data to HTML, JAVA, and PHP Platforms

Goran Vorotović
University of Belgrade, Serbia

Časlav Mitrović
University of Belgrade, Serbia

Nebojša Petrović
University of Belgrade, Serbia

Vesna Šešum-Čavić
Vienna University of Technology, Austria

ABSTRACT

This chapter identifies and describes the key concepts and techniques for BLOB and CLOB integration into the IoT core. Data system centralization has sped up the solution of problems with large amounts of data storage and processing, particularly if the data is large by its nature. In that sense, everyday stream of photos, audio

DOI: 10.4018/978-1-5225-2437-3.ch009

and video content, large textual data files led to new concepts BLOB and CLOB. Adequate examples of stored procedures, views, C#, JAVA, HTML5 i PHP languages, follow the establishing communication methods. Finally, the chapter will illustrate two practical examples of IoT: the example for pagination on a large database with million BLOB and CLOB objects, and the example for dynamic mechatronic system of a fire truck with feedback.

BLOB

Although historically speaking the term "Blobbing", is usually related to the process of moving a large amount of data from one database to another, that is from one location to another, the existing definitions are overbuilt and in the direction of object-oriented paradigm. It should be noted that the transfer of a large amount of data from one database to another is still primarily associated with the definition of a "large" object but in terms of large quantities of objects. This practically means that, for example, transferring a large number of small files (size 10 kB, number of files 1.000.000) remains the field of "Blobbing". This concept does not include any primary data error checking, or any form of a filter. Error checking and potential filters represent the task of the newly formed base, that is a new host, which ensures the possibility of fast data transfer. The justification for this approach is reflected in modern systems of client-server orientation. The term originated from the image of someone grabbing the material from a container and putting it into another without thinking how much material is "grabbed", that is how big is the lump (blob) taken for transfer.

Modern understanding of the issue is related to BLOB as data type. Namely, one of BLOB definitions is that BLOB (engl. Binary large object) or large binary object is a type of data that represents a possible structure element for data storing. Blob are large variable sequences of bites that represent an image, a sound or a video recording (multimedia objects) (Figure 1).

The objects are "intelligent" data that can be found in certain states. These states can be changed using certain methods. Set of objects with the same properties makes one class. Classes are analogue to data types, such as integers or real numbers, but may represent arbitrarily complex abstract objects (e.g. geometric figures, images, audio recordings, etc.).

The above said represents a revolution in the field of data manipulation. Namely, by describing the binary large object with object-oriented paradigm postulates a complete analogy with a large number of programming languages of the same

Figure 1. Binary large objects

concept is achieved. In that way it is achieved that the individuals or development teams, regardless of whether they use some form of PSP[1] or TSP[2] philosophy can simply access the problem that involves the formation, distribution and storage of large amounts of data – the developers understood the databases, and database administrators and designers became familiar with the stream of thinking of clients applications that rely on their databases. (Humphrey, Personal Software Process (PSP), 2000) (Humphrey, Team Software Process (TSP), 2000)

Why Is It Important to Describe BLOB as Data Type?

In order to answer this question it is important to look back at some of the basic features of object-oriented paradigm through the prism of SmallTalk – the first successful object-oriented language. Namely, among other features, Alan Kay said (Bergin & Gibson, 1996):

- Everything is an object. Think about the object as of a suitable variable; it stores data, but you can also ask from it to perform the operations on itself by making requests. In theory, you can take any conceptual component of a problem you are trying to solve (dogs, buildings, services, etc.) and present it as an object in your program.

- The program is a bunch of objects that tell each other what to do by sending messages. In order to send a request to some object, you "send a message" to that object. More specifically, you can think about the message as of a request for a function that belongs to a particular object.
- Each object has its own memory consisting of other objects. In other words, you make a new type of object by making a package that consists of existing objects. In that way you can build complexity within the program while simultaneously hiding it behind the simplicity of objects.
- Each object is a type. Each object is an instance of a class and class is a synonym for type. The most significant characteristic of a class is "which message can you send to it?".
- All objects of a certain type can receive the same messages. Since the object of a circle type is at the same time the object of a shape, it is certain that the circle will receive messages for the shape as well. This means that you can write a code that is related to the shapes and it automatically performs everything that corresponds to the description of shape. This substitutability is one of the most important concepts of OOP[3] (Kraus, 1996).

The data type and the definition of the data type that is introduced to describe the data are not originally defined in traditional database systems, especially because the data were too large to store during 70-s i 80-s of the 20th century when databases were introduced. The data type was practically applicable when the disc space became less expensive. This definition became popular with DB2[4] IBM.

Blob (BLOB) can be viewed as a collection of binary data stored as a single entity in the database management system. BLOB are usually images, audio or other multimedia objects, although sometimes the binary executable code is also stored as a BLOB. *Database support for BLOB is not universal.*

All operations related to working with multimedia data can be classified into two logical levels. At the lower level, operations on poorly structured record are performed (ADT BLOB). Typical operations assigned to BLOB are creating, reading and deleting the BLOB content, without considering the internal organization and structure of media data. At a higher level, operations specific to each media type (presentation, editing) are performed.

Blob contains an attribute that appears in the application as a sequence of bites. Database management system provides the connection and interface. By means of interface the application reads and adds the data into BLOB. Memory space that BLOB occupies is large, which is why a specific support is required.

BLOB can occupy linear or non-linear address space of the operating memory, and the method of storing is not relevant for media data modelling (but it affects the performances).

CLOB

A Character Large Object (or CLOB) is a collection of character data in a database management system, usually stored in a separate location that is referenced in the table itself. Oracle[5] and IBM DB2 provide a construct explicitly named CLOB, and the majority of other database systems support some form of the concept, often labeled as text, memo or long character fields (Character Large Object, 2017).

CLOBs usually have very high size-limits, of the order of 2 GB or more. The tradeoff for the capacity is usually limited access methods. In particular, some database systems[which?] limit certain SQL clauses and/or functions, such as LIKE or SUBSTRING from being used on CLOBs. Those that permit such operations may perform them very slowly.

Alternative methods of accessing the data are often provided, including means of extracting or inserting ranges of data from the CLOB.

Database systems vary in their storage patterns for CLOBs. Some systems always store CLOBs as a reference to out-of-table data, while others store small CLOBs in-table, changing their storage patterns when the size of the data grows beyond a threshold. Other systems are configurable in their behavior.

CLOBs differ from BLOBs by having a specified character encoding, and also by the capability to permit some string-oriented operations on them.

LOBs PHILOSOPHY

DB2 Philosophy of Large Objects (LOBs)

The term large object and the generic acronym LOB refer to the BLOB, CLOB, or DBCLOB data type. In a Unicode database, NCLOB can be used as a synonym for DBCLOB (Large Objects, 2017).

LOB values are subject to restrictions, as described in Varying-length character strings. These restrictions apply even if the length attribute of the LOB string is 254 bytes or less.

LOB values can be very large, and the transfer of these values from the database server to client application program host variables can be time consuming. Because application programs typically process LOB values one piece at a time, rather than as a whole, applications can reference a LOB value by using a large object locator.

A large object locator, or LOB locator, is a host variable whose value represents a single LOB value on the database server.

An application program can select a LOB value into a LOB locator. Then, using the LOB locator, the application program can request database operations on the

LOB value (such as applying the scalar functions SUBSTR, CONCAT, VALUE, or LENGTH; performing an assignment; searching the LOB with LIKE or POSSTR; or applying user-defined functions against the LOB) by supplying the locator value as input. The resulting output (data assigned to a client host variable) would typically be a small subset of the input LOB value.

LOB locators can represent more than just base values; they can also represent the value associated with a LOB expression. For example, a LOB locator might represent the value associated with:

```
SUBSTR(<lob 1> CONCAT <lob 2> CONCAT <lob 3>, <start>,
<length>)
```

When a null value is selected into a normal host variable, the indicator variable is set to -1, signifying that the value is null. In the case of LOB locators, however, the meaning of indicator variables is slightly different. Because a locator host variable can itself never be null, a negative indicator variable value indicates that the LOB value represented by the LOB locator is null. The null information is kept local to the client by virtue of the indicator variable value - the server does not track null values with valid locators.

It is important to understand that a LOB locator represents a value, not a row or a location in the database. Once a value is selected into a locator, there is no operation that one can perform on the original row or table that will affect the value which is referenced by the locator. The value associated with a locator is valid until the transaction ends, or until the locator is explicitly freed, whichever comes first. Locators do not force extra copies of the data to provide this function. Instead, the locator mechanism stores a description of the base LOB value. The materialization of the LOB value (or expression, as shown previously) is deferred until it is actually assigned to some location - either a user buffer in the form of a host variable, or another record in the database.

A LOB locator is only a mechanism used to refer to a LOB value during a transaction; it does not persist beyond the transaction in which it was created. It is not a database type; it is never stored in the database and, as a result, cannot participate in views or check constraints. However, because a LOB locator is a client representation of a LOB type, there are SQLTYPEs for LOB locators so that they can be described within an SQLDA structure used by FETCH, OPEN, or EXECUTE statements.

DB2 defines the value of variables (Table 1).

Table 1.

Description	Limit
Maximum length of CHAR (in bytes or OCTETS)	254
Maximum length of CHAR (in CODEUNITS32)	63
Maximum length of VARCHAR (in bytes or OCTETS)	32 672
Maximum length of VARCHAR (in CODEUNITS32)	8 168
Maximum length of LONG VARCHAR (in bytes)	32 700
Maximum length of CLOB (in bytes or OCTETS)	2 147 483 647
Maximum length of CLOB (in CODEUNITS32)	536 870 911
Maximum length of serialized XML (in bytes)	2 147 483 647
Maximum length of GRAPHIC (in double-byte characters or CODEUNITS16)	127
Maximum length of GRAPHIC (in CODEUNITS32)	63
Maximum length of VARGRAPHIC (in double-byte characters or CODEUNITS16)	16 336
Maximum length of VARGRAPHIC (in CODEUNITS32)	8 168
Maximum length of LONG VARGRAPHIC (in double-byte characters)	16 350
Maximum length of DBCLOB (in double-byte characters or CODEUNITS16)	1 073 741 823
Maximum length of DBCLOB (in CODEUNITS32)	536 870 911
Maximum length of BLOB (in bytes)	2 147 483 647
Maximum length of character constant 32 672	32 672
Maximum length of graphic constant 16 336	16 336
Maximum length of concatenated character string 2 147 483 647	2 147 483 647
Maximum length of concatenated graphic string 1 073 741 823	1 073 741 823
Maximum length of concatenated binary string 2 147 483 647	2 147 483 647
Maximum number of hexadecimal constant digits 32 672	32 672
Largest instance of a structured type column object at run time (in gigabytes)	1
Maximum size of a catalog comment (in bytes)	254

SQL Server Philosophy of Large Objects

Modern versions of SQL server[6] include three solutions (Binary Large Object (Blob) Data (SQL Server), 2017):

- FILESTREAM.
- FileTables.
- Remote Blob Store.

FILESTREAM (SQL Server)

FILESTREAM enables SQL Server-based applications to store unstructured data, such as documents and images, on the file system. Applications can leverage the rich streaming APIs and performance of the file system and at the same time maintain transactional consistency between the unstructured data and corresponding structured data.

FileTables (SQL Server)

The FileTable feature brings support for the Windows file namespace and compatibility with Windows applications to the file data stored in SQL Server. FileTable lets an application integrate its storage and data management components, and provides integrated SQL Server services - including full-text search and semantic search - over unstructured data and metadata.

In other words, you can store files and documents in special tables in SQL Server called FileTables, but access them from Windows applications as if they were stored in the file system, without making any changes to your client applications.

Remote Blob Store (RBS) (SQL Server)

Remote BLOB store (RBS) for SQL Server lets database administrators store binary large objects (BLOBs) in commodity storage solutions instead of directly on the server. This saves a significant amount of space and avoids wasting expensive server hardware resources. RBS provides a set of API libraries that define a standardized model for applications to access BLOB data. RBS also includes maintenance tools, such as garbage collection, to help manage remote BLOB data.

RBS is included on the SQL Server installation media, but is not installed by the SQL Server Setup program.

Structurally, similar to other database platforms SQL server defines the limits for entering large objects (Table 2).

MySQL[7] Philosophy of Large Objects

A BLOB is a binary large object that can hold a variable amount of data. The four BLOB types are TINYBLOB, BLOB, MEDIUMBLOB, and LONGBLOB. These differ only in the maximum length of the values they can hold. The four TEXT types are TINYTEXT, TEXT, MEDIUMTEXT, and LONGTEXT. These correspond to the four BLOB types and have the same maximum lengths and storage requirements (The BLOB and the TEXT Types, 2017).

Table 2.

Data Type	Description
char(n)	Fixed width character string. Maximum 8,000 characters
varchar(n)	Variable width character string. Maximum 8,000 characters
varchar(max)	Variable width character string. Maximum 1,073,741,824 characters
text	Variable width character string. Maximum 2GB of text data
nchar	Fixed width Unicode string. Maximum 4,000 characters
nvarchar	Variable width Unicode string. Maximum 4,000 characters
nvarchar(max)	Variable width Unicode string. Maximum 536,870,912 characters
ntext	Variable width Unicode string. Maximum 2GB of text data
bit	Allows 0, 1, or NULL
binary(n)	Fixed width binary string. Maximum 8,000 bytes
varbinary	Variable width binary string. Maximum 8,000 bytes
varbinary(max)	Variable width binary string. Maximum 2GB
image	Variable width binary string. Maximum 2GB

BLOB values are treated as binary strings (byte strings). They have no character set, and sorting and comparison are based on the numeric values of the bytes in column values. TEXT values are treated as nonbinary strings (character strings). They have a character set, and values are sorted and compared based on the collation of the character set.

If strict SQL mode is not enabled and you assign a value to a BLOB or TEXT column that exceeds the column's maximum length, the value is truncated to fit and a warning is generated. For truncation of nonspace characters, you can cause an error to occur (rather than a warning) and suppress insertion of the value by using strict SQL mode.

Truncation of excess trailing spaces from values to be inserted into TEXT columns always generates a warning, regardless of the SQL mode.

For TEXT and BLOB columns, there is no padding on insert and no bytes are stripped on select.

If a TEXT column is indexed, index entry comparisons are space-padded at the end. This means that, if the index requires unique values, duplicate-key errors will occur for values that differ only in the number of trailing spaces. For example, if a table contains 'a', an attempt to store 'a ' causes a duplicate-key error. This is not true for BLOB columns.

In most respects, you can regard a BLOB column as a VARBINARY column that can be as large as you like. Similarly, you can regard a TEXT column as a

VARCHAR column. BLOB and TEXT differ from VARBINARY and VARCHAR in the following ways:

For indexes on BLOB and TEXT columns, you must specify an index prefix length. For CHAR and VARCHAR, a prefix length is optional.

BLOB and TEXT columns cannot have DEFAULT values.

If you use the BINARY attribute with a TEXT data type, the column is assigned the binary collation of the column character set.

LONG and LONG VARCHAR map to the MEDIUMTEXT data type. This is a compatibility feature.

MySQL Connector/ODBC defines BLOB values as LONGVARBINARY and TEXT values as LONGVARCHAR.

Because BLOB and TEXT values can be extremely long, you might encounter some constraints in using them:

Only the first max_sort_length bytes of the column are used when sorting. The default value of max_sort_length is 1024. You can make more bytes significant in sorting or grouping by increasing the value of max_sort_length at server startup or runtime. Any client can change the value of its session max_sort_length variable:

```
mysql> SET max_sort_length = 2000;
mysql> SELECT id, comment FROM t
    -> ORDER BY comment;
```

Instances of BLOB or TEXT columns in the result of a query that is processed using a temporary table causes the server to use a table on disk rather than in memory because the MEMORY storage engine does not support those data types. Use of disk incurs a performance penalty, so include BLOB or TEXT columns in the query result only if they are really needed. For example, avoid using SELECT *, which selects all columns.

The maximum size of a BLOB or TEXT object is determined by its type, but the largest value you actually can transmit between the client and server is determined by the amount of available memory and the size of the communications buffers. You can change the message buffer size by changing the value of the max_allowed_packet variable, but you must do so for both the server and your client program. For example, both mysql and mysqldump enable you to change the client-side max_allowed_packet value. You may also want to compare the packet sizes and the size of the data objects you are storing with the storage requirements.

Each BLOB or TEXT value is represented internally by a separately allocated object. This is in contrast to all other data types, for which storage is allocated once per column when the table is opened.

In some cases, it may be desirable to store binary data such as media files in BLOB or TEXT columns. You may find MySQL's string handling functions useful for working with such data. For security and other reasons, it is usually preferable to do so using application code rather than giving application users the FILE privilege.

MySQL defines the following limits for entering large objects (Table 3).

ORACLE Philosophy of Large Objects

A BLOB (binary large object) is a varying-length binary string that can be up to 2,147,483,647 characters long. Like other binary types, BLOB strings are not associated with a code page. In addition, BLOB strings do not hold character data (BLOB Data Type, 2017).

The length is given in bytes for BLOB unless one of the suffixes K, M, or G is given, relating to the multiples of 1024, 1024*1024, 1024*1024*1024 respectively.

Note: Length is specified in bytes for BLOB.

Table 3.

Data Type	Description
CHAR(size)	Holds a fixed length string (can contain letters, numbers, and special characters). The fixed size is specified in parenthesis. Can store up to 255 characters
VARCHAR(size)	Holds a variable length string (can contain letters, numbers, and special characters). The maximum size is specified in parenthesis. Can store up to 255 characters. **Note:** If you put a greater value than 255 it will be converted to a TEXT type
TINYTEXT	Holds a string with a maximum length of 255 characters
TEXT	Holds a string with a maximum length of 65,535 characters
BLOB	For BLOBs (Binary Large OBjects). Holds up to 65,535 bytes of data
MEDIUMTEXT	Holds a string with a maximum length of 16,777,215 characters
MEDIUMBLOB	For BLOBs (Binary Large OBjects). Holds up to 16,777,215 bytes of data
LONGTEXT	Holds a string with a maximum length of 4,294,967,295 characters
LONGBLOB	For BLOBs (Binary Large OBjects). Holds up to 4,294,967,295 bytes of data
ENUM(x,y,z,etc.)	Let you enter a list of possible values. You can list up to 65535 values in an ENUM list. If a value is inserted that is not in the list, a blank value will be inserted.
	Note: The values are sorted in the order you enter them.
	You enter the possible values in this format: ENUM('X','Y','Z')
SET	Similar to ENUM except that SET may contain up to 64 list items and can store more than one choice

```
Syntax
{ BLOB | BINARY LARGE OBJECT } [ (length [{K |M |G }]) ]
Default
A BLOB without a specified length is defaulted to two gigabytes
(2,147,483,647).
```

Note: Use the getBlob method on the java.sql.ResultSet to retrieve a BLOB handle
to the underlying data.

POSTGRESQL[8] Philosophy of Large Objects

Binary Data Types

The bytea data type allows storage of binary strings.

```
bytea          1 or 4 bytes plus the actual binary
string          variable-length binary string
```

A binary string is a sequence of octets (or bytes). Binary strings are distinguished from character strings in two ways. First, binary strings specifically allow storing octets of value zero and other "non-printable" octets (usually, octets outside the range 32 to 126). Character strings disallow zero octets, and also disallow any other octet values and sequences of octet values that are invalid according to the database's selected character set encoding. Second, operations on binary strings process the actual bytes, whereas the processing of character strings depends on locale settings. In short, binary strings are appropriate for storing data that the programmer thinks of as "raw bytes", whereas character strings are appropriate for storing text (Binary Data Types, 2017).

The bytea type supports two external formats for input and output: PostgreSQL's historical "escape" format, and "hex" format. Both of these are always accepted on input. The output format depends on the configuration parameter bytea_output; the default is hex. (Note that the hex format was introduced in PostgreSQL 9.0; earlier versions and some tools don't understand it.)

The SQL standard defines a different binary string type, called BLOB or BINARY LARGE OBJECT. The input format is different from bytea, but the provided functions and operators are mostly the same.

BLOB TRANSFER

Concept of BLOB Transfer (From Client to Server)

One of the most suitable methods for BLOB transfer from client to server involves the use of two levels:

- Server level
- Client level

Server level is the key concept of this approach. Namely, the use of stored procedures and views is the basis of distribution of data in the corresponding table. Regardless of whether the table is relationally associated with other tables, the concept provides the control of entry only on server side (Figure 2).

This approach implies that stored procedure is responsible for the quality distribution of data into the appropriate field. Therefore, the first level of entering BLOB in the database is defining the field where a binary large object will be entered. As an example a database called TEST is created within SQL server. Within it BLOBexample table was created with three fields. The first field contains the primary key entry for field identification, while the other field contains BLOB itself whose type is defined as varbinary(max) in accordance with the limits defined in the Table 2. In order to understand and decode the binary object by the operating system, the next field will contain the name and file extension that will be distributed into the base (Guo, 2002).

Figure 2. Basic concept of BLOB and CLOB distribution into IoT core

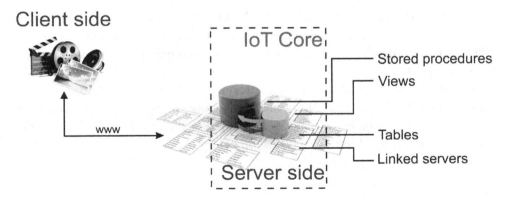

List 1. Code for creating a demo table

```
USE [IoT]
GO
/****** Object:  Table [dbo].[BLOBexample]    Script Date:
##/##/#### ##:##:## ******/
SET ANSI_NULLS ON
GO
SET QUOTED_IDENTIFIER ON
GO
SET ANSI_PADDING ON
GO
CREATE TABLE [dbo].[BLOBexample](
        [IDblob] [bigint] IDENTITY(1,1) NOT NULL,
        [BLOB] [varbinary](max) NOT NULL,
        [Filename] [nvarchar](max) NOT NULL
 CONSTRAINT [PK_BLOBexample] PRIMARY KEY CLUSTERED
(
        [IDblob] ASC
)WITH (PAD_INDEX  = OFF, STATISTICS_NORECOMPUTE  = OFF, IGNORE_
DUP_KEY = OFF,
ALLOW_ROW_LOCKS  = ON, ALLOW_PAGE_LOCKS  = ON) ON [PRIMARY]
) ON [PRIMARY]
GO
SET ANSI_PADDING OFF
GO
```

Entering the data is performed by standard INSERT statement (statement).

Previous SQL Codes fully describe the server side of entering the BLOB. All other solutions are only variations on this subject, including the solutions described in the section 4.2.

The client side, regardless of the platform used, involves the formation of a connection to a subject base. The connection can be formed locally, as well as at a remote location, which is the essence of IoT. For the purposes of this text the connection is formed through TCP/IP protocol by the SQL server on a modified port 1533 (the default port is 1433).

List 2. Stored procedure that performs entering the BLOB in the table BLOBexample has the following form

```
USE [IoT]
GO
/****** Object:  StoredProcedure [dbo].[BLOBInsert]     Script
Date: ##/##/#### ##:##:## ******/
SET ANSI_NULLS ON
GO
SET QUOTED_IDENTIFIER ON
GO
-- ================================================
-- Author:                  IoT
-- Create date: ##/##/####
-- Description:             BLOB Insert in database
-- ================================================
CREATE PROCEDURE [dbo].[BLOBInsert]
        -- Add the parameters for the stored procedure here
        @BLOB varbinary(max),
        @Filename nvarchar(max)

AS
BEGIN
        SET NOCOUNT ON;
            INSERT INTO dbo.BLOBexample (BLOB, Filename)
VALUES
        (@BLOB, @Filename)
END
GO
```

Applicative Solution of BLOB Transfer (VB 6.0) (Direction Client-Server)

In order to illustrate the above mentioned stored procedure an example code in Visual Studio VB 6.0. is given as a basis (Cornell, 1998). The code is interesting from the aspect of using the connections to the database from somewhat older programming languages. Two basic objects are given as an example (a window with the folders list and a window with the folders content) (Figure 3). By pressing the send button,

Figure 3. An example of the developed form VB 6.0

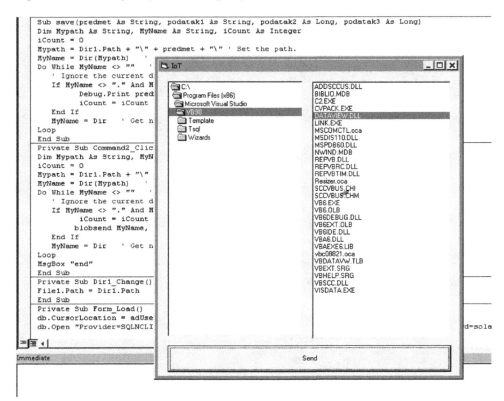

sending of all files from the selected folder into the database is performed by means of stored procedure.

The key feature of the presented solution is based on providing a connection to the database server, defining the memory stream that takes content from the file stream and as such it is passed to stored procedure by using ADODB connection (marked in red).

Applicative Solution of BLOB Transfer (.NET VB) (Direction Client-Server)

This technique is based on the .NET Framework, which similar to the previous concept, performs the connection of applications with the database server using ready-made libraries System.Data.SqlClient. The application, like the previous one, contains two lists (the folders list and the list of the selected folder content), as well as the button for sending the selected file into the database (Figure 4.).

List 3. Applicative solution has the form

```
Option Explicit
Dim db As New ADODB.Connection
Dim cmd As New ADODB.Command
Dim mstream As ADODB.Stream
Sub save(predmet As String, podatak1 As String, podatak2 As
Long, podatak3 As Long)
Dim Mypath As String, MyName As String, iCount As Integer
iCount = 0
Mypath = Dir1.Path + "\" + predmet + "\" ' Set the path.
MyName = Dir(Mypath)    ' Retrieve the first entry.
Do While MyName <> ""    ' Start the loop.
   ' Ignore the current directory and the encompassing
directory.
   If MyName <> "." And MyName <> ".." Then
        Debug.Print predmet + " - " + MyName
        iCount = iCount + 1
   End If
   MyName = Dir   ' Get next entry.
Loop
End Sub
Private Sub Command2_Click()
Dim Mypath As String, MyName As String, iCount As Integer
iCount = 0
Mypath = Dir1.Path + "\" ' Set the path.
MyName = Dir(Mypath)    ' Retrieve the first entry.
Do While MyName <> ""    ' Start the loop.
   ' Ignore the current directory and the encompassing
directory.
   If MyName <> "." And MyName <> ".." Then
        iCount = iCount + 1
        blobsend MyName, Mypath
   End If
   MyName = Dir   ' Get next entry.
Loop
MsgBox "end"
End Sub
Private Sub Dir1_Change()
```

continued on following page

List 3. Continued

```
File1.Path = Dir1.Path
End Sub
Private Sub Form_Load()
db.CursorLocation = adUseClient
db.Open "Provider=SQLNCLI10;Server=YYY.YYY.YYY.YYY,1533;Databas
e=IoT;Uid=username;Pwd=pass"
End Sub
Private Sub blobsend(imefajla As String, putanja As String)
cmd.ActiveConnection = db
cmd.CommandType = adCmdStoredProc
cmd.CommandText = "BLOBInsert"
Set mstream = New ADODB.Stream
mstream.Type = adTypeBinary
mstream.Open
mstream.LoadFromFile putanja + "\" + imefajla
cmd.Parameters.Append cmd.CreateParameter("BLOB",
adLongVarBinary, adParamInput, mstream.Size)
cmd.Parameters.Append cmd.CreateParameter("Filename",
adVarChar, adParamInput, 50, imefajla)
cmd.Parameters("BLOB").Attributes = adFldLong
cmd.Parameters("BLOB").AppendChunk mstream.Read
cmd.Execute
cmd.Parameters.Delete ("BLOB")
cmd.Parameters.Delete ("Filename")
End Sub
```

Unlike the solution that is used in VB 6.0, sql string is here defined with integrated parameters without subsequent addition which is suitable in cases when there is a great number of parameters.

Applicative Solution of BLOB Transfer (.NET C#)

Using the .NET Framework is also represented in this programming language under the Visual Studio environment (Figure 5). The dialogue control is here used where the selected file via the generated stored procedure is sent to the database. The main library is the same as in the previous example.

Adding parameters to the stored procedure is performed in the same way as in the first example VB 6.0. From all the previous examples it is obvious that defining

Figure 4. An example of developed form .NET VB

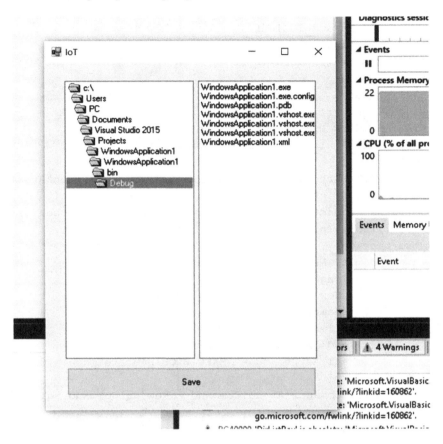

the size of the files is essential in order to clearly define the buffer and prepare it for sending BLOB into the database.

SQL and the Applicative Solution of Clob Transfer (JAVA)

For demonstration purposes of entering the data type character which are the basis of CLOB, a table employee is generated (Roberts, 2008):

```
USE [IoT]
GO
/****** Object:  Table [dbo].[employee]    Script Date: YY/YY/
YYYY YY:YY:YY ******/
SET ANSI_NULLS ON
```

List 4. Applicative solution has the form

```
Imports System.Data.SqlClient
Imports System.Drawing
Imports System.Drawing.Drawing2D
Imports System.IO
Public Class Form1
    Private Sub DirListBox1_Change(sender As Object, e As
EventArgs) Handles DirListBox1.Change
        FileListBox1.Path = DirListBox1.Path
    End Sub
    Private Sub Button1_Click(sender As Object, e As EventArgs)
Handles Button1.Click
        Using connection As New SqlConnection("Data Source=YYY.
YYY.YYY.YYY,1533; Initial Catalog=IoT; User Id=username
;Password=pass;")
            Dim fs As System.IO.FileStream
            Dim imagedata() As Byte
            fs = New FileStream(DirListBox1.Path + "\" +
FileListBox1.FileName, FileMode.Open)
            ReDim imagedata(fs.Length)
            fs.Read(imagedata, 0, fs.Length)
            Dim sql As String = "EXEC BLOBInsert @imgdata,@
nazivfajla"
            Dim command2 As SqlCommand = New SqlCommand(sql,
connection)
            Dim sqlpara As New SqlParameter("imgData", SqlDbType.
Image)
            Dim sqlparb As New SqlParameter("nazivfajla",
FileListBox1.FileName)

            sqlpara.SqlValue = fs
            command2.Parameters.Add(sqlpara)
            command2.Parameters.Add(sqlparb)

            connection.Open()
            command2.ExecuteNonQuery()
            connection.Close()
            fs.Close()
        End Using
    End Sub
End Class
```

Figure 5. An example of developed form .NET C#

```
GO
SET QUOTED_IDENTIFIER ON
GO
CREATE TABLE [dbo].[employee](
        [employeeId] [bigint] IDENTITY(1,1) NOT NULL,
        [string] [nvarchar](50) NOT NULL,
 CONSTRAINT [PK_employee] PRIMARY KEY CLUSTERED
(
        [employeeId] ASC
)WITH (PAD_INDEX  = OFF, STATISTICS_NORECOMPUTE  = OFF, IGNORE_
DUP_KEY = OFF,
ALLOW_ROW_LOCKS  = ON, ALLOW_PAGE_LOCKS  = ON) ON [PRIMARY]
) ON [PRIMARY]
GO
```

The task of the stored procedure is to return the primary entry key to the client for each entered data on the employee.

In case of using JAVA to communicate with the SQL servers it is necessary to integrate the JDBC driver to the development environment. The applicative solution,

List 5. Applicative solution has the form

```
using System;
using System.Collections.Generic;
using System.ComponentModel;
using System.Data;
using System.Data.SqlClient;
using System.Drawing;
using System.IO;
using System.Linq;
using System.Text;
using System.Threading.Tasks;
using System.Windows.Forms;
namespace WindowsFormsApplication3
{
    public partial class Form1: Form
    {
        public Form1()
        {
            InitializeComponent();
        }
        private void button1_Click(object sender, EventArgs e)
        {
            openFileDialog1.ShowDialog();
            using (SqlConnection conn = new SqlConnection("Data
Source=YYY.YYY.YYY.YYY,1533;Initial Catalog=IoT;User
Id=username;Password=pass;"))
                {
                    conn.Open();
                    SqlCommand cmd = new SqlCommand("BLOBInsert",
conn);
                    cmd.CommandType = CommandType.StoredProcedure;
                    byte[] buffer;
                    FileStream fileStream = new
FileStream(openFileDialog1.InitialDirectory + openFileDialog1.
FileName,
 FileMode.Open, FileAccess.Read);
                    try
                    {
                        int length = (int)fileStream.Length;   //
```

continued on following page

List 5. Continued

```
get file length
                buffer = new byte[length];              //
create buffer
                int count;                               //
actual number of bytes read
                int sum = 0;                             //
total number of bytes read
                // read until Read method returns 0 (end of
the stream has been reached)
                while ((count = fileStream.Read(buffer,
sum, length - sum)) > 0)
                    sum += count;   // sum is a buffer
offset for next reading
                }
                finally
                {
                    fileStream.Close();
                }
                cmd.Parameters.Add(new SqlParameter("@BLOB",
buffer));
                cmd.Parameters.Add(new SqlParameter("@
Filename", openFileDialog1.FileName));
                cmd.Parameters.Add(new SqlParameter("@
Extension", openFileDialog1.FileName));
                cmd.ExecuteNonQuery();
                conn.Close();
            }
        }
    }
}
```

as all the previous, is based on the object-oriented paradigm with precise orientation of the flow of data to the database.

Web Applicative Solution of BLOB Transfer (ASP, HTML5)

Web applicative solution of the desired blob transfer from server to client includes past analyses with the basic segment of the data type distribution using the stored

List 6. The stored procedure GenerateID for entering the data into the database is also generated

```
USE [IoT]
GO
/****** Object:  StoredProcedure [dbo].[GenerateID]    Script
Date: YY/YY/YYYY YY:YY:YY ******/
SET ANSI_NULLS ON
GO
SET QUOTED_IDENTIFIER ON
GO
-- =============================================
-- Author:              IoT
-- Create date: today
-- Description:            -
-- =============================================
CREATE PROCEDURE [dbo].[GenerateID]
        -- Add the parameters for the stored procedure here
        @String nvarchar(50)
AS
BEGIN
        -- SET NOCOUNT ON added to prevent extra result sets
from
        -- interfering with SELECT statements.
        SET NOCOUNT ON;
    -- Insert statements for procedure here
        Insert into employee (string) VALUES (@String)

        SELECT scope_identity() as employeeId, 1 as test


END
GO
```

procedure. The procedure that is shown here based on the primary key of document distributes the BLOB to the client (web page) which is controlled by Internet Information Server (ASP 4.0). IIS communicates with the SQL server using the connection configuration string:

List 7. Applicative solution developed in te environment Eclipse has the form

```
                    package newPackage;
// Import required packages
import java.sql.CallableStatement;
import java.sql.Connection;
import java.sql.DriverManager;
import java.sql.ResultSet;
import java.sql.SQLException;
public class yadarr {
    // JDBC driver name and database URL

    public static void main(String[] args) {
          Connection con = null;
        CallableStatement proc_stmt = null;
        ResultSet rs = null;
        try {

            Class.forName("com.microsoft.sqlserver.jdbc.
SQLServerDriver");

            con = DriverManager.getConnection
("jdbc:sqlserver://YYY.YYY.YYY.YYY:1534;databaseName=IoT",
"username", "pass");

            proc_stmt = con.prepareCall("{ call generateID(?)
}");

            proc_stmt.setString(1, "employee");
            rs = proc_stmt.executeQuery();

            if (rs.next()) {
                int employeeId = rs.getInt(1);
                System.out.println("Generated employeeId: " +
employeeId);
            } else {
                System.out.println("Stored procedure couldn't
generate new Id");
```

continued on following page

259

List 7. Continued

```java
        }
    } catch (ClassNotFoundException ex) {
        ex.printStackTrace();
    } catch (SQLException ex) {
        ex.printStackTrace();
    } finally {

        try {

            rs.close();
            proc_stmt.close();
            con.close();

        } catch (SQLException ex) {
            ex.printStackTrace();
        }

    }

    System.out.println("Goodbye!");
}//end main
}
```

```xml
<?xml version="1.0"?>
<configuration>
  <system.web>
    <compilation debug="true" targetFramework="4.0"/>
    <customErrors mode="Off" defaultRedirect="~/greska.cshtml">
              <error statusCode="404" redirect="~/
Nepostojeca.cshtml" />
        </customErrors>
    <httpRuntime maxRequestLength="10240" />
        <sessionState timeout="180" />
  </system.web>
  <connectionStrings>
   <add name="DBkonekcija-Poglavlje" connectionString="Data
Source=XXX.XXX.XXX.XXX,XXXX;Initial Catalog=Iot;User
Id=username;Password=pass;" providerName="System.Data.
```

```
SqlClient"/>
  </connectionStrings>
  <system.data>
    <DbProviderFactories>
      <remove invariant="System.Data.SqlServerCe.4.0"/>
      <add name="Microsoft SQL Server Compact Data Provider
4.0" invariant = "System.Data.SqlServerCe.4.0" description
= ".NET Framework Data Provider for Microsoft SQL Server
Compact" type = "System.Data.SqlServerCe.SqlCeProviderFactory,
System.Data.SqlServerCe, Version = 4.0.0.0, Culture=neutral,
PublicKeyToken = 89845dcd8080cc91"/>
      <add name="SqlClient Data Provider"
        invariant="System.Data.SqlClient"
        description=".Net Framework Data Provider for SqlServer"
        type="System.Data.SqlClient.SqlClientFactory, System.
Data,
      Version=2.0.0.0, Culture=neutral, PublicKeyToken=b77a5c561
934e089"/>
    </DbProviderFactories>
  </system.data>
  <appSettings>


  </appSettings>
</configuration>
```

Source code of displaying the documents for constant value of the primary key and displaying the given BLOB (assuming that there is a support in the browser for a particular extension) has the form:

```
@{
    var db = Database.Open("DBkonekcija-Poglavlje");
    var upit = "select * from BLOBexample where IDblob=36";
    var rez = db.QuerySingle(upit);
    Response.ContentType = "image/png";
        Response.AddHeader("content-disposition",
"inline;filename=" + Request["Filename"]+"."+Request["Extensi
on"]);
    Response.Cache.SetCacheability(HttpCacheability.NoCache);
    Response.BinaryWrite((byte[])rez.BLOB);
```

```
}
PHP solution:
<?php
error_reporting(1);
error_reporting(E_ALL);
$connectionInfo = array("UID"=>"username","PWD"=>"pass", "Datab
ase"=>"IoT","CharacterSet" => "UTF-8");
$conn = sqlsrv_connect("XXX.XXX.XXX.XXX,XXXX",
$connectionInfo);
if($conn === false)
{
        echo "Konekcija neuspesna.</br>";
        die();
}
$sql = "select * from BLOBexample where IDblob=?";
$params = array(36);
$stmt = sqlsrv_query($conn, $sql, $params);
header("Content-type: image/jpeg");
while($row = sqlsrv_fetch_array($stmt, SQLSRV_FETCH_ASSOC)) {
    echo $row['BLOB'];
}
sqlsrv_free_stmt($stmt);
?>
```

The Feedback Server-Client (Pagination)

As it is known, the distribution of data over the Internet is limited by throughput capacity of the net itself. Despite the fact that new technologies bring ever increasing speed of information flow, taking into account that large strings of data are BLOB, it is vital that return data sets be packet form. Taking into consideration the intentions of multiplatform use of web browser (orientation toward web applications) it becomes clear that infinitely long strings of data (for example table) are not practical for display on one browser screen. Previously mentioned also applies on the network flow itself. This practically means that displaying of data is dictated by the terms of pagination which is practically applied in modern web.

The solution that is shown here relies only on SQL software platform. The basic idea is that the conditions of pagination are dictated from the client side, while the server side by standard SELECT statement, using local memory space, generates the selected data package dictated by the client side. Previously mentioned is achieved using the two stored procedures:

The first stored procedure generates the data package based on the dictated conditions:

```
USE [IoT]
GO
/****** Object:  StoredProcedure [dbo].[Pagination]    Script
Date: YY/YY/YYYY YY:YY:YY ******/
SET ANSI_NULLS ON
GO
SET QUOTED_IDENTIFIER ON
GO
-- =============================================
-- Author:                IoT
-- Create date:    Today
-- Description:          -
-- =============================================
CREATE PROCEDURE [dbo].[Pagination]
        -- Add the parameters for the stored procedure here
        @Page int,
        @RecsPerPage int,
        @Col int,
        @AscDesc nvarchar(10),
        @Question nvarchar(50)
AS
DECLARE
@FirstRec int,
@LastRec int,
@Kolona nvarchar(100),
@cmd nvarchar(4000),
@REZ datetime
BEGIN
        -- SET NOCOUNT ON added to prevent extra result sets
from
        -- interfering with SELECT statements.
        SET NOCOUNT ON;
SELECT @FirstRec = (@Page - 1) * @RecsPerPage
SELECT @LastRec = (@Page * @RecsPerPage + 1)
```

```
CREATE TABLE #TempItems
(
employee nvarchar(50))
CREATE TABLE #TempItems1
(RowNum int IDENTITY PRIMARY KEY,
employee nvarchar(50))
INSERT INTO #TempItems (employee)
SELECT     TOP (100) PERCENT dbo.employee.string
FROM          dbo.employee
WHERE

        (string Like '%' + @question + '%')
SET @cmd = 'Select * from #TempItems ORDER BY ' +
CONVERT(varchar(20),@col)+ ' ' +@AscDesc
INSERT INTO #TempItems1 EXEC(@cmd)
SET @cmd = '              SELECT TOP  ('+CONVERT(varchar(20),@
LastRec -1)+') employee
        FROM #TempItems1
        WHERE RowNum >'+ CONVERT(varchar(20),@FirstRec) +'
        AND RowNum <'+ CONVERT(varchar(20),@LastRec)
EXEC(@cmd)
---- Drop the temp table
    DROP TABLE #TempItems
    DROP TABLE #TempItems1
END
GO
```

It can be seen from the previous code that the initial conditions are dictated by the page which is necessary to be displayed, by the type number per page, by the column number on which sorting will be done (ASC or DESC), as well as by the query based on which a complete database search will be performed. Generating of the first temporary table with the search results of the basic query (question) is performed based on the initial conditions. The second temporary table contains the results of additional filter with conditions that describe pagination itself (page number, type number, column by which sorting is done). Finally the results are returned to the client.

Since it remained unclear from the first stored procedure how large is the sample that is at the clients disposal, in order to complete the logic of pagination the second stored procedure returns the total number of types that are necessary to be displayed, tht is how large is the CLOB sample:

```
USE [IoT]
GO
/****** Object:  StoredProcedure [dbo].[ PaginationCounter]
Script Date: YY/YY/YYYY YY:YY:YY ******/
SET ANSI_NULLS ON
GO
SET QUOTED_IDENTIFIER ON
GO
-- ================================================
-- Author:                IoT
-- Create date:   Today
-- Description:           -
-- ================================================
CREATE PROCEDURE [dbo].[ PaginationCounter]
        -- Add the parameters for the stored procedure here

        @Page int,
        @RecsPerPage int,
        @Col int,
        @AscDesc nvarchar(10),
        @question nvarchar(50)



AS
DECLARE
@FirstRec int,
@LastRec int,
@Kolona nvarchar(100),
@cmd nvarchar(4000),
@REZ datetime
BEGIN
        -- SET NOCOUNT ON added to prevent extra result sets
from
        -- interfering with SELECT statements.
        SET NOCOUNT ON;
SELECT @FirstRec = (@Page - 1) * @RecsPerPage
SELECT @LastRec = (@Page * @RecsPerPage + 1)
SELECT    TOP (100) PERCENT COUNT(dbo.employee.employeeId) as
Countt
```

```
FROM        dbo.employee
WHERE
        (string Like '%' + @question + '%')
END
GO
```

Practically, the client get two sets of information:

- The size of a sample that is at disposal and
- The data set for the intended sample size.

This means that the server returns only a limited data set, which overcomes the problem of uncontrolled flow of large amounts of information that leads to the liberation of network resources.

MECHATRONIC SYSTEM WITH FEEDBACK

Special civil protection services such as firefighting units, ambulance and police are the most important segments of the program for protection of people and property within which the benefits of fleet management is crucial. Vehicle tracking in real time provides coordination of all vehicles of the fleet as well as sending the closest vehicles with the possibility of selecting the shortest paths which are some of the advantages that IoT system offers and that are of vital importance for the quality functioning of the services and timely delivery of necessary assistance.

The electronic device installed in the vehicle in order to enable the owner or a third party to monitor and determine the location of the vehicle is the basis for the work of this type of IoT system. The most modern vehicle tracking systems use GPS modules with implemented algorithms for increasing the precision to locate the vehicles as accurately as possible (Mohinder S. Grewal, 2001). Many systems combine communication modules such as cellular or satellite transmitters to establish the connection between the device installed in the vehicle and a remote information system for data collection. The information collected on the vehicle are displayed on electronic maps via the Internet or specialized softwares. Modern vehicle tracking systems originate from the ship industry that required some sort of a system that would allow it to determine at any time where each of the vessels are, in order to facilitate the locating of the vessels in the event of danger, damage or disaster. Another of the important functions and advantages of these systems is the possibility of an early warning against bad weather conditions based on meteorological data and the position of the vessel, which protects the vessels, the material goods that are transported and the most important, the human lives.

As an example of the above, a dynamic database can be made that in real time continuously updates the data obtained from the system that collects data on vehicle. The operator can, for example, seek the information on all the vehicles that consume more than a certain level of fuel per 100 km on a fuel consumption sensor that is installed . In this situation it may occur that some of the vehicles unusually consume a great deal which can be an alarm and indicate that there is a problem with the operation of the vehicle itself, which gives the operator the information that the vehicle must be sent to a premature technical inspection. The operator can also ask for a list of all vehicles that within a certain period exceeded a smaller number of kilometers than instructed, which in turn may indicate that those vehicles are little or not at all used. This information is very important for business and further planning, because if some vehicles ar not in use and require a certain maintenance, that only brings unnecessary cost to the company. The operator may decide to sell the vehicle, to put it in operation or to make an analysis of the vehicle utility based on which its further use will be determined. The operator can also ask for the inspection of the vehicles that exceeded over certain number of kilometers because this may indicate that the vehicles are close to break down or their replacement should be considered. In the companies that manage a large numbers of vehicles the listed items are very important for further planning and business development. Another solution offered by this type of software is the alarm adjustment that will somewhat earlier, for example 10-20 days, warn the operator that the vehicle is approaching the regular service or the time of registration.

Defining the authoritative parameters of monitoring (Blagojević Ivan, 2004) the conditions of fire engines is essential for reliable operating of this critical system. The necessary analysis of the objective possibilities for realization of the required hardware-software support is the starting point of the design and later the implementation of the developed solution. Conceptual setting of the monitoring system which is in theory required to be developed, includes several methods of data collection:

1. Positioning of the fire engine on the city map, route tracking of its movement when leaving to intervene, with the possibility to record these trajectories and their subsequent simulation at any time. Availability of data is also implied:
    a. Distance travelled,
    b. The time of departure to the intervention from the fire-fighting unit,
    c. The time of arrival to the location of intervention,
    d. The start time of acting with the fire engine.

2. Monitoring the data from the fire engine incomplete vehicle, where the world leading manufacturers of fire-fighting equipment, pursuant to the needs include the following parameters:
    a. Operating time of the incomplete vehicle engine and distance travelled,
    b. Incomplete vehicle engine rmp
    c. Pressure in the pneumatic installation of the vehicle,
    d. Incomplete vehicle engine oil pressure,
    e. Incomplete vehicle engine coolant temperature,
    f. Incomplete vehicle fuel level.
3. Monitoring the acquisition parameters additionally set on the upgrade, that is the equipment in the fire engine:
    a. Water pressure in the water pump (normal pressure, high pressure, recirculation),
    b. Temperature in the water pump housing (normal pressure, high pressure)
    c. Water pump number of rotations, with the possibility of monitoring the synchronicity of the pump drive
    d. Water pump operating time,
    e. Level of extinguishing agents (water, foaming agent), with the alert that the remaining capacity of extinguishing agents is at 10% of nominal and the estimation of the remaining operating time of the water pump in the current mode of operation. It also implies the availability of data on the expenditure of fire-fighting agents.
4. Monitoring the daily activities of fire-fighting personnel on the implementation of procedures and verification of characteristic systems functionality, where in addition to the effects of inclusion of particular devices, it is monitored and noted the compliance of firefighting personnel with defined protocols of putting them into function.
    a. Identification with the record of operator command on the water pump starting button,
    b. Identification with the record of operator command on the water pump main valve starting button,
    c. Identification with the record of operator command on recirculation starting button,
    d. Identification with the record of operator command on vacuum device starting button.

GPS receivers may use different form of communication with the microcontroller or computer. The usual form of communication is via the serial port, while the most commonly used protocol for transmitting these information is precisely NMEA protocol (Мирослав Демић, 2006).

NMEA (National Marine Electronics Association) defined the specification of communication protocol for exchanging data between different electronic devices used in maritime transport. The data is in this case transmitted in the form of sentences which are made up of a series of data and together constitute an independent set of data in relation to other sentences.

Each sentence starts with a special symbol <$> (ASCII 36), and ends with the characters for moving to a new line <CR> (ASCII 13) and <LF> (ASCII 10). The sentence consists of multiple words separated by a comma <,>. The first word in each sentence determines the type of sentence based on which sentence parsing can be performed in order to get the desired parameters. For example, a sentence that starts with $GPGLL provides information on latitude and longitude, the exact time (shown as UTC – (Universal Coordinated Time) and the data validity (A - Active or V - Void). Character that is used to define the end of the sentence <*> after which two more characters are sent that represent (eng. checksum) the value that provides the possibility to check whether the previously received data is valid. By applying the binary operation exclusively-or on all characters sent after the character <$>, and before the character <*>, a value is obtained as a result that can be in hexadecimal notation compared with the checksum field obtained in the sentence and thus check the validity of the data.

GPS receiver sends a set of NMEA sentences each second. In the event that data on latitude and longitude are not fixed (if the GPS receiver is not able to determine its position) and in the event that other data are not specified, GPS receiver will still continue to send the same set of sentences but reduced by the missing data.

There is a great number of different NMEA sentences that are used in maritime, and some of them can be applied to data received from the GPS receiver.

NMEA sentence that provides basic information on position after fixing the satellite is $GPGGA sentence. Since GPGGA sentences do not contain data on the speed of the vehicle it is necessary to parse GPRMC sentence as well.

$GPGGA – basic information about fixing the satellite, 3D coordinates of the position and accuracy of data. $GPRMC – minimum recommended data to locate – in addition to geographical position it contains the data on the speed of the vehicle, the exact time and date.

An example of $GPGGA sentence:

```
$GPGGA,105955.000,3150.6731,N,11711.9399,E,1,09,1.0,37.3,M,0.0
,M,,0000*57
```

Since the solution also involves monitoring other relevant parameters of the fire engine it is necessary to extend the sentence for those values. Some of the parameters are described in the text above, and for the purpose of this demonstration a parameter for monitoring the high pressure pump temperature is taken, whose proper functioning is essential for the actual firefighting.

Therefore, for the purpose of monitoring the vehicle and forming the potential feedback it is necessary to implement an electronic device that should perform the acquisition of the vehicle parameters such as its position (geographic coordinates), speed of the vehicle and measuring one of the parameters that indicate proper functioning f the vehicle during operation. After acquisition, the device should establish a connection with information system that collects data on the vehicles.

In addition to the data obtained using GPS receiver such as the position, the satellite time and the vehicle speed, the device also performs acquisition of the high pressure pump temperature whose increasing temperature would indicate a potential problem to the monitoring system, which would be capable of sending another vehicle to the intervention. This is only one of the parameters that indicates the proper functioning of the vehicle, but it is certainly very important because detection of the peak value of this parameter can timely alert the driver and the supervising authority and prevent a greater breakdown of the vehicle, as well as provide the normal functioning of the firefighting intervention as a whole.

Owing to the rapid development of techniques, availability of the elements necessary for the development of such electronic device is increasing. The basis of the device realization are microcontrollers, GPS and GSM modules. The device is basically divided into two units, acquisition and communication module. Communication is established between the above mentioned modules and each of these units is controlled by a microcontroller. There is plenty of space for further development and upgrade of the device due to this organization of the electronic device.

The main function of the acquisition module is collecting and selecting the data from the GPS monitoring system as well as measuring the temperature using a digital temperature sensor. When iteration of the data collection is completed, extended NMEA sentence that contains notification of the relevant information necessary for quality control of the vehicle is formed. The notification formed in that way is forwarded to the communication module.

The communication module is primarily intended for establishing and maintaining a connection to the server on which there is a part of the information system responsible for collecting and monitoring the condition of the vehicle. When the communication module receives notification from the acquisition module, the relevant data are being prepared for wireless transmission over the GPRS protocol of the GSM network. When establishing the a successful connection with the server, the data are sent to the server where they are permanently stored in the database, which allows their further processing. The general principle of the device operation is illustrated in Figure 6.

Figure 6. Layout of the developed IoT core for the present case

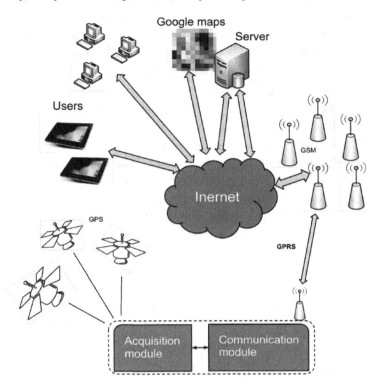

The primary task of the microcontroller that controls the operation of the acquisition module is receiving data from the GPS module, such as latitude and longitude, the exact satellite time and the speed of the vehicle. The data that can be obtained from the GSM module are grouped into standard NMEA sentences. The moment when GPS module fixes the sufficient number of satellites for accurate parameters determining it starts sending NMEA sentences with a period of one second. Since the communication protocol that microcontroller uses to communicate with GSM module is asynchronous serial UART communication, a mechanism of external interruption is used that provides a secure communication between the microcontroller and GSM module.

Hardware communication UART module that is located on microcontroller itself holds the buffer of three bytes which is unfortunately not enough for storing the complete NMEA sentence that could be several dozen characters long. The mechanism of interruption is used in order to solve this problem. When the NMEA sentence is stored into buffer, parsing is performed as well as data extracting that are of interest to control the vehicle.

In addition to communication with the GPS module, the microcontroller reads the digital temperature sensor. A chip with the tag MICROCHIP DS1820 is used for controlling the high pressure pump temperature in the vehicle. Operating range of measuring temperature for this chip is (-50 ÷ +125) °C, with an increment of 0,5 °C.

The device communication module is of great importance because the information system depends on it that needs data to be stored based on which the system users will have a complete overview of the condition and position of the vehicle.

The microcontroller communicates with the GSM module via an asynchronous serial UART connection. Communication is achieved using AT commands, which are defined by the manufacturer of the module. The interruption option is used for communication between the microcontroller and GSM module ensuring that communication is complete, i.e. without data loss.

After the connection to the server, the microcontroller sends a request to the server which contains the vehicle parameters. If the server receives all the data sent via the GPRS network, it will return the response "GPS OK", otherwise it will send a description of the error that occurred when receiving data. Depending on the response received from the server the microcontroller decides whether it is necessary to re-send the request to the server with the same data. The microcontroller will continue to send data to the server until it responds with the message "GSM OK"

Figure 7. Developed acquisition module

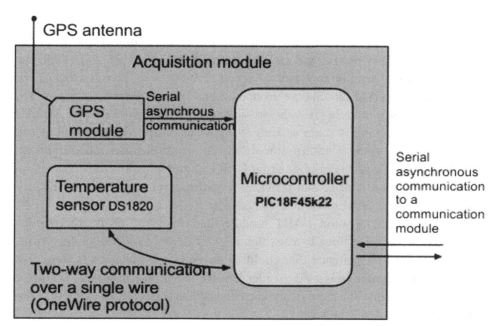

or until it receives, in the meantime, a new set of data from the acquisition module. The functional scheme of the communication module is shown in Figure 8.

After the distribution of extended NMEA sentence in SQL server database, the integrated stored procedure performs the decoding of the input string to specific columns (latitude, longitude, vehicle speed, temperature, ...). The table with operative information on the level of relational connectivity via the primary key defines the particular vehicle and provides access to the second stored procedure that has an integrated algorithm of pagination that is previously described.

At the request of web application, after establishing communication the SQL server distributes the information on the specific vehicle based on which the position is defined that is associated with the API maps and shows the position of the vehicle, as well as all the relevant information about it (Figure 9).

BLOB and CLOB objects integration, evidently, includes the development of systems and the application for monitoring the vehicles in real time represents a challenge from both software (James Bret Michael, 1995) and hardware point of view. The twenty-first century and the rapid development of programming along with the Internet have brought benefits in almost every aspect of life. Considering only one its part that includes development of the application GoogleMap as well as GSM and GPRS systems, the transmission of photos and videos, their storage and direct access, it can be said that it is hard to imagine life and work without them. The above mentioned systems are support not only to big companies but to

Figure 8. Functional scheme of the communication module

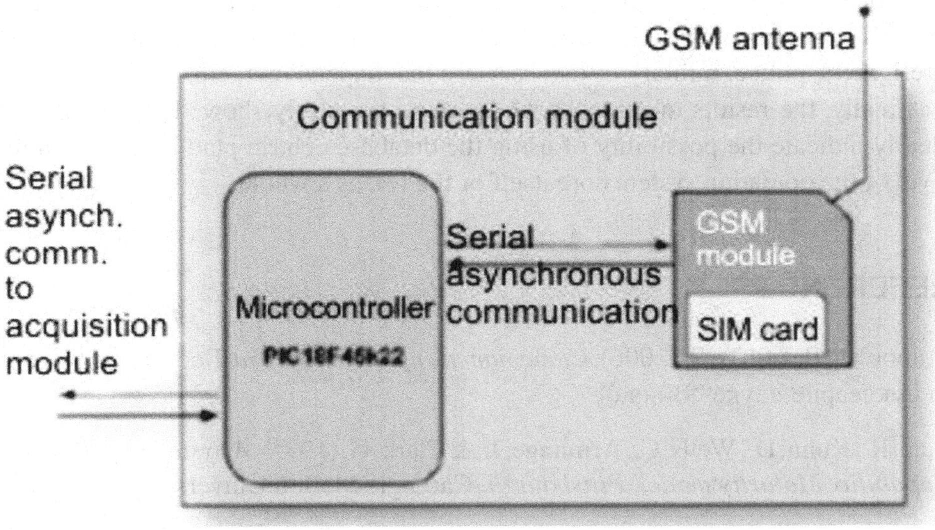

Figure 9. Layout of the output screen

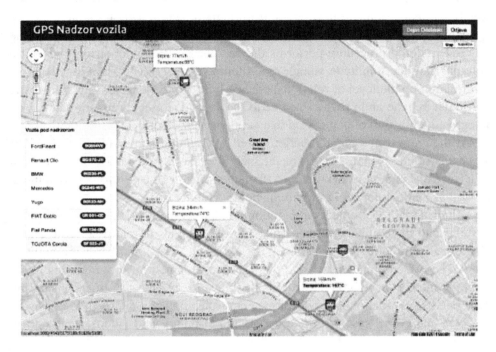

each individual as well. The material is aimed at contributing to the development of platform that will be an available, secure and stable support to the previously mentioned clients, developers, database administrators and engineers with an emphasis on critical systems (Blanchard B.S., 1998) such as emergency services, firefighters, police, military or taxi services that depend on them.

Finally, the results of research whose parts are partly showed in this chapter clearly indicate the possibility of using the database centric platforms and on the level of the operating system core itself or the IoT as a whole.

REFERENCES

Мирослав Демић Ђ. Д. (2006). *Сателитско праћење возила.* Београд: Институт за нуклеарне науке "Винча".

Bate, R., Kuhn, D., Wells, C., Armitage, J., & Clark, G. (1995). *A Systems engineering Capability Maturtiy model. Pittsbourgh.* Carnegie Mellon University.

Bergin, T. J., & Gibson, R. G. (1996). *History of programming languages---II*. Washington, DC: The American University.

Binary Data Types. (2017). Retrieved from www.postgresql.org: http://www. postgresql.org/docs/9.1/static/datatype-binary.html

Binary Large Object (Blob) Data (SQL Server). (2017). Retrieved from Microsoft: https://msdn.microsoft.com/en-us/library/bb895234.aspx

Blagojević Ivan, V. G. (2004). The possibilities for acquisition and usage of data concerning a large number of vehicles functioning, in real terms of exploitation using OBD technology. In *Virtual Product Development in Automotive Engineering*. Grac: Tehnički univerzitet Grac.

Blanchard, B. S. F. W. (1998). Systems Engineering and Analysis. Prentice Hall Inc.

BLOB Data Type. (2017). Retrieved from Oracle: http://docs.oracle.com/ javadb/10.8.2.2/ref/rrefblob.html

Character Large Object. (2017). Retrieved from wikipedia: https://en.wikipedia. org/wiki/Character_large_object

Cornell, G. (1998). *Visual Basic 6 from the Ground UP*. Toronto: Osborne/McGraw-Hill.

Guo, G. (2002). *High Performance Data Mining*. New York: Kluwer Academic Publishers. doi:10.1007/b116461

Humphrey, W. S. (2000). *Personal Software Process (PSP)*. Carnegie Mellon University.

Humphrey, W. S. (2000). *Team Software Process (TSP)*. Carnegie Mellon University.

James Bret Michael, A. C. (1995). Validation of Testing Results for Vehicle Control Software. *Intellimotion*, 2-15.

Kraus, L. (1996). *Programsko okruženje Delphi sa rešenim zadacima*. Beograd: Mikro Knjiga.

Large Objects. (2017). Retrieved from IBM: https://www.ibm.com/support/ knowledgecenter/SSEPGG_9.7.0/com.ibm.db2.luw.sql.ref.doc/doc/r0008473.html

Larman, C. (1998). *Applying UML and Patterns*. Prentice Hall PTR.

Mohinder, S., & Grewal, L. R. (2001). Global Positioning Systems, Inertial Navigation, and Integration. New York: John Wiley & Sons, Inc. Publication.

Roberts, E. (2008). *The Art and Science of Java*. Boston: Addison-Wesley.

Šunderić, D. (2003). SQL Server 2000, Stored Procedure & XML Programming (2nd ed.). New York: McGraw-Hill/Osborne.

The BLOB and the TEXT Types. (2017). Retrieved from MySQL: http://dev.mysql.com/doc/refman/5.7/en/blob.html

ENDNOTES

1. Personal Software Process
2. Team Software Process
3. Object Oriented Paradigm
4. Is a family of database server products developed by IBM. These products all support the relational model, but in recent years some products have been extended to support object-relational features and non-relational structures like JSON and XML
5. Oracle Database (commonly referred to as Oracle RDBMS or simply as Oracle) is an object-relational database management system produced and marketed by Oracle Corporation.
6. Microsoft SQL Server is a relational database management system developed by Microsoft.
7. is an open-source relational database management system (RDBMS)
8. is an object-relational database management system (ORDBMS) with an emphasis on extensibility and standards-compliance

Chapter 10
Cognitive Internet of Everything (CIoE):
State of the Art and Approaches

Gopal Singh Jamnal
Edinburgh Napier University, UK

Lu Fan
Edinburgh Napier University, UK

Xiaodong Liu
Edinburgh Napier University, UK

Muthu Ramachandran
Leeds Beckett University, UK

ABSTRACT

In today's world, we are living in busy metropolitan cities and want our homes to be ambient intelligent enough towards our cognitive requirements for assisted living in smart space environment and an excellent smart home control system should not rely on the users' instructions (Wanglei, 2015). The ambient intelligence is a sensational new information technology paradigm in which people are empowered for assisted living through multiple IoTs sensors environment that are aware of inhabitant presence and context and highly sensitive, adaptive and responsive to their needs. A noble ambient intelligent environment are characterized by their ubiquity, transparency and intelligence which seamlessly integrated into the background and invisible to surrounded users/inhabitant. Cognitive IoE (Internet of Everything) is a new type of pervasive computing. As the ambient smart home is into research only from a couple of years, many research outcomes are lacking potentials in ambient intelligence and need to be more dug around for better outcomes. As a result, an effective architecture of CIoE for ambient intelligent space is missing in other researcher's work. An unsupervised and supervised methods of machine learning

DOI: 10.4018/978-1-5225-2437-3.ch010

can be applied in order to classify the varied and complex user activities. In the first step, by using fuzzy set theory, the input dataset value can be fuzzified to obtain degree of membership for context from the physical layer. In the second step, using K-pattern clustering algorithms to discover pattern clusters and make dynamic rules based on identified patterns. This chapter provides an overview, critical evaluation of approaches and research directions to CIoE.

MOTIVATION: DIGITAL EVERYTHING AND DIGITAL EVERYWHERE

In recent years, impressive hardware technologies have been developed that let mobile and embedded devices to better exploit the web-internet features to ensure an enhanced interactive experience with the physical world. As earlier, Satyanarayanan (2001) suggested that great technology inventions are those, who dissolve themselves into everyday life and be invisible for human consciousness. Such research developments are making futuristic scenarios of Ambient Intelligence and smart environments into the reality of everyday lives by integrating research contribution from the fields of pervasive computing, sensor networking, IOTs, artificial intelligence, machine learning and context-aware computing. These smart spaces extend the functionality of ambient intelligence toward more proactive possibilities, where the smart environment not only monitors people for tasks or support them by executing their requests, but also influences and changes their plans and intentions. Also by the EU report, pervasive computing will be the next wave of new ICT innovation in the next five years, and it is said by 2020 pervasive computing will be one major type of ICT system (Ricci et al, 2015).

As, it is a great statement by EU 2020 report on IoTs that, pervasive computing will be the next wave of new ICT innovation in the next five years, and it's said by 2020 is will be one major type of ICT system. Many researchers all around the world are working on Context aware IoTs projects and many of them proposed their research findings but still this process is in iterative in nature which makes research to involve and investigate more about smart home, smart cities and urban computing projects. Furthermore, Taylor et al. (2015), stated that there will be a significant increase in the rate of change in the electronics industry as the Internet of Things (IoTs) becomes a reality, an explosion of sensor technology will take place. The challenges to integrate smart grids and cities, for semi-autonomous automobiles, smart manufacturing, building and home automation and to offer improved health care via remote monitoring or drug tracking; securely, offer tremendous opportunities to the electronics industry.

Figure 1. Predicted growth of IoT
(Taylor et al. 2015)

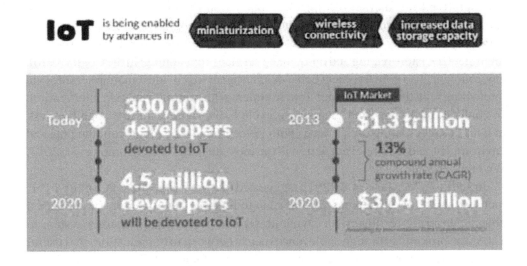

Overall, IoT is an enabling technology, whereas the internet and current communication networks connect People to People (P2P), it will connect Machine to Machine (M2M).Examples of applications include: wearable's, building and home automation, smart cities, smart manufacturing, health care and automotive. From cars and homes that respond to our every wish and want, to appliances that think for themselves, to interconnected geographies – from the most remote farmlands to bustling cities – we will all be digitally directed "Imagine the day when the entire continent of Africa is completely, digitally connected. That day will come by 2025" (Taylor et al. 2015).

As top computing schools and blue chip companies are working hard to capture this ready market, it becomes quite understandable that it will not only help human's daily life but will also boost financial economy around the world. Therefore big IT giants like IBM Watson, Samsung, Panasonic and Microsoft are building large research group and infrastructure to embrace the demand of 2020 for IoTs. As we know, it was year 2011 when IBM's Watson won the jeopardy championship trophy and challenged the human cognition intelligence in jeopardy game show on national TV and beat the human brains to quickly extract information and find the right/relevant answer in much shorter time. It was an alert indication that with knowledge engineering and context aware computing can reveal insights, patterns and relationships across large data sets to quickly extract the key information to answer the questions being asked.

RESEARCH BACKGROUND

As cognitive IoT (internet of things) is foundation of smart spaces, Somav et al. (2013) recommended six fundamental key tasks of cognitive IoT as perception-action cycle, massive data analysis, semantic derivation, knowledge discovery, intelligent decision making and on-demand service provisioning. In the Cognitive IoT environment, every smart object behaves as an agent to provide dynamic services via interacting with the physical/social environment with minimum human intervention. In contrast, they suggested, perception cycle is the most primitive cognitive task in CIoT as anticipating user's needs with perception as the input from the physical environment and take relevant action is the most difficult work (Somov et al. 2013; Wu et al. 2014).

In addition, Vlacheas et al. (2013) suggested that the framework of Cognitive IoT, focuses mainly on three areas such as plan to hide the heterogeneity of connected objects, ensuring resiliency for Dynamic service provisioning, instruct system to assess the proximity through a relevance metric between IoT applications and useful objects. They emphasize on the concept of Virtual Object (VO), which provides a virtual representation of real world object(RWO) and such VO can be dynamically created and destroyed as well (Vlacheas et al. 2013).

Turning to context-aware expert systems, as Chen et al. (2004) proposed "CoBrA" as a broker-centric agent architecture, where broker agent efficiently maintains a shared model of context on the behalf of a community of agent and devices and protect the privacy of users by enforcing the user defined policies. Cobra address four important issues such as (i) Context knowledge Base (ii) Context Reasoning Engine (iii) Context acquisition module (iv)Privacy and Policy management module. In their proposed architecture, the burdens of reasoning over contextual information is shifted away from the resource-limed mobile device to the centralized resource-rich broker device (Chen et al. 2004).

On the other hand, Gu et al. (2004) also proposed a service oriented context-aware middleware architecture called "SOCAM". They claimed that "SOCAM" deal with contextual task very efficiently via acquiring context from various sources, interpreting context and carrying out the dissemination of contextual knowledge. The main feature of the "SOCAM" architecture is to support context reasoning where high-level implicit contexts derived from low-level explicit context as a result, applications can be derived from low-level explicit contexts. The "SOCAM" architecture is divided into five layers including: Context providers, Context interpreter, Context database, Service location and context-aware services. While on the other side, Lee and Lin (2010) offered a context management framework for real time SOA, introducing context manager and context agent. They claimed that a context manager performs context reasoning by utilizing Q-Broker for service composition and managing adaptation for service reconfiguration. Likewise, Hong et al. (2009) used a slightly different approach as meticulously analyzing user preferences, habits from historical database to provide more personalized service in agent-based framework. They outlined framework into four layers such as data gathering, context management, preference management and application layer to provide more personalized service as an outcome.

As further, we studied about various context aware expert systems, Tennehouse (2000) emphasized on the elimination of human-in-loop computing life cycle pattern and raised a research question on how can we move from human-centered to human-supervised computing. In following years, Want et al. (2003) and Salovarra et al. (2004) argued that a proactive system can be designed to anticipate user's needs or environment only if it is provided with a hypothesis about what are the user's goals and intentions. While in latest, Vansyckel and Becker (2014) further claimed that in the near future, human interaction with computing resources will be minimum and to achieve such proactive dynamic architecture will be required to build smart context- proactive applications for pervasive computing environment. Furthermore, Negnevitsky (2011) suggested that choosing the right tool for the job is undoubtedly the most critical part of building an intelligent expert system for smart spaces. The process of building an intelligent system begins with gaining an understanding of the problem domain to access the problem and determine the availability nature of input data. It has six phases as problem assessment, data and knowledge acquisition, prototype development, complete system development, revised evaluation, Integration and maintenance of the system. However, we learnt and embraced them as guidelines into our proposed architecture, but still building an intelligent expert system is a very challenging task and need to dig deeper for solutions to tackle six major problems such as (i) Semantic description of Raw data (ii) Opaque relation between rules (iii) Ineffective search strategy (iv) Inability to learn.

Fuzzy Logic for Handling Uncertainty and Vagueness

In a human cognition system, some values and experiences are not crisp but rather more vague and ambiguous in their terms, which means it have some level of uncertainty. Fuzzy logic embraces the idea that all things admit of degrees, for example really hot, very tall, not very fast, and very rapid, quite a short etc. Hence, it is very important to represent such multi-valued logic for approximate reasoning in a formal system called fuzzy logic. It provides a mathematical formation for dealing with imprecision and uncertainty in term of degree of membership whereas crisp membership or values of classical binary logic fails. (Negnevitsky, 2005; Zaheeruddin & Garima, 2006).

Furthermore in the fuzzy theory, fuzzy set A of universe X can be defined by function Ma(x) known as membership function of set A.

```
Ma(x): X -[0,1]
Where
Ma(x) = 1 if x is totally in A;
Ma(x) = 0 if x is not in A;
0 < Ma(x) < 1 if x is partly in A;
```

Where the value between 0 and 1, represents the degree of membership, also known as membership value, of element x in set A.

Operation of fuzzy set is categorized as classical sets such as compliment, intersection, union.

- **Complement:** How much of element not belong to the set?

$$\mu_A(u) = 1 - \mu_A(u)$$

- **Intersection:** How much of the element is in both sets?

$$\mu_{A \cap B}(u) = \min\{\mu_A(u), \mu_B(u)\}$$

- **Union:** How much of the element is in either set?

$$\mu_{A \cup B}(u) = \max\{\mu_A(u), \mu_B(u)\}$$

As fuzzy logic embrace human linguistic variables, so it capture human knowledge into fuzzy rules as conditional statement such as

If x is A.
Then y is B.

Here, x, y are linguistic variables and A, B are linguistic values.

Fuzzy rules are divided in two parts as antecedent (if part) and consequent (then part). As compared with classical rule based system where, if antecedent is true then consequent will also be true, is not fully applicable in fuzzy rule based system. Instead, in fuzzy system where antecedent is true to some degree of membership, then the consequent will also be true that same degree.

Fuzzy Rule: 1

```
IF   speed is fast
Then  stopping_distance is long
```

Fuzzy Rule: 2

```
IF   speed is slow
Then  stopping_distance is short
```

Here we noticed that, antecedent (speed) and consequent (stopping_distance) are fuzzy values (ranges).

Fuzzy rule based systems give a single crisp output by aggregating all outputs fuzzy sets into a single output fuzzy set and then defuzzify the resulting fuzzy set into a single number. The most commonly used fuzzy inference system is invented in 1975 by Professor Ibrahim Mamdani from London University to control a steam engine and boiler Combination. Mamdani -style inference system is divided into four parts as (i) fuzzification of input values (ii) rule evaluation (iii) aggregation of the rule output (iv) and finally defuzzification. (Negnevitsky, 2005)

Fuzzy Logic Application in Cognitive IoT and Pervasive Computing

In the cognitive IoT environment and pervasive computing environment, uncertainty and vagueness of sensors generated data, is well handled by the fuzzy set theory using membership function- to what degree an element belongs to fuzzy set values. The degree of similarity/fuzziness can be described in linguistic variable such as low, medium and high. Furthermore, mapping sensor data to linguistic variables increase human social/conceptual thinking to evaluate degree of concepts/membership. A domain expert or user experience can provide probability values of low, medium, high to reflect the linguistic reliability of data. It allows imprecise knowledge to be modelled, such that an approximation of a numerical value, or a vague information is expressed. For example in the domain of temperature, fuzzy functions on temperature terms like 'cold', 'lukewarm', and 'warm' can be mapped to a (possibly overlapping) range of temperature degrees. A temperature degree 15 °C could be evaluated against these fuzzy functions and inferred as 'cold' with the fuzzy value 0.3, 'lukewarm' with 1.0, and 'warm' with 0.1. It is the preferred way to deal with knowledge numerically provided by measuring devices, and knowledge symbolically expressed by a human observer. As we discussed above that Fuzzy logic supports

Figure 2. Mamdani fuzzy inference system
(Negnevitsky, 2005)

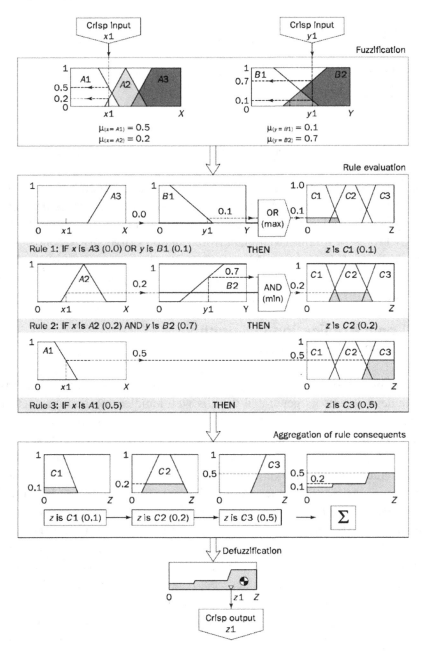

the operations including intersection, union, complement and modifier of fuzzy sets to make such information overlapping easier for further inferencing. (Ye et al. 2012)

Artificial Neural Network

Neural networks represent the complex reasoning model of a biological human brain which consist highly interconnected processors known as neurons. These neurons lies in adjacent layers and are connected with each other with certain numerical weights, such weights express the importance, strength of each neutron inputs. As human learn from experience, ANN also learn through their repeated adjusted weights by comparing output values with desired goals values to obtain error values.

Therefore, based on obtained error values, neurons weights are adjusted to reduce the error (difference between input and output). Such iterative approach of adjusted weights to minimize error is known as Back-propagation algorithm. Once training stage over, ANN saves the weight values for last time for testing stage to get results according to the input data and conserved weights values. (Wu et al. 2013 and Negnevitsky, 2005)

Figure 3. An example of three layer BP neural network
(Negnevitsky, 2005)

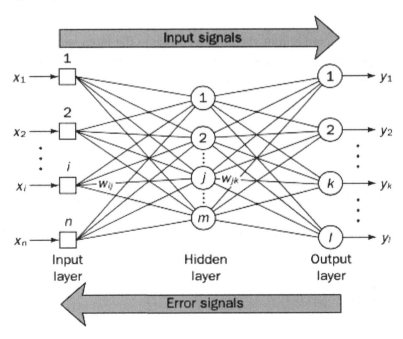

Error Correction (Delta) Rule: Back Propagation Learning Algorithmes

In an error correction rule, the weights that connect the nodes are modified by calculating the difference between the desired output and that produced by the node

```
Error at the node= 1/2 * (Desired Output, O - Produced Output,
P)
```

The modified weight at edge connecting from input xi

```
= learning rate * error at the node * xi + old weight
```

Mathematically, the error (E) for each input vector is calculated as follows:

$$E = \sum_s E_S$$

where,

$$E_S = \frac{1}{2}\sum_i (O_i - P_i)^2$$

where, Oi is the desired output vector in response to the input vector representing the input sequences *x1, x2, ..., xn* and *w1, w2, ..., wn* are the weights connecting the input to the node/neuron. Therefore the initial out, Pi created by the neuron is given as:

$$P = f(\sum_{i=1}^{n} W_i X_i)$$

where, f (.) =activation function, more practically applicable are Step, Sign, and Linear and Sigmoid functions.

According to the delta rule the modified weight at each edge is obtained using the following equation:

$$w_i(new) = w_i(old) + \partial w_i$$

Figure 4. Single layer two input perceptron
(Negnevitsky, 2005)

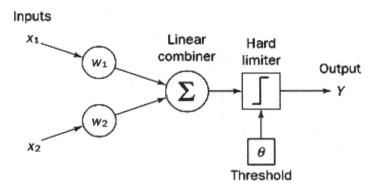

where,

$$\partial w_i = \eta E_i x_i (\eta = \text{Learning Rate})$$

In a back propagation algorithm, the weights are modified first by calculating the error via some suitable error function. If a differentiable function is chosen as an error function, gradient descent on such a function will naturally lead to a learning rule. (Begg & Hassan, 2006)

ANFIS (Adaptive Neuro-Fuzzy Inference System)

Neuro fuzzy computing is a judicious integration of merits of neural and fuzzy approaches. This incorporate the generic advantages of artificial neural network like massive parallelism, robustness and learning in data-rich environments into the system. The modeling of imprecise and qualitative knowledge as well as the transmission of uncertainty is possible through the use of fuzzy logic. Beside these generic advantages, the neuro fuzzy approach also provides the corresponding application specific merits. It consists two major component namely, fuzzy inference system and adaptive neural network. In order to incorporate the capability of learning form input/output data sets in fuzzy inference system, a corresponding adaptive neural network is generated. An adaptive network is a multi-layer feed-forward network consisting of nodes and directional links through which nodes are connects. (Zaheeruddin & Garima, 2006)

Neural networks are used to tune the membership functions of fuzzy systems even for complex systems. Communicating weight of the neural net using fuzzy

Figure 5. Conceptual diagram of ANF IS
(Zaheeruddin & Garima, 2006)

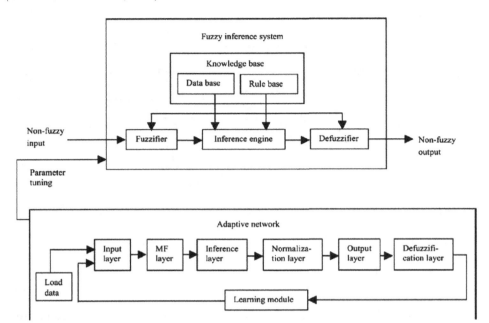

rules provides deep insight into the neural net, thus easier to a design of better neural networks. The non-linear membership function of neuro-fuzzy approach reduces the rule based and saved memories, hence reduces implementation cost. Neuro-fuzzy hybrid systems integrate the advantages of fuzzy systems for dealing with explicit knowledge which can be explained and understood, and neural networks for dealing with implicit knowledge which can be acquired by learning. (Singh et al. 2012).

Furthermore, using a given input/output data set, the toolbox function ANFIS constructs a fuzzy inference system (FIS) whose membership function parameters are tuned (adjusted) using either a back-propagation algorithm alone or in combination with a least squares type of method. Agreeing to the structure of the consequent parts and the inference method to compute the output of the model, rule based model can be classified mainly in four groups such as *(i)* fuzzy relational models *(ii)* linguistic models *(iii)* neural network based models *(iv)* and Takagi–Sugeno–Kang (TSK) fuzzy models. The most commonly used systems are Mamdani-type and Takagi–Sugeno-type which is also known as Takagi–Sugeno–Kang-type . In Mamdani-type fuzzy inference system, both premise (if) and consequent (then) parts of a fuzzy, if–then rule are fuzzy propositions whereas a Takagi–Sugeno-type fuzzy inference system where the premise part of a fuzzy rule is a fuzzy proposition, the consequent part is a mathematical function, usually a zero- or first-degree polynomial function. (Singh et al. 2012)

For simplicity, assume that FIS under consideration has two inputs *(x, y)* and one output *(f)* .Then governing rule set with two if–then rule of Takagi and Surgeon's type as illustrated.

Rule 1: If x is A1 and y is B1, then f1 = p1x + q1y + r1.
Rule 2: If x is A2 and y is B2, then f2 = p2x + q2y + r2.

The node functions in the same layer are of the same function family as described:

Layer 1: Every node *i* in this layer is a square node with a node function:

$$O_i^1 = \mu_{Ai}(x)$$

where x is input to node *i,* is the membership grade of a fuzzy set and it specifies the degree to which the given input x satisfies the quantifier *A* and is Gaussian membership function and it is given by:

$$\mu_{Ai}(x) = \exp\left[-\left(\frac{x - c_i}{a_i}\right)^2\right]$$

where *ai* and *ci* are parameter set. parameters in this layer are referred to as premise parameters.

Layer 2: Every node in this layer is a circle node labeled Π whose output is product of all incoming inputs:

$$w_i = \mu_{Ai}(x) \times \mu_{Bi}(x), i = 1, 2$$

Each node output represents the firing strength of a rule.

Layer 3: Every node labeled as encircled N. The *i-th* node calculates the ratio of the *i-th* rule's firing strength to the sum of all rules' firing strengths:

$$\overline{w}_i = \frac{w_i}{w_1 + w_2}, i = 1, 2$$

Outputs of this layer will be called normalized firing strengths.

Layer 4: Including adaptive nodes:

$$O_1^4 = \overline{w}_i f_i = \overline{w}_i (p_i x + q_i y + r_i)$$

Parameters in this layer will be referred to as consequent parameters.

Layer 5: Including a single labeled encircled $\sum$ with function of summation.

$$\text{Overall Output} = O_1^5 \sum_i \overline{w}_i f_i = \frac{\sum_i w_i f_i}{\sum_i w_i}$$

(Singh et al. 2012)

Cognitive Computing: Embedded Intelligence for CIoE

As Wu et al. (2014) claimed that *"Without cognitive capability, IoT is just like an awkward stegosaurs: all brawn, no brains"*. To fulfil its potential and deal with growing challenges, we must take the cognitive capability into consideration and empower IoT with high-level intelligence as we say brain-empowered internet of things or cognitive internet of things. In contrast, as human, our mind takes input from outer world to sense, hear, touch taste and smell to make decision and initiate sophisticated coordinated actions as results. In cognitive computing, aim is to mimic human decision making capability with the help of computational theory. In the same way, Cognitive Internet of Everything is a new network paradigm, where (physical/virtual) things or objects are interconnected and behave as agents, with minimum human intervention, the things interact with each other following a context-aware perception-action cycle, use the methodology of understanding-by-building to learn from both the physical environment and social networks, store the learned semantic and/or knowledge in kinds of databases, and adapt themselves to changes or uncertainties via resource-efficient decision-making mechanisms. The prime objective of such CIoE, is to bridge the gap between physical world (with objects, resources, etc.) and the social world (with human demand, social behavior, etc.) to form an intelligent physical-cyber-social (iPCS) system by enabling smart resource allocation, automatic network operation, and intelligent service provisioning. (Wu et al. 2014)

Similarly, suggested by Taylor et al. (2015) cognitive computers are expected to learn through experience to find correlation, create hypothesis and remember outcome to learn from. Such cognitive computing mimic the human brain's structure and synaptic plasticity. They proposed a SyNAPSE (System of neuromorphic adaptive plastic scalable electronics) project to create a system that not only analyses complex information from multiple sensors but also dynamically rewires itself according to the environment, while keeping reduced computing complexity and power usage.

Therefore, we are living in a world where world wide effort from academic community, service providers, network operators and standard development organization etc. contributing their effort to make life easier. Briefly, cognitive Internet of Things enhances the current Internet of Things by mainly integrating the human cognition process into the system design. The advantages are multi-fold, e.g., saving people's time and effort, increasing resource efficiency, and enhancing service provisioning, to just name a few of many more. As Wu et al. (2014) proposed framework of CIoT and Fundamental Cognitive tasks where CIoT serves as a transparent bridge between physical world (with general physical/virtual things, objects, resources, etc.) and social world (with human demand, social behavior, etc.), together with itself form an intelligent physical-cyber-social (iPCS) system: With a synthetic methodology learning-by-understanding located at the heart, the framework of CIoT includes five fundamental cognitive tasks, sequentially, Perception-action cycle, Massive data analytics, Semantic derivation and knowledge discovery, Intelligent decision-making, and On-demand service provisioning. (Wu et al. 2014)

Likewise, Guo et al. (2011) suggested that such embedded intelligence in CIoT aims at extracting individual behaviors, space contexts, and social dynamics from off-the-shelf or emerging smart things. The various smart things weave themselves deeply into the fabric of everyday life. The diverse features of them, nevertheless, present us unprecedented opportunities to understand various aspects of interaction patterns between human and real-world entities, incorporating human-object interaction, human-environment interaction, and human to human interaction. The learned embedded intelligence cannot only, from the micro-scale, improves the quality of human life by anticipating user needs and environmental changes, but also from the macro-scale, provides real time decision support for the crowd as well as urban managers. (Guo et al. 2011)

K-Means Clustering: Pattern Recognition in Smart Home

Smart home control can learn about inhabitant activities, previous and current behavior of operation to household appliances with the help of sensory data.

To improve the learning ability we can take the help of K-means clustering algorithms to find patterns and anomalies in inhabitant behavior. As we know,

Figure 6. Framework of Cognitive Internet of Things (CIoT)
(Wu et al. 2014)

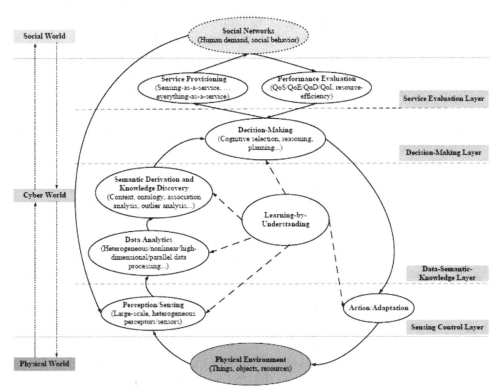

K-means clustering algorithms is a typical distance based clustering algorithm, using the distance as the similarity index, namely that the closer of the two objects, the greater its similarity. K-means clustering algorithms principle is simple, and easy to implement, with good clustering speed and effect. Its main disadvantage is the need to determine in advance the K value(k data point as the initial cluster center). In the smart home control system, it depend on the simulation of human experience to make intelligent home control. Human beings may usually perceptually make judgement to the external environment variable, which are very strong, moderate, and very weak. Thus, ANFIS can use the maximum, minimum and intermediates values as three initial cluster center on K-means algorithms such as:

- In the data input, the maximum, minimum and intermediates values are selected as three initial cluster centers $c1, c2, c3$.
- For other data object in the data set, below equation is used to cluster the Euclidean distance with all cluster centers. According to the principle

Figure 7. The characteristics of embedded intelligence for CIoT
(Guo et al. 2011)

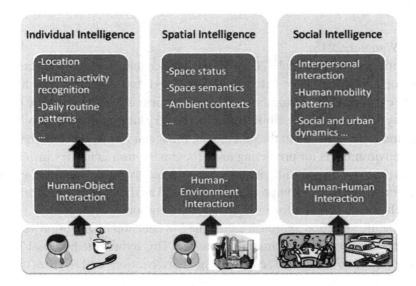

of nearest neighbor, the data will be put to the nearest cluster, wherein xj represent the *j-th* data points, ci the *i-th* cluster center.

$$d_{ij} = \left| x_j - c_i \right| (i = 1, 2, 3)$$

- The equations above and below are used to re-calculate the cluster centers, wherein di in (14) represents the mean value for all the data points in the *i-th* cluster; n represents the number of data points in the *i-th* cluster; xj represents the data point in the *i-th* cluster. The new cluster center is xj, with xj meeting min{*f(xj)*}.

$$d_i = \frac{\sum x_j}{n} (x_j \in c_i)(i = 1, 2, 3)$$

$$f(x_j) = \left| x_j - d_i \right| (i = 1, 2, 3)$$

- Steps 2 and step 3 are to be repeated, until E is less than a given threshold and the algorithm ends.

$$E = \sum_{i=1}^{3} \sum_{x_j \in c_i} (x_j - c_i)^2 \, (i = 1, 2, 3)$$

(Shao & Wanglei, 2015)

In addition, Bourobou et al. (2015) also suggested that in order to detect repeated patterns or anomalous user behavior from varied and complex user activities, K-pattern clustering algorithm shows the best performance in terms of the temporal complexity and cluster set flexibility even for the very large amount of data in the IoT smart home environment. On the other hand, the second step describes the training of smart environments for predicting and recognizing user activities inside his/her personal space in order to mitigate the issues related to that activity recognition in the real world. The Allen's temporal relations based artificial neural network (ANN) gives the highest accuracy for user activity recognition. The additional use of an efficient feature selection approach called the J48 decision tree to improve both the average accuracy and the run-time performance. This hybrid method deals with the activity recognition challenges, considering the restrictions and features of the IoT based smart home environment. (Bourobou et al. 2015)

In most cases, the existing clustering algorithms have some ambiguity in processing noisy data. Indeed, this noise makes it difficult to include an object into a certain cluster because it affects the results of the algorithms. In contrast, the K-pattern clustering algorithm has the ability to overcome this drawback. On the other hand,

Figure 8. Architecture of hybrid method
(Bourobou et al. 2015)

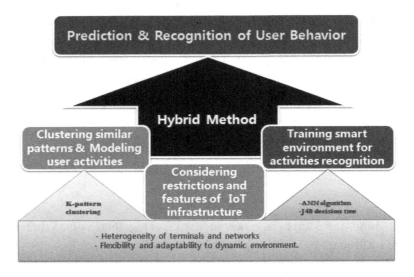

some works integrate user behavior through activity recognition. Detecting user activities usually implies the collection of observation sequence in order to recognize new events. Also, Bourobou et al. (2015) explained the pseudo code for methodology analysis is described in the following Algorithms 1–3. The set of frequent activity patterns and the number of clusters are the input, while the set of clusters is the output of the algo- rithm as shown in Figure 9 (Bourobou et al. 2015).

The second stage gets different items from this input pattern and the cluster center to check the priority table in order to get the sequence with the highest priority (Lines 8–9). Finally, the items formed at Lines 8 and 9 are combined to create a new cluster center (Line 11) (Bourobou et al. 2015).

Temporal Features of Activity Pattern: Spatial and Temporal Reasoning

In contrast, Cook et al. (2009) suggested that a very little can be done in smart home environment without an explicit or implicit reference to where and when the meaningful events occurred. For an intelligent system to make sensible decisions it has to be aware of where the users are and have been during some period of time. Spatial and temporal data reasoning can be used to analyze trajectories of people within a room and classify them as having a clear goal or being unsettled.

Prevent hazardous situation at home:

Figure 9. Process of forming frequent activity patterns
(Bourobou et al. 2015)

Algorithm 1: K-PATTERN CLUSTERING (NC, cP)

```
Input: NC- Number of Clusters      - Initially is zero
         C1set- set of Cluster Centers
         P1set- set of Input Patterns
   Output: Set of Clusters
1 Read the Input dataset
2 begin
3      for each Pattern P in dataset do
4          if NC=0 then
5              C1 ← P1               - First Pattern as Cluster Center
6              i ← 1                 - Index of the Pattern
7              NC ← 1
8          else
9              i ← i+1
10         Get next Pattern Pi
11         Assign Pi to Cluster
12         Cluster (NC, Ci, Pi)
13 return Cluster
```

Figure 10. Process of forming clustering
(Bourobou et al. 2015)

Algorithm 2: CLUSTER (NC, Ci, Pi)

Input: NC- Number of Clusters
C- set of Cluster Centers
P- Input Pattern
Output: Patterns are assigned to Clusters

1	l: Cluster label for each pattern
2	for each Cluster center Ci do
3	if dif f <= threshold then
4	lc ← cluster id
5	recompute cluster center
6	center (Ci, Pi)
7	else
8	Assign it as a new cluster
9	nc ← nc+1
10	return clusters - Patterns are assigned to clusters

Figure 11. Process of re-computing new center
(Bourobou et al. 2015)

Algorithm 3: CENTER (Ci,Pi)

Input: Ci- Clusters Center
Pi- Input Pattern
Output: new cluster center

1 q: common sequence in both patterns
2 pq: Priority table of the sequence
3 s: itemsets that differ in both sequence
4 g: length of the pattern
5 begin
6   for g do
7   q ← compare Ci and Pi   - Common sequence in both patterns
8   s ← itemsets differ
9   d ← compare q and pq   - Get sensor items with high priority
10   Form the new cluster center
11   C[i] ← q+d
12   return Ci   - new Cluster Center

1. Consider a scenario in which the AMI environment sensed the cooker has been turned on, after which a sequence of sensor signals (e.g., movement sensors combined with RFID sensors) was captured detecting the location of U moving from the kitchen to a reception area and then into the bedroom. Finally, the bed occupancy sensor (a pressure pad) detects the person is in bed. By the point at which the person is in bed the condition that more than 10 units have

left the cooker unattended is satisfied. All the conditions will be fulfilled for the warning rule to be triggered.

2. Let's consider another situation in which the doorbell has been rung and the resident does not respond within 5 min. However, the AMI system detects that the person is at home and knows the resident is not hearing impaired. This can be identified as a potential emergency and may trigger a procedure where caregivers are notified and will try to contact the individual visually or by telephone.

An alternative formalism for reasoning about time is based on Allen's temporal logic. Allen suggested that it is more common to describe scenarios by time intervals than by time points, and defined thirteen relations that comprise a temporal logic: before, after, meets, meet-by, overlaps, overlapped-by, starts, started-by, finishes, finished-by, during, contains, and equals. These temporal relations play a beneficial role in prediction and anomaly detection for ambient environments. (Cook et al. 2009)

Furthermore, Nazerfrad et al. (2010) proposed a temporal model for discovering temporal feature and relation of activity patterns from sensor data called, "DTFRA" (Discovering of Temporal Features and Relation of Activities)" which discovers the usual start times of the each activity patterns in form of a normal mixture distribution. Using a k-means clustering technique. DTFRA discovers a similar representation for duration of activities using a normal mixture distribution. The temporal information that is discovered by algorithms can be beneficial in many different applications such as reminder systems, anomaly detection, context aware system networks. The activity patterns in smart environment also include a timestamp. The timestamp indicates when a particular activity has occurred, or more specifically when specific sensor was triggered. Just like the association rule mining, adding the concept of temporal features to the activity patterns can be quite useful, and in some cases necessary.

Temporal Activity Feature Discovery

Next, Nazerfrad et al. (2010) suggested that in this study, we consider two temporal features for every activity: the *start time* of the activity and the *duration* of the activity. For this purpose, we extract the start times of every activity instance, and then we cluster the start times to obtain a canonical representation for the start time of a specific activity.

Here, we can use the k-means clustering algorithm to construct a mixture model for each activity ai. If we denote the start time of an activity instance ai as ti, then the probability that ti belongs to a certain cluster k with parameters

$$\Theta_k = (\mu, \sigma)$$

Figure 12. DTFRA architecture
(Nazerfrad et al. 2010).

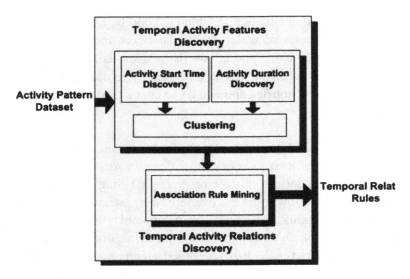

Figure 13. Discovering start time and duration of activity

Cluster #	Start Time (hh:mm)	Duration (hh:mm)
1	[8:37 – 10:29]	[0:02 – 0:04]
2	[6:32 – 9:12]	[0:06 – 0:08]
3	[18:56 – 22:18]	[0:02 – 0:06]

Which can be expressed as a normal probability density function

$$prob(t_i \mid \Theta_k) = \frac{1}{\sqrt{2\pi\sigma^2}} e^{-\frac{(t_i-\mu)^2}{2\sigma^2}}$$

Temporal Activity Relations Discovery

Second, Nazerfrad et al. (2010) suggested that after the canonical forms of start time and duration have been discovered, next we can discover the order of activities. The input to this stage is the features discovered in the previous stage such as the canonical start time and duration. The output of this stage is a set of temporal relations between activities. The temporal relations will determine the order of activities with respect to their start time such as for a specific time point, what activity would be the most probable. Such results can be useful in a variety of activity prediction scenarios, such as home automation.

Overall, to discover the temporal relations of activities, we use the Apriori algorithm. Let's denote an instance I of an activity a by ai and its successor activity in the dataset by b. as mentioned in the previous section, each activity instance belongs to specific cluster Θk, with respect to its start time. To denote an activity belonging to a specific cluster Θk, we will show it as . We will show the temporal relation "$b\ follow\ a$" as a $\rightarrow$ b. The dataset length will also be shown by $|D|$. Then we can define the support of the "follows" relation as in first equation and its confidence in second equation

$$\text{supp}(a^k \rightarrow b) = \frac{\sum i, j(a_k^i \rightarrow b_j)}{|D|}$$

$$conf(a^k \rightarrow b) = \frac{\sum i, j(a_k^i \rightarrow b_j)}{|a|}$$

(Nazerfrad et al. 2010)

Figure 14. Discovering temporal relation of activity

Cluster #	Start Time	Duration	Next Activity	Conf
1	[8:37 – 10:29]	[0:02 – 0:04]	Eating	0.90
2	[6:32 – 9:12]	[0:06 – 0:08]	Eating	0.81
			Meal Preparation	0.11
3	[18:56 – 22:18]	[0:02 – 0:06]	Personal Hygiene	0.50
			Sleeping Not in Bed	0.25
			Eating	0.25

Urban Computing

Urban Computing

Urban computing is an interdisciplinary field where computer sciences meet conventional city related fields, like transportation, civil engineering, environment, economy, ecology and sociology in the context of urban spaces. Compared with other systems (e.g., web search engines) that are based on a single (modal)-data/single-task framework (i.e. information retrieval from web pages), urban computing holds a multi (modal)-data/multitask framework. The tasks of urban computing include improving urban planning, easing traffic congestion, reducing energy consumption, and reducing air pollution. Different tasks can be fulfilled by combining different data sources with different data acquisition, management and analytics techniques from different layers of the framework. As a result, Sun et al. (2014) suggested that, traffic congestion on city's road has impacted on the city development seriously, and became the crux which constrained the city development. An intelligent urban traffic management system is needed urgently. An intelligent collaborative urban traffic management system based on SOA and cloud computing is proposed to solve above problems. Architecture combined with perception layer, network layer and application layer by modification. Network layer contained data processing and intelligent computing. Intelligent computing was realized on cloud computing platform. Application layer packaged solution into service, and realized intelligent collaborative management of urban traffic by intelligent service request and response dispatching strategy. (Sun et al. 2014)

Government Interest and Investment in Smart City Projects in India

In the approach of the smart cite mission, the object is to promote cities that provide core infrastructure and give decent quality of life to its citizens. A clean and sustainable environment and application of smart solutions. The core infrastructure element in a smart city would include:

- Adequate water supply.
- Assured electricity supply.
- Sanitation, including solid waste management.
- Efficient urban mobility and public transport.
- Affordable housing, especially for the poor.
- Robust IT connectivity and digitalization.
- Good governance, especially e-Governance and citizen participation.
- Sustainable environment.

Figure 15. Structural figure of intelligent collaborative urban traffic management system based on SOA
(Sun et al. 2014)

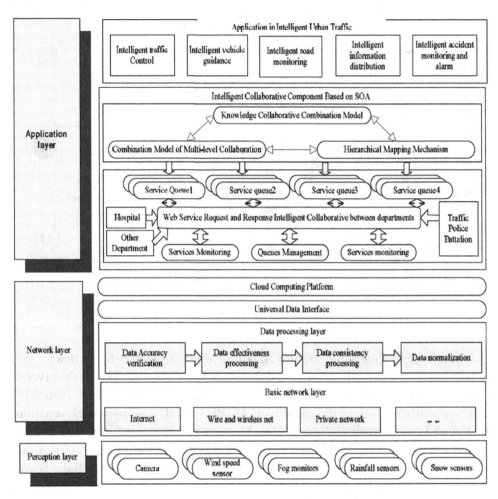

- Safety and security of citizens, particularly women, children and the elderly, and Health and education.

Application of Smart Solutions will enable cities to use technology, information and data to improve infrastructure and services. Comprehensive development in this way will improve quality of life, create employment and enhance incomes for all, especially the poor and the disadvantaged, leading to inclusive Cities. Smartcities (2016)

Figure 16. Smart solution aspects for smart city in India
(Smartcities, 2016)

Furthermore, Prime Minister, Shri Narendra Modi, strongly believes that for the first time in the country, the people, and the urban leadership would play the pivotal role in deciding the future course of their cities. He was speaking at the launch of three major urban development initiatives: AMRUT (Atal Mission for Rejuvenation and Urban Transformation); Smart Cities Mission; and Housing for All (Urban), at Vigyan Bhawan in New Delhi. The Prime Minister explained that for the first time in India, a challenge was being floated, in which the citizens of urban India could contribute in the formulation of development visions of their cities. Those cities which were able to competitively meet the required parameters would be developed as smart cities. Hence, the Prime Minister said, this competitive mechanism would end the top-down approach, and lead to people-centric urban development. Pmindia (2016)

On the other hand, Makeinindia (2016) with this context suggested that Prime Minister Narendra Modi's vision "Digital India," has set an ambitious plan to build 100 smart cities across the country. Modi in his speech quoted, "Cities in the past were built on riverbanks. They are now built along highways. But in the future, they will be built based on availability of optical fiber networks and next-generation infrastructure." The Government of India allocated INR70.6 billion (US$1.2 billion) for Smart Cities in Budget 2014–15. India has also been inviting foreign partnership in developing the smart cities and has signed deals to build eight cities — three with Germany, three with the US, and one each with Spain and Singapore. (Makeinindia, 2016)

Related IoTs Devices and Projects

Panasonic Smart Home Device

The smart hub sits at the heart of every Panasonic smart home system, connected wirelessly to all you other smart home device. It can be setup through one push pairing, and communicate with other devise as far as 300m away. It also can record to micro SD/micrsoSDHC card any footage it receives from triggered smart home cameras. Your camera, sensors and smart plugs will be able to communicate with each other via the smart home hub at the distance. Panasonic smart home devices communicate with each other using a DECT Ultra low energy (ULE) wireless standard that's invisible to regular consumer products rather than Wi-Fi based products. Panasonic (2016)

Figure 17. The initial funding for smart city project based on state and central government funding
(Smartcities, 2016)

Summing up, Additional Resources for financing Smart Cities

- Gol funds: Rs.500 cr
- Matching contribution by States/ ULBs: Rs.500 cr
- User fees
- Public-Private Partnerships
- FFC recommendations (incl land based instruments)
- Municipal bonds
- Borrowings from bilaterals and multilaterals
- National Investment and Infrastructure Fund (NIIIF)
- Convergence with other Government schemes

IBM Watson

IBM Watson technology represents the leading edge of cognitive computing, using natural language to communication with people, Watson eliminates the need for users to know complex coding and have specialized IT expertise. IBM Watson, expand the input, deepen the understanding and broaden the possibilities.

Watson IoT learns from, and infuses intelligence into, the physical world to transform business and enhance the human experience. Traditional programmable computing system are designed to handle specific scenarios and data sets. IoT data doesn't play by traditional rules. Images, video, sound and machine data of many types are combined with social media, weather and enterprise data, providing context and relevance that sharpens insights. (IBM, 2016)

i-Dorm (Intelligent Dormitory) at Essex University

The IIE research group at the University of Essex is researching new ways for mankind to interface with the technology that surrounds them. The i-Dorm (intelligent dormitory) represents an application of the grid architecture, whereby the effecters and sensors found inside represent different service with the room. The intelligent dormitory was an office in the computer science department at the University of Essex. It has been converted into a student dormitory, the design of which is based on the campus accommodation at Essex. iDorm uses three main communication protocols to allow its device to communicate with each other to show its network independent. (Cornish and Holmes, 2002)

Such as; LonTalk, 1-Wire and IPv4.

LonTalk is a twisted pair network, similar to IP that comes in two flavors-one that provides power to the device through the network and another that requires device to have an external power supply. The network is laid out in a ring arrangement; there is no central server.

1-Wire is designed for small-scale applications where the distances between devices on the network are relatively small. Unlike LonTalk, this network required a central server that takes the form of a small piece of hardware called a Tiny Internet Interface board (TINI). . The TINI board acts a gateway to the 1-Wire network. It is addressable on the IP as well as on the 1-Wire network. A java Virtual Machine is embedded on the board and the research group has written a small server that accepts HTTP requests. (Cornish and Holmes, 2002)

IPv4

The protocol that has been produced is an XML definition for the iDorm. All information requested form the iDorm must go through a central server. The server communicates with the iDorm's LonTalk and 1-Wire network across IP using HTTP request to get information. The interfaces can request information about the iDorm in the form of an empty XML tag pair. This pair then gets returned to the interface with the blank part of the request filled with the appropriate data. The XML definition is stored on the central server and can be retried by any interface.

CONCLUSION

We have investigated the existing approaches and technologies in areas related to recognizing situations in CIoE environments in an extensive literature review. Based on the analysis, it would be suitable to use hybrid approach for situation classification and self-learning algorithms procedures, where a data classification based technique would be responsible for knowledge representation and sharing and a learning based technique is responsible for deriving new knowledge and dealing with uncertainties in sensor data in a smart home environment. On the other hand, the importance of domain knowledge is nowhere more apparent than the field of assistive living as

Figure 18. The Incremental Synchronous Learning architecture as learning engine in the iDorm embedded agent
(Hagras et al. 2004)

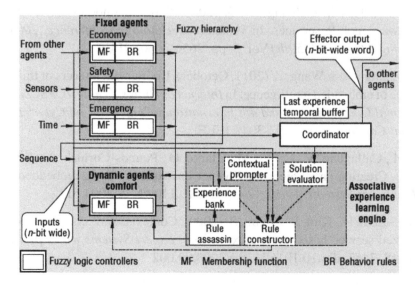

every individual has their own way of performing activities. As a result, it would be advantageous to embrace knowledge driven approach for formulating rule-based system to achieve this task. While with the prominent pattern recognition algorithms from supervised and unsupervised machine learning-artificial neural network and subtractive clustering will be extensively devised. The k-means clustering is efficient to group and identify the user activity model with temporal information of interleaved activities. In the meantime, a learning environment can be created using, artificial neural network into the system architecture for predication of activity recognition.

REFERENCES

Begg, R., & Hassan, R. (2006). Artificial neural networks in smart homes. In *Designing Smart Homes* (pp. 146–164). Springer Berlin Heidelberg. doi:10.1007/11788485_9

Bourobou, S. T. M., & Yoo, Y. (2015). User activity recognition in smart homes using pattern clustering applied to temporal ANN algorithm. *Sensors (Basel, Switzerland)*, *15*(5), 11953–11971. doi:10.3390/s150511953 PMID:26007738

Chen, H., Finin, T., & Joshi, A. (2003). An ontology for context-aware pervasive computing environments. *The Knowledge Engineering Review*, *18*(03), 197–207. doi:10.1017/S0269888904000025

Cook, D. J., Augusto, J. C., & Jakkula, V. R. (2009). Ambient intelligence: Technologies, applications, and opportunities. *Pervasive and Mobile Computing*, *5*(4), 277–298. doi:10.1016/j.pmcj.2009.04.001

Gu, T., Pung, H. K., & Zhang, D. Q. (2004, May). A middleware for building context-aware mobile services. In *Vehicular Technology Conference, 2004. VTC 2004-Spring. 2004 IEEE 59th* (Vol. 5, pp. 2656-2660). IEEE.

Guo, B., Zhang, D., & Wang, Z. (2011, October). Living with internet of things: The emergence of embedded intelligence. In *Internet of Things (iThings/CPSCom), 2011 International Conference on and 4th International Conference on Cyber, Physical and Social Computing* (pp. 297-304). IEEE.

Hagras, H., Callaghan, V., Colley, M., Clarke, G., Pounds-Cornish, A., & Duman, H. (2004). Creating an ambient-intelligence environment using embedded agents. *IEEE Intelligent Systems*, *19*(6), 12–20. doi:10.1109/MIS.2004.61

Hong, J., Suh, E. H., Kim, J., & Kim, S. (2009). Context-aware system for proactive personalized service based on context history. *Expert Systems with Applications*, *36*(4), 7448–7457. doi:10.1016/j.eswa.2008.09.002

IBM. (2016). Retrieved from http://www.ibm.com/internet-of-things/images/watson-iot-point-of-view.pdf

Lee, J., & Lin, K. J. (2010, July). A context management framework for real-time SOA. In *Industrial Informatics (INDIN), 2010 8th IEEE International Conference on* (pp. 559-564). IEEE. doi:10.1109/INDIN.2010.5549682

Makeinindia. (2016). Retrieved from http://www.makeinindia.com/article/-/v/internet-of-things

Nazerfard, E., Rashidi, P., & Cook, D. J. (2010, December). Discovering temporal features and relations of activity patterns. In *Data Mining Workshops (ICDMW), 2010 IEEE International Conference on* (pp. 1069-1075). IEEE. doi:10.1109/ICDMW.2010.164

Negnevitsky, M. (2005). *Artificial intelligence: a guide to intelligent systems*. Pearson Education.

Negnevitsky, M. (2011). Artificial intelligence: a guide to intelligent systems, Pearson education limited (3rd ed.). Academic Press.

Panasonic. (2016). Retrieved from https://www.panasonic.com/uk/consumer/smart-home-learn/smart-home/giving-you-peace-of-mind.html

Pmindia. (2016). Retrieved from http://pmindia.gov.in/en/news_updates/pms-remarks-at-the-launch-of-amrut-smart-cities-mission-and-housing-for-all-urban/

Pounds-Cornish, A., & Holmes, A. (2002, May). The idorm-a practical deployment of grid technology. In *Cluster Computing and the Grid, 2002. 2nd IEEE/ACM International Symposium on* (pp. 470-470). IEEE. doi:10.1109/CCGRID.2002.1017192

Ricci, A., Piunti, M., Tummolini, L., & Castelfranchi, C. (2015). The Mirror World: Preparing for Mixed-Reality Living. *IEEE Pervasive Computing / IEEE Computer Society [and] IEEE Communications Society*, *14*(2), 60–63. doi:10.1109/MPRV.2015.44

Salovaara, A., & Oulasvirta, A. (2004). Six modes of proactive resource management: a user-centric typology for proactive behaviors. In *Proceedings of the third Nordic conference on Human-computer interaction* (pp. 57-60). ACM. doi:10.1145/1028014.1028022

Satyanarayanan, M. (2001). Pervasive computing: Vision and challenges. *Personal Communications, IEEE*, *8*(4), 10–17. doi:10.1109/98.943998

Shao, P., & Wanglei. (2015). Intelligent control in smart home based on adaptive neuro fuzzy inference system. In *Chinese Automation Congress (CAC), 2015* (pp. 1154-1158). IEEE.

Singh, R., Kainthola, A., & Singh, T. N. (2012). Estimation of elastic constant of rocks using an ANFIS approach. *Applied Soft Computing*, *12*(1), 40–45. doi:10.1016/j.asoc.2011.09.010

Smartcities. (2016). Retrieved from http://smartcities.gov.in/

Somov, A., Dupont, C., & Giaffreda, R. (2013). *Supporting Smart-city Mobility with Cognitive Internet of Things*. Academic Press.

Sun, F., Yu, X., Liu, S., & Lu, F. (2014, May). Intelligent collaborative urban traffic management system based on SOA and cloud computing. In *Control and Decision Conference (2014 CCDC), The 26th Chinese* (pp. 1692-1695). IEEE. doi:10.1109/CCDC.2014.6852441

Taylor, R., Baron, D., & Schmidt, D. (2015, October). The world in 2025-predictions for the next ten years. In *Microsystems, Packaging, Assembly and Circuits Technology Conference (IMPACT), 2015 10th International* (pp. 192-195). IEEE.

VanSyckel, S., & Becker, C. (2014). A survey of proactive pervasive computing. In *Proceedings of the 2014 ACM International Joint Conference on Pervasive and Ubiquitous Computing: Adjunct Publication* (pp. 421-430). ACM.

Vlacheas, P., Giaffreda, R., Stavroulaki, V., Kelaidonis, D., Foteinos, V., Poulios, G., & Moessner, K. (2013). Enabling smart cities through a cognitive management framework for the internet of things. *Communications Magazine, IEEE*, *51*(6), 102–111. doi:10.1109/MCOM.2013.6525602

Want, R., Pering, T., & Tennenhouse, D. (2003). Comparing autonomic and proactive computing. *IBM Systems Journal*, *42*(1), 129–135. doi:10.1147/sj.421.0129

Wu, Q., Ding, G., Xu, Y., Feng, S., Du, Z., Wang, J., & Long, K. (2014). Cognitive Internet of Things: A New Paradigm beyond Connection. *IEEE Internet of Things Journal*, 1–1. http://doi.org/.10.1109/JIOT.2014.2311513

Wu, X., Wu, J., Cheng, B., & Chen, J. (2013, September). Neural Network Based Situation Detection and Service Provision in the Environment of IoT. In *Vehicular Technology Conference (VTC Fall), 2013 IEEE 78th* (pp. 1-5). IEEE. doi:10.1109/VTCFall.2013.6692303

Ye, J., Dobson, S., & McKeever, S. (2012). Situation identification techniques in pervasive computing: A review. *Pervasive and Mobile Computing*, 8(1), 36–66. doi:10.1016/j.pmcj.2011.01.004

Zaheeruddin, , & Garima, . (2006). A neuro-fuzzy approach for prediction of human work efficiency in noisy environment. *Applied Soft Computing*, 6(3), 283–294. doi:10.1016/j.asoc.2005.02.001

Compilation of References

3rd Generation Partnership Project. (2016). *Specification Release 13*. Retrieved from http://www.3gpp.org/release-13

Aazam, M., Khan, I., Alsaffar, A., & Huh, E. (2014). Cloud of Things: Integrating Internet of Things and cloud computing and the issues involved. *Proceedings of 11th International Bhurban Conference on Applied Sciences & Technology (IBCAST)*, 414-419.

ActualTech Media. (2016). *2016 State of Hyperconverged Infrastructure Market*. ActualTech Media.

Al-Fuqaha, A., Guizani, M., Mohammadi, M., Aledhari, M., & Ayyash, M. (2015). Internet of Things: A survey on enabling technologies, protocols, and applications. *IEEE Communications Surveys and Tutorials*, *4*(17), 2347–2376. doi:10.1109/COMST.2015.2444095

Allseen aliance. (n.d.). Retrieved April 5, 2016, from https://allseenalliance.org/alliance/members

Apache Cassandra Database. (2016). Retrieved from http://cassandra.apache.org

Apache Flume. (2016). *Service for collecting, aggregating, and moving large amounts of log data*. Retrieved from https://flume.apache.org

Apache Hive Data Warehouse Platform. (2016). Retrieved from https://hive.apache.org

Apache Kafka. (2016). *Publish-subscribe messaging rethought*. Retrieved from http://kafka.apache.org

Apache Software Foundation. (2016). *Apache Hadoop*. Retrieved from http://hadoop.apache.org/

Apache Spark. (2016). *General engine for large-scale data processing*. Retrieved from https://spark.apache.org

Apple. (2017). *Working with HomeKit*. Retrieved Jan 12, 2017, from https://developer.apple.com/homekit/

Arnold, W. C., Arroyo, D. J., Segmuller, W., Spreitzer, M., Steinder, M., & Tantawi, A. N. (2014). Workload orchestration and optimization for software defined environments. *IBM Journal of Research and Development*, *58*(2/3), 11–1. doi:10.1147/JRD.2014.2304864

Artik. (2016). Retrieved April 24, 2016, from https://www.artik.io/hardware

Compilation of References

Ashton, K. (2009). *That "Internet of Things" Thing*. RFID Journal.

Augoyard, J.-F., & Torgue, H. (2006). *Sonic Experience: A Guide to Everyday Sounds*. Quebec, Canada: McGill-Queen's University Press.

Azure IoT HUM. (2016). Retrieved April 24, 2016, from https://azure.microsoft.com/en-us/services/iot-hub/

Bate, R., Kuhn, D., Wells, C., Armitage, J., & Clark, G. (1995). *A Systems engineering Capability Maturtiy model. Pittsbourgh*. Carnegie Mellon University.

Beecham Research. (2011). *M2M Sector Map*. Beecham Research. Retrieved Jan 12, 2017, from http://www.beechamresearch.com/download.aspx?id=18

Begg, R., & Hassan, R. (2006). Artificial neural networks in smart homes. In *Designing Smart Homes* (pp. 146–164). Springer Berlin Heidelberg. doi:10.1007/11788485_9

Belissent, J. (2010). *Getting Clever About Smart Cities: New Opportunities Require New Business Models*. Forrester Research.

Bell, A. G. (1876). *Patent No. US 174 465*. USA.

Bell, E. C. (2010). *Measuring Attitudes about Blindness: The Social Responsibility about Blindness Scale*. Research Report of the Professional Development and Research Institute on Blindness. Ruston: Louisiana Tech University. Retrieved from http://www.pdrib.com/downloads/Measuring%20Attitudes%20Social%20Responsibility%20about%20Blindness%20Scale.doc

Bergin, T. J., & Gibson, R. G. (1996). *History of programming languages---II*. Washington, DC: The American University.

Binary Data Types. (2017). Retrieved from www.postgresql.org: http://www.postgresql.org/docs/9.1/static/datatype-binary.html

Binary Large Object (Blob) Data (SQL Server). (2017). Retrieved from Microsoft: https://msdn.microsoft.com/en-us/library/bb895234.aspx

Blagojević Ivan, V. G. (2004). The possibilities for acquisition and usage of data concerning a large number of vehicles functioning, in real terms of exploitation using OBD technology. In *Virtual Product Development in Automotive Engineering*. Grac: Tehnički univerzitet Grac.

Blanchard, B. S. F. W. (1998). Systems Engineering and Analysis. Prentice Hall Inc.

BLOB Data Type. (2017). Retrieved from Oracle: http://docs.oracle.com/javadb/10.8.2.2/ref/rrefblob.html

Bluetooth. (2016). Retrieved April 5, 2016, from https://www.bluetooth.com/what-is-bluetooth-technology/bluetooth-technology-basics/low-energy

Botta, A., De Donato, W., Persico, V., & Pescapé, A. (2014). On the integration of cloud computing and internet of things. *The 2nd International Conference on Future Internet of Things and Cloud (FiCloud)*, 23-30.

Bourobou, S. T. M., & Yoo, Y. (2015). User activity recognition in smart homes using pattern clustering applied to temporal ANN algorithm. *Sensors (Basel, Switzerland)*, *15*(5), 11953–11971. doi:10.3390/s150511953 PMID:26007738

BrainPort V100 Device Helps People who are Blind See with Tongue. (2015). Retrieved from https://brailleworks.com/brainport-v100/

Brassai, S. T., Bakó, L., & Losonczi, L. (2011). Assistive Technologies for Visually Impaired People. *Journal of Electrical and Mechanical Engineering*, *3*, 39–50.

Breiter, G., Behrendt, M., Gupta, M., Moser, S. D., Schulze, R., Sippli, I., & Spatzier, T. (2014). Software defined environments based on TOSCA in IBM cloud implementations. *IBM Journal of Research and Development*, *58*(2/3), 1–10. doi:10.1147/JRD.2014.2304772

Brown, L. R. (2010). *World on the Edge: How to Prevent Environmental and Economic Collapse*. New York: W.W. Norton and Company.

Bruce, I., McKennell, A., & Walker, E. (1991). *Blind and Partially Sighted Adults in Britain: The RNIB Survey* (Vol. 1). London: Her Majesty's Stationery Office.

Bryant, M. (2015, August). *The Things Network wants to make every city smart – starting with Amsterdam*. Retrieved April 24, 2016, from http://thenextweb.com/insider/2015/08/19/the-things-network-wants-to-make-every-city-smart-starting-with-amsterdam/#gref

Bucherer, E., Eisert, U., & Gassmann, O. (2012). Towards Systematic Business Model Innovation: Lessons from Product Innovation Management. *Creativity and Innovation Management*, *21*(2), 183–198. doi:10.1111/j.1467-8691.2012.00637.x

Buratti, C., & Gardasevic, G. (2016). Testing protocols for the Internet of Things on the EuWin platform. *IEEE Internet of Things Journal*, *3*(1), 124–133. doi:10.1109/JIOT.2015.2462030

Buyya, R. V., & Dastjerdi, A. (2016). *Internet of Things: Principles and paradigms*. Morgan Kaufmann.

Cappagli, G., Cocchi, E., & Gori, M. (2015). Auditory and Proprioceptive Spatial Impairments in Blind Children and Adults. *Developmental Science*, (Nov): 1–12. doi:10.1111/desc.12374 PMID:26613827

Character Large Object. (2017). Retrieved from wikipedia: https://en.wikipedia.org/wiki/Character_large_object

Chen, H., Finin, T., & Joshi, A. (2003). An ontology for context-aware pervasive computing environments. *The Knowledge Engineering Review*, *18*(03), 197–207. doi:10.1017/S0269888904000025

Chen, M. (2013). Towards Smart City: M2M Communications with Software Agent Intelligence. *Multimedia Tools and Applications, 67*(1), 167–178. doi:10.1007/s11042-012-1013-4

Chen, S., Xu, H., Li, D., Hu, B., & Wang, H. (2014). A Vision of IoT: Applications, Challenges, and Opportunities With China Perspective. *The Internet of Things Journal, 1*(4), 349–359. doi:10.1109/JIOT.2014.2337336

Chesbrough, H., & Rosenbloom, R. S. (2002). *The role of the business model in capturing value from innovation: Evidence from Xerox Corporation's technology.* Academic Press.

Cisco. (2015). *IoT System.* Retrieved from http://www.cisco.com/c/m/en_us/solutions/internet-of-things/iot-system.html

Cisco. (2017). *Internet of Things (IoT), Connecting everything drives positive business results.* Retrieved Jan 12, 2017, from http://www.cisco.com/c/en/us/solutions/internet-of-things/overview.html

Clark-Carter, D. D., Heyes, A. D., & Howarth, C. I. (1986). The Efficiency and Walking Speed of Visually Impaired Pedestrians. *Ergonomics, 29*(6), 779–789. doi:10.1080/00140138608968314 PMID:3743536

Clifton, L., Clifton, D. A., Pimentel, M. A. F., Watkinson, P. J., & Tarassenko, L. (2014). Predictive Monitoring of Mobile Patients by Combining Clinical Observations With Data From Wearable Sensors. *Biomedical and Health Informatics. IEEE Journal, 18*(3), 722–730.

Connect the apps you love. (2016). Retrieved April 24, 2016, from https://ifttt.com/

Cook, D. J., Augusto, J. C., & Jakkula, V. R. (2009). Ambient intelligence: Technologies, applications, and opportunities. *Pervasive and Mobile Computing, 5*(4), 277–298. doi:10.1016/j.pmcj.2009.04.001

Cornell, G. (1998). *Visual Basic 6 from the Ground UP.* Toronto: Osborne/McGraw-Hill.

Czarnecki, K., & Eisenecker, U. W. (2000). *Generative Programming: Methods, Tools, and Applications.* Addison-Wesley.

D'Atri, E., Medaglia, C. M., Serbanati, A., Ceipidor, U. B., Panizzi, E., & D'Atri, A. (2007). A System to Aid Blind People in the Mobility: A Usability Test and its Results. In *Proceedings of 2nd International Conference on Systems (ICONS'07).* Sainte-Luce, Martinique, France: IEEE. doi:10.1109/ICONS.2007.7

DASH 7 Alliance. (n.d.). Retrieved April 5, 2016, from http://www.dash7-alliance.org/

Devices, A. (n.d.). Retrieved April 12, 2016, from http://www.ambientdevices.com/

Dijkman, R. M., Sprenkels, B., Peeters, T., & Janssen, A. (2015). Business models for the Internet of Things. *International Journal of Information Management, 35*(6), 672–678. doi:10.1016/j.ijinfomgt.2015.07.008

Docker. (2016). *Platform for distributed applications.* Retrieved from https://www.docker.com

Docker. (2017). *Docker Use Cases*. Retrieved Jan 12, 2017, from https://www.docker.com/use-cases

Doukas, C. (2012). Building Internet of Things with the Arduino. Seattle, WA: CreateSpace Independent Publishing Platform.

Dzenowagis, J. (2005). *Connecting for Health. Global Vision, Local Insight*. Geneva: World Health Organization.

EIT Climate-KIC. (2015). *Knowledge & Innovation Community*. Retrieved from http://www.climate-kic.org/

ENDNOTES

Engineering Recommendations and Minimal Standards v4.0. (2011). Hyatt International Technical Services.

Enocean Alliance. (n.d.). Retrieved April 5, 2016, from https://www.enocean-alliance.org/en/home/

ETSI Technical Specification. (2010). *Machine-to-Machine Communications (M2M); M2M Service Requirements*. ETSI TS 102 689 V1.1.1(2010-08).

European Commission. (2015). *Policy*. Retrieved December 27, 2014, from http://ec.europa.eu/health/ehealth/policy/

Evans, D. (2011). *The Internet of Things - How the Next Evolution of the Internet is Changing Everything*. Cisco Internet Business Solution Group.

Evans, D. (2011). *The Internet of Things. How the Next Evolution of the Internet Is Changing Everything*. San Jose, CA: Cisco.

Evans, M. (2011). *Internet of Things*. Cisco.

Eysenbach, G. (2001). What is e-health? *Journal of Medical Internet Research, 3*(2), 20. doi:10.2196/jmir.3.2.e20 PMID:11720962

Feamster, N., Rexford, J., & Zegura, E. (2014). The road to SDN: An intellectual history of programmable networks. *Computer Communication Review, 44*(2), 87–98. doi:10.1145/2602204.2602219

Fernandez-Luque, F., Zapata, J., & Ruiz, R. (2013). PIR-Based Motion Patterns Classification for AmI Systems.*Proc. of Conference on the Interplay Between Natural and Artificial Computation, IWINAC 2013*, 355-364. doi:10.1007/978-3-642-38622-0_37

Fire and Smoke Protection Control System. (2010). Retrieved April 24, 2016, from http://euroicc.com/solutions/ringbus/

Fleisch, E., Weinberger, M., & Wortmann, F. (2015). Business Models and the Internet of Things. In P. Z. Ivana, P. Krešimir, & S. Martin (Eds.), *Interoperability and Open-Source Solutions for the Internet of Things, 9001* (pp. 6–10). Berlin: Springer.

Fowler, M. (2010). *Domain-specific languages*. Addison-Wesley Professional.

G 9959-Series G: Transmission Systems and Media, Digital Systems and Networks - Short Range Narrow-Band Digital Radiocommunication Transceivers – PHY, MAC, SAR and LLC Layer Specifications. (2015). ITU.

Gantz, J., & Reinsel, D. (2012). The digital universe in 2020: Big data, bigger digital shadows, and biggest growth in the far east. *IDC iView: IDC Analyze the Future, 2007*, 1-16.

Gardasevic, G., Veletić, M., Maletić, N., Vasiljević, D., Radusinović, I., Tomović, S., & Radonjić, M. (2017). The IoT architectural framework, design issues and application domains. *Springer Journal Wireless Personal Communications*, *92*(1), 127–148. doi:10.1007/s11277-016-3842-3

Gardner, G. (2009). *Bycicle Production Reches 30 Billion Units*. Washington, DC: Worldwatch Institute.

Gartner (2015). Retrieved from http://www.gartner.com/newsroom/id/3165317

Gartner. (2015). *Gartner Says 6.4 Billion Connected "Things" Will Be in Use in 2016, Up 30 Percent From 2015*. Retrieved 01.03.2016 from: http://www.gartner.com/newsroom/id/3165317

Gartner. (2016). Magic Quadrant for Integrated Systems. ID: G00291000

Gassmann, O., Frankenberger, K., & Csik, M. (2014). Revolutionizing the Business Model. In O. Gassmann & F. Schweitzer (Eds.), *Management of the Fuzzy Front End of Innovation* (pp. 89–98). New York: Springer; doi:10.1007/978-3-319-01056-4_7

Gazis, V. (2016). A survey of standards for Machine to Machine (M2M) and the Internet of Things. *IEEE Communications Surveys and Tutorials, 99*.

Gazis, V., Gortz, M., Huber, M., Leonardi, A., Mathioudakis, K., Wiesmaier, A., & Vasilomanolakis, E. et al. (2015). A survey of technologies for the Internet of Things. *Wireless Communications and Mobile Computing Conference (IWCMC)*, 1090–1095. doi:10.1109/IWCMC.2015.7289234

George Antheil, H. M. (1942). *Patent No. 2292387 A*. Washington, DC: US Patent Office.

Golledge, R. G. (1993). Geography and the Disabled: A Survey with Special Reference to Vision Impaired and Blind Populations. *Transactions of the Institute of British Geographers*, *18*(1), 63–85. doi:10.2307/623069

Goodwyn, M., Bell, E. C., & Singletary, C. (2009). Factors that Contribute to the Success of Blind Adults. Research Report of the Professional Development and Research Institute on Blindness. Ruston: Louisiana Tech University. Retrieved from http://www.pdrib.com/downloads/Factors%20 that%20Contribute%20to%20the%20Success%20of%20Blind%20Adults.doc

Google Trends. (n.d.). Retrieved April 17, 2016, from https://www.google.com/trends/ explore#q=internet%20of%20things%2C%20%2Fm%2F07v58%2C%20wireless%20 sensors&cmpt=q&tz=Etc%2FGMT-2

Google. (2017). *Internet of Things (IoT) Solutions*. Retrieved Jan 12, 2017, from https://cloud. google.com/solutions/iot/#learn

Goria, M., Cappaglia, G., Tonellia, A., Baud-Bovyb, G., & Finocchietti, S. (2016). Devices for Visually Impaired People: High Technological Devices with Low User Acceptance and no Adaptability for Children. *Neuroscience and Biobehavioral Reviews*, *69*, 79–88. doi:10.1016/j.neubiorev.2016.06.043 PMID:27484870

Gu, T., Pung, H. K., & Zhang, D. Q. (2004, May). A middleware for building context-aware mobile services. In *Vehicular Technology Conference, 2004. VTC 2004-Spring. 2004 IEEE 59th* (Vol. 5, pp. 2656-2660). IEEE.

Gubbi, J., Buyya, R., Marusic, S., & Palaniswami, M. (2013). Internet of Things (IoT): A vision, architectural elements, and future directions. *Future Generation Computer Systems*, *29*(7), 1645–1660. doi:10.1016/j.future.2013.01.010

Guo, B., Zhang, D., & Wang, Z. (2011, October). Living with internet of things: The emergence of embedded intelligence. In *Internet of Things (iThings/CPSCom), 2011 International Conference on and 4th International Conference on Cyber, Physical and Social Computing* (pp. 297-304). IEEE.

Guo, G. (2002). *High Performance Data Mining*. New York: Kluwer Academic Publishers. doi:10.1007/b116461

Hagras, H., Callaghan, V., Colley, M., Clarke, G., Pounds-Cornish, A., & Duman, H. (2004). Creating an ambient-intelligence environment using embedded agents. *IEEE Intelligent Systems*, *19*(6), 12–20. doi:10.1109/MIS.2004.61

Heikkila, M., & Kuivaniemi, L. (2012). *Ecosystem Under Construction: An Action Research Study on Entrepreneurship in a Business Ecosystem*. Technology Innovation Management Review.

Hersent, O., Boswarthick, D., & Elloumi, O. (2012). *The Internet of Things: Key applications and protocols* (2nd ed.). Wiley.

Hersh, M., & Johnson, M. A. (2008). *Assistive Technology for Visually Impaired and Blind People*. London, UK: Springer-Verlag. doi:10.1007/978-1-84628-867-8

Hinden, R. (1998). *IP Version 6 Addressing Architecture*. Cisco Systems. doi:10.17487/rfc2373

Hong, J., Suh, E. H., Kim, J., & Kim, S. (2009). Context-aware system for proactive personalized service based on context history. *Expert Systems with Applications*, *36*(4), 7448–7457. doi:10.1016/j.eswa.2008.09.002

Hui, G. (2014). How the Internet of Things Changes Business Models. *Harvard Business Review*.

Humbly, C. (2006). *Data is the New Oil, ANA Senior marketer's summit*. Kellogg School.

Humphrey, W. S. (2000). *Personal Software Process (PSP)*. Carnegie Mellon University.

Humphrey, W. S. (2000). *Team Software Process (TSP)*. Carnegie Mellon University.

IBM. (2016). Retrieved from http://www.ibm.com/internet-of-things/images/watson-iot-point-of-view.pdf

IBM. (2017). *Simplify development for networked devices.* Retrieved Jan 12, 2017, from http://www-03.ibm.com/software/products/en/internet-of-things-foundation

IEEE Global History Network. (2009, May 18). Retrieved March 1, 2016

IEEE Standard for Local and metropolitan area networks—Part 15.4: Low-Rate Wireless Personal Area. (2011). New York: IEEE Computer Society.

iGlasses Ultrasonic Mobility Aid. (2016). Retrieved from https://www.maxiaids.com/iglasses-ultrasonic-mobility-aid-clear-lens

Institute of Electrical and Electronics Engineers. (2015). *Towards a definition of the Internet of Things (IoT).* Retrieved from http://iot.ieee.org/definition

Institute of Electrical and Electronics Engineers. (2016). *Internet of Things (IoT) related standards.* Retrieved from http://standards.ieee.org/innovate/iot/stds.html

Institute of Electrical and Electronics Engineers. (2017). *Time-Sensitive Networking Task Group.* Retrieved from http://www.ieee802.org/1/pages/tsn.html

Intel. (2016). *IoT Platform: Secure, scalable, interoperable.* Retrieved from http://www.intel.com/content/www/us/en/internet-of-things/overview.html

Intel. (2017). *IoT Security and Scalability on Intel® IoT Platform.* Retrieved Jan 12, 2017, from http://www.intel.com/content/www/us/en/internet-of-things/iot-platform.html

Intel, W. P. (2009). *Rise of the Embedded Internet.* Intel Corporation.

Interaxon Inc. (2015). *Muse, the brain sensing headband.* Retrieved November 16, 2015, from http://www.choosemuse.com/

Internet of Things World Forum. (2014). *Reference Model.* Retrieved from https://www.iotwf.com/resources

Internet Research Task Force. (2016). *Thing-to-Thing Research Group.* Retrieved from https://irtf.org/t2trg

Internet Society. (2015). *The Internet of Things (IoT): An overview - Understanding the issues and challenges of a more connected world.* Retrieved from http://www.internetsociety.org/doc/iot-overview

Internet Society. (2016). *Internet of Things: Standards and guidance from the IETF.* Retrieved from https://www.internetsociety.org/publications/ietf-journal-april-2016/internet-things-standards-and-guidance-ietf

IoTivity. (2017). *IoTivity, a Linux Foundation Collaborative Project.* Retrieved Jan 12, 2017, from https://www.iotivity.org/

Islam, R., Kwak, D., Kabir, H., Hossain, M., & Kwak, K.-S. (2015). The Internet of Things for Health Care: A Comprehensive Survey. *IEEE Access, 3,* 678–708. doi:10.1109/ACCESS.2015.2437951

ISO/IEC JTC1/SC29/WG11 MPEG. (2016). *Internet of Media Things and Wearables*. Retrieved from http://mpeg.chiariglione.org/standards/exploration/internet-media-things-and-wearables

ISO/IEC JTC1/WG10. (2015). *Internet of Things*. Retrieved from http://isotc.iso.org/livelink/livelink/open/jtc1wg10

ITU-Telecommunication Standardization Sector. (2015). *Study Group 20 at a glance*. Retrieved from http://www.itu.int/en/ITU-T/about/groups/Pages/sg20.aspx

ITU-Telecommunication Standardization Sector. (n.d.). *Internet of Things: Global Standards Initiative*. Retrieved from http://www.itu.int/en/ITU-T/gsi/iot/

Jacobson, R. D., & Kitchin, R. M. (1997, December). GIS and People with Visual Impairments or Blindness: Exploring the Potential for Education, Orientation, and Navigation. *Transactions in GIS*, 2(4), 315–332. doi:10.1111/j.1467-9671.1997.tb00060.x

James Bret Michael, A. C. (1995). Validation of Testing Results for Vehicle Control Software. *Intellimotion*, 2-15.

Kafle, V. P., Fukushima, Y., & Hara, H. (2016). Internet of Things Standardization in ITU and prospective networking technologies. *IEEE Communications Magazine*, 54(9), 43–49. doi:10.1109/MCOM.2016.7565271

Kalantar, M. H., Rosenberg, F., Doran, J., Eilam, T., Elder, M. D., Oliveira, F., & Roth, T. et al. (2014). Weaver: Language and runtime for software defined environments. *IBM Journal of Research and Development*, 58(2/3), 1–12. doi:10.1147/JRD.2014.2304865

Kamala, J., & Joseph, A. (2014). Solar Tracking for Maximum and Economic Energy Harvesting. *International Journal of Engineering and Technology*, 5(6), 5030-5037. Available from http://www.enggjournals.com/ijet/docs/IJET13-05-06-338.pdf

Kelly, S., & Tolvanen, J. P. (2008). *Domain Specific Modeling*. Wiley. doi:10.1002/9780470249260

King, R. (2015). *Performance Dashboard for Lean Startups*. Retrieved 01.03.2016 from: http://www.slideshare.net/RodKing/business-model-dashboard-for-lean-startups

Kovar, J. F. (2015). *13 Powerful Hyper-Converged Infrastructure Solutions*. Retrieved Jan 12, 2017, from http://www.crn.com/slide-shows/virtualization/300076666/13-powerful-hyper-converged-infrastructure-solutions.htm/pgno/0/13

Kraus, L. (1996). *Programsko okruženje Delphi sa rešenim zadacima*. Beograd: Mikro Knjiga.

Large Objects. (2017). Retrieved from IBM: https://www.ibm.com/support/knowledgecenter/SSEPGG_9.7.0/com.ibm.db2.luw.sql.ref.doc/doc/r0008473.html

Larman, C. (1998). *Applying UML and Patterns*. Prentice Hall PTR.

Lee, J., & Lin, K. J. (2010, July). A context management framework for real-time SOA. In *Industrial Informatics (INDIN), 2010 8th IEEE International Conference on* (pp. 559-564). IEEE. doi:10.1109/INDIN.2010.5549682

Leminen, S., Westerlund, M., Rajahonka, M., & Siuruainen, R. (2012). Towards IOT Ecosystems and Business Models. In S. Andreev, S. Balandin, & Y. Koucheryavy (Eds.), *Internet of Things, Smart Spaces, and Next Generation Networking, 7469* (pp. 15–26). Heidelberg, Germany: Springer. doi:10.1007/978-3-642-32686-8_2

Lengyel, Ekler, Ujj, Balogh, & Charaf. (2015). SensorHUB – An IoT Driver Framework for Supporting Sensor Networks and Data Analysis. *International Journal of Distributed Sensor Networks*.

Lengyel, L., Ekler, P., Ujj, T., Balogh, T., Charaf, H., Szalay, Zs., & Jereb, L. (2015). ICT in Road Vehicles – The VehicleICT Platform. *4th International Conference on Models and Technologies for Intelligent Transportation Systems*, 457-462. doi:10.1109/MTITS.2015.7223294

Li, C., Brech, B. L., Crowder, S., Dias, D. M., Franke, H., Hogstrom, M., & Rao, J. et al. (2014). Software defined environments: An introduction. *IBM Journal of Research and Development*, *58*(2/3), 1–11. doi:10.1147/JRD.2014.2298134

Lightman, K. (2016, March). Silicon Gets Sporty. *IEEE Spectrum*, 44–48.

Liu, J., Li, Y., Chen, M., Dong, W., & Jin, D. (2015). Software-defined internet of things for smart urban sensing. *IEEE Communications Magazine*, *53*(9), 55–63. doi:10.1109/MCOM.2015.7263373

Lopez Research. (2013). *An Introduction to the Internet of Things (IoT). Part 1. of "The IoT Series"*. San Francisco: Lopez Research.

Lopez, J. (2012). *Internet of Things Scenario: When Things Negotiate*. Stamford, CT: Gartner.

LoRa Alliance. (2016). *Technology*. Retrieved from https://www.lora-alliance.org/what-is-lora/technology

LoRa Technology. (2016). Retrieved April 5, 2016, from https://www.lora-alliance.org/What-Is-LoRa/Technology

Mahoney, J., & LeHong, H. (2012). *Innovation Insight: The 'Internet of Everything*. Stamford, CT: Gartner.

Makeinindia. (2016). Retrieved from http://www.makeinindia.com/article/-/v/internet-of-things

Manyika, Chui, Bisson, Woetzel, Dobbs, Bughin, & Aharon. (2015). *The internet of things: Mapping the value beyond the hype*. McKinsey Institute.

Manyika, J., Chui, M., Brown, B., Bughin, J., Dobbs, R., Roxburgh, C., & Byers, A. H. (2011). *Big data: The next frontier for innovation, competition, and productivity*. McKinsay Global Institute.

Manyika, J., Chui, M., Bughin, J., Dobbs, R., Bisson, P., & Marrs, A. (2013). *Disruptive technologies: Advances that will transform life, business, and the global economy*. Mc Kinsey Global Institute.

Marsh, P. (1978). Sonic Aids for the Blinds – Do They Work? *J. New Scientist, 13,* 114–117. Retrieved from https://books.google.com.mx/books?id=PhxDVgkDfuwC&pg=PA116&lpg=P A116&dq=Sonicguide+price+blinds&source=bl&ots=AbU1ehCMQq&sig=rSbdoz1KpJq88u HYauhoDVndf4E&hl=en&sa=X&ved=0ahUKEwjhpeerpf7PAhWJSyYKHa6PCYAQ6AEIGz AA#v=onepage&q=Sonicguide%20price%20blinds&f=false

Meddeb, A. (2016). Internet of Things standards: Who stands out from the crowd?. *IEEE Communications Magazine - Communications Standards Supplement, 7*(54), 40–47.

Mejtoft, T. (2011) Internet of Things and Co-Creation of Value. *Proceedings of the 2011 International Conference on and 4th International Conference on Cyber, Physical and Social Computing,* 672-677. doi:10.1109/iThings/CPSCom.2011.75

Mesarovic, M. D., Macko, D., & Takahara, Y. (1970). *Theory of Hierarchical, Multilevel Systems.* New York, NY: Academic Press.

Microsoft. (2016a). *Install Nano Server.* Retrieved Jan 12, 2017, from https://technet.microsoft. com/windows-server-docs/get-started/getting-started-with-nano-server

Microsoft. (2016b). *Windows Containers.* Retrieved Jan 12, 2017, from https://docs.microsoft. com/en-us/virtualization/windowscontainers/about/index

Microsoft. (2017). *4 steps to start your IoT solution.* Retrieved Jan 12, 2017, from https://www. microsoft.com/en-us/server-cloud/internet-of-things/overview.aspx

Middleton, P., Kjeldsen, P., & Tully, J. (2013). *Forecast: The Internet of Things, Worldwide, 2013.* Stamford, CT: Gartner.

Minerva, R. (2015). Internet of Things and the 5th Generation Mobile Network. *IEEE Internet of Things .*

Mohinder, S., & Grewal, L. R. (2001). Global Positioning Systems, Inertial Navigation, and Integration. New York: John Wiley & Sons, Inc. Publication.

Morris, M., & Aguilera, A. (2012). Mobile, Social, and Wearable Computing and the Evolution of Psychological Practice. *Professional Psychology, Research and Practice, 43*(6), 622–626. doi:10.1037/a0029041 PMID:25587207

Morris, M., Schindehutte, M., & Allen, J. (2005). The entrepreneurs business model: Toward a unified perspective. *Journal of Business Research, 58*(6), 726–735. doi:10.1016/j.jbusres.2003.11.001

Morse, S. (1840). *Patent No. US1647 A.* Washington, DC: US Patent Office.

MQTT. (2016). *A machine-to-machine (M2M)/"Internet of Things" connectivity protocol.* Retrieved from http://mqtt.org

Nabaztag. (n.d.). Retrieved April 12, 2016, from http://www.nabaztag.com/

Nazerfard, E., Rashidi, P., & Cook, D. J. (2010, December). Discovering temporal features and relations of activity patterns. In *Data Mining Workshops (ICDMW), 2010 IEEE International Conference on* (pp. 1069-1075). IEEE. doi:10.1109/ICDMW.2010.164

Negnevitsky, M. (2011). Artificial intelligence: a guide to intelligent systems, Pearson education limited (3rd ed.). Academic Press.

Negnevitsky, M. (2005). *Artificial intelligence: a guide to intelligent systems*. Pearson Education.

NEST. (2016). Retrieved April 24, 2016, from https://nest.com/

Network Computing. (2015). *10 Hyperconvergence Trendsetters*. Retrieved Jan 12, 2017, from http://www.networkcomputing.com/storage/10-hyperconvergence-trendsetters/1523423309

Norris, D. (2015). *The Internet of Things: Do-It-Yourself at Home Projects for Arduino, Raspberry Pi, and BeagleBone Black*. New York: McGraw-Hill Education.

Nutanix. (2017). *Nutanix Products Series*. Retrieved Jan 12, 2017, from https://www.nutanix.com/products/hardware-platforms/

One App + One Hub + All Your Things. (2016). Retrieved April 24, 2016, from https://www.smartthings.com/how-it-works

OpenFog Consortium. (2016). Retrieved April 5, 2016, from http://www.openfogconsortium.org/

Openshaw, E., Hagel, J., Wooll, M., Wigginton, C., Brown, J. S., & Banerjee, P. (2014). The Internet of Things ecosystem: unlocking the business value of connected devices. *Technical report*. Deloitte.

Osterwalder, A., Pigneur, Y., & Tucci, C. L. (2005). Clarifying business models: Origins, present, and future of the concept. *Communications of the Association for Information Systems, 16*(1), 1.

Panasonic. (2016). Retrieved from https://www.panasonic.com/uk/consumer/smart-home-learn/smart-home/giving-you-peace-of-mind.html

Pantelopoulos, A., & Bourbakis, N. G. (2010). A survey on wearable sensor-based systems for health monitoring and prognosis, IEEE Trans. *Systems, Man, and Cybernetics, Part C: Applications and Reviews, 40*(1), 1–12. doi:10.1109/TSMCC.2009.2032660

Paper, E. W. (2011). *More Than 50 Billion Devices Connected*. Ericson.

Part 11: Wireless LAN Medium Access Control (MAC) and Physical Layer (PHY) Specifications Amendment 4: Enhancements for Very High Throughput for Operation in Bands below 6 GHz. (2013). New York: IEEE.

Pavel Schilling. (n.d.). Retrieved 11 1, 2015, from https://en.wikipedia.org/wiki/Pavel_Schilling

Pmindia. (2016). Retrieved from http://pmindia.gov.in/en/news_updates/pms-remarks-at-the-launch-of-amrut-smart-cities-mission-and-housing-for-all-urban/

Pomdevices, LLC. (2015). *Sonamba, Medical Alert System*. Retrieved November 15, 2015, from http://sonamba.com/

Porter, E. M., & Heppelmann, E. J. (2015). How Smart, Connected Products Are Transforming Companies. *Harvard Business Review*.

Pounds-Cornish, A., & Holmes, A. (2002, May). The idorm-a practical deployment of grid technology. In *Cluster Computing and the Grid, 2002. 2nd IEEE/ACM International Symposium on* (pp. 470-470). IEEE. doi:10.1109/CCGRID.2002.1017192

Prinsloo, G., & Dobson, R. T. (2014). *Solar Tracking: High precision solar position algorithms, programs, software and source-code for computing the solar vector, solar coordinates & sun angles in Microprocessor, PLC, Arduino, PIC and PC-based sun tracking devices or dynamic sun following hardware*. Available from https://www.researchgate.net/publication/263085113_Solar_Tracking_High_precision_solar_position_algorithms_programs_software_and_source-code_for_computing_the_solar_vector_solar_coordinates_sun_angles_in_Microprocessor_PLC_Arduino_PIC_and_PC-based_sun

Quinn, J. B. (2000). Outsourcing innovation: The new engine of growth. *Sloan Management Review*, *41*(4), 13–28.

Raga Lavima, P., & Subhramanya Sarma, G. (2015). Aa IoT based intelligent medicine box. *International Journal of Computer Science and Mobile Computing*, *4*(10), 186–191.

Ranck, J. (2012). *The wearable computing market: a global analysis*. San Francisco: GigaomPRO.

Raskino, M., & LeHong, H. (2011). *Exploit the Democratization of the Internet of*. Stamford, CT: Gartner.

REN21. (2015). *Renewables 2015 Global Status Report*. Available online: http://www.ren21.net/status-of-renewables/global-status-report/

Reports. I. I. (2005). Internet of Things. Geneve: ITU.

Ricci, A., Piunti, M., Tummolini, L., & Castelfranchi, C. (2015). The Mirror World: Preparing for Mixed-Reality Living. *IEEE Pervasive Computing / IEEE Computer Society [and] IEEE Communications Society*, *14*(2), 60–63. doi:10.1109/MPRV.2015.44

Roberts, E. (2008). *The Art and Science of Java*. Boston: Addison-Wesley.

Rolik, A. I. (2013a). Decomposition-Compensation Method of Service Level Management of Corporate IT Infrastructures. *Visnyk NTUU "KPI" Informatics, Operation and Computer Science, 58*, 78-88.

Rolik, A. I. (2013b). Service Level Management of Corporate IT Infrastructure Based on the Coordinator. *Visnyk NTUU "KPI" Informatics, Operation and Computer Science, 59*, 98–105.

Rong, K., Hu, G.Y., Lin, Y., Shi, Y.J. & Guo, L. (2015). Understanding Business Ecosystem Using a 6C Framework in Internet-of-Things-Based Sectors. *International Journal of Production Economics, 159*, 41-55.

Salovaara, A., & Oulasvirta, A. (2004). Six modes of proactive resource management: a user-centric typology for proactive behaviors. In *Proceedings of the third Nordic conference on Human-computer interaction* (pp. 57-60). ACM. doi:10.1145/1028014.1028022

Samsung Smart Thing. (2016). Retrieved April 5, 2016, from https://www.smartthings.com/

Samsung. (2017a). *SmartThings*. Retrieved Jan 12, 2017, from https://www.smartthings.com/

Samsung. (2017b). *The ARTIK End-to-end IoT Platform*. Retrieved Jan 12, 2017, from https://www.artik.io/

Satyanarayanan, M. (2001). Pervasive computing: Vision and challenges. *Personal Communications, IEEE, 8*(4), 10–17. doi:10.1109/98.943998

Scale Computing. (2017). *Hardware Platforms*. Retrieved Jan 12, 2017, from https://www.scalecomputing.com/products/hardware-platforms/

Shao, P., & Wanglei. (2015). Intelligent control in smart home based on adaptive neuro fuzzy inference system. In *Chinese Automation Congress (CAC), 2015* (pp. 1154-1158). IEEE.

Sheng, Z., Yang, S., Yu, Y., Vasilakos, A., Mccann, J., & Leung, K. (2013). A survey on the IETF protocol suite for the internet of things: Standards, challenges, and opportunities. *IEEE Wireless Communications, 20*(6), 91–98. doi:10.1109/MWC.2013.6704479

SIGFOX - The Global Communication Service Provider. (n.d.). Retrieved April 5, 2016, from www.sigfox.com

Singh, A., Ong, J., Agarwal, A., Anderson, G., Armistead, A., Bannon, R., & Kanagala, A. et al. (2015). Jupiter rising: A decade of clos topologies and centralized control in googles datacenter network. *Computer Communication Review, 45*(4), 183–197. doi:10.1145/2829988.2787508

Singh, R., Kainthola, A., & Singh, T. N. (2012). Estimation of elastic constant of rocks using an ANFIS approach. *Applied Soft Computing, 12*(1), 40–45. doi:10.1016/j.asoc.2011.09.010

Slama, D., Puhlmann, F., Morrish, J., & Bhatnagar, R. M. (2015). *Enterprise IoT: Strategies and Best Practices for Connected Products and Services*. O'Reilly Media. Available from http://enterprise-iot.org/book/enterprise-iot/

Slama, D., Puhlmann, F., Morrish, J., & Bhatnagar, R. M. (2015). Enterprise IoT: Strategies and Best Practices for Connected Products and Services. Sebastopol, CA: O'Reilly Media.

Smart Hotel Control. (2015). Retrieved April 24, 2016, from http://euroicc.com/solutions/smart-hotel-control/

Smartcities. (2016). Retrieved from http://smartcities.gov.in/

Sohail, N. (2013). Stress and Academic Performance Among Medical Students. *Journal of the College of Physicians and Surgeons--Pakistan, 23*(1), 67–71. PMID:23286627

Somov, A., Dupont, C., & Giaffreda, R. (2013). *Supporting Smart-city Mobility with Cognitive Internet of Things*. Academic Press.

Sonnier, J., & Riesen, A. H. (1985). Developmental Brain Research, Deprivation, and Sensory Aids. In Electronic Spatial Sensing for the Blind. *Proc. of the NATO Advanced Reseasrch Workshop on Visual Spatial Prosthesis for the Blind.*

Spire. (2015). Retrieved November 15, 2015, from https://www.spire.io/

Stankovic, J. A. (2014). Research directions for the Internet of Things. *IEEE Internet of Things Journal, 1*(1), 3–9. doi:10.1109/JIOT.2014.2312291

Stankovic, J. A. (2014). *Research Directions for the Internet of Things. IEEE Internet of Things Journal.*

State of the World Cities 2012/20132013United Nations.

Sun, F., Yu, X., Liu, S., & Lu, F. (2014, May). Intelligent collaborative urban traffic management system based on SOA and cloud computing. In *Control and Decision Conference (2014 CCDC), The 26th Chinese* (pp. 1692-1695). IEEE. doi:10.1109/CCDC.2014.6852441

Šunderić, D. (2003). SQL Server 2000, Stored Procedure & XML Programming (2nd ed.). New York: McGraw-Hill/Osborne.

Sundmaeker, H., Guillemin, P., Friess, P., & Woelfflé, S. (2010). *Vision and challenges for realising the Internet of Things. Cluster of European Research Projects on the Internet of Things.* Brussels: European Commision.

Sun, Y., Yan, H., Lu, C., Bie, R., & Thomas, P. (2012). A Holistic Approach to Visualizing Business Models for the Internet of Things. *Communications in Mobile Computing, 1*(1), 1–7. doi:10.1186/2192-1121-1-4

Swagger. (2016). *RESTful API representation.* Retrieved from http://swagger.io

Swan, M. (2013). The Quantified Self: Fundamental Disruption in Big Data Science and Biological Discovery. *Big Data, 1*(2), 85–99. doi:10.1089/big.2012.0002 PMID:27442063

Taivalsaari, A., & Mikkonen, T. (2015). Cloud technologies for the Internet of Things: Defining a research agenda beyond the expected topics. *Proc. Euromicro Conference on Software engineering and advanced applications (SEAA)*, 484–488.

Tao, F., Cheng, Y., Da Xu, L., Zhang, L., & Li, B. H. (2014). CCIoT-CMfg: Cloud computing and internet of things-based cloud manufacturing service system. *IEEE Transactions on Industrial Informatics, 10*(2), 1435–1442. doi:10.1109/TII.2014.2306383

Compilation of References

Taylor, R., Baron, D., & Schmidt, D. (2015, October). The world in 2025-predictions for the next ten years. In *Microsystems, Packaging, Assembly and Circuits Technology Conference (IMPACT), 2015 10th International* (pp. 192-195). IEEE.

Temperton, J. (2015, May 15). *A 'fourth industrial revolution' is about to begin (in Germany)*. Retrieved April 12, 2016, from http://www.wired.co.uk/news/archive/2015-05/21/factory-of-the-future/viewgallery/474960

Tesla, N. (1898). *Patent No. US 613809 A*. Washington, DC: US Patent Office.

Tesla, N. (1926, January 30). *When Woman is Boss*. 21st Century Books.

The BLOB and the TEXT Types. (2017). Retrieved from MySQL: http://dev.mysql.com/doc/refman/5.7/en/blob.html

The City of Chicago Technology Plan. (2013). Chicago: City of Chicago.

The Discovery of the Molecular Structure of DNA - The Double Helix. (2003, September 30). Retrieved April 18, 2016, from https://www.nobelprize.org/educational/medicine/dna_double_helix/readmore.html

The SensorHUB Project Website. (2015). Retrieved from https://www.aut.bme.hu/ SensorHUB/

The SOLSUN Project Website. (2015). Retrieved from http://solsun.co.uk/index.php/SOLSUN/

The URBMOBI Project Website. (2015). Retrieved from http://www.climate-kic.org/case-studies/urban-resistance-to-the-effects-of-climate-change/

The VehicleICT Project Website. (2015). Retrieved from https://www.aut.bme.hu/VehicleICT/

The VMTS Project Website. (2015). Retrieved from https://www.aut.bme.hu/VMTS/

Thibodeau, P. (2014). *The ABCs of the Internet of Things*. Computerworld US. Retrieved from http://www.techworld.com/networking/abcs-of-internet-of-things-3516134/3/

Thread Group. (2016). Retrieved April 5, 2016, from http://www.threadgroup.org/

Timmer, J. (2011, February 11). *World's total CPU power: one human brain*. Retrieved April 12, 2016, from http://arstechnica.com/science/2011/02/adding-up-the-worlds-storage-and-computation-capacities/

Turber, S., Brocke, J. V., Gassmann, O., & Flesich, E. (2014) Designing Business Models in the Era of Internet of Things.*9th International Conference, DESRIST 2014*, 17-31. doi:10.1007/978-3-319-06701-8_2

Turner, W. P., Seader, J. H., & Renaud, V. E. (2010). *Data center site infrastructure tier standard: Topology*. New York, NY: Uptime Institute.

Unification Will Combine the Best of Both Organizations under Open Connectivity Foundation Name and Bylaws. (2016, October 10). Retrieved November 30, 2016, from https://openconnectivity. org/press-releases/allseen-alliance-merges-open-connectivity-foundation-accelerate-internet-things

User Manual for ESP-12E DevKit based on ESP8266. (2016). Retrieved from https://smartarduino. gitbooks.io/user-manual-for-esp-12e-devkit/content/index.html

VanSyckel, S., & Becker, C. (2014). A survey of proactive pervasive computing. In *Proceedings of the 2014 ACM International Joint Conference on Pervasive and Ubiquitous Computing: Adjunct Publication* (pp. 421-430). ACM.

Velosa, A., Shulte, W. R., & Lhereux, B. J. (2015). *Hype Cycle for the Internet of Things, 2015.* Stamford, CT: Gartner.

Vermesan, O. (2013). Internet of Things beyond the Hype: Research, innovation and deployment. In O. Vermesan & P. Friess (Eds.), *Internet of Things: Converging technologies for smart environments and integrated ecosystems* (pp. 15–118). Aalborg, Denmark: River Publishers.

Vermesan, O., & Friess, P. (2014). *Internet of Things - From Research and Innovation to Market Deployment.* Aalborg: River Publishers.

Visual Impairment and Blindness. (2016). World Health Organization. Retrieved from http://www.who.int/mediacentre/factsheets/fs282/en/

Vlacheas, P., Giaffreda, R., Stavroulaki, V., Kelaidonis, D., Foteinos, V., Poulios, G., & Moessner, K. (2013). Enabling smart cities through a cognitive management framework for the internet of things. *Communications Magazine, IEEE, 51*(6), 102–111. doi:10.1109/MCOM.2013.6525602

Vladimir Brusic, J. Z. (1999). Knowledge discovery and data mining in biological databases. *The Knowledge Engineering Review, 14*(3), 257–277. doi:10.1017/S0269888999003069

VMware. (2017). *VMware Hyper-Converged Infrastructure (HCI) - VMware Products.* Retrieved Jan 12, 2017, from https://www.vmware.com/products/hyper-converged-infrastructure.html

Want, R., Pering, T., & Tennenhouse, D. (2003). Comparing autonomic and proactive computing. *IBM Systems Journal, 42*(1), 129–135. doi:10.1147/sj.421.0129

Warren, J.-D., Adams, J., & Molle, H. (2011). *Arduino Robotics.* New York: Apress Media LLC. doi:10.1007/978-1-4302-3184-4

Weiser, M. (1991). The Computer for 21st Century. *Scientific American, 265*(September), 94–104. doi:10.1038/scientificamerican0991-94

Welbourne, E., Battle, L., Cole, G., Gould, K., Rector, K., Raymer, S., & Borriello, G. et al. (2009). *Building the Internet of Things Using RFID - The RFID Ecosystem Experience* (pp. 48–55). IEEE Computer Society.

Westerlund, M., Leminen, S., & Rajahonka, M. (2014). Designing Business Models for the Internet of Things. *Technology Innovation Management Review*, *4*, 5–14.

What the Internet of Things (IoT) needs to be a Reality2014Retrieved from freescale.com/arm.com.

WHO. (2006). *Building foundations for eHealth: progress of Member States: report of the WHO Global Observatory for eHealth*. Geneva: World Health Organization. Retrieved December 27, 2014, from http://whqlibdoc.who.int/publications/2006/9241563354_eng.pdf

Wi-Fi Alliance. (2016). *Introduces low power, long range Wi-Fi HaLow*. Retrieved from http://www.wi-fi.org/news-events/newsroom/wi-fi-alliance-introduces-low-power-long-range-wi-fi-halow

Wilson X Connected Basketball - All Day. (2015, September 10). Retrieved April 5, 2016, from https://www.youtube.com/watch?v=qRvAXsaHNkY

Wu, Q., Ding, G., Xu, Y., Feng, S., Du, Z., Wang, J., & Long, K. (2014). Cognitive Internet of Things: A New Paradigm beyond Connection. *IEEE Internet of Things Journal*, 1–1. http://doi.org/.10.1109/ЛОТ.2014.2311513

Wu, X., Wu, J., Cheng, B., & Chen, J. (2013, September). Neural Network Based Situation Detection and Service Provision in the Environment of IoT. In *Vehicular Technology Conference (VTC Fall), 2013 IEEE 78th* (pp. 1-5). IEEE. doi:10.1109/VTCFall.2013.6692303

Ye, J., Dobson, S., & McKeever, S. (2012). Situation identification techniques in pervasive computing: A review. *Pervasive and Mobile Computing*, *8*(1), 36–66. doi:10.1016/j.pmcj.2011.01.004

Zaheeruddin, , & Garima, . (2006). A neuro-fuzzy approach for prediction of human work efficiency in noisy environment. *Applied Soft Computing*, *6*(3), 283–294. doi:10.1016/j.asoc.2005.02.001

Zubov, D., Barbosa, H. A., & Duane, G. S. (2015). *A Nonanticipative Analog Method for Long-Term Forecasting of Air Temperature Extremes*. Available from http://arxiv.org/abs/1507.03283

Zubov, D., Volponi, F., & Khosravy, M. (2015). D-Wave Quantum Computing Ising Model: A Case Study for the Forecasting of Heat Waves. In *Proceedings of Fourth International Conference on Control, Automation and Information Sciences (ICCAIS 2015)*. Changshu, China: IEEE. doi:10.1109/ICCAIS.2015.7338651

ZWave Alliance. (2016). Retrieved April 5, 2016, from http://z-wavealliance.org/

Мирослав Демић Ђ. Д. (2006). *Сателитско праћење возила*. Београд: Институт за нуклеарне науке "Винча".

Index

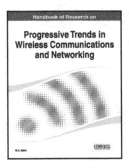

Stay Current on the Latest Emerging Research Developments

Become an IGI Global Reviewer for Authored Book Projects

Premier Reference Source

Solutions for High-Touch Communications in a High-Tech World

Premier Reference Source

Advanced Research on Biologically Inspired Cognitive Architectures

Premier Reference Source

Workforce Development Theory and Practice in the Mental Health Sector

Premier Reference Source

Resource Management and Efficiency in Cloud Computing Environments

The overall success of an authored book project is dependent on quality and timely reviews.

In this competitive age of scholarly publishing, constructive and timely feedback significantly decreases the turnaround time of manuscripts from submission to acceptance, allowing the publication and discovery of progressive research at a much more expeditious rate. Several IGI Global authored book projects are currently seeking highly qualified experts in the field to fill vacancies on their respective editorial review boards:

Applications may be sent to:
development@igi-global.com

Applicants must have a doctorate (or an equivalent degree) as well as publishing and reviewing experience. Reviewers are asked to write reviews in a timely, collegial, and constructive manner. All reviewers will begin their role on an ad-hoc basis for a period of one year, and upon successful completion of this term can be considered for full editorial review board status, with the potential for a subsequent promotion to Associate Editor.

If you have a colleague that may be interested in this opportunity, we encourage you to share this information with them.

Printed in the United States
By Bookmasters